AF681367

THE CROSSWORD BOOK

Parragon

First published 2007 Parragon Books, Ltd.

Copyright © 2018 Cottage Door Press, LLC
5005 Newport Drive, Rolling Meadows, Illinois 60008

Individual puzzles © 2006 Dell Magazines, Inc.,
A Division of Crosstown Publications. Used with permission.

All Rights Reserved

Cover Design by: Talking Design

10 9 8 7

ISBN: 978-1-68052-486-4

Parragon Books is an imprint of Cottage Door Press, LLC.
Parragon Books® and the Parragon® logo are
registered trademarks of Cottage Door Press, LLC.

1

ACROSS

1. Comfy couch
5. Move back and forth, as a dog's tail
8. Chore
12. Where cakes are baked
13. Drink-cooling cube
14. He played Hawkeye, with 9-Down
15. University official
16. Robert E. or Bruce
17. Lazy
18. Take into police custody
20. Raise the spirits of
21. Putting into service
24. Supermarket lane
28. Hen's mate
33. Notion
34. Flying mammal
35. "Present!"
36. Canoe's kin
38. Chin whiskers
39. Amphitheater, perhaps
41. Smack on the behind
45. Revised (copy)
50. Do, re, or mi
51. Cut the grass
53. Car for hire
54. A singing voice
55. Citrus beverage
56. Applaud
57. "Where have you ____ all my life?"
58. For each
59. Skirts' borders

DOWN

1. Drugstore fountain drink
2. "The Party's ____"
3. Scared state
4. Ms. Bancroft
5. Droops, as a flower
6. Expert pitcher
7. "Golly!"
8. Peacock's pride
9. See 14-Across
10. A table seasoning
11. A proposer gets down on this
19. Take to court
20. Freudian self
22. Incensed
23. Word of negation
24. Atmosphere
25. Marriage-vow words
26. Stitch together
27. Chemist's workplace
29. Feminine pronoun
30. Chinese beverage
31. Make mistakes
32. Tomato color
34. Soap unit
37. Durable wood
38. Unsatisfactory
40. More recent
41. Dagger thrust
42. Fishing rod
43. Poker fee
44. Bright sign-gas
46. Poison-ivy symptom
47. "A ____ of Two Cities," novel
48. School test
49. Dunks
51. Road chart
52. Lyric poem

2

ACROSS

1. Mimicked
5. Fitting, as a remark
8. Level
12. Depend (on)
13. Mr. Gershwin
14. Meshed fabric
15. Create
16. Steal from
17. Matured
18. Chips' partner
20. Bartender on "Cheers"
22. Health resort
25. Solemn promise
27. Unwanted plants
31. That girl's
32. Wipe the slate clean?
34. Allow
35. Flattering poem
36. Pencil point
37. Like: 2 wds.
38. Cooking vessel
39. "Stubborn" beasts
41. Roofing goo
42. Cut quickly
44. Golfer's gadget
45. Observe intently
46. Chum
48. Morning moisture
50. "Handle with ____"
53. Boxing great
55. Barbecue bugs
59. Actor Alda
60. "A Few Good ____"
61. Des Moines' state
62. Curve
63. Wooden pin
64. Horse's gait

DOWN

1. Supply with weapons
2. Carrot go-with
3. Large deer
4. Tinted
5. LAX and JFK
6. Paid athlete
7. Soda-can rings
8. What a moth is drawn to
9. Hang (behind)
10. High card
11. Media mogul Turner
19. "____ got an idea!"
21. Fill with astonishment
22. Small stores
23. Bicycle footrest
24. 53-Across's match site
26. Midsection
28. Make happy
29. Postpone
30. Gaze (at)
33. Highway violation
39. "Gotcha!"
40. Perceive
43. Consume
47. Table light
49. "Hold it!"
50. Taxi
51. Pub quaff
52. Moved quickly
54. Civil War general
56. Neither's partner
57. Number to tango
58. Used (a chair)

3

ACROSS

1. Like some school reports
5. 2,000-pound weight
8. Sleep spot for a baby
12. Rich source of ore
13. Be regretful
14. Strong dislike
15. Coloring chemicals
16. Curving path
17. "____ upon a time . . ."
18. Big, blue expanse above us
20. Dragon slayer
22. Consents (to)
25. Paving stuff
26. Mr. Eastwood
27. Christmas-tree choice
28. Tiny, green veggie
31. Chart for a traveler
32. Root for the home team
34. Fall behind
35. Sullivan and Asner
36. Do a garden chore
37. Stood up
39. Campaign (for office)
40. Packed away
41. Zebra feature
44. Permit
45. Transport by truck
46. Health spot
48. Eve's mate
52. "Can you think of anyone ____?"
53. Food can
54. Mosaic component
55. Act of heroism
56. However
57. Home to 48-Across

DOWN

1. Outdated
2. Film-cowboy Rogers
3. Lemon drink
4. Diminish
5. Waiters' serving platters
6. "____ Love Is Here to Stay"
7. Gift for Dad
8. Church singing group
9. Sounded, as a bell
10. Mosquito-bite feeling
11. Borscht ingredient
19. Tomato-based condiment
21. Tell (a 42-Down)
22. Highest peak
23. Elated
24. Tears to shreds
27. Monetary charge
28. Create furrows in (a field)
29. Relieve (pain)
30. Got older
33. Truthfulness
38. Turn, as the earth
39. Stirred (up)
40. Slope
41. Storage building
42. Word after "folk" or "fairy"
43. Bit of deception
47. Dessert pastry
49. Accomplished
50. Lager's kin
51. Boys, as adults

4

ACROSS

1. At any time
5. Mr. Alda
9. Resort for pampering
12. River in Egypt
13. Sneaker tie
14. Warm embrace
15. Slightly wet
16. "____ Island," classic novel
18. Take a gander (at)
20. Compared
21. Tartan patterns
24. Encountered
25. Felt sick
26. In favor of
27. Public transport
30. Poverty
31. Upper limb
32. Throw with force
33. McMahon and Bradley
34. Attempt
35. Hot ____ sundae
36. Physician: slang
37. Washed out (shampoo)
38. Sandal thong
41. ____ over matter
42. Vows to keep
44. Steals from
48. Help
49. Return to health
50. Revise (copy)
51. Negative replies
52. Observed
53. Say (something) isn't so

DOWN

1. Conclusion
2. By way of
3. Lawn tree
4. Answered
5. Choir voices
6. "Happy" songbird
7. Untouchable tennis serve
8. At less of a distance
9. Close
10. Unadulterated
11. Quite old
17. Used a chair
19. Not even
21. Window section
22. Fibbed
23. Brewery products
24. Dad's darling
26. Sizzle in oil
27. Unopened flowers
28. Inner drive
29. Winter vehicle
31. Circle part
32. Ten times ten
34. Subjects
35. Fish propeller
36. Beaver's construction
37. Up and about
38. Length, as of time
39. Small music group
40. Metal poles
41. Humble
43. Take to court
45. Lyric poem
46. Storage container
47. Messy place

5

ACROSS

1. Leak, as a faucet
5. Crooner Torme
8. Partner of crafts
12. Helper
13. Mine product
14. Bait contraption
15. Castle's watery ditch
16. By means of
17. "How have you ____?"
18. Bird's chirp
20. Previously owned
21. Reached accord
24. That guy
26. Ice-skate runner
27. Patriot Franklin, familiarly
28. Play segment
31. Produce (eggs)
32. Cherished ones
34. Spooky shout
35. Asner and Sullivan
36. Wrap up
37. Mental formulations
39. Citrus drink
40. Grownups
41. Specialty store
44. Stags, for example
46. Mama's mate
47. Igloo material
48. Rocker Turner
52. By any chance
53. Go astray
54. Home of Eve
55. Fender damage
56. Fix, as a price
57. Parka filling

DOWN

1. Beaver's building project
2. ____ de Janeiro
3. Ms. Lupino
4. Stroked (a dog)
5. Changed residences
6. Cleveland's Great Lake
7. Tanned cowhide
8. Snapshot book
9. Feels regret
10. Arbor Day planting
11. Transmit
19. Removed dandelions
21. Skilled enough
22. Elated
23. Beams (of light)
25. Not out of doors
27. Good's opposite
28. Adam's shepherd son
29. Layer (of paint)
30. Throw gently
33. Foes
38. Wiped off bookshelves
39. To one side
40. Vigilant
41. Exceeded the posted limit
42. "To ____ and to hold . . ."
43. Ready for customers
45. Farmland measure
49. Altar vow: 2 wds.
50. Never before seen
51. Advice columnist Landers

6

ACROSS

1. Criminal catchers
5. One of New York's football teams
9. Captain's diary
12. An acting Baldwin
13. Steel ingredient
14. Fold female
15. Cruel Roman emperor
16. Doctor's field
18. Dorothy's dog
19. Sleeveless coat
20. Flavorful
23. Caustic liquids
27. Stein filler
30. School vehicle
31. Mitten's cousin
32. Bachelor of arts, for one
34. Bake-sale treat
35. Haloed harp-player
36. Grown boy
37. "A Nightmare on ____ Street," flick
38. Catholic church service
39. Courtroom VIP
41. Makes (a bow)
43. Copied
47. Battled with (one's conscience)
51. Sticky strip
52. Cattle food
53. Help for Holmes
54. Guitarist Clapton
55. Wallet find
56. Church song
57. Upper spine part

DOWN

1. "You ____ Take It With You"
2. Toast topping
3. Bold; saucy
4. "Scram!"
5. Muppets creator Henson
6. Builds
7. Now
8. Quick, short cut
9. Hawaiian garland
10. Be the possessor of
11. "Well, I'll be!"
17. Viola's larger cousin
21. One of Eve's sons
22. Take to court
24. Harness for oxen
25. Wicked
26. Look (like)
27. First man
28. Horne of song
29. Omelet need
31. Disk-shaped bell
33. Takes it easy
34. Rude fellow
36. Tourist attraction
39. See 2-Down
40. Consumed
42. Urge to scratch
44. Peel (potatoes)
45. Sweeping drama
46. Floor of a ship
47. "Which person?"
48. Sprinted
49. Needle opening
50. Cozy room

7

ACROSS

1. Female chicken
4. Small store
8. Hollywood celebrity
12. Anger
13. Marching-band instrument
14. Extremely large
15. Had significance
17. Single things
18. Depend (on)
19. Brown (bread)
20. Classify
23. Self
25. "Mighty" trees
26. In a lazy way
27. Pig's home
30. Emulated Tara Lipinski
32. Onto dry land
34. "Hello!"
35. Require
37. Actor Alda
38. Moving truck
39. Lets go
40. Bowling lane
44. Therefore
46. TV's Rivers
47. Fellow from Dublin
51. Fervent
52. Outdoor shelter
53. Actress Gabor
54. Cincinnati baseball team
55. Fixes firmly
56. Knock lightly

DOWN

1. That man
2. Epoch
3. Butterfly catcher
4. Sheer, as a slope
5. Fling
6. Followed the orders of
7. Gym mat
8. "Get away!"
9. Common food fish
10. Matures
11. Take it easy
16. Have faith in
19. Child's playthings
20. "Golly!"
21. Leaf gatherer
22. "Will do!"
24. Very pleased
26. Thought
27. Aria, for one
28. Lobster catcher's device
29. Strong longings
31. Covet
33. Grating
36. Main course
39. Wipes the furniture
40. Slightly open
41. Extreme adoration
42. Set down
43. Concludes
45. Helpful tip
47. "_____ a boy!"
48. Came upon
49. Ms. Gardner
50. Short sleep

8

ACROSS

1. Use a key
5. Reclined in a chair
8. Make changes in (copy)
12. Persian rug source
13. Bakery pastry
14. Dwell (at)
15. Window section
16. In the tradition of: 2 wds.
17. Unwrap, as a gift
18. Catch some "shut-eye"
20. Sharp knock
22. Below freezing
25. Dog's strap
29. Part of a disguise
32. Targets
34. Slugger DiMaggio
35. Enjoyed a meal
36. High card
37. Every last one
38. Japanese currency
39. Different
41. Fishing pole
42. Catch a whiff of
44. Give it a shot
45. Like 3, 5, or 7
47. Our planet
52. Sound reverberation
55. That thing's
58. Attract irresistibly
59. Negative replies
60. Procured
61. Beloved
62. Hemispherical roof
63. Undercover operative
64. Wee vipers

DOWN

1. "Loose ____ sink ships"
2. Involving the mouth
3. Tap dancer's prop
4. Leg bender
5. Pampering resort
6. Sicken
7. Eye droplet
8. Wed in secret
9. Brief swim
10. "____ Got a Secret"
11. Twice five
19. Sow or boar
21. Jolson and Pacino
23. Warm winter garment
24. Luxury boat
26. Not quite closed
27. Song for one
28. Embraced
29. Methods
30. News bit
31. Mr. Hackman
33. Malicious look
39. Antique
40. Bread grain
43. Wiggly, as a tooth
46. Excavates
48. "Same Time Next Year" costar
49. Feels regret
50. Pitfall
51. That lady's
52. Finale
53. Sound from a pigeon
54. ____ and haw
56. Spinning toy
57. Messy room

9

ACROSS

1. Set of tools
4. Touches lightly
8. Insult by ignoring
12. Marriage words
13. Revise (a manuscript)
14. Gardening tube
15. Recently made
16. Small horse
17. Kitchen appliance
18. Ballerina, for one
20. Be in debt to
21. Listened to (a warning)
24. Cow's noise
27. Fido's annoyance
30. Roll (of bills)
31. Coal storage place
32. Desk light
33. For every
34. Actor Hackman
35. Adam's mate
36. Young lady
37. Boats like Noah's
38. Military conflict
39. Permits
42. Egypt snake
44. Syrup-producing trees
48. Skilled
50. Monkeys' relatives
52. Drink-cooling cubes
53. Traveled by bicycle
54. Tenant's payment
55. That woman
56. Throw
57. Lawyer's concern
58. Spinning toy

DOWN

1. Merciful
2. Mental conception
3. Urban settlement
4. Plains Indian's traditional dwelling
5. Love greatly
6. Sewing fastener
7. Pigs' enclosure
8. Demonstrate
9. Turkey time
10. Employ
11. Founding father Franklin, familiarly
19. Become rough, as lips
20. Strange
22. Reside (in)
23. Serving of corn
25. Cry from a 7-Down
26. Washington bills
27. Took a plane
28. Volcano flow
29. Green precious gems
33. Buddy
34. Shocked inhalation
36. Blank space
40. Prophets' signs
41. "Haste makes ____"
43. Uses the eyes
45. Shopper's reminder
46. Repeated sound
47. Leak slowly
48. Museum sight
49. Startling shout
50. Rainbow's shape
51. Tiny, round vegetable

10

ACROSS

1. Pull by rope
4. Plumbing tube
8. Unlocked
12. Mine find
13. Persia, now
14. Impel
15. Damage slightly
16. Table seasoning
17. Horn's sound
18. Mixture of rain and snow
20. Woodland sprite
22. Neither's partner
24. Lifted
28. Small child
32. Kitchen range
33. "Gotcha!"
34. Work with a shovel
36. Adult boys
37. Citrus fruits
40. Word after "down" or "car"
43. Sports defeats
45. "Golly!"
46. Used a chair
47. Danger signal
51. Carbonated drink
54. Slightly 8-Across
57. Female deer
58. Out of town
59. Bouncing orb
60. Actress Gardner
61. Animals' lairs
62. Move back and forth
63. Came upon

DOWN

1. Male cats
2. Spoken
3. Existed
4. Small gun
5. Composer Gershwin
6. Chum
7. Go into
8. Costume
9. In favor of
10. Self
11. Fishing snare
19. Conclude
21. ____ Vegas, Nevada
23. Stop-sign color
25. Indefinite quantity
26. Level
27. Fender blemish
28. Far from short
29. Columbus's state
30. Water barriers
31. Tear
35. Practical joke
38. Students' compositions
39. Ocean
41. Occurring every 365 days
42. Singer Torme
44. Uses a dagger
48. Eve's mate
49. Wander
50. Beef or pork
51. Unhappy
52. Have debts
53. Newsman Rather
55. Mouth bone
56. In the style of: 2 wds.

11

ACROSS
1. Cone-bearing evergreen trees
5. Curved doorway
9. Pacino and Gore
12. False god
13. Apple's center
14. Far from high
15. Infant
16. Sound of grief
17. Health resort
18. Hostile opponent
20. Overly curious
21. Gets up
24. Miner's find
26. Jolly North Pole resident
27. Winter-weather action
31. Equipment set
32. Crispy, browned bread
34. Brazilian city, for short
35. Least rapid
37. A couple of times
39. Creative skill
40. Rents
41. Far-reaching
44. Showers from the sky
46. Expression of surprise
47. The missing ____
48. Strikes softly
52. Shrill bark
53. Skin condition
54. Departure
55. Distress code
56. Storage shack
57. Refute (an allegation)

DOWN
1. Lie
2. Ms. Lupino
3. Steal from
4. Most cunning
5. Peaks
6. Enclosure with walls and a ceiling
7. Children's coloring sticks
8. Female chicken
9. Additionally
10. Cuts (off)
11. Move side to side
19. More organized
20. Recent
21. Poses a query
22. Train track
23. Concerned with
25. Spoiled
27. Used a chair
28. Eye part surrounding the pupil
29. Friendly
30. Leaves
33. Large, flightless bird
36. Swing, as a tail
38. Squandered
40. Had a fondness for
41. Sets (down)
42. Akron's state
43. Snoozes
45. Ms. Bancroft
47. Scale tones
49. Chopping tool
50. Bowling target
51. Pigpen

12

ACROSS

1. Young fellow
4. Wharf
8. One-dish meal
12. Actor Vigoda
13. Inner drive
14. Gondolier's oar
15. Affleck or Gazzara
16. From ____ to riches
17. Convenience
18. Most like a trickster
20. Dealt the baseball cards?
22. Expected, as a baby
23. Furniture wood
24. Phase
27. "Give it the old college ____!"
28. Vessel for a 8-Across
31. On this site
32. Take to court
33. Fish eater's find
34. As of now
35. Large
36. Stared open-mouthed
37. IRS concern
38. Bit of wordplay
39. Choker locale
42. Supermarket lanes
46. Tree's "foot"
47. English nobleman
49. Ms. Lupino
50. TV's Alan
51. Polish (copy)
52. Hombres
53. Citrus rind
54. Prying
55. Terminate

DOWN

1. Research facilities
2. Cain's victim
3. Contradict
4. Chase after
5. Incensed
6. Omelet ingredient
7. Work with antiques, perhaps
8. Command to Fido
9. Despicable person
10. Otherwise
11. Dandelion, for one
19. Sidle (over)
21. Shaft of light
24. Introverted
25. Woods widget
26. Gallery hanging
27. Pull (on)
28. Burst, as a balloon
29. Individual
30. Danson of "Cheers"
32. Sweet birthday?
33. Prohibits
35. Rural sound
36. Having pangs of conscience
37. Entire
38. The City of Light
39. Leave with no way out
40. Cavity
41. Busted a bronco
43. Shade of green
44. Unspoiled spot
45. Beach grit
48. Major fuss

13

ACROSS

1. Ladd of classic movies
5. Couple
8. Performs like 1-Across
12. "Get up!"
13. "That's amazing!"
14. Cut (coupons)
15. Create a sweater
16. Columnist Landers
17. Lion's hair
18. Spring, summer, winter, or autumn
20. Cried like a kitten
21. House of snow
24. Tin or iron
28. Officer in the navy
33. Kitchen appliance
34. Conclude
35. Entice
36. Wound covering
38. Choose (a politician)
39. Defeated one
41. Wood-working tool
45. Concern
50. Traveled by bus
51. Bottle cap, for one
53. Rant
54. Ajar
55. Away from home
56. Mimics
57. Pod vegetables
58. Attempt
59. Annoyance

DOWN

1. Boats like Noah's
2. Fishing string
3. Largest continent
4. New Jersey basketball team
5. Banjo sound
6. Was victorious
7. Possess
8. Summit
9. Eagle's talon
10. Fork prong
11. Moved (away)
19. Lubricate
20. Female parent
22. Bowling alleys
23. Uncommon
24. Riotous group
25. Ms. Perón
26. Hamilton's bill
27. In addition to
29. Sick
30. Regret
31. Curved line
32. Permit
34. Self
37. Everything
38. Historic period
40. Unoccupied
41. Allow to fall
42. Heavy cord
43. Thought
44. Camera glass
46. Snare
47. Adhesive strip
48. Nights before holidays
49. Period of relaxation
51. Small child
52. Belonging to us

14

ACROSS

1. Atlas picture
4. Elongated circle
8. Genesis man
12. In the tradition of: 2 wds.
13. Harsh sentence
14. Soda-machine possibility
15. Signal for help
16. Be bold
17. Exam
18. Blasting compound: abbr.
19. Part of "MFA"
21. Furry sea mammal
23. Serving receptacle
24. Mr. King Cole
27. Very enthusiastic
29. Newport, ____ Island
31. TV dog
34. Got misty-eyed
35. Revises (copy)
36. Typical freshman
37. Uppermost point
38. Remove wrinkles from
40. Be aware of
44. Bit of gossip
45. Rhyming heavy-weight champ
46. Jab
49. Operation reminder
52. Fool (around)
53. Fence bar
54. City vehicle
55. Mate of 8-Across
56. Nothing but
57. Daisy stalk
58. Family room

DOWN

1. Poles on schooners
2. Without any company
3. Fettuccine or ziti
4. Like Father Time
5. By means of
6. Scared
7. Sly glances
8. Plays a role
9. Fawn's mother
10. Gore and Jolson
11. Bathroom rug
20. Age after two
22. Final
23. Expire
24. Word with "neither"
25. Summer citrus drink
26. TV's Koppel
28. Call on
30. Singer Williams
31. "____ sleeping dogs lie"
32. Fuss
33. Wee swallow
34. The ____ Commandments
36. Male feline
39. Takes five
41. Not wearing any clothes
42. Pimento-filled food
43. Become broader
44. In a nonchalant way
46. Old hand
47. Was a cross-country competitor
48. Petroleum product
50. Lumberjack's tool
51. Cup edge

15

ACROSS

1. "____ Shoot Me," TV show
5. Play divisions
9. Male child
12. Japan's continent
13. Word before "beer" or "canal"
14. A pair
15. Choker site
16. Thick, strong cord
17. Picnic pest
18. Igloo dwellers
20. Rhyming lines, often
22. "ASAP!"
23. Guitar-tuning pin
24. Lottery game
27. Tina Turner's skill
31. Expert pilot
32. Large storage container
33. Payable
34. Michigan city
37. "All Quiet on the Western ____," book
39. Mimic
40. ____ de Janeiro
41. Immense
44. Ship robbers
48. Muhammad of boxing
49. Gas found in signs
51. Fizzy drink
52. Under the weather
53. Preholiday nights
54. Short journey
55. Hair-coloring solution
56. Estimate the value of
57. Matched groups

DOWN

1. Ms. Fonda
2. Utilizes
3. See 52-Across
4. Stealer's action
5. Bow's partner
6. Speaks gently and lovingly
7. Child's spinning toy
8. "E.T." director Spielberg
9. Headliner
10. Possesses
11. Music symbol
19. Cow sound
21. Omelet ingredient
23. Deep hole
24. Wicked
25. Frozen water
26. Meshed trap
27. Took a chair
28. Altar vow: 2 wds.
29. Mother Teresa, for one
30. Obtain
32. Compete
35. Dusting cloth
36. Device that unseals cans
37. Cone-bearing evergreen tree
38. Cooks (meat) in an oven
40. Wash lightly
41. Deposited (a 21-Down)
42. Wartime friend
43. Provoke
44. Writer of 20-Across
45. Pulled apart
46. Prepare (copy) for print
47. Weakens
50. A Gabor

16

ACROSS

1. Adhesive strip
5. Neptune's domain
8. Current of air
12. Cain's brother
13. Bonnet, for one
14. Cooking byproduct
15. Lively joy
16. Museum exhibit
17. _____ Tyler Moore
18. Played a waiter's role
20. Gabor sister
22. Fruity drink
23. Watched over (a baby)
27. Worries
30. King Kong is one
31. Shaft of light
32. Abiding passion
33. High explosive: abbr.
34. Nothing more than
35. Pub order
36. Produce (eggs)
37. Young stags, perhaps
38. Native of Berlin
40. Soft roll
41. It may be fried or scrambled
42. Rubs out
46. Brains
49. Great deal
51. Capricorn symbol
52. Wallet bills
53. Dine
54. ". . . or _____!," threat ending
55. "Fine!"
56. "Wild, blue yonder"
57. Appear

DOWN

1. Pricing labels
2. Competent
3. Look intently (into)
4. Raise up
5. Shelter from the sun
6. Lobe location
7. Make an effort
8. A lass, at last?
9. Actress Lupino
10. Neither's sidekick
11. Parched
19. Sullivan and McMahon
21. Fight one another (for)
24. Made a sketch
25. Work for (a salary)
26. Colors (hair)
27. Old Glory or Union Jack
28. Part to portray
29. By any chance
30. Some
33. Knots in long hair
34. Makes do
36. Dawdle
37. Dog's coat
39. In a state of disorder
40. "Golden Girl" White
43. Shoe bottom
44. Convenience
45. Plant stalk
46. Pay court to
47. Writing liquid
48. Afternoon social
50. Furniture wood

17

ACROSS

1. Vocal composition
5. Opposite of on
8. Dressing gown
12. Through
13. Dove's cry
14. At any time
15. Tardy
16. Hearing organ
17. Rude look
18. Choice word
19. Pub brew
20. Actress Jillian and columnist Landers
21. Metal food container
23. Blend together
25. Tacked on
28. Owns
29. Scot's cap
32. Light-hearted
33. Unfastens
35. Ms. Gardner
36. Dollar bill
37. Competed in a race
38. Word before "class" or "hand"
40. That woman
41. Steeped beverage
42. Storage tower
45. Health resort
47. Volcano's output
51. Spoken
52. ____ Vegas, Nevada
53. Cain's brother
54. Thin sheet of metal
55. European moose
56. Cut with scissors
57. Actor Griffith
58. "All right!"
59. Slippery swimmers

DOWN

1. Bottom of the foot
2. Egg-shaped
3. Meshed traps
4. Sparta's country
5. Sea
6. Baby horse
7. Factory leader
8. Become less tense
9. Baking chamber
10. Existed
11. Makes mistakes
22. Love greatly
24. Magazine edition
25. In the past
26. Marino of football
27. Hair-coloring solution
28. Female chicken
29. Strike lightly
30. "____ Maria," hymn
31. Deface
34. Aromatic garnish
39. Emperor's residence
40. Shrub with sharp-pointed leaves
41. Pieces of work
42. Uphol-stered couch
43. Press (clothes) smooth
44. Deposited (eggs)
46. Ashen
48. Competent
49. Bride's headdress
50. Swiss mountains

18

ACROSS

1. Major furniture purchase
4. Entreat
8. Glance at quickly
12. Reverence
13. Golf-pin place
14. Jay of late-night TV
15. Philadelphian Franklin
16. Is in debt to
17. Concludes
18. Expensive homes
20. Speedy plane
21. Fishing pole
22. Public transit "coins"
25. Candle cords
28. Oily nutrient
29. Waterway: Spanish
30. Historic span
31. Coffee cup
32. Yuletide helper
33. Loud knock
34. Enthusiast
35. Police trainee
37. Main dinner course
39. "Do, re, mi, fa, ____ . . ."
40. Give a hand to
41. Garment experts
45. Make a web
47. Human spirit
48. Brewing vessel
49. Egg layers
50. ____ in a blue moon
51. Adam's mate
52. Convenience
53. Crab grass, for one
54. Inexperienced

DOWN

1. Paul Bunyan's blue ox
2. Female sheep
3. Slight hollow
4. Camera images
5. Used oars
6. Pub choices
7. "Absolutely!"
8. Smooth; glossy
9. Balanced
10. As well as
11. Alternatives to yeses
19. Boat for Noah
20. Notate quickly
22. Hanging label
23. Egypt flooder
24. Downy
25. Streisand hit, "The Way We ____"
26. Tehran's nation
27. Military officers
28. Amusement
31. West of Hollywood?
34. Gave nourishment to
35. Ready to strike
36. Everything
38. Wash in clear water
39. Spaghetti topping
41. Sound quality
42. Pizza chamber
43. Rant's partner
44. Meat-and-potatoes dish
45. Ship's pronoun
46. Pod find
47. Boar's mate

19

ACROSS

1. Sailor's home
4. Mama's main man
8. Opening on a mailbox
12. European peak
13. Had financial obligations
14. Dracula's garment
15. Cabbie's bonus
16. Nighttime bugle call
17. Potato baker
18. Requiring little effort
20. "United we ____ . . ."
21. Boat's mast
23. "You ____ Your Life," old game show
25. Fishing bait, often
27. Gardner of movies
28. An explosive: abbr.
31. Draft serving
32. Now
34. ____ de Janeiro
35. Signal "yes"
36. Be on the sick list
37. Skin of the head
39. House pest
40. Serves without return
41. Fill (a turkey)
45. Financial deficit
47. Make (muscles) firmer
48. Dog's tormentor
50. Like 1, 3, or 5
53. A Great Lake
54. Back (of the bus)
55. Feel bad about
56. Dampens
57. Raise one's voice
58. Stitch up

DOWN

1. Used a sofa
2. Mr. Whitney
3. Seemed (to be)
4. Kitchen vessels
5. Out of town
6. Liveliness
7. Paid notices
8. Perth native
9. Etna output
10. Not closed
11. Be inclined (to)
19. Give weapons to
20. Hangs around
21. Graceful bird
22. Horseback "hockey"
23. Without skill
24. Actress Marie Saint
26. Work force
28. Farm machines
29. River of Egypt
30. Goes one better
33. Olive extract
38. Truck-driver's seat
41. Cook by simmering
42. Ripped (off)
43. Condominium division
44. Service charges
45. Give out (the cards)
46. Noble Englishman
48. Cook in oil
49. Actor Majors
51. Owing
52. Lawn moisture

20

ACROSS

1. Young goat
4. Also
7. Make 15-Across
11. Gershwin brother
12. Chest bone
13. Honking bird
14. Paving goo
15. Malt beverage
16. Great civilization of the ancient Middle East
17. Journal recording
19. Strong longing
21. Declare
23. Whirlpool bath
26. Animal companion
28. Sacred image
29. Mouth part
30. Neighbor-hood bar
32. Take away
34. Monkey's kin
35. Look boldly at
37. Annoy
38. Golf score
39. Sharp sides of knives
41. Wager
42. Stage-struck artiste
46. Got up
50. McMahon and Sullivan
52. Paul Bunyan's tool
53. One who gives generously
54. Take to court
55. Pod vegetable
56. Has a debt
57. Mr. Danson
58. Conclude

DOWN

1. Flying toy
2. Tehran's land
3. Pub missile
4. Serving platters
5. Lubricate
6. Followed (orders)
7. Marshy place
8. Cowboy Rogers
9. Psychic's gift
10. Dry's opposite
13. Kind
18. Fixed price
20. Disinte-grated
22. Unmarried
23. Harmful remark
24. Choose
25. Likely (to)
26. Mama's mate
27. Always
30. Light touch
31. Bank thief
33. Phono-graph record, for one
36. Most recent
40. Relieved, as pain
43. Adhesive strip
44. Beasts of burden
45. Peruse
46. Fuss and bother
47. Group of seats
48. Undivided
49. Distress call
51. Payable

21

ACROSS

1. Word on a gift card
5. Suit's shoulder enlarger
8. Money on hand
12. Talk crazily
13. Inspire with reverence
14. Provoke
15. Distinctive time periods
16. Siesta
17. Characteristic smell
18. "Electric" fishes
19. Coloring substance
20. Dampens
21. One of Zsa Zsa Gabor's sisters
23. Cloistered woman
25. Rodeo rope
28. Notices of sales
29. Roll (of paper money)
32. High mountain
33. From the Emerald Isle
35. Scuba-tank filler
36. Cheerful
37. Food fish
38. Ahead of time
40. Just bought
41. Monet creation
42. Swing to and fro
45. Grocery sack
47. Drags behind
51. Mountain's little cousin
52. Belonging to us
53. Tied
54. Concerned with
55. Had a cookie
56. Roman tyrant
57. Times Square light-gas
58. Boot tip
59. Attracted (a crowd)

DOWN

1. At no charge
2. Steak order
3. Football shape
4. Untidy conditions
5. Chinese bear
6. On vacation, perhaps
7. Relies (on)
8. Ruler's headdress
9. Helper
10. Narrow opening
11. Towel word
22. Express, as an opinion
24. One who seats theater patrons
25. Hang (behind)
26. In the manner of: 2 wds.
27. Watch in secret
28. Lend a hand to
29. "____ and Peace"
30. Become sick
31. Needing water
34. Craft with oars
39. Go to (a party)
40. Stockings fabric
41. Be of like mind
42. Lower leg
43. Chablis or merlot
44. Choir member
46. Car
48. Finished
49. Existed
50. Peak topper

22

ACROSS

1. Requires
6. Newsman Rather
9. ____ talk, coach's speech
12. Arctic shelter
13. ____ de Janeiro
14. Fruity beverage
15. Gambling card game
16. Total (up)
17. Barbecuing site, sometimes
18. Cliff's border
20. Fence exit
21. Close friend
24. Swiss Alps song
26. Make a hole in one
27. Author's implement
28. Homes for birds
32. Protected from the sun
34. Wide thoroughfare
35. Native American tent
36. Weep
37. Tap-dancing Miller
38. Clock's buzzer
40. Flat cushion
41. Arrange beforehand
44. Light beams
46. Cut (off)
47. Make an attempt
48. Ewes' offspring
53. Poem of praise
54. Ply with candy and flowers
55. Expect
56. Tied the knot
57. Have
58. White or Ford

DOWN

1. Puppy's "attack"
2. Self-love
3. Big deer
4. Female 3-Down
5. Tender, as skin
6. Puff of song fame
7. Gave a hand to
8. Signal agreement
9. Mama's mate
10. Revise text
11. Baseball's Rose
19. Tinted
20. Lively joy
21. It's history!
22. Be 5-Down
23. Jump, frog style
25. Desire for something another has
27. Remove the rind from
29. Break sharply
30. Food fish
31. Dispatch (a letter)
33. College head
34. Military branch
36. Child's coloring stick
39. Missile for Cupid
41. Snow remover
42. Mineral source
43. Mimicked
45. Thick slice
47. A couple
49. Reverential dread
50. "Welcome" rug
51. Took the bait
52. Pig's place

23

ACROSS

1. Arrange (items)
5. Compact ____, music-store find
9. Marker cover
12. Thought or opinion
13. Spoken
14. President Lincoln, to some
15. Mountain's summit
16. Egypt's river
17. Trapping fabric
18. Morning mist
20. Frighten suddenly
22. Camera bulb
24. A Gershwin
25. Research room
26. Not closed
29. Mama's husband
33. Feel sick
34. Burrowing animals
36. Helpful hint
37. Got larger
39. Ascend
40. Actor Majors
41. Picnic pest
43. Recognition of achievement
45. Attorneys
49. Adult boy
50. Ms. Gardner
51. Adam's son
53. Wound by piercing
56. Young person
57. Flying toy
58. Heap
59. Asner and Sullivan
60. Meat-and-vegetable dish
61. Examine quickly

DOWN

1. Use a straw
2. Lyric poem
3. Easily deciphered, as hand-writing
4. Gets possession of
5. Mr. Rickles
6. Eye part surrounding the pupil
7. Flat, crisp crackers
8. Free from obstacles
9. Is unable to
10. Brother of 51-Across
11. Hitting star Rose
19. "To ____ it may concern . . ."
21. Strike, as on the knuckles
22. National banner
23. Animal's "house"
27. Artful rendering of a person's face
28. Yale alum
30. East Coast's ocean
31. Docking spot
32. Mimicked
35. Line of stitches
38. "Where there's a will, there's a ____"
42. Parts between heads and bodies
44. Hornet relatives
45. Erie, for one
46. Eager
47. Gum units
48. Location
52. Recent
54. In the style of: 2 wds.
55. Mr. Franklin, familiarly

24

ACROSS

1. Bring up (children)
5. Feedbag bits
9. Make inquiries
12. Inactive
13. Pest, to Rover
14. Neptune's domain
15. Heap (on)
16. Native of Helsinki
17. Bit of butter
18. Current fashion
20. Sample the flavor of
22. Utter
24. What a boy becomes
25. Scrap of cloth for dusting
28. Mountain climbers' lifeline
30. Show sleepiness
34. Rink material
35. The "N" in "R.N."
37. Female deer
38. Office note
40. Prying
41. Morning dampness
42. What happy dogs' tails do
44. Affirmative vote
46. Beijing's country
49. Strikes at (a fly)
53. Parking area
54. Uncontrolled anger
58. Feel sore
59. Mr. Lincoln, familiarly
60. Horned beasts of burden
61. Tehran's land
62. Dad's wife
63. Be unable to do without
64. Give medical attention to

DOWN

1. Tears; splits
2. Revise (text)
3. Comrade
4. Staggers
5. Opposite of on
6. The Greatest of boxing
7. Nine plus one
8. Mr. Claus
9. Egyptian snakes
10. Bicycle part
11. "Kiss Me, ____," musical
19. Work for, as wages
21. ". . . have you ____ wool?"
23. Of few years
24. Far from neat
25. Cup's edge
26. First-rate
27. Sapphire, for one
29. Paid athlete
31. Do sums
32. Deep sorrow
33. Never used
36. Baby blues?
39. Possess
43. Man of Exodus
45. Be in store
46. Chowder tidbit
47. Trainyard tramp
48. Catalog article
50. Farmland measure
51. Comparison word
52. Transmit
55. Wood-splitter's tool
56. "Gosh!"
57. Closing chapter

25

ACROSS

1. Fairy-tale opening
5. College cheer
8. Roasting rod
12. Lion's "hello"
13. In the past
14. Ripped
15. India's continent
16. Lair
17. Actor Alda
18. Camera glass
19. Hubbub
20. Repair, as clothing
21. Make a blunder
23. Sharp knock
25. Extra
28. For each
29. Weird
32. Chicken's mom
33. One of the seven deadly sins
35. "All's fair in love and ____"
36. Have breakfast
37. Ship's journal
38. Nursemaid
40. Workout room
41. Deface (a surface)
42. Run away from
45. The Greatest of boxing
47. Reason for scratching
51. Went by camel
52. Dogcatcher's snare
53. Store's markdown event
54. Lyric poems
55. Persian or Siamese
56. School test
57. DNA strand
58. McMahon and Asner
59. Small bites

DOWN

1. Spoken
2. Organ of smell
3. A son of Adam
4. Chalk-removing pad
5. Detecting device
6. Ripened, as cheese
7. Acceptance-speech word
8. Postage sticker
9. Warsaw native
10. Tehran's land
11. Take care of (the sick)
22. Answer
24. Sports venue
25. That girl
26. Small, round vegetable
27. Industrious insect
28. Sty animal
29. Have the title to
30. Quarterback Marino
31. Waterless
34. Novel of love
39. Ascended
40. "Silly" birds
41. Catchers' gloves
42. Grown tadpole
43. Mining source
44. Bible spot
46. Take charge of (a discussion)
48. City cab
49. Applaud
50. Shortens, as a skirt

26

ACROSS

1. Actor Alan
5. Wood sprite
8. Knowing
12. Bridle strap
13. Feel under the weather
14. At rest
15. The Bluegrass State
17. Scaloppine meat
18. That girl
19. Dines
20. Navajo group
24. Building sites
27. Give a job to
28. Use a keyboard
29. Cup rim
32. Magazine VIP
34. Complete
36. "Sure!"
37. Frayed
39. Sturdy trees
40. Poker stake
41. Least satisfactory
42. Sandwich shop
45. In the style of: 2 wds.
47. Enthusiastic
48. Child's friend
53. Street entertainer
54. Large deer
55. Beasts of burden
56. Snow vehicle
57. Pastrami bread
58. Unwanted plant

DOWN

1. Noah's boat
2. Civil War general
3. Confused noise
4. Social insect
5. Every one
6. Apt (to)
7. Go by plane
8. Husbands' partners
9. Thought
10. Narrow opening
11. Snakelike fishes
16. Put into service
20. Those people
21. Carnival attraction
22. Spring flower
23. Wager
25. Not closed
26. Five plus five
28. Horse's gait
29. Fibber
30. Annoys
31. 4-Down, at a picnic
33. Possess
35. As well
38. "No kidding?"
40. Helped
41. Path
42. Beavers' projects
43. Morally depraved
44. Cocktail flavoring
46. Large pond
48. For each
49. Cut (grass)
50. Woodsman's chopping tool
51. Golfer's peg
52. Finish

27

ACROSS

1. Ripped
5. Distress-signal letters
8. Shrub
12. Unnecessary fusses
13. A couple
14. Pakistan's continent
15. Signals agreement
16. Cease
17. Gave temporarily
18. Axle oil
20. Become sicker
22. High-pitched bark
23. _____ away, hid aboard a ship
27. Speak in an undertone
31. Gaze steadily
32. Scuba supply
33. Largish rodent
35. Apply, as rouge (with "on")
36. Boise's state
39. Least wealthy
42. High male voices
44. _____ Grande
45. Gents
46. Puts (a seed) into the soil
50. Land measurement unit
53. Lincoln or Vigoda
55. Mature female horse
56. 60-minute period
57. Young goat
58. Equal
59. Certain colonists?
60. Self-pride
61. Colored permanently

DOWN

1. Distinctive flavor
2. Smell
3. Went by horse
4. Writing assignments
5. More sharply sloping
6. Hold the title to
7. Fizzy beverages
8. What a voter casts
9. Exploit for selfish purposes
10. Immorality
11. Sombrero or chapeau
19. Drink a little
21. Impersonal pronoun
24. Get one's feet wet?
25. Ages
26. Financial obligation
27. Be patient
28. Take cover
29. Tehran's land
30. Knock sharply
34. Submarine weapon
37. Baseball's "round trips"
38. Prospector's quest
40. Slippery liquid
41. Wandered
43. Serpent
47. Dark blue
48. Orchard growth
49. Convey
50. "I've found it!"
51. Pro's foe
52. Road groove
54. Massive

28

ACROSS

1. Mr. Newhart
4. Glasgow native
8. Close, as a door
12. Fearful wonder
13. Angel's topper
14. Window square
15. Mediterranean or Caribbean
16. "Raggedy" doll
17. Parched
18. Northern native
20. Worries
21. More sunken
24. Baby's first word, often
27. Sailor's affirmative reply
28. Do simple math
31. Word after "Iron" or "Ice"
32. Half of six
34. Beam of sunshine
35. Heavy weight
36. Have brunch
37. Wile E. Coyote's supplier
38. Fashions
41. Moved sneakily
45. Licked (up)
49. Strong affection
50. Historic periods
52. "Without further ____ . . ."
53. Chimps, for example
54. Sour fruit
55. Parishioner's seat
56. "Go ____, young man!"
57. Baby horse
58. Landers of advice columns

DOWN

1. Softball bag
2. Is in arrears
3. Bird's "nose"
4. Humiliation
5. Birch-bark boat
6. Antique
7. Child's plaything
8. Shadowbox
9. Rabbit's relative
10. Single part
11. Turner and Knight
19. Ms. Lupino
20. Release from jail
22. Celebration
23. Needle's hole
24. Wrestling surface
25. In the past
26. Grown-up lads
28. Curved line
29. Beaver's construction
30. Color-changing liquid
32. Examination
33. Bonnet, for one
37. Egyptian viper
39. Andes animal
40. Artist's stand
41. Talon
42. Lariat material
43. Preholiday nights
44. Bothersome person
46. Dad
47. Genesis garden
48. Parka filling
50. Magical being
51. ____ Grande

29

ACROSS

1. Cut, as the grass
4. Pub drinks
8. Tacks on
12. Humble admiration
13. Aching
14. Imperial Roman fiddler
15. Delightful
17. Sports group
18. Dancer Kelly
19. Fence made of shrubs
20. Boxes in an exhibition
23. Sun's domain
25. Glazed ceramic square
26. Plant support
27. By way of
30. Most ancient
32. Conclusion
34. Little legume
35. Light source
37. Skin disorder
38. Gershwin of songwriting
39. Full-court ____
40. Thunder-and-lightning display
44. Real
46. Dracula's garment
47. Usual
51. Monkey house residents
52. Superman's alter ego
53. Bring to court
54. Canvas shelter
55. Annoys
56. Porker's abode

DOWN

1. Atlas page
2. Night-hunting bird
3. Tiny
4. Donkeys
5. Mortgage, perhaps
6. Writer Hemingway
7. Place; arrange
8. Start a kitty
9. Title of ownership
10. Go too slowly, as time
11. Indefinite quantity
16. Be of like mind
19. "Ave Maria," for one
20. React to a red light
21. Mound
22. "M*A*S*H" star
24. Save
26. Broadway headliner
27. "Miami ____," 1980s TV show
28. Country hotels
29. Gets on in years
31. Thin
33. Had the courage (to)
36. Substance
39. Football kicks
40. "Get out of here!"
41. Sticky strip
42. Ajar, at least
43. Take one's ease
45. Military status
47. Enjoy a snow sport
48. Cleo's serpent
49. Feel regret over
50. Scout group

30

ACROSS

1. Revise (copy)
5. Taste (a drink)
8. Munch on
12. Fishing string
13. Neither's partner
14. Deep affection
15. Gym pads
16. Be indebted to
17. Prayer ending
18. Coin opening
19. Sharp knock
20. Relax
21. Dine
23. Inquire
25. Asian bear
28. Museum display
29. Auction offer
32. Self
33. More mature
35. At least one
36. "Bam!"
37. Dollar bill
38. Alert
40. Dancer Miller
41. Pastrami bread
42. Juicy fruit
45. Anger
47. "Woe is me!"
51. Land unit
52. Affirmative gesture
53. Abundant, as vegetation
54. Slender
55. Deity
56. Musical ensemble
57. Bubbly drink
58. Pigpen
59. Miami basketball team

DOWN

1. Shade trees
2. Control knob
3. Dividing word
4. Evaluated
5. Express derision
6. Des Moines' state
7. Get ready
8. Superman's alter ego Kent
9. Catcher's plate
10. Holiday precursors
11. Took off
22. Hammerin' Hank
24. Wander away
25. Vigor
26. In the past
27. At this time
28. Imitate
29. Sheep's sound
30. Pen liquid
31. Tint
34. A baseball game has nine, usually
39. Riches
40. Sports stadium
41. "I Am Woman" singer Helen
42. Taps lightly
43. Repeated sound
44. Very dry
46. Plant anchor
48. Tempt
49. Largest continent
50. Fired (a pistol)

31

ACROSS

1. Relieve (pain)
5. Male turkey
8. Vaccine injection
12. Grows old
13. "____ Got a Secret," TV show
14. City cab
15. Hauls
16. Gents
17. Cooking appliance
18. Watchful
20. Tenant's monthly payment
21. Remained
24. Annoy
26. Usual place for a belt
27. Slugger DiMaggio
28. Solid H_2O
31. Everything
32. Nasal sound
34. Negative vote
35. Reply of consent
36. To do this "is human"
37. Part of the wash cycle
39. Anger
40. Sight, touch, etc.
41. Cuts (the lawn)
44. Lovers' quarrels
46. Friends of Tarzan
47. 2,000-pound weight
48. Sunrise direction
52. Restaurant's bill of fare
53. Parking area
54. Tip, to Sherlock Holmes
55. Poker stake
56. Period in history
57. Docile

DOWN

1. Devour
2. In the past
3. Make a fine seam
4. Short, nonfiction writings
5. Used a stopwatch
6. Ended
7. Refer to
8. Long-legged bird
9. " . . . to ____ and to hold . . ."
10. Yoked beasts
11. Dye (hair)
19. Piece of mail
21. Swing gently to music
22. Narrative account
23. Feels sick
25. Rueful feeling
27. Glass container
28. Rural lodgings
29. Violin box
30. Vision organs
33. Try to pin an opponent to the mat
38. Six-legged critter
39. Put forth
40. Christmas visitor
41. Doll's cry
42. Unseal
43. Departed
45. Needy
49. Like: 2 wds.
50. Addition result
51. Golf-ball holder

32

ACROSS

1. Slant
5. Pig enclosure
8. Yarn mop
12. Smell
13. Weeding implement
14. Use a stopwatch
15. Adhesive strip
16. Colony insect
17. Puts to work
18. Get forty winks
20. Fender dimple
21. Sell door to door
24. Weep
26. Opposite of most
27. Payable
28. Place for pampering
31. Park tree
32. Goofed up
34. Lock-opening device
35. Cleopatra's undoing
36. Beam of light
37. Join together
39. Blaze remnant
40. Play parts
41. In good health
44. Chinese drink
45. Crop-destroying weather
46. Doctor's bill
48. "____ Me Out to the Ball Game"
52. Teen's skin woe
53. Frosty brew
54. Immoral
55. Yonder folks
56. Playful bite
57. Official military position

DOWN

1. Little kid
2. Filmdom's Lupino
3. Cut (a branch)
4. Fashions
5. Physical form
6. Cargo weight
7. As ____, up until now
8. Prepare for a test
9. Very learned
10. Ending to some prayers
11. Most excellent
19. Changes
21. Urgent appeal
22. Slippery swimmers
23. Slight wetness
24. Billiards stick
25. Make smaller
27. Use a towel
28. Fruit rind
29. Sampras of tennis
30. Favorable votes
33. Stadium sound
38. Less messy
39. Narrow urban street
40. High, as prices
41. "____ do you mean?"
42. Apiece
43. Highway marking
46. Devotee
47. Famous inventor Whitney
49. Gardner of Hollywood
50. Relatives
51. Large North American deer

33

ACROSS

1. Golf score
4. Thick chunk
8. Assess
12. High card
13. Made a basket
14. Egg-shaped
15. High explosive: abbr.
16. Paradise
17. Becomes victorious
18. That girl
19. Writing tool
20. Border
21. Have lunch
23. Consumed
26. Trade
28. Rip
29. Mature
32. Not as cold
34. Drank like Lassie
36. "Def- initely!"
37. Bad habit
39. Mimics
40. Short note
41. Tavern brew
42. Coura- geous one
45. Chess piece
47. Fire residue
50. Very dry
51. Money owed to another
52. Cowboy Rogers
53. Aspect
54. Lazy
55. Shade tree
56. Command to Spot
57. Coloring agents
58. Actor Knotts

DOWN

1. Forest trail
2. Skin condition
3. Falls back
4. Used a broom
5. Mine find
6. City road
7. Performer Vereen
8. Moved a canoe
9. Eager
10. Sharp flavor
11. Otherwise
22. Likely (to)
24. Bargain event
25. Historic time period
26. Timid
27. "Alas!"
28. Neat
29. Became visible
30. "Golly!"
31. Asner and Sullivan
33. First woman
35. Buddy
38. Funny movie
40. Sit for an artist
41. Poker stakes
42. Corned- beef dish
43. A Great Lake
44. Go by bus
46. Qualified
48. Diva's perform- ance
49. Church song
51. Accom- plished

34

ACROSS

1. Never seen before
4. Mature tadpole
8. Legendary slugger's nickname
12. Wood chopper
13. Competent
14. Had a debt
15. Prohibit (from)
16. Hawaiian garlands
17. Jungle homes
18. Having a bad odor
20. Utter
22. "The world is my ____!"
24. Beaver's blockade
27. Opening for inserting letters
30. Be a pest to
31. Yale student
32. Hardwood tree
33. Catchers' gloves
35. Certain musical tones
36. Actress Gardner
37. "That's ____, folks!"
38. Milk measure
39. Disburse, as money
40. Magic word?
43. Employ
44. San Francisco team
48. Sudden break
51. Trot or gallop
53. Be in poor health
54. Tramp
55. Skin affliction
56. Anger
57. Paradise
58. Lower limbs
59. Conducted, as a band

DOWN

1. Captures (a fugitive)
2. School test
3. Used to be
4. Add up, as points
5. Pays heed to
6. Boxing legend
7. Meal's sweet finish
8. Human form
9. Amazement
10. Big ____, London landmark
11. Asner and Bradley
19. Parking area
21. Boats like Noah's
23. Earl or Lord
24. Pastrami store
25. Actor Alda
26. Thin fog
27. Detergent
28. Hot, molten rock
29. "All right!"
33. Directional aids
34. Against the regulations
38. Green vegetable
41. Getting older
42. Locales
43. Atop
45. Hammer's target
46. Wheel cover
47. Luge, for one
48. That lass
49. Doze off
50. Mr. Lincoln, familiarly
52. Aviation expert

35

ACROSS

1. Increase in size
5. Distress signal
8. Throw
12. Helper
13. Couple
14. Largest continent
15. Home for lads and lasses?
17. Holiday of fasting
18. For each
19. Anger
20. Move to avoid a blow
21. Audio equipment
23. Unruffled
26. Idle chatter
31. Except
34. Athens' country
35. Sell
36. Adolescent
37. Medals of valor
41. Skin on top of the head
45. Small inlet
46. High explosive: abbr.
49. Game played on horseback
50. More beautiful
52. Exclamation of sorrow
53. "_____ got a secret!"
54. Choir voice
55. Canvas shelter
56. Family room
57. Sunset direction

DOWN

1. Sound of surprise
2. Cereal grain
3. Smell
4. Saturate
5. Look intently
6. Person who possesses
7. Rich earth
8. Angel's headgear
9. Consumed
10. Wedding band
11. Tardy
16. Illuminated
20. Hinged entryway
21. Winter vehicle
22. Breakfast food
23. Drinking vessel
24. Single
25. Ancient
27. Matched collections
28. View
29. Frozen water
30. Writing tool
32. Strike with an open hand
33. Stitch
38. Higher than
39. Black bird
40. Hair coloring
41. Formal footwear
42. Nat King _____
43. Actor Alda
44. Misplaced
46. Roofing square
47. Catches
48. Horse's pace
50. Jar covering
51. Code of conduct

36

ACROSS

1. Heap
5. Horses' grains
9. Angry
12. Moistureless
13. ____ as a pancake
14. Boxer Muhammad
15. Sounded (a bell)
16. Celebrity status
17. Auto
18. Prepare to propose
20. Visualize
21. Colony insect
22. Everything but the kitchen ____
24. For each
26. Director's directive
29. Froth
31. Sailor's cord
34. Concurs (with)
36. Merited
38. Those people
39. Three-foot measure
41. "____ about time!"
42. Gibson of "Braveheart"
44. Burst (of laughter)
46. Brush (on)
48. Horned viper
50. Candle lighter
54. Squeaky-hinge fix
55. Pinball foul
57. Sneaker or pump
58. Poem of praise
59. Bible garden
60. Cultivate, as land
61. Fiery color
62. Sit a spell
63. Breaking-twig sound

DOWN

1. City play area
2. Tehran's land
3. Facial crease
4. Photo borders
5. On's opposite
6. Juneau's state
7. Subdue
8. Dropping off sharply
9. Pasta often cooked with a cheese sauce
10. Alda or Arkin
11. Potting soil
19. Existence
23. Overly curious
25. Be human?
26. A 32-Down
27. "Yuck!"
28. Quaked
30. Nothing other than
32. Pampered animal
33. Bradley and McMahon
35. Hole in a needle
37. Eve's man
40. Crisp fruits
43. After a time
45. Endures
46. Closet closer
47. Assistant
49. Face of a cube
51. Slender
52. Soft-drink favorite
53. Beatles song and film
56. Dynamite's cousin: abbr.

37

ACROSS

1. Be boastful
5. Total up
8. Piece of living-room furniture
12. Frilly trim
13. Use a weeding tool
14. Capture by cunning
15. Cooking chamber
16. North Pole employee?
17. Steak order
18. Where the sun sets
19. "____ Baba and the Forty Thieves"
20. Tavern choices
21. Coffee-can cover
23. Freshly created
25. Watched secretly (with "on")
28. Gibson of "Lethal Weapon"
29. Fashion craze
32. Silvery metal
33. Entertain
35. Whitney who invented the cotton gin
36. Strong longing
37. Ham source
38. Dairy product
40. It may be vacant
41. Had breakfast
42. Pop
45. Feminine pronoun
47. Pesters incessantly
51. Consequently
52. Slip up
53. Become weary
54. Soybean extracts
55. ____ Grande
56. Revise (text)
57. Equestrian game
58. Make a hem
59. Lions' lairs

DOWN

1. Sound, as a whistle
2. Favorable review
3. Certain cards
4. Mild
5. In front (of)
6. Tea-party guest?
7. Gives the meaning of (a word)
8. Mare's bedding
9. Of the mouth
10. Taxi rider
11. Monkeys' kin
22. Boise's state
24. Vote into office
25. Place for pigs
26. Crusty pastry
27. Rural lodging
28. Stein's cousin
29. Charge for a service
30. In the style of: 2 wds.
31. Lower, as the lights
34. Fathers' mates
39. Leased
40. Cattle-roping loop
41. Bow's missile
42. "Quit it!"
43. Akron's state
44. Boring
46. A Great Lake
48. Assistant
49. Toothy smile
50. TV receivers

38

ACROSS

1. Word of woe
5. Felines
9. Mouthful of gum
12. City cab
13. Agree to employ
14. Super tennis serve
15. Earthly paradise
16. "May it be so!"
17. That woman
18. Baseball hat
20. Or's partner
22. Catholic clergyman
25. Scatter (seeds)
26. Curtain holder
27. Coop resident
29. Bake (chicken)
33. Fuss and bother
34. Tear
36. Halloween shout
37. Dissolves
40. Tap fondly
42. Bradley and Asner
43. Of that thing
45. Texas city
47. Far from rare
50. Lacking rain
51. "So that's it!"
52. Lunch or dinner
54. Showy spring flower
58. Ignited
59. Lacking color
60. Three times three
61. Angeles lead-in
62. Slip on ice
63. Departed

DOWN

1. Had a 52-Across
2. Young fellow
3. Chopping tool
4. Because
5. Novel section
6. Purpose
7. Oaks and elms
8. One about to graduate
9. Cleanse
10. Be sore
11. Forest creature
19. Fire residue
21. One plus one
22. British baby buggy
23. Went by bus
24. Object of worship
28. ____ and tuck
30. Cain's brother
31. Ginger ale, for one
32. Lob
35. Rowed a canoe
38. "Tiny" hero of "A Christmas Carol"
39. Walks heavily
41. Paving goo
44. Move stealthily
46. Telling untruths
47. Use the phone
48. State by Lake Erie
49. Grappling pads
53. ____ Baba
55. Brazil port, for short
56. Rural hotel
57. "Monkey ____, monkey do!"

39

ACROSS

1. Chemist's workplace
4. Melt, as 12-Across
8. Unblemished
12. Frozen water
13. Judge's garment
14. Large continent
15. Picnic pest
16. Imitated
17. Take it easy
18. Dwell (at)
20. Legal suits
21. Lucille Ball, for one
24. Students' tables
27. Takes into custody
31. Strong tree
32. Canine coat
33. Tool set
34. Mineral formation
37. Cold and ____, weather forecast
39. Pray to
41. Let
44. Comes in
48. Sidelong glance
49. High cards
51. Large rodent
52. Shoreline grit
53. Singer Nat King
54. Mature
55. Bettor's concern
56. Fling
57. Use a needle

DOWN

1. Fibber
2. Teen's skin condition
3. Wagers
4. Exchanges (for)
5. Fervently wished
6. Honest ____, Presidential nickname
7. Marry
8. Thanksgiving march
9. Employs
10. Elevate
11. Has lunch
19. Annoy
20. Automobile
22. Moves by truck
23. Make a mistake
24. "What's up, ____?"
25. Hearing organ
26. Wild blue yonder
28. Hit the slopes
29. Can metal
30. Pigpen
32. From a distance
35. Fencing blades
36. Pull behind
37. Washes soap out of
38. Likely
40. Shoe parts
41. As well
42. Show the way
43. Give temporarily
45. Epochs
46. Raving fury
47. Thick soup
49. Play part
50. Dove's call

40

ACROSS

1. Self-important one
5. Energy
8. Punch or slap
12. Plumbing tube
13. Grow older
14. Steak order
15. Experts
16. Neither's partner
17. Was indebted to
18. Leased
20. "A ____ Good Men"
22. Brother of Moses
24. Actress Marie Saint
27. No longer together
31. Gave a command
33. Country road
34. Confection for chewing
35. Territory
36. Rainy-day pools
38. Light fogs
39. Sneaky
40. Sports stadium
42. Phys-ed room
43. Writer Hemingway
48. County lock-up
51. TV commercials
53. Finished
54. "M*A*S*H" star Alan
55. Negative word
56. Construction locale
57. Use the library
58. "Absolutely!"
59. Otherwise

DOWN

1. Practice boxing
2. Pleasant
3. Honest; candid
4. Superior to all others
5. Black-and-white bear
6. Self-image
7. Play for an audience
8. Forehead
9. "Stop in the name of the ____!"
10. Mine find
11. Marry
19. Have a snack
21. Finale
23. Awaken
24. Historic periods
25. Small window in a car
26. Says further
27. Swiss peaks
28. Letter-writing apostle
29. Griffith of TV
30. Lipstick shade
32. Inventor Whitney
34. Berlin's country
37. Produce (eggs)
38. Make imperfect
41. Birds' homes
42. Pleased
44. Smelling organ
45. Wrong-doing
46. Fixes, as a date
47. Maple, for one
48. Glass container
49. Beer's kin
50. Lupino of film
52. Fawn's mom

41

ACROSS

1. An evergreen
4. Made a basket
8. Look for a bargain
12. Wedding reply: 2 wds.
13. Tehran's land
14. Ms. Turner
15. Game-show host Barker
16. Allow to borrow
17. Biblical paradise
18. Frozen precipitation
20. V-formation flyers
21. Venomous snake
23. Swiss mountain
24. "Stop!"
27. Plead
29. Possess
32. Cotton-gin inventor Whitney
33. Trap
34. Female deer
35. Tear
36. Pain
37. Curved
38. "Nasty!"
39. Time period
41. Brief arguments
44. Mad
48. Desire
49. Higher than
52. Regret
53. Teens' skin condition
54. Six minus one
55. Sick
56. Equal
57. Terror
58. Actor Gibson

DOWN

1. Lies
2. Worshiped object
3. Dressing gown
4. Droops
5. Mine find
6. Moving vehicle
7. Conclude
8. Soak
9. Conceal
10. Singles
11. Window section
19. Dine
20. Joy
22. Fruit drink
23. Concur
24. That woman
25. The Greatest
26. Mouth part
28. Pep-squad word
29. Lyric poem
30. Was victorious
31. Mesh snare
33. Loses firmness
37. Prohibit
38. Express
40. Less common
41. Trade
42. Stride
43. Actress Bancroft
45. Unpleasant
46. Regulation
47. Scream
49. Light-switch position
50. Compete
51. Ms. Perón

42

ACROSS

1. Party giver
5. Rubies and diamonds
9. Wild blue yonder
12. Skunk's defense
13. Uniform
14. Individual
15. Hollywood's Hackman
16. Notorious Roman Emperor
17. Take the gold medal
18. "____ on your life!"
20. Bread-slice borders
22. Open-toed shoe
25. However
26. One who plays for money
27. Beer barrel
29. Took a risk
33. Performs in a movie
35. L.L. Cool J's music
37. ____ and seek
38. Of those people
40. House plant container
42. Bowling target
43. ____ down, disappoint
45. Freedom from danger
47. U.S. currency
50. Large whirlpool bath
51. Hatchet's kin
52. Sports event
54. Under-the-mistletoe event
58. Two plus eight
59. Hullabaloos
60. Canyon effect
61. Finish
62. Informative report
63. Colored, as hair

DOWN

1. Greedy person
2. Poem of tribute
3. Daddy's boy
4. Current style
5. Less harsh
6. Preholiday night
7. Compassion
8. Slept noisily
9. Scatters (seeds)
10. Make a sweater
11. Strong urges
19. Durable tree
21. State next to Nevada
22. Little fight
23. Bridge's curve
24. High C, for one
28. Hole in a fence
30. Mature
31. Revise (text)
32. Contradict (charges)
34. Window ledge
36. Own
39. U.S. President Ronald
41. Faucet; spigot
44. Exchange goods
46. Counterfeited
47. Calendar square
48. Strong animals
49. Give for a while
53. Cut the grass
55. Frozen
56. This woman
57. Lawn strip

43

ACROSS

1. Destiny
5. Sheep's sound
8. Rock's Turner
12. Alda of "The West Wing"
13. "Get ____ of it!"
14. Dollar bills
15. Take a break
16. Aged
17. Alongside of
18. Natives of Greenland
20. Allow
21. Basketball hoop
22. More sacred
25. Express with words
28. Chest bone
29. Chopping tool
30. "That's neither here ____ there"
31. Tiny particles
33. Jar top
34. Anger
35. Food fish
36. Classroom exams
38. Building for worship
40. Feminine pronoun
41. Spelling contest
42. Distant
46. Bundle (of hay)
48. Cut apart roughly
49. Alike in every way
50. Higher than
51. Swiss mountain
52. Level
53. Rolls of cash
54. Attention-getting call
55. Animals' "houses"

DOWN

1. Transportation cost
2. Pub drinks
3. Assignment
4. Whole
5. Sweeping instrument
6. Feels sick
7. Find a sum
8. Cloth for drying
9. First letters of a name
10. Attachment to a 21-Across
11. Cigar residue
19. "____ on 34th Street," film
20. Seafood favorite from Maine
22. That man
23. Way out
24. Crimson and maroon
25. Single part
26. Pulled apart
27. Shook, as if in fear
28. Fishing pole
32. Foot digit
37. Rubbed out
39. Individuals of equal rank
40. Far from sad
42. Arrange (papers)
43. "Goodbye" gesture
44. Prayer conclusion
45. Longings
46. Bend respectfully
47. Ms. Gardner
48. Football cheer

44

ACROSS

1. Mama's mate
5. Baseball hat
8. Construction location
12. Egg-shaped
13. Everyone
14. Opera solo
15. Desire; crave
16. ____ Grande
17. Delicate hue
18. Organ of vision
20. Makes fun of
22. Breathed noisily during sleep
25. Light brown
26. Bee homes
27. That girl
28. Was victorious
31. Frosted (a cake)
32. Pea shell
33. Hillside hollow
34. Writer's implement
35. Crow's cry
36. Military student
37. Worthless thing
38. Pours H_2O on (plants)
39. Frightened
42. Exist
43. Openwork fabric
44. Fall behind
46. Cost per unit
50. Picnic pests
51. Conceit
52. Biblical paradise
53. Untidy condition
54. Male heir, often
55. Feat of skill

DOWN

1. Comic-book sound
2. Gardner of "Mogambo"
3. Frying vessel
4. Modified
5. Worried (about)
6. Boxer Muhammad
7. Engaged in a conspiracy
8. The devil
9. 18-Across part
10. Pitchfork prong
11. Dines
19. "Definitely!"
21. Corn spike
22. Big boat
23. Friendly
24. Baking chamber
27. "By what means?"
28. Walk in the shallows
29. Higher than
30. Mesh snares
32. Uses oars
33. Provided food for (a party)
35. Pool stick
36. Detroit product
37. Frock or gown
38. Child's cart
39. Shut forcefully
40. Sugar source
41. Plays a role
45. In the past
47. Fruit drink
48. Golfer's mound
49. Finale

45

ACROSS

1. Bestow upon
5. Scottish girl
9. Carbonated beverage
12. Refreshing drinks
13. Cathedral-doorway shape
14. Bustle
15. Search for
16. Guided actors in a movie
18. Fashion capital of the world
20. Boring
21. Cut (a lawn)
23. Uses dynamite
27. Gymnastic circus performer
31. Utter
32. Ghost's shout
33. Puppy's cry
35. Mr. Whitney of the cotton gin
36. Folks who tell fibs
39. Mail-carrying guys
42. Story's conclusion
44. Orange pekoe or oolong
45. Warming first course
47. Dentist's request
51. Fabric
55. "Saturday Night ____," TV comedy show
56. Indivisible
57. Outer border
58. Cooking appliance
59. Weird
60. Act of bravery
61. Part of "R and R"

DOWN

1. Sound of shock
2. Concept; thought
3. Swerve
4. Northern native
5. Boy
6. Desert-dry
7. Clean with a scouring pad
8. Clam casings
9. Tap affectionately
10. Poem of tribute
11. Pea's locale
17. Applaud
19. Weep loudly
22. Sinatra song, "My ____"
24. Appear
25. Narrative account
26. Body's covering
27. Competent
28. Nickel or dime
29. Highway
30. "In the know" information
34. Pasta-boiling vessel
37. "Early to bed, early to ____ . . ."
38. "Sawed wood"
40. Work as a 41-Down
41. One who alters suits
43. Sight-seeing-tour conductor
46. Magazine leaf
48. Jackknife or gainer
49. 12/24 and 12/31
50. Lease
51. Sound of a cow
52. In addition to
53. Danson or Williams
54. Was winning

46

ACROSS

1. Tom-tom, for example
5. "To ____ is human . . ."
8. Ooze (out) slowly
12. Greeted the dawn
13. Vote on the Senate floor
14. Acting Alan
15. Think-tank's output
16. Omelet necessity
17. Wooden pins
18. Flies or fleas
20. Fire residue
22. Doctor for livestock
23. Heavenly body
25. Have overdue bills
27. Fedora, for one
30. Do some easy math
31. Territories
34. Take a breath
36. Revolver
37. Play platform
38. Roll out the ____ carpet
39. "You, there!"
40. Verbal refusals
41. Outstanding periods
43. Pose a question
45. Involuntary motion
47. Luxury craft
51. Seat in the den
53. Tear
55. Run for it
56. Hole stopper
57. Gibbon or gorilla
58. Deserve, as a salary
59. Mild-tasting fish
60. Never seen before
61. Stain

DOWN

1. Act like a leaky faucet
2. Was a jockey
3. Exploits
4. Butcher's display
5. Center (of a storm)
6. Esteem
7. Tatters
8. Maple "juice"
9. ____ hour, latest possible time
10. Outer border
11. Gone by, as time
19. Least fresh
21. Special occasion
24. Summer cooler
26. Used to be
27. That fellow's
28. Industrious insect
29. Filled with gratitude
32. Bambi's ma, for one
33. Cunning
35. In the past
36. For each
38. Cookbook entry
42. Bank vaults
43. Venomous snakes
44. Song for one
46. Tehran's country
48. Sound of thunder
49. Story's protagonist
50. Circus shelter
52. Become older
54. Church bench

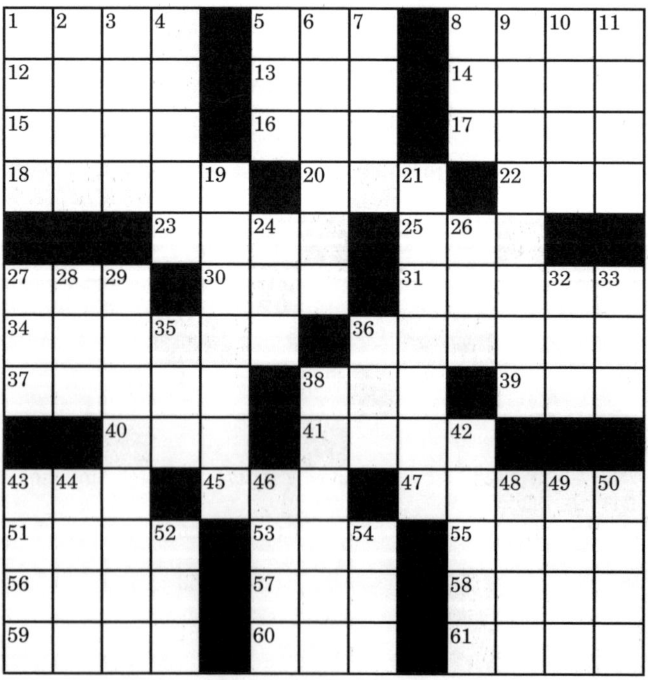

47

ACROSS

1. Lawn builder
4. See 1-Across
8. Man's spouse
12. Fruit-filled pastry
13. Cambodia's continent
14. Pressing appliance
15. Green around the gills
16. Head's support
17. Frying fat
18. Boy Scout's skill with knots
20. Grasped in the hand
22. Like Methuselah
24. Playground favorite
28. Withdrawal, as of troops
32. Steered (the car)
33. Woodshed tool
34. "Merry" month
36. Help
37. Parlor instrument
40. Certain incentives
43. Sipping tubes
45. Tic-____-toe
46. Concerned with
48. Catalog entries
52. Involving the mouth
55. Sinister
57. Brazilian port, for short
58. Social engagement
59. Surfer's quest
60. In addition to
61. Given a new color
62. Winter amusement
63. Ocean

DOWN

1. Barbecue skewer
2. Like 17-Across
3. Sandwich shop
4. Snarl, as hair
5. Apply
6. Extremely wealthy
7. Counterfeits
8. Less tame
9. Lyric-writing Gershwin brother
10. On account of
11. Conclusion
19. "Neither a borrower ____ a lender be . . ."
21. Was a guide
23. Water barrier
25. Fly high
26. Enthusiastic
27. Joins in matrimony
28. Sharp knocks
29. Sign in a movie theater
30. Rip
31. Roofing goo
35. As of today
38. Hammered down
39. Be the proprietor of
41. Cried mournfully
42. Play a part
44. Cooks slowly
47. Racetrack shape
49. Notable times
50. Coal source
51. Soft drink
52. Strange
53. Bit of sunshine
54. Munched on
56. "Now ____ seen everything!"

48

ACROSS

1. A Gershwin
4. Play division
7. Make very happy
12. "What's up, ____?"
13. Bashful
14. Felt deep affection for
15. Tall shade tree
16. Pelvis part
17. Graceful birds
18. Beerlike beverages
20. Four plus five
22. Liberace's instrument
24. Health resort
27. "Excellent!"
30. Obtained
32. Foot the bill
33. Uttered a loud, deep sound
35. Original inhabitant
37. Fitting
38. Furious
40. Flying toys
41. "Of course!"
42. More fully developed
44. Headliner
45. Apiece
49. Not together
53. Round cooking vessel
55. Montana of football
56. Boombox, for one
57. Holiday night
58. In the style of: 2 wds.
59. Scout unit
60. Bloodshot
61. Strike sharply

DOWN

1. Thought
2. Small piece of bread
3. Highest point
4. Volcanic dust
5. Beijing's country
6. Data processor's action
7. Otherwise
8. Close to the ground
9. Ms. Gardner
10. Gymnast's perfect score
11. McMahon and Sullivan
19. Practice boxing
21. Midday
23. Bit of news
24. Meat-roasting rod
25. Cover with tar
26. Affirmative votes
27. Drab color
28. Strong cord
29. Gobbles up
31. Seize
34. Pub missile
36. Wheel cover
39. Cloth for a baby
43. Establish as true
44. Discontinue
46. Slightly open
47. Carbonated drink
48. Jumbled pile
49. Museum attraction
50. Skillful golf score
51. Fuss
52. Carnival city, for short
54. Actor Danson

49

ACROSS

1. Horse food
4. Qualified
8. Slip
12. Conceit
13. Distribute cards
14. Actor Griffith
15. Head signal
16. Halloween wear
17. Smoothing tool
18. Prepares a script
20. Despised
21. Breaks apart
23. Atmosphere
24. Forest growths
25. Helps
29. Jug handle
30. Writing fluid
31. Soda, to some
32. Enigma
35. Cost
37. Noah's boat
38. Esteem
39. Scrub
42. Drills holes in
43. Respiratory organ
44. In addition to
45. Easter meat
48. Rounded entryway
49. Love's flower
50. Hurricane's center
51. Red veggie
52. Has debts
53. Collection

DOWN

1. Egg layer
2. In the past
3. Alpine vocalists
4. Acknowledges
5. Plays on a drum
6. Irish girl
7. Moose's kin
8. Jungle excursion
9. Create a sweater
10. Lazy
11. Colored, as hair
19. Expire
20. Belonging to that man
21. Plant stalk
22. Beseech
23. Inquire
25. Some
26. Scatters (water)
27. Sightseeing trip
28. Drove too quickly
30. Bother
33. Instructed
34. Make a mistake
35. Song divisions
36. Mature
38. Awaken
39. Hunk of bacon
40. Heal
41. A single time
42. Inflate, ____ up
44. In favor of
46. Sailor's affirmative
47. Encountered

50

ACROSS

1. Little bit (of paint)
4. Mimicked
8. Dancer Astaire
12. Drink-cooling cubes
13. Innermost section
14. One who tells fibs
15. Boy who "won't grow up": 2 wds.
17. In addition
18. Actor Majors
19. "____ off the grass!"
20. Hard-shelled mollusk
23. Verbalized
27. Small carpets
28. Reverent dread
29. Ship's diary
32. Anger; wrath
33. Ahead of time
35. Citrus thirst-quencher
36. Place to sleep
37. Compete
38. Where cakes are baked
39. Cloth measures
41. Great in magnitude
42. Grain-storage tower
45. Metal source
47. Matinee ____, old-time movie star
48. Help-wanted ads' offers
53. Disclose a secret
54. Covetous feeling
55. Emulate 8-Across
56. Young whipper-snappers
57. Vision organs
58. Piggery

DOWN

1. Quick swim
2. Great tennis serve
3. Put money (on)
4. Unit of land
5. John Paul I and Pius VI
6. Memorable epoch
7. Study room
8. Snow particle
9. Anger
10. Relieve; comfort
11. Bit of rain
16. Shade givers
20. Baby's bed
21. Entice
22. Antiquated
24. Peeled, as an apple
25. Wide-eyed bird
26. Lock-opening device
29. Fluid rock
30. Poems of praise
31. Fellow
33. Gabor sister
34. Ventilate, as a room
38. Finished
39. Egg centers
40. Crack (a mystery)
42. Window part
43. Thought; concept
44. Fill with cargo
46. Light beams
48. "Get it?"
49. Some
50. "____ about time!"
51. Have a salad
52. Sneaky character

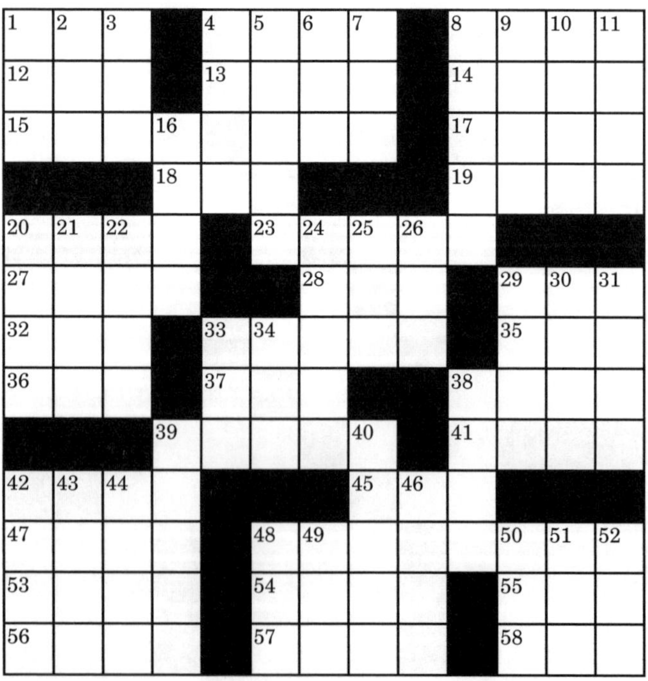

51

ACROSS

1. Simple
5. Big fuss
8. Sluggish
12. Persia, now
13. Jogged
14. Cover (a road)
15. Real estate
16. Deli bread choice
17. Had debts
18. Some Alaskans
20. Country hotels
21. Currently
22. "My ____ Sal"
24. Boasts
27. Sports enthusiast
28. Lie
31. Ventilate
32. Pie shell
34. Raw metal
35. Small child
36. "____ Town," play
37. Enticed
39. Fearful wonder
40. Mr. Franklin, familiarly
41. Break in two
44. African ape
48. 60-minute period
49. IRS's "take"
50. Frog's kin
51. Concerned with
52. "____ Been Working on the Railroad"
53. New York canal
54. Colorful sign gas
55. For each
56. Cozy retreats

DOWN

1. Footrace unit
2. Historic times
3. Corporal or sergeant
4. Happy finale to a fairy tale
5. Bow's missile
6. Most years have 365 of them
7. Dollar bill
8. Ruin
9. Manicured yard
10. Baking chamber
11. Marries
19. Kremlin's city
22. Fuel for a Ferrari
23. Stag's horn
24. Flying mammal
25. Brazil port, for short
26. Museum display
27. Cat's coat
28. In favor of
29. Wrath
30. Sleeping spot
33. Regret
38. Joined together
39. Cook's "bib"
40. Muhammad Ali, for one
41. Lower-leg bone
42. Zilch
43. Car
44. Bestowed upon
45. Folk wisdom
46. Stretched out
47. Fruit drinks
49. Waiter's bonus

52

ACROSS

1. Common skin disorder
5. Soup cooking vessel
8. Marine crustacean
12. Lower leg
13. Brazilian seaport, for short
14. Freight-yard vagabond
15. Male ruler
16. Lawn tree
17. With no purpose
18. Magic charms
20. Leg joints
21. Vienna's land
24. Surrounded by
27. Came in first
28. In the past
31. Conduct (an expedition)
32. Relieved (of)
33. Persia, today
34. Pen fluid
35. Neither's partner
36. Mom's brother
37. Release in print
39. Madrid's country
42. Harvested (a crop)
46. Sound an alarm
47. Certain Gabor
49. Volcanic rock
50. Highest point
51. Set on fire
52. Eternally
53. Untidy condition
54. Fixed charge
55. Fender boo-boo

DOWN

1. Poses a question
2. A ____ off the old block
3. Six plus three
4. Jolly Old ____
5. Printing machine
6. Cooking fat
7. Fowl fellow?
8. Fine porcelain
9. Went by horse
10. Competent
11. Lads
19. Struggle to carry
20. Family members
22. Spin, as a baton
23. Angler's pole
24. ____ Baba
25. Gents
26. It was once an acorn
28. Rainbow's shape
29. Young lady
30. The loneliest number?
32. Thieve from
33. Took a breath
35. Cloistered one
36. Employ
37. Evergreen trees
38. Very angry
39. Did the backstroke
40. Stride back and forth
41. Hugging appendages
43. Do some road repairs
44. Well matched
45. Pub missile
47. Little, magical being
48. Compete (with)

53

ACROSS

1. Car horn's sound
5. Afternoon parties
9. Not on
12. Involving the mouth
13. St. Louis landmark
14. West of old Hollywood
15. Uncovered
16. Dock
17. A Gershwin
18. "You said it!"
20. Following
22. Pursued
25. Small bill
26. Tablecloth fabric, often
27. Clumsy
31. Big coffeepot
32. Indisposed
33. TV's Leno
34. Honey-farm sight
37. Knowing (of)
39. Some, no matter which
40. Distress signals
41. Says "Grace"
44. Lubricates
45. "____ Town," play
46. Omelet ingredients
48. Made a knot in
52. Actor Wallach
53. Young stallion
54. Rim
55. Mr. Turner
56. "Rings on her fingers and bells on her ____ . . ."
57. Before long

DOWN

1. Hope of comedy
2. Historic time
3. Corn unit
4. Magic word?
5. Recorded
6. The Emerald Isle, in verse
7. High playing card
8. Became smaller
9. Leave out
10. Taxi charge
11. Horror-movie emotion
19. Grown-up guys
21. Some
22. "Welcome to the ____!"
23. Add to the payroll
24. Bancroft of "The Miracle Worker"
25. Hooting bird
27. Sudsy brew
28. Open a bit
29. Steak request
30. Hair tints
32. Climbing plant
35. Horse fodder
36. Fly or cricket
37. Everyone
38. Uses recklessly
40. Boxer's "dukes"
41. Keats or Yeats
42. Govern
43. Very dry
44. Stare at
47. Sticky stuff
49. Bride's words
50. Conceit
51. Thieves' haunt

54

ACROSS

1. 40 winks
4. Circle portions
8. Became taller
12. Long time
13. Wan
14. The ____ Star State, Texas
15. 2,000 pounds
16. Mob scene
17. Chances (of winning)
18. Brads or tacks
20. Three-piece suit part
21. Stable unit
23. Otherwise
26. Fingers' locale
27. The Beehive State
28. Lamb's lament
31. Sacrificial tables
33. Minute fraction
35. Moines preceder
36. Casual "Uh-huh"
38. Catch, as a fish
39. Annoying person
40. Urban transports
41. "Go away!"
44. Bird's sound
46. Proceed to the terminal, in a way
47. Assign a chair to
48. Lupino of movies
51. Smooth
52. Make sweaters
53. Tiny taste
54. Sallied forth
55. In a casual way
56. Procure

DOWN

1. ____ King Cole
2. In the past
3. Triangular flags
4. Spring month
5. Track part
6. Cloakroom
7. Prepare (the table)
8. Hand covering
9. Went on horseback
10. Winds up
11. Compass direction
19. "M*A*S*H" star
21. Source of prized roe
22. Nursery story
24. Mascara's target
25. Pronoun for Eve
27. Puts into service
28. Being a braggart
29. Green Gables gal
30. Does some arithmetic
32. Bread variety
34. Hint in a crossword puzzle
37. Be a guest
39. Sharp end
40. Mrs. Ford, former White House resident
41. Thick, souplike dish
42. "To ____ and to hold . . ."
43. Cart-pulling beasts
45. Cry plaintively
47. Glide down a mountain
49. Go out, as a flame
50. Liable (to)

55

ACROSS

1. "____ upon a time . . ."
5. Harden, as concrete
8. 46-Across's partner
12. Sheep's fleece
13. Sailor
14. Racetrack-shaped
15. English nobleman
16. Period in history
17. Shoulder enhancers
18. Cold symptom
20. "____ got an idea!"
22. Tiny wave on a pond's surface
24. Bustle
27. Skin on top of the head
30. Permit
31. Fellows
32. Actor Randall
33. Chocolate unit
34. Film spool
35. Likely (to)
36. Rainbow's shape
37. Actor Fonda
38. "Golly!"
39. Was overflowing (with)
41. Ocean
42. Entertained with humor
46. Daddy
49. Blasting compound: abbr.
51. Sheltered inlet
52. Final or midterm
53. Garden implement
54. Adam and Eve's home
55. Unit of heredity
56. Bradley and Sullivan
57. Pub missile

DOWN

1. Hooting birds
2. Time for lunch, for some
3. Center
4. Aged
5. Sloping suddenly
6. Hearing organ
7. Mobile home
8. Be morose
9. Acting Gardner
10. Angry
11. Gore and Pacino
19. ____ code, address part
21. Animal doctor
23. Location
24. Prayer closer
25. Forest animal
26. "____ the Lonely"
27. Male 25-Down
28. Deal (with)
29. Poker stake
33. Use the lungs
34. Made smaller
36. Had dinner
37. Skirt's edge
40. Spouses
41. Identical
43. Bubbly soft-drink
44. At any time
45. Fender depression
46. Wooden nail
47. Lumberjack's tool
48. Skillet
50. Nonverbal "yes"

56

ACROSS

1. Golfer's norm
4. Performs in a play
8. Cease
12. Bride's vow: 2 wds.
13. Weaving machine
14. Des Moines' state
15. Cut (off)
16. Shoe bottom
17. Land title
18. Miner's find
19. Tardy
21. Try out
23. "The Way We ____," Streisand movie
24. Cry of discovery
27. Took advantage of
29. Stocking material
31. World
34. Tricked
35. Like some beavers?
36. British noble
37. Deli bread choice
38. Air duct
40. Smooch
44. Hit (a drum)
45. "Ready or ____, here I come!"
46. Floor square
49. Moreno or Hayworth
52. Pair of singers
53. Admired one
54. Catch in a snare
55. Country sleepover spot
56. Sail's pole
57. Roll-call response
58. Summer fruit drink

DOWN

1. Airline captain
2. Love greatly
3. Catches, cowboy style
4. Gore and Pacino
5. Dove's soft sound
6. Sounded, as a church bell
7. Put (on) messily
8. Flank
9. Foot part
10. Be obliged to
11. Cushion
20. Certain male vocalist
22. Melody
23. Sopping
24. Everybody
25. Chop weeds
26. Connecting word
28. Dish out
30. Egg's center
31. For each
32. Reclined
33. Grow old
34. Oily nutrient
36. Whole; complete
39. Our 31-Across
41. Calcutta's land
42. What the ear hears
43. Quarry material
44. Pants accessory
46. Comedian Allen
47. Lupino of the big screen
48. ____ Angeles
50. Paving stuff
51. King Kong, for one

57

ACROSS

1. Became more mature
5. Use a chair
8. Read quickly
12. Clean with a sponge
13. Shed tears
14. Narrative account
15. Wicked
16. Took place
18. Make a choice
20. Corn spike
21. Detergent foam
23. Passed out (cards)
27. Rooster's mate
30. "Stubborn" beast
32. High woodwind
33. Bride's words
34. Accuse
36. Young fellow
37. Immoral acts
39. Eternally
40. Asner and Bradley
41. Water vapor
43. Part of "HOMES"
45. Swab the floor
47. Corners of a square, basically
51. Rank below sergeant
55. Harvard's chief rival
56. Involving the mouth
57. Ancient
58. Heap
59. Tennis star Sampras
60. Female sibling, for short
61. Snare

DOWN

1. Astonished
2. Pass along
3. Sweeping drama
4. Cold-cuts shops
5. List of events
6. Mr. Gershwin
7. Use a word processor
8. Sound system
9. Knows how to
10. Malt drink
11. Actor Beatty
17. Cushion
19. Stupid
22. Work extremely hard
24. Qualified
25. Fill with cargo
26. Danson and Koppel
27. Reaction to the villain
28. Prepare (copy)
29. Nary a soul
31. Green gems
35. Colleen's land, to poets
38. Specimen
42. Cow's call
44. Cairo's country
46. Paid athletes
48. Dragon's den
49. Fitzgerald of jazz
50. Ooze (out of)
51. Police officer
52. Raw metal
53. Mouse's kin
54. Boxer Muhammad

58

ACROSS

1. Young goat
4. Plate or saucer
8. Become rough, as lips
12. Anger
13. Fascinated by
14. Conceal
15. Tic-_____-toe
16. Sing like Ella
17. Mr. Alda
18. Like a mosquito bite
20. Motion pictures
21. Donkeys and burros
23. Work for, as wages
25. Wet weather
26. Unemployed
27. That girl
30. Clothes-hanging place
32. Star of "Sesame Street"?
34. Biddy
35. To a great extent
37. Get word of
38. Office reminder
39. Garden invaders
40. Log home
43. Vagabond
45. Of the mouth
46. Leave speechless
47. Sung syllables
50. Be fond of
51. Annoying one
52. Moose kin
53. Citrus drinks
54. _____ in the pants, restlessness
55. 007, for one

DOWN

1. Set of tools
2. Lyricist Gershwin
3. Difficult choice, often
4. Spinal column components
5. One-twelfth of a foot
6. Remained
7. Sweltering
8. Word before "saw" or "letter"
9. Rise in the terrain
10. Eden resident
11. Graduation gifts, often
19. Hamilton bills
20. At liberty
21. It may be fallen
22. Bargain event
24. One who's on your side
26. Shopping list entry
27. Church spires
28. Noggin
29. Slips up
31. Neck and neck
33. Those people
36. Decayed
38. Highway measurements
39. Has a yen for
40. Soda choice
41. Desertlike
42. Create muffins
44. Corrode, as iron
46. Health club
48. European peak
49. Blue yonder

59

ACROSS

1. New York football team
5. Luxury resort
8. "Scram!"
12. Feel sore
13. Ignited
14. Detective's guide
15. "At what time?"
16. Everyone
17. Price; value
18. Daddy's boys
19. Drink with crumpets
21. "Beauty is in the ____ of the beholder"
23. Weep aloud
25. Baseball-card transaction
28. Invigorate (with "up")
29. See 23-Across
32. Convent dweller
33. Came up
35. Affirmative vote
36. Five plus five
37. Singer Stewart
38. Student's jottings
40. Colony-building insect
41. Egyptian cobra
42. Displeases
45. Skilled, as a pupil
47. Comes to a close
51. Baby's "piggies"
52. Little one
53. Civil disturbance
54. Razor's cutting part
55. Actor Wallach
56. Pinnacle
57. Soldier's meal
58. "What's up, ____?"
59. Appear

DOWN

1. Spielberg's shark movie
2. Sound reflection
3. At the time
4. Detected
5. Small chalkboard
6. Stack (up)
7. Geography reference books
8. Scour clean
9. Applaud
10. Garage occupant?
11. Adolescent
22. Long (for)
24. Unlocks
25. Blasting compound: abbr.
26. Feel remorse about
27. Columnist Landers
28. Bean casing
29. Panther or puma
30. Deli bread choice
31. "Absolutely!"
34. Turned on an axis
39. Musical dramas
40. Wild donkeys
41. Upper room in some houses
42. Catalog entry
43. Played 46-Down
44. Beer barrels
46. Horseback game
48. Pleasant
49. Rounded roof
50. Flower support

60

ACROSS

1. Smile widely
5. High-calorie nutrient
8. Teen's skin woe
12. Motorcar
13. "____ got an idea!"
14. Furnace fuel
15. Decreased
17. Clip neatly
18. Ms. Landers
19. "Electric" swimmers
20. Brief
24. Secondhand
27. Singer Horne
28. Villain's 1-Across
29. Light, explosive sound
32. Jughead's pal
34. Show up
36. Peg for a Player?
37. Shopper's wagon
39. "What a shame!"
40. Do some clerical work
41. Received a dubbing
42. Bottom of a shoe
45. Hit the slopes
47. Comparison word
48. Apple-pie spice
53. Goals
54. Excitement
55. A Midwest state
56. Dressing gown
57. Worshiper's seat
58. Opposite of 20-Across

DOWN

1. Young woman
2. Have regret for
3. "____ a Wonderful Life," film
4. Verbal rejections
5. Helsinki native
6. Wide thoroughfare
7. Slugger Williams
8. Portrayed a character
9. Center of the earth
10. Bit of hardware
11. Shade trees
16. Have a bowl of chowder
20. Bed board
21. In this location
22. Formerly
23. Cheer sound
25. Bench or stool
26. Goof up
28. "Look before you" do this
29. Mound
30. Egg-shaped
31. Annoying insect, for one
33. Like a slick winter road
35. Did a marathon
38. Live (at)
40. Strained
41. Relatives
42. Headliner
43. Buckeyes' home
44. Young sheep
46. Be sure of
48. Top for a pen
49. Feel sick
50. Barnyard quote
51. Be the proprietor of
52. Jaded horse

61

ACROSS

1. A son of Adam and Eve
5. Stayed in place
8. Lobster's cousin
12. Possess
13. Yalie
14. Curtain material
15. Momentous times
16. Badger ceaselessly
17. Poker stake
18. Sloppy conditions
20. Cut and dried alfalfa
22. Chooses by ballot
24. Touch affection-ately
27. Express gratitude to
30. Swiss peak
31. Possessive pronoun
32. St. Louis pros
33. Travel like a bird
34. Sandwich fish
35. Angry feeling
36. Starfish part
37. Eight times five
38. Some are husbands
39. Try to hear
41. Put into play
42. Revised (copy)
46. Fellow
49. Acknowl-edge silently
51. Rainy-day color
52. Motor vehicle
53. Father
54. Put on the payroll
55. Adult-in-training
56. Heavens
57. Spilled the beans

DOWN

1. Throat-clearing sound
2. Like many trees in winter
3. Perón and Gabor
4. Decreases
5. Intelli-gence
6. In the style of: 2 wds.
7. In a snug way
8. Potter's supply
9. Took off on foot
10. Be in a play
11. Posy pollinator
19. A lodge member
21. Nile biter
23. Pacifies
24. Serve (the tea)
25. Parent's sister
26. Cafeteria carrier
27. Neat and tidy
28. Rabbitlike creature
29. Prayer's last word, often
33. Popular sitcom
34. This evening
36. Capone and Pacino
37. Gave lunch to
40. Cuddly bear
41. At the top of
43. Small music group
44. James ____ Jones, actor
45. Tinted (hair)
46. Lion or tiger
47. Color variation
48. Had supper
50. Shade tree

62

ACROSS

1. Cider bottle
4. Summit
8. Open-hand blow
12. Single
13. Tehran's land
14. Musical sound
15. Card game
16. Completed
17. Give an evaluation of
18. Hi-fi sound system
20. More vicious
22. Inquire
23. Clinging plant
24. Bunch of hoodlums
27. Playground rides
31. In the past
32. Go to the other side
34. Golf peg
35. Sold from a cart
37. Money owed
38. Sprinted
39. Enjoy a Vail vacation
41. Cookbook entry
44. Christmas tree "icicles"
48. Rounded shape
49. Sound the alarm
51. Raw metal
52. Invoice
53. Eager; enthusi-astic
54. Take the prize
55. Shady trees
56. Drinks like Lassie
57. Ocean

DOWN

1. Trots
2. Army group
3. Actor Hackman
4. Assistants
5. Lawbreaker
6. Bloke; chap
7. Foes
8. Wanders off the path
9. Bank offering
10. Poker pot
11. Social equal
19. Tattered cloth
21. Preholiday nights
24. Hole in a fence
25. How old one is
26. Signal "yes"
27. Instant lawn
28. Devoured
29. Spider's snare
30. Matching collection
32. Applaud
33. Fresh beginning
36. Marching practices
37. Constant racket
39. Narrow piece of cloth
40. Categories
41. Dressing gown
42. Morally bad
43. Tranquil
45. Scatters (seeds)
46. One of the Great Lakes
47. Singer Horne
50. Gardner of the movies

1	2	3	■	4	5	6	7	■	8	9	10	11
12			■	13				■	14			
15			■	16				■	17			
18			19			■	20	21				
■	■	■	22			■	23			■	■	■
24	25	26		■	■	27				28	29	30
31			■	32	33				■	34		
35			36				■	■	37			
■	■	■	38			■	39	40		■	■	■
41	42	43				■	44			45	46	47
48				■	49	50			■	51		
52				■	53				■	54		
55				■	56				■	57		

63

ACROSS

1. Colt or filly
5. Health-and-beauty retreat
8. Sound repetition
12. Having nothing to do
13. Kept out of sight
14. Edible stuff
15. Cola, for one
16. Closing
17. Celebrities have it
18. Goes on a journey
20. Burrowing animals
21. Magical being
22. In favor of
23. True's opposite
26. Less rough
30. Wedding words
31. Looks at
33. Climbing plant
34. Substitute for
36. Plains Indian's home
38. Helped oneself to food
39. Part of "mph"
40. Dish
43. Distant
47. Every single one
48. Belonging to that fellow
49. "____ Enchanted Evening"
50. Prince Charles's sister
51. Colony builder
52. Equally matched
53. Bold look
54. Pekoe or oolong
55. Family rooms

DOWN

1. Clenched hand
2. Smell
3. "M*A*S*H" actor Alan
4. Departs
5. Place for books
6. Sewing articles
7. Total (up)
8. Exertion
9. Carbon-based fuel
10. Dwelling place
11. Keats poems
19. Raise
20. Godzilla, for one
22. "A ____ Good Men," film
23. Evergreen tree
24. Fruit cooler
25. Cut off (branches)
26. Cry of surprise
27. Mouth part
28. Festive night before
29. Deli bread variety
32. Frost crystals
35. Shampoo suds
37. Rubbed out, as a pencil mark
39. Ravioli, for one
40. Ring, as a bell
41. Highway division
42. Common skin disorder
43. Reply to "How are you?"
44. Used a loom
45. Word in some prayers
46. Longs (for)
48. Head covering

64

ACROSS

1. Item to play with
4. Far from fat
8. Tiny branch
12. Wondering fear
13. Evergreen tree
14. Agree to employ
15. Least rough
17. Single condominium
18. Expansive
19. Soldier's meal
20. Own up to
23. Membership organization
26. Become part of a 23-Across
27. Doe's mate
28. British drink
31. In dreamland
33. Stock portions
35. Matador's cape color
36. Sleeveless garment
38. Pout
39. Manufactured
40. Game with pawns and kings
41. Sandwich shop
44. Apple center
46. Plow-pulling animals
47. Grounds or spanks
51. Fork prong
52. Circle segments
53. In the manner of: 2 wds.
54. Telescope target
55. Cry audibly
56. Heavens

DOWN

1. Clothing label
2. Be beholden to
3. Japanese currency
4. Cut in half
5. Told fibs
6. Beetle, for one
7. Got acquainted with
8. Tom ____, tiny fellow
9. Beverage kept in a cellar
10. Tall, showy flower
11. Acquires
16. Sturdy string
20. Not quite closed
21. Medicine measurement
22. Gentle in disposition
24. Final
25. Exclamation of disgust
27. Hastened
28. Loyal, as a friend
29. Slippery swimmers
30. Inquires (about)
32. Ms. Gabor
34. Fire's remnants
37. Protected from danger
39. Gold-rush participant
40. Like a potato chip
41. Connect the ____
42. Leave (a room)
43. Singer Horne
45. A single time
47. Bear's "foot"
48. Is the owner of
49. Large, antlered deer
50. Express in words

65

ACROSS

1. Taste an ice-cream cone
5. Jewel
8. Restaurant list
12. Mideast nation
13. Anger
14. Matures
15. Catholic leader
16. Family vehicle
17. Short letter
18. Allergy symptom
20. Arid
22. New Delhi's land
24. Flock noise
27. Animal that produces a 24-Across
31. Part of Great Britain
33. Last testament
34. Price label
35. Concerned with
36. Naval officer
38. Dress hems
39. "Definitely!"
40. Before
42. Beer barrel
43. Executive's workplace
48. Skin condition
51. Rules of conduct
53. Worshiped person
54. In a little while
55. Ms. Gabor
56. Oceans
57. Wooden support
58. ____ Francisco
59. Fairy story?

DOWN

1. Mouth parts
2. Smooth wrinkles
3. Batman's accessory
4. Leg joint
5. Donated
6. Time period
7. Repairing (socks)
8. Several
9. Conceit
10. Butterfly catcher
11. Employ
19. Metal fastener
21. Dusting cloth
23. Coped (with)
24. Gun noise
25. Poker stake
26. Troubles
27. Swing
28. Conceal
29. Shade trees
30. Inventor Whitney
32. Jar covering
34. Snarls
37. Regret
38. Christmas-toy maker?
41. Corn-Belt resident, maybe
42. Superman's surname
44. Closed hand
45. Thought
46. Furnace fuel
47. Otherwise
48. Poisonous snake
49. Dove's call
50. Flat refusals
52. Actress Gardner

66

ACROSS

1. Is an annoyance
5. Put a question to
8. Forest trail
12. Hammer's target
13. Go out, as a fire
14. Land unit
15. Extremely small
16. Desertlike
17. Lower leg
18. Quite mature
19. Put into play
20. Staircase parts
21. Singer King Cole
23. Brief letter
25. Used, as cash
27. Bring civil action against
28. Deplete (strength)
31. It follows Lent
33. Make less
35. Sullivan and McMahon
36. Floor covering
38. Less polluted
39. Tennis's Sampras
40. Cut (off)
41. Dish of greens
44. Mine extraction
46. Large rodent
49. Person who fibs
50. One who's an expert
51. Dwell (at)
52. Prepare (copy) for print
53. Sense of self
54. Big continent
55. Claim it is not so
56. Animal companion
57. Gets married

DOWN

1. Division word
2. Fence bar
3. Affectionate generosity
4. Sneaky
5. Tacks on
6. Ambulance warning devices
7. Door unlocker
8. School glue
9. Steady pain
10. Excursion
11. Egg-laying chickens
19. Spoke
20. Church tower
22. Picnic spoiler
24. Owned by us
25. Look at
26. Gym mat
28. Unexpected occurrence
29. Winning tennis serve
30. For each
32. Wheel furrow
34. Pair of performers
37. President Bush's first name
39. Celebratory get-together
41. Coasting vehicle
42. Nurse's helper
43. Reclined
45. Plant's underground anchor
47. Keenly interested
48. Afternoon socials
50. Liveliness
51. Government regulation

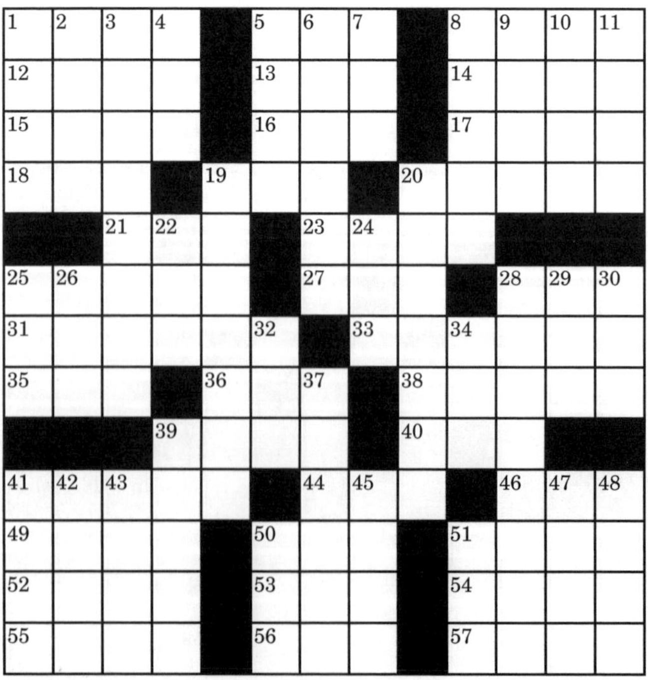

67

ACROSS

1. Titled woman
5. Place (bricks)
8. Boast
12. Smell
13. Common contraction
14. Furious spell
15. Marinara sauce ingredients
17. Baking chamber
18. Country hotel
19. Sunset direction
20. Group of bees
24. "Once ____ a time . . ."
27. Des Moines' state
28. Sandwich shop
29. A Gabor
32. Religious blessing
34. Martini fruits
36. Airplanes' area
37. Enormous
39. Flat, circular object
40. Obligation to pay
41. Stops temporarily
42. Angel's "headpiece"
45. Boxing legend
47. Employs
48. Indoor shoes
53. Ore spot
54. Writing stick
55. A Great Lake
56. Butter servings
57. Noah's boat
58. Become bigger

DOWN

1. Round speck
2. Hubbub
3. Dad's mate
4. Time period
5. Powerful jungle cat
6. Main thoroughfare
7. Affirmative response
8. Coffee-colored
9. Talk wildly
10. Gets older
11. Polite man
16. "Home Improvement" star Allen
20. Drinks slowly
21. Labor for pay
22. In another place
23. Beam of light
25. Sequence of events in a novel
26. Car grease
28. Dull
29. Wicked
30. Sleeveless garment
31. Inquires
33. Woman of Eden
35. Ms. Lupino
38. Not as fresh
40. Portions (of medicine)
41. Joint between the waist and the thigh
42. Feature of a camel's back
43. China's continent
44. Fasting period
46. The missing ____
48. Health resort
49. Score-keeping device
50. Mess up
51. Brazilian city, for short
52. Stitch clothing

68

ACROSS

1. Perform a fancy trampoline stunt
5. Tour vehicle
8. Bargain-hunt
12. Nursing assistant
13. Cleopatra's snake
14. A Corn Belt state
15. Negative replies
16. Golf-ball prop
17. Money for the landlady
18. Grab
20. Organ of vision
22. Out of the way
24. Dairy farm sound
27. Unobscured
31. Give an answer
33. Paper-towel unit
34. Substance we breathe
35. Copied (one's actions)
36. Helps
38. Gown or shift
39. Honey insect
40. Alternative option
42. Be indebted (to)
43. All by ____, toddler's phrase
48. Multiple vitamin additive
51. Cleaning implement
53. Egg-shaped
54. Drab
55. Placed
56. Fair, as weather
57. Griffith or Garcia
58. Have a go at
59. Lively joy

DOWN

1. Team supporters
2. African predator
3. Brainstorm outcome
4. Gnat, for one
5. Tub soaks
6. Avail oneself of
7. One who drives too fast
8. Address for the king
9. Gardening tool
10. Have
11. Tap lightly
19. Automobile
21. "Indeed!"
23. From Dublin
24. Be sulky
25. Wallet bills
26. Partner of "ends"
27. Seafood treat
28. Fail to win
29. Otherwise
30. Boxer Muhammad
32. ____ for the course
34. Make an effort (to)
37. Scatter (seeds)
38. Towel off
41. Vacant, as a lot
42. No more than
44. Ditty
45. Wickedness
46. Frilly trim
47. Escape
48. Lupino of films
49. Flee (from)
50. Young's opposite
52. Belonging to us

1	2	3	4	■	5	6	7	■	8	9	10	11
12				■	13			■	14			
15				■	16			■	17			
18				19		■	20	21		■	■	■
■	■	■	■	22		23			■	24	25	26
27	28	29	30		■	31			32			
33				■	34			■	35			
36				37			■	38				
39			■	40			41		■	■	■	■
■	■	■	42			■	43		44	45	46	47
48	49	50		■	51	52		■	53			
54				■	55			■	56			
57				■	58			■	59			

69

ACROSS

1. Cakes (of soap)
5. Record on cassette
9. Carbonated drink
12. Condo apartment
13. Unlocked
14. Hooting night bird
15. Use an office keyboard
16. Give care to
17. Confederate general
18. Whiskey grain
20. Alan of TV
21. Little river
24. Baronet's title
26. Boy Scout group
27. Article of clothing
31. Become sick
32. Parlor instrument
34. Compete (for)
35. They haunt the links
37. Female relative
39. Praise poem
40. Specs parts
41. Pony prodder
44. Billboard displays
45. Tavern spigot
46. Stay a bit
49. Salt Lake City's locale
53. In the past
54. Keep from view
55. Solitary
56. Patriot Franklin
57. Funky smell
58. Actor Curtis

DOWN

1. Except for
2. One of several
3. Tear
4. Sound system
5. ____ pole, tribal symbol
6. Gorilla, for one
7. It's "mightier than the sword"
8. Finish
9. Opinion census
10. Was in debt
11. Earnest request
19. Barked shrilly
20. Upper limb
21. Antler-bearing animal
22. Small jazz combo
23. Hot-dog item
24. Diego preceder
25. Pressed (clothes)
27. Oxygen or hydrogen
28. Holiday nights
29. Agreeable
30. Pegs for 35-Across
33. Extreme anger
36. Favoring
38. Speak to disrespectfully
40. Further behind schedule
41. Thrust a knife into
42. Book part
43. At the top of
46. "____ was that masked man?"
47. Lend a hand
48. Words for tying the knot
50. Also
51. Landers of column fame
52. Call for attention

70

ACROSS

1. Snake's tooth
5. Have a go at
8. Live in a tent (with "out")
12. Admired one
13. Sailor's affirmative
14. A Great Lake
15. Roman tyrant
16. Allow
17. Citrus fruit
18. Contend (for)
20. More antique
21. House buyer's bid
24. Hit the slopes
26. Famous boxer
27. Bend down in prayer
29. That female
32. Four plus six
33. Hold, as personal property
34. One ____, street sign
35. Downcast
36. Composers of 45-Down
38. Fill with great wonder
39. "All for one ____ one for all!"
40. Sounds from the sty
42. Arm joint
46. Opposite of subtract
47. Share a bedtime story
48. Crooner Torme
50. Not completely closed
54. Bancroft of "The Miracle Worker"
55. In the style of: 2 wds.
56. Tramp on a freight train
57. Droops
58. Ruckus
59. Heed (a command)

DOWN

1. Fish "limb"
2. Fruit-juice drink
3. Neither's companion
4. Hand warmer
5. Narrative story
6. Dark bread
7. Up to now
8. Prisoner's room
9. Parched
10. Silent performer
11. Look (at)
19. Bother
20. Frying fluid
21. Feedbag bits
22. Tiny dog-tormentor
23. Locate
24. Made a quilt
25. Superman's alter ego
28. Midday
29. Graceful waterfowl
30. Soaring hunter
31. Needle slits
36. Fido's "foot"
37. Turf
41. State famous for its potatoes
42. Historic time periods
43. Jazz legend Horne
44. Gun sound
45. Lyric verses
46. Mr. Alda
48. Angry
49. Inventor Whitney
51. Task
52. Honest ____ Lincoln
53. Dale Evans' husband

71

ACROSS

1. Actor Beatty
4. Fire remnant
7. Once existed
10. Dry
12. By means of
13. Fence support
14. Road material
16. Unattractive
17. Farm tower
18. Taste and smell
20. Shiny fabric
22. Help signal
23. Boxer Muhammad
25. Lawn moisture
27. Stands up
31. Entryway
33. Believe it or ____
35. Unit of land
36. Person in possession
38. One of a reporter's questions
40. Wrath
41. Drink holder
43. Many millennia
45. Ark passenger
48. Soldier's station
50. Toss (a coin)
51. Travel document
54. Speed contest
55. Adam's mate
56. Canal of song
57. Dollar bill
58. Mouse's kin
59. Turf

DOWN

1. Short snooze
2. Historic ages
3. Mathematical process
4. "____ Maria"
5. Religious misdeeds
6. Loathes
7. Earn a living ____
8. Declines, in a way
9. Cunning; wily
11. Cold-cuts shop
13. Putin's country
15. Stale-bread growth
19. Neither's partner
21. Olin or Howard
23. Commotion
24. Not high
26. "Amazing!"
28. Cutting tool
29. Make a blunder
30. Perceive
32. Cook's formula
34. Common article
37. Pirate drink
39. Clumsy one's cry
42. Writer's need
44. Slangy denial
45. Comedian King
46. Pleasant
47. Volcano output
49. Peter, Paul and Mary are one
50. To's sidekick
52. TV receiver
53. Newsman Koppel

72

ACROSS

1. Scorch
5. Average
8. Matured
12. Largest continent
13. Wedding words
14. Actor's part
15. Superman's alter ego, Clark ____
16. Allow
17. Violin box
18. Igloo dweller
20. Sampled
22. Furnish
24. Magnificent
27. Single
28. Ignited
31. Is troubled
32. Embrace
33. Rate of movement
34. Health resort
35. Moving vehicle
36. Helped
37. Diner requests
39. Tossed
43. Go to (a party)
47. Enjoy a book
48. Sullivan and Asner
50. Smell
51. Dry
52. Litigate in court
53. Green fruit
54. Veggie casings
55. Rich earth
56. Chunky soup

DOWN

1. Cook a cake
2. Consumes
3. Skating arena
4. United ____, world organization
5. Flying ace
6. Summer cooler
7. Decaying
8. Circle parts
9. Farm animal
10. Otherwise
11. Proof of ownership
19. Dampened earth
21. Consumed
23. Discovered
24. Car fuel
25. Tear
26. Like: 2 wds.
28. Young boy
29. Frozen water
30. Newsman Koppel
32. Plow-pulling equipment
33. Small firearms
35. Solemn promise
36. Museum hanging
38. Comforted
39. Snare
40. Brave one
41. Sudden attack
42. Gambling stats
44. Fix (text)
45. Alaskan city
46. Sketched
49. Pair

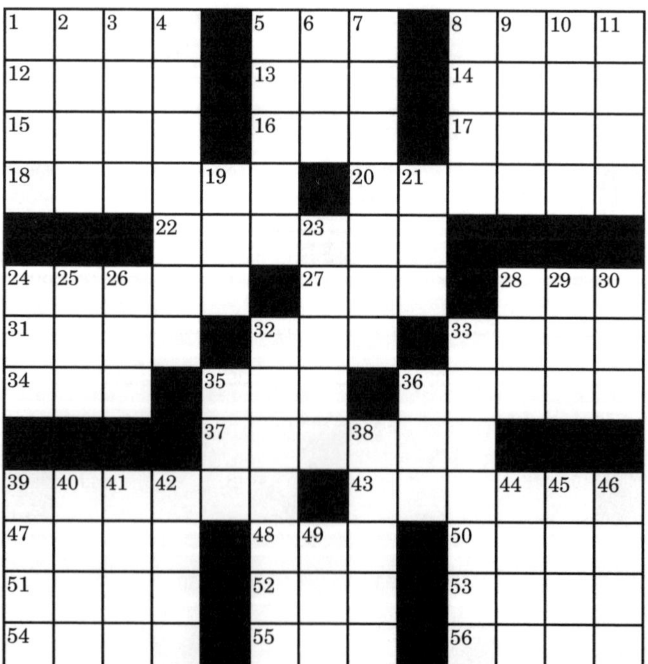

73

ACROSS

1. "Once ____ a time . . ."
5. The lady in question
8. Be in a sulky mood
12. Identical
13. Roofing goo
14. Strong metal
15. At any time
16. Inspect closely
17. Come gently down to earth
18. Colorado city
20. Friendly nation
21. Ones holding title to something
24. Cherish
27. Fence opening
28. Corn serving
31. Ripens
32. Workout spot
33. Choir voice
34. Signal "yes"
35. Bunny's jump
36. Requested
37. Says
39. Make a sweater
42. Outline quickly
46. Plant origin
47. Used to be
49. Part for a player
50. Apple skin
51. Malt brew
52. Band's cross-country excursion
53. Williams or Garcia
54. Car fuel
55. Snow toy

DOWN

1. Employed
2. Fix (a driveway)
3. Fortune-teller's sign
4. Fidgety
5. Severe
6. Horse fodder
7. Before, to Burns
8. Grain-grinding machine
9. Spoken
10. The ____ Express
11. Conclude
19. Source of wool
20. Deadly snake
22. Pharaohs' land
23. See 19-Down
24. Cargo carrier
25. In the past
26. Was in the forefront
28. Lodge member
29. Had brunch
30. Angler's need
32. Acquired
33. Says positively
35. Small shelter
36. "Raiders of the Lost ____"
38. Curved letters
39. Sharp-witted
40. Requirement
41. Without much interest
43. Wrench or saw
44. Hint
45. Cattle group
46. Mineral spring
47. Move like a dog's tail
48. In the manner of: 2 wds.

74

ACROSS

1. Close friend
4. Virginia pork products
8. Penetrate with a dagger
12. In the past
13. Part of a catalog order
14. Minuscule
15. Veggie eaten on a knife?
16. Cold-cuts shop
17. Teen's skin disorder
18. Put into the mix
20. Set (down)
22. Seasoned soldier
24. Happenings
28. Snacks for monkeys
32. Worship
33. Top gun
34. Art student's tablet
36. This second
37. Do a bloodhound's job
40. Places for vendors
43. Jason and Hercules
45. Go out, as a candle
46. Cry of distaste
47. Stockings material
51. Move, as emotions
54. Mimics
57. "So that's it!"
58. Possesses
59. Extreme anger
60. Sauce for chips
61. Emerged from slumber
62. Poke
63. Distress signal

DOWN

1. Father
2. Grew older
3. Burden
4. Out of sight
5. Banished hunger
6. Gibson of Hollywood
7. Happy expression
8. Stuck around
9. Facial twitch
10. Beloved columnist Landers
11. "Adios!"
19. ____ Marie Saint
21. Gardner of films
23. Dance like Gene Kelly
25. Nary a soul
26. Horse's gait
27. Makes seams
28. Cleansing soak
29. Unit of land
30. Close to
31. Sleuth Spade
35. See 1-Down
38. Hangout for Tiger Woods
39. Small barrel
41. Washed off
42. Door opener
44. Keen
48. Young fellows
49. Neighbor of Kentucky
50. Snoozes
51. Piglets' mom
52. "Tea for ____"
53. Printer's fluid
55. Golfing standard
56. Freudian self

75

ACROSS

1. Created
5. Carpet of grass
8. Of great height
12. Child of 55-Across
13. Hint for an actress
14. Dayton's locale
15. Shut noisily
16. Consumed (food)
17. Track circuits
18. Less relaxed
20. Writing tablet
22. Before's opposite
24. This woman
27. Rub (on) messily
31. Ran away, as from jail
33. Cab
34. Occupied a chair
35. "West Side Story" group
36. Zoo residents
38. Zebra's kin
39. Acquire
40. Female relative
42. Aardvark's snack
43. Pearl-producing shellfish
48. Cut with scissors
51. Shorten (a skirt)
53. Broad
54. Peel (apples)
55. Adam's mate
56. "So be it!"
57. Mellowed
58. Lab rodent
59. Campsite sight

DOWN

1. Sailboat's sail-supporter
2. Ready, willing, and ____
3. University personage
4. Shade-giving trees
5. Silk neck-wrap
6. Not in
7. Most profound
8. Tattled (on)
9. "I found it!"
10. Place to apply gloss
11. ____ Angeles, California
19. Corn serving
21. Rainbow's curve
23. Harass playfully
24. Do some light boxing
25. Chicks' moms
26. Razor's sharp part
27. Mate for a doe
28. Lion's ruff
29. Go offstage
30. Shoot (for)
32. In the past
34. Move like a snake
37. Ms. Landers
38. "You there!"
41. Sky streaker
42. Mimicked
44. Hit, as a housefly
45. Clock (a race)
46. Original sin setting
47. Tenants' payments
48. Exercise club
49. Bother repeatedly
50. Wrath
52. Gabor or Perón

76

ACROSS

1. Luggage lugging device
5. Resort for unwinding
8. Hayworth of old films
12. Aroma
13. Be unhealthy
14. Condominium division
15. Ashen
16. "The honor of your ____ is requested . . ."
18. Spread (on) messily
20. Make a query
21. Set at a slant
23. Luxury boat
28. Broiling
31. Prompted (an actor)
33. Earnest request
34. Gets up
36. Come back
38. Army status
39. Tresses
41. Make a 33-Across
42. Braid
44. Squabble
46. "Wise" night bird
48. Scattered (seeds)
52. Age for a college student, often
57. Ocean crest
58. Daredevil Knievel
59. Steeped drink
60. Adam's garden
61. Seven-day stretch
62. 007, for one
63. Eyeglasses part

DOWN

1. Law enforcers
2. Actor Sandler
3. Part to play
4. Foot the bill
5. Plant juice
6. Captain Kidd was one
7. Barroom choices
8. Be regretful
9. B & B, maybe
10. Facial twitch
11. Had a meal
17. Place for stars
19. Asian grain
22. Lavish, as growth
24. Skilled, as a pupil
25. Membership organization
26. At this location
27. Strong flavor
28. "Heavenly" instrument
29. Spoken
30. Ms. Turner of rock
32. Leaky faucet's sound
35. Participate in a slalom
37. Historical periods
40. Napping
43. Little one
45. Beach blanket, often
47. Moistens
49. Walk in the shallows
50. Tied
51. Foxes' homes
52. Unused
53. "____ Got a Secret"
54. Born
55. Deer's cousin
56. Negative vote

77

ACROSS

1. Noah's vessel
4. Highlands resident
8. Remain
12. Garden tool
13. Crossword hint
14. Reside
15. Lyric poem
16. Trumpet, for one
17. Zoo favorites
18. Sunny color
20. Water barrier
22. Long time
23. Firefly or cricket
27. Flower part
30. Conclude
31. Stag's mate
32. Press (pants)
33. Tail movement
34. Manicurist's tool
35. Struck (a match)
36. Baseball club
37. The Devil
38. Looked slyly
40. Sprinted
41. Unusual
42. Heavenly messengers
46. "Woe is me!"
49. Set down (a plane)
51. Round speck
52. Wedding shower?
53. Verge; border
54. 43-Down dweller
55. Golf pegs
56. Plant start
57. Recent

DOWN

1. Sailor's cry
2. Went by bus
3. ____ over, capsize
4. Learning site
5. Circus comic
6. Your and my
7. Caring for
8. Shuts noisily
9. Pencil point
10. Roman greeting
11. "Positively!"
19. Slant
21. Not to mention
24. Revise copy
25. Soda flavor
26. Adolescent
27. Medicine tablet
28. A Great Lake
29. Carry
30. Have lunch
33. Walks like a duck
34. Vampire tooth
36. Sleeping place
37. Smoothed wood
39. Thorny flowers
40. Kitchen appliance
43. Genesis garden
44. Adore
45. Hearty soup
46. Mr. Carney
47. Fib
48. High card
50. Fruity drink

78

ACROSS

1. Floor wiper
4. Speak indistinctly
8. Auction offers
12. Night bird
13. Randall of "The Odd Couple"
14. New York canal
15. Billfold bill
16. Start a poker pot
17. Contribute
18. Fury
20. Army camps
21. Otherwise
23. "Once ____ a time . . ."
25. Crowd's sound
26. Snaky sea creatures
27. Used a sofa
30. Mr. Schwarzenegger
32. Take for granted
34. Prepare (a table)
35. Repulsive
37. Mimicked
38. Costing nothing
39. Camera part
40. Frown's opposite
43. Go into
46. Hook, ____, and sinker
47. One less than a quartet
48. Chart for a motorist
51. Actress Bancroft
52. Departed
53. In the manner of: 2 wds.
54. Untidy condition
55. Poems by Keats
56. Tennis-court barrier

DOWN

1. Cow's sound
2. "Mind your ____ business!"
3. Nice
4. Male elk
5. Unaccompanied
6. False
7. Bread grain
8. Commenced
9. Showy bloom
10. Plunge, as into water
11. Witnesses
19. Roman emperor
20. Employer
21. Notable time periods
22. Community knowledge
24. Drama-club production
26. Cutting side of a blade
27. Lois Lane's hero
28. End of some prayers
29. Koppel and Danson
31. Attract using bait
33. Shopper's bonanza
36. Looked at lustfully
38. Escapes from danger
40. Bang noisily
41. Coal diggers' workplace
42. Rural lodgings
44. Six plus three
45. Small children
47. A couple
49. Pub refreshment
50. Tap gently

ACROSS

1. Ask for earnestly
4. Gleeful shouts
8. "Scram!"
12. Zodiac feline
13. Spiral
14. Septet minus four
15. Significant period
16. Former NYC mayor Giuliani
17. Like hens' teeth?
18. Feel under the weather
19. Output of a mine
20. Kindled
21. Takes on a trial run
23. Unlocks (a door)
26. Classify
30. ____ de Janeiro, Brazil
31. Harpo or Chico
34. Marriage words
35. Venomous vipers
36. Freudian self
37. Welcomes
39. Ready for rest
41. "What person's?"
45. Total (up)
46. Metal-cutting tool
48. Cook's vessel
49. Crawling insects
51. Baby in pink
52. Tire track
53. Song for a pair
54. Tel ____, Israeli seaport
55. First-rate; expert
56. Final points
57. Military installation
58. The lady

DOWN

1. Sheep's cry
2. Weird
3. Aims; objects
4. Word at the top of this page
5. Sixty minutes
6. Teacher's helper
7. Tricky
8. Dismantle
9. Moon-surface features
10. Lung filler
11. Boot tip
20. Great deal
22. IRS's demand
24. Small taste of
25. Coded call for help
27. Form of address for a knight
28. Lofty poem
29. Caviar source
31. Kitten's cry
32. "The ____ of Aquarius"
33. Prepared coffee beans
35. Fireplace remainder
37. Coach's domain
38. Six plus six
40. Corrodes
42. Ms. Winfrey
43. Spaghetti topping
44. "Come in!"
46. Leontyne, for one
47. Eye part
49. Picnic cooler?
50. Convent member
51. Chew the fat

79

80

ACROSS

1. Choir voice
5. Table seasoning
9. Spider's creation
12. Wild pig
13. Urgent request
14. Pub beverage
15. Parcel of earth
16. Pull
17. Popular card game
18. Border
19. Comic Martin
21. Dish-drying stand
24. Compass direction
27. Fireplace residue
30. Fly like an eagle
32. Rubber wheel
33. Wall Street's concerns
35. First game in a series
37. Sport on horseback
38. Band instrument
40. "Golly!"
41. Acciden-tally tip over
43. Cruel emperor
45. Gave out (cards)
47. Fellow
51. Ms. Lupino
53. Lure
55. Contend (with)
56. Sunbeam
57. Always
58. Consumes
59. Sullivan and Asner
60. Lord's mate
61. Relax

DOWN

1. Qualified
2. Put on board, as cargo
3. Sour taste
4. Restaurant request
5. Secret agent
6. Juneau's state
7. Time of fasting
8. Kidnapped
9. Betting
10. Inventor Whitney
11. Actor Kingsley
20. Choose (with "for")
22. Inquire
23. Price
25. Elm or pine
26. This place
27. Venomous snakes
28. "Halt!"
29. 12/25 and 1/1
31. Dressing gown
34. Nat King ____
36. Average
39. Loosened
42. Price tag
44. Happen
46. Molten rock
48. Gardening tube
49. Plays the mimic
50. Annoyance
51. Strong anger
52. Father
54. Attempt

1	2	3	4	■	5	6	7	8	■	9	10	11
12				■	13				■	14		
15				■	16				■	17		
18				■	■	19			20		■	■
■	■	■	21	22	23		■	24			25	26
27	28	29	■	30			31	■	32			
33			34			■	35	36				
37				■	38	39			■	40		
41				42	■	43			44	■	■	■
■	■	45			46		■	■	47	48	49	50
51	52		■	53			54	■	55			
56			■	57				■	58			
59			■	60				■	61			

81

ACROSS

1. Wide ocean inlet
4. Does some math
8. Handles roughly
12. Hole in one
13. Warm winter garment
14. Buffalo's Great Lake
15. "I found it!"
16. Pitchfork prong
17. Land measure
18. Religious lecture
20. Was in a hurry
22. Pianos' relatives
24. Some choir members
27. "Golly!"
28. "You, there!"
31. Told a whopper
32. Evergreen tree
33. Small, sheltered 1-Across
34. Rejuvenating retreat
35. Animal enclosure
36. Native of a Corn Belt state
37. Consider
39. Place of instruction
43. Some female kin
47. Genesis youth
48. Vexes
50. Ms. Gardner
51. Actress Bancroft
52. Where Baby Moses floated
53. Subject of an 18-Across
54. Fishing snares
55. Departs
56. Mooselike critter

DOWN

1. Sheepish replies?
2. Soreness
3. 365-day stretch
4. Members of a troupe
5. "What on earth are you ____?"
6. Rather of CBS
7. Less lenient
8. Pod finds
9. Architectural feature
10. Pipe-cleaner's core
11. Feed-store purchase
19. Emotional state
21. Bring into play
23. Becoming elderly
24. Jolson and Pacino
25. Site for gloss
26. Chinese brew
28. "In what manner?"
29. Gabor or Perón
30. Japanese currency
32. Sensation
33. Set of secret symbols
35. In favor of
36. Subject for Van Gogh
38. Place for a brace
39. Read swiftly
40. Sugar source
41. Clue
42. Individuals
44. Violin carrier
45. Wickedness
46. Dropped beneath the waves
49. Brazil port, for short

82

ACROSS

1. Sticky strip
5. Having a level surface
9. Police officer
12. Untamed
13. Attract irresistibly
14. Glamour girl Gardner
15. Some poems by Keats
16. "____ upon a time..."
17. Bloke; chap
18. Mediterranean, for one
19. Comedian's joke
20. Syrup tree
22. Highlander, maybe
24. Jewel
25. In pieces
27. Takes off weight
31. Eat by candlelight, maybe
32. Gardening tool
33. Sofa or chair
34. Went into
36. Auto magnate Ford
37. Golf norm
38. Rapid
39. Like potato chips
42. Verbalize
43. Historic age
46. Free (of)
47. Settled a debt
49. Tiny bird
50. Sick
51. Cliff's border
52. Warm up (leftovers)
53. Buzzing insect
54. Puts on, as a uniform
55. Track statistic

DOWN

1. Groupings for Noah
2. Helper
3. Nice
4. McMahon and Bradley
5. Levitate
6. Breathing organ
7. Circle fragment
8. Abounded (with)
9. Place to pitch tents
10. ____ Office, President's workplace
11. Window section
19. Obtained
21. Entertains
23. Crawls
24. "Turn right, mule!"
25. Fruit beverage
26. Brooch, maybe
27. Metal bar
28. Balanced
29. Hearing organ
30. Place for pigs
32. That woman
35. Knocked sharply
36. Stack contents
38. Loses coloring
39. Bed for a baby
40. Make angry
41. Not at all busy
42. Write one's name on
44. Enjoy a novel
45. Tunneling insects
48. Trouble
49. "Which person?"

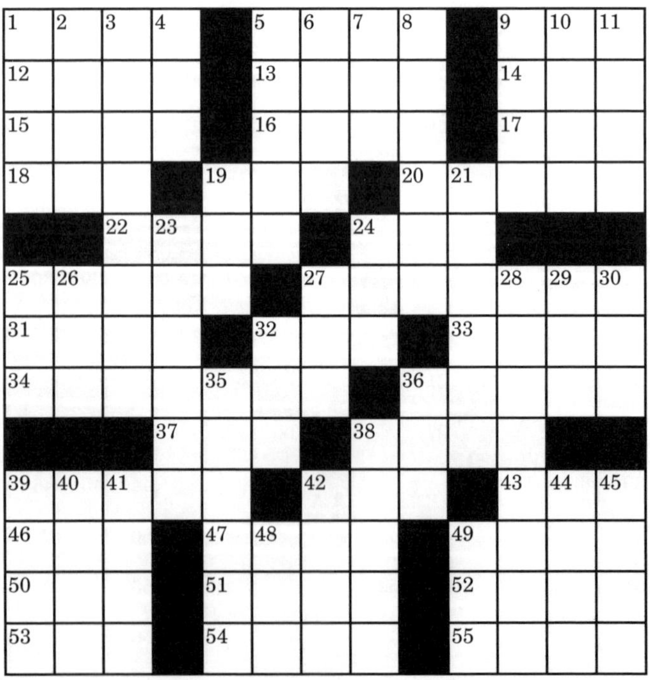

83

ACROSS

1. The thing mentioned
5. Asner and Bradley
8. Soda choice
12. Narrow's opposite
13. ____ rummy, card game
14. Needed to repay
15. Metal attracted to a magnet
16. Complained
18. Birds' homes
20. Self
21. Circle fragment
23. Word before "day" or "stone"
28. Hot beverage
31. Insect that eats woolens
33. Infamous Roman emperor
34. One of a bread-crumb-dropping pair
36. Sprain sites, often
38. Skin condition
39. What Cupid's arrows inspire
41. But still
42. Bread grain
44. Adored animal
45. Mined matter
47. Perspiration
52. Commencing
57. Uncommon
58. Des Moines, ____
59. Golfing gadget
60. Poses a query
61. Rhymester, perhaps
62. Summertime cooler
63. Irritating person

DOWN

1. Identical sibling, often
2. Take on (an employee)
3. Unnecessary fusses
4. Nomad's home
5. Breakfast favorite
6. Straightforward
7. Cozy
8. Corn core
9. Pussycat's companion of rhyme
10. Martial artist Bruce
11. Find the sum
17. Unruly crowd
19. Unchanged
22. Hot-dog bun
24. Pen filler
25. Count (on)
26. Oak or fir
27. Giver of a party
28. Melt, as snow
29. "To ____ his own"
30. Bancroft of film
32. Possess
35. Briny deep
37. Fishing traps
40. Unlocked (a door)
43. Little kid
46. Glamorous Hayworth
48. Cover (a gift)
49. Lessen (pain)
50. Boats like Noah's
51. Exam
52. Drink slowly
53. As well
54. Amazement
55. Mouse's kin
56. "Oh, my!"

84

ACROSS

1. Nevada city
5. Moved in water
9. Young dog
12. Finished
13. Certain soda
14. Commit a blunder
15. Information
16. Always
17. Conceit
18. Adjust (a piano)
20. Used a keyboard
22. Most unusual
25. ____ Grande
26. Stanza
27. First month
31. In the style of: 2 wds.
32. Practical joke
33. Grant's foe
34. Less dark
37. Bravery award
39. Exist
40. Bring back to mind
41. Move smoothly
44. Cloth-devouring pest
45. Have lunch
46. Region
48. Klutz's word
52. "____ Maria"
53. Browns in the sun
54. One of the Great Lakes
55. Male sheep
56. Close (a door)
57. Fender mark

DOWN

1. Fishing pole
2. Gabor of "Green Acres"
3. Mesh fish-trap
4. Gives a speech
5. Fragrance
6. Used a loom
7. Tavern brew
8. Actor Sheen
9. Chick's chirp
10. Impulse
11. Goad
19. Function
21. "____ Ought to Be in Pictures"
22. Track shape
23. Salami shop
24. Pull with effort
25. Dustcloth
27. Jelly holder
28. "M*A*S*H" star
29. Genuine
30. Shout; scream
32. "Golly!"
35. Owned
36. Foots the bill
37. Encountered
38. Reverberated
40. Cook (a turkey)
41. Bike part
42. Volcanic flow
43. News article
44. Bill of fare
47. Crowd's cheer
49. Mine product
50. Brooch
51. TV unit

85

ACROSS

1. Word after "teacher's" or "nurse's"
5. Swiss peaks
9. Luxury retreat
12. Press out wrinkles
13. Anything but shallow
14. Pester nonstop
15. Lease
16. Swerve suddenly
17. Cold cubes
18. First name in U.S. inventors
20. Harvested, as wheat
22. Musical plays
25. Occupied a bench
26. Family member
27. Soaked in liquid
29. Fabric for jeans
33. Ply a shovel
34. Hurried on foot
36. Actress Lupino
37. Eskimo vehicles
40. ____ squad, cheer-leading group
42. Edible fish
43. *Oui* or *sí*
45. Briny cucumber
47. Menace
50. That girl
51. Garden weeder
52. After-bath attire
54. Absence of obstacles
58. Boxing great
59. Gang of workers
60. Have fun
61. One-fourth of forty
62. Chicks' moms
63. Make less wild

DOWN

1. Atmos-phere
2. Anger
3. Put on (clothes)
4. Go into
5. One who counsels
6. Civil War general
7. Squints (at)
8. Pâté, perhaps
9. Clip
10. Gait
11. Grew older
19. Legal rule
21. Gobbled down
22. Bookie's info
23. Bucket
24. Verge
28. Faucet
30. Shaving mishap
31. Pagan image
32. Created
35. Certain male relatives
38. Color, as cloth
39. Hunt (for)
41. Pastry with a crust
44. Place with goods for sale
46. Moved quietly
47. The one yonder
48. Golfer's goal
49. Horse-guiding strap
53. Mr. Franklin, informally
55. Similar to: 2 wds.
56. Donaldson of the news
57. Center of a storm

86

ACROSS

1. Metal spike
5. Far from fat
9. Used to be
12. Common skin problem
13. Volcanic flow
14. Cheering cry
15. Dancer Kelly
16. Follow (orders)
17. Intense anger
18. Ready to eat
20. Pedicure digit
21. Broadcast on TV
24. Depend (upon)
26. Dollar fraction
27. House-building material
29. Grain-storage tower
31. "Bald" birds
33. Royal abode
37. In an offhand way
39. Christmas song
40. Faucet leak
43. Strong pull
45. Male cat
46. Have lunch
47. "Wild" American region
49. Fruit beverage
50. Has in one's collection
52. Puts into service
56. Cup lip
57. Count calories
58. Singer Nat
59. Signal for help
60. Comes to a close
61. Make a sweater

DOWN

1. Feeble, old horse
2. King topper
3. Rural hotel
4. Knowing look
5. Skier's trail
6. Mailing stickers
7. "____ Been Working on the Railroad"
8. The fifth month
9. Be an author
10. Baseball great Hank
11. Bedding need
19. Annoyed
21. Actor Vigoda
22. Wordsmith Gershwin
23. Trucker's tractor
25. Small dog's yelp
26. Soft-drink choice
28. Hair holder
30. Doesn't have
32. Crafty; calculating
34. Museum display
35. Sound of a dove
36. Shade tree
38. Exhibited sleepiness
40. Cherished ones
41. Transistor ____
42. Articles on a checklist
44. Birds' homes
48. "____ in that shirt-tail, young man!"
50. Lyric poem
51. Finish in first place
53. Abel, to Adam
54. Whitney of the cotton gin
55. Matched pair

87

ACROSS

1. Door handle
5. Health resort
8. Open-handed hit
12. The Hawkeye State
13. April 15 payment
14. Walk back and forth
15. Stored valuables
17. At all times
18. Picnic pest
19. Final
20. Inanimate object
24. British nobleman
27. Give a job to
28. In an inactive way
29. Exclamation of triumph
32. Newspaper VIP
34. President, for one
36. "Abso-lutely!"
37. Annoyingly inquisitive
39. Common songbird
40. Car accident result
41. Office notes
42. Sandwich shop
45. Epoch
47. Beasts of burden
48. Least arid
53. Fork prong
54. Not ordinary
55. Leaf-gathering tool
56. Night-sky feature
57. "Farewell!"
58. A Great Lake

DOWN

1. Set of tools
2. Neither's mate
3. Be indebted to
4. Sheep's call
5. Shock deeply
6. Left
7. Wood chopper
8. Wizard's enchant-ment
9. Molten rock
10. Expert pilots
11. Sassy
16. Droop
20. Those folks over there
21. Conceal
22. Spring flower
23. Butterfly catcher
25. Friendly nation
26. Bread grain
28. Press (pants)
29. Eve's mate
30. Superman or Batman
31. Boats like Noah's
33. Dollar bill
35. Pub draft
38. On an even keel
40. Restaurant patron
41. Checkers piece
42. Small, round specks
43. Doorway leading out
44. Singer Horne
46. Go by car
48. Steal from
49. Anger
50. Hearing organ
51. Hit the slopes
52. Golf peg

88

ACROSS

1. Deal (with)
5. Barbecue skewer
9. Burst, as a balloon
12. Very dry
13. Actor Alan
14. Regret
15. Sharp flavor
16. Relate (a story)
17. Make a gaffe
18. Snooze
20. Sandwich shops
22. Composer's work
24. Butterfly catchers
27. Auto
30. Majors and Marvin
32. Musical group
33. Word after "bottle" or "can"
35. Estab-lished
37. Office 34-Down
38. The Buckeye State
40. Sullivan and Asner
41. Revise (copy)
42. "You ____ Live Twice," Bond movie
44. At no time
47. Dawdles
51. Passing fashion
53. Teen's skin condition
55. Bait
56. Holiday precursor
57. Those people
58. Leg joint
59. Prolonged battle
60. Painful
61. Plant support

DOWN

1. Felines
2. Spoken
3. Evergreen tree
4. Outer rims
5. Used a chair
6. Avow
7. Inactive
8. Like a redwood
9. Keep from harm
10. "Days of ____ Lives"
11. For each
19. Fishing rod
21. Division word
23. Cruel Roman emperor
25. Bound with rope
26. Male offspring
27. Arrive
28. Imitated
29. Memory aid
31. Rotate
34. Written message
36. Hamburger bun
39. "Little Jack ____," nursery rhyme
43. Egg centers
45. Containers for liquid
46. Repeated sound
48. Uncle's wife
49. Liberate
50. Appear (to be)
51. Not many
52. Gardner of film
54. Seeing organ

ACROSS

1. Scientist Whitney
4. America's Uncle
7. Sample (food)
12. Invention of 1-Across
13. A Gershwin
14. Dodge
15. "I ____ You, Babe"
16. Cowboy Rogers
17. Pants heavily
18. Ski-slope covering
20. Feltlike plant
22. Separated
24. Play segment
27. Path for hiking
30. Adjust (a clock)
32. Ghostly shout
33. Corroded, as iron
35. Irrigates
37. The Greatest
38. Be in poor health
40. Heaps
41. Green veggie
42. Planted (seeds)
44. Clog or pump
45. Scream
49. Spot to pin a carnation
53. Tree fluid
55. Compete (for)
56. Martini garnish
57. One of the Gabors
58. Country hotel
59. Haste
60. Not yet used
61. Rent to tenants

DOWN

1. Hen products
2. King of the Beasts
3. Fascinated by
4. Noble's title
5. Fragrance
6. Urban political leaders
7. Price labels
8. Ms. Gardner
9. Signal for trouble at sea
10. Reward the waiter
11. Sullivan and McMahon
19. "Stay there!"
21. Hearty meat-and-vegetable dish
23. Urgent request
24. Cain's victim
25. Discarded apple center
26. Mix (a salad)
27. Animal snare
28. Directive
29. China's continent
31. Sticky sealing strip
34. Plate, for one
36. Neat
39. Reduce the tightness of
43. Work a loom
44. Winter toy
46. Sinful
47. Fishing cord
48. Pre-Easter period
49. ____ Angeles, California
50. Swiss mountain
51. Pumpkin dessert
52. Preholiday night
54. Cat's "foot"

89

1	2	3	■	4	5	6	■	7	8	9	10	11
12			■	13			■	14				
15			■	16			■	17				
18			19	■	20		21		■	■	■	■
■	■	■	22	23				■	■	24	25	26
27	28	29			■	30		31	■	32		
33					34	■	35		36			
37			■	38		39	■	40				
41			■	■	42		43			■	■	■
■	■	■	■	44				■	45	46	47	48
49	50	51	52		■	53		54	■	55		
56					■	57			■	58		
59					■	60			■	61		

90

ACROSS

1. It's cut by a barber
5. Sahara grains
9. Mediter-ranean or Aegean
12. "M*A*S*H" star
13. Urgent appeal
14. Young man
15. Travel on foot
16. Three-foot measure
17. Memorable time period
18. Get down to pray
20. Piece of turf
21. Sheltering tree
22. Vex
24. Bark from a small dog
26. ____ Angeles
29. Close to
31. Maiden
34. Owns up to
36. Wide city thorough-fare
38. Necklace orb
39. Car's spare
41. Receive
42. Movie cowboy Rogers
44. Fishing mesh
45. Play a part
47. Fire remnant
49. Sipping aid
54. Deep sorrow
55. "____ is your name?"
57. Lasso
58. Notices in the classifieds
59. River of Egypt
60. Bubbly beverages
61. As of now
62. Exceeded the posted limit
63. Annoying one

DOWN

1. Predatory bird
2. First name of 12-Across
3. Not in use
4. Leaf-gathering tool
5. CIA agent
6. Nome's state
7. Cruel emperor
8. Father, to a child
9. Taking a nap
10. British noble
11. Eden inhabitant
19. Clothes-dryer fuzz
23. Relief from toil
25. Birthday concern
26. Scientist's workplace
27. Lyric tribute
28. Most intelligent
30. Not often seen
32. Feel remorse for
33. Beatles song, "____ It Be"
35. Marriage vow: 2 wds.
37. Doctors for pets
40. Take a deep breath
43. Gapes groggily
45. Out of town
46. Secret language
48. Ocean liner, for one
50. Mouse catcher
51. Function
52. Friends of Tarzan
53. Toward sunset
56. Kennedy or Turner

91

ACROSS

1. Pester persistently
4. Untidy person
8. Nile serpents
12. Like: 2 wds.
13. Sticky strip
14. Dark-brown soda
15. Accepted as true
17. Move by truck
18. Back (of the line)
19. Poetic writing
20. Trans-parent
23. Wonder
25. Tenant's fee
26. Applies
27. Lamb's cry
30. Design something new
32. Thin thread
34. Sea inlet
35. Sunrise direction
37. Deep female voice
38. "What person?"
39. Legal records
40. Puts a blanket around
44. Press, as slacks
46. Assistant
47. Agreeable
51. Bridge section
52. Genuine
53. ____ Grande, Texas border
54. Skirt edges
55. Horse-race chances
56. Fitting, as a remark

DOWN

1. Seize (a fugitive)
2. Pub drink
3. Guy's partner
4. Guide, as a ship
5. Molten volcano flow
6. Musical dramas
7. Flower plot
8. Throbbing head pain
9. Fly high, as a bird
10. In addition to
11. Discount event
16. Filled with rage
19. Sleeveless garment
20. Place for a baby to sleep
21. Singer Horne
22. Jealous feeling
24. Opposite of 35-Across
26. Salt Lake City's state
27. Rubber sphere
28. Opening stake
29. Major fusses
31. Current-events report
33. Drizzles, perhaps
36. Covered with mud
39. Young horses
40. Use soap and water
41. Ready to be picked, as fruit
42. Eve's mate
43. Writing utensils
45. Enjoy a magazine article
47. In support of
48. Mr. Gershwin
49. Small bite
50. "I ____ You, Babe"

92

ACROSS

1. Miner's bonanza
5. Unruly child
9. Lyricist Gershwin
12. Major fusses
13. Scarce
14. Signal "yes"
15. Strong longings
16. Points (a weapon)
17. Front of a boot
18. Enthusi-astic
20. Jogs
22. Remained
25. Doctor's charge
26. Farthest from good
27. Very young child
31. Provoke
32. Jolt
33. Glamorous Gardner
34. Less tidy
37. Made on a loom
39. Monet's creation
40. Decreased in size
41. Keyboard instrument
44. Mental state
45. Strange
46. Close at hand
48. Nights before holidays
52. Little green veggie
53. One of the Great Lakes
54. Make irritable
55. USA's Uncle
56. Male parents
57. ____ and sound, secure

DOWN

1. Produce (an egg)
2. Poetic tribute
3. Get into (clothes)
4. Writing assign-ments
5. Plait (hair)
6. Police attack
7. Elbow's site
8. Tried out
9. Division word
10. Plant's anchor
11. Citrus coolers
19. Old soldier
21. Lipstick shade
22. Go for a dip
23. Pulled apart by force
24. Large boats
25. In honor of
27. Black goo
28. Volcanic substance
29. Uniform
30. Sergeant or admiral
32. Fast plane
35. ____ Diego, California
36. Pressed (shirts)
37. "Which person?"
38. Cafe patrons' requests
40. Tender spots
41. Bursts, as a balloon
42. Brainstorm outcome
43. Eve's mate
44. Hotel house-keeper
47. Epoch
49. By means of
50. One of a shoemaker's helpers, in a tale
51. Use the eyes

93

ACROSS

1. Pout
5. Tree fluid
8. Clean (clothes)
12. British nobleman
13. Crusted dessert
14. The Buckeye State
15. Corral problem
17. Tolled, as a bell
18. Timid
19. Ogled (at)
21. More irate
22. Number to tango
25. Narrow walkways
28. Moved quickly (with "off")
30. Stretched out
31. Plumbing tube
32. Yearly
35. Garden residents
37. Witness
38. Less of a 1-Down
40. Pattern
41. Lyricist Gershwin
44. Ms. Hayworth
47. Wobbled
49. Finished
50. Self
51. Wind indicator
52. Word after "kidney" or "pinto"
53. Put on (clothes)
54. Picnic pests

DOWN

1. Unclean state
2. Solemn promise
3. Say "Grace"
4. Shade tree
5. Drives too fast
6. Helped
7. Looked searchingly
8. Sentence part
9. "Gotcha!"
10. Moral transgression
11. Pen resident
16. "All work and no ____ . . ."
20. Epoch
21. Bill of fare
22. Lean
23. Sobbed
24. Lyric poems
25. "Woe is me!"
26. Country road
27. Cover the inside of
29. Shadowbox
33. Had lunch
34. Catalogued
35. Ledge dweller
36. Gave temporarily
39. San ____, California
40. "Drat!"
41. Persia, now
42. Lease
43. Summer drinks
44. Steal from
45. "____ Got a Secret"
46. Brewed beverage
48. A Gabor

94

ACROSS

1. Secret scheme
5. Slide, as tires on ice
9. Camp bed
12. Feel great affection for
13. Bancroft of "The Turning Point"
14. Mined material
15. Pre-owned, as a car
16. Bit of music
17. Damage the surface of
18. Fix (torn clothes)
19. Northern food fish
20. Shade-giving tree
21. Egg's center
24. Grass carpet
26. Jewel
29. Eyelid hair
31. Mental faculties
34. Steers clear of
36. Napping
38. Knitter's raw material
39. Song for one
41. Express in words
42. Explosive substance: abbr.
44. Soup dish
46. Piglet's parent
48. Suitable
50. Not at home
54. "The light has dawned!"
55. Surf's noise
57. Hardly cooked
58. Trucker's vehicle
59. Quartet with one missing
60. Broad smile
61. Bambi's mom, for one
62. Post (a letter)
63. Terminates

DOWN

1. Small, purple fruit
2. Suffer a defeat
3. Baker's hot spot?
4. Name for a toy bear
5. ____ Antonio, Texas
6. Raps (on a door)
7. Division term
8. Property documents
9. Plays with happy endings
10. Of the mouth
11. Semester
22. Ancient
23. Scottish maiden
25. Hooting bird
26. Light-hearted
27. Actress Gabor
28. Housing loan
30. Angelic glow
32. Asian beverage
33. Intelligence agent
35. Country hotel
37. Female hog
40. Get
43. Small pies
45. Sweater size
46. Difficult
47. Cleveland's state
49. Tiny skin opening
51. Alert (someone) to danger
52. Dry and desolate
53. Desires; wants
56. Curtain holder

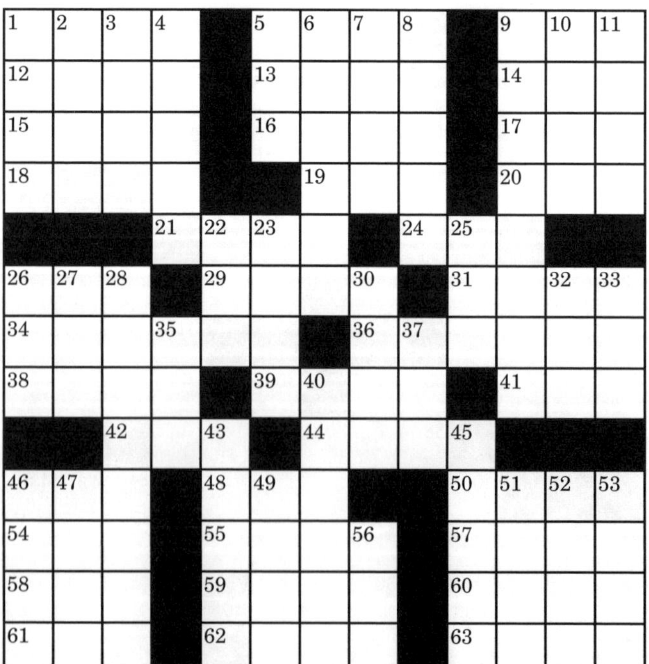

95

ACROSS

1. Carnation color
5. Ready money
9. Suited to a particular purpose
12. Petroleum exporting nation
13. Skilled
14. Try to win the heart of
15. Record on a cassette
16. Authentic
17. Everyone
18. Potato bud
20. Partici-pated in a sport
22. Long-haired dog
25. Message in a bottle, maybe
26. One of the Gabor sisters
27. Expert
29. Mold
33. Volleyball barrier
34. Evil act
36. Food tin
37. Cornered in a conifer?
40. Parking area
42. Kept secret
43. By way of
45. Ones in possession
47. Apply, as peanut butter
50. Bambi's mom, for one
51. Murmur lovingly
52. Public-opinion survey
54. Hermit ____, sea critter
58. Swiss mountain
59. Historic canal
60. Toy for a windy day
61. Boot tip
62. Cincinnati baseballers
63. Went rapidly

DOWN

1. Barbe-cuing site, some-times
2. Gershwin brother
3. Doze
4. Prepare to propose
5. Professions
6. Mr. Vigoda
7. Smacks
8. Verbal greetings
9. Out of town
10. Vaulting aid
11. Tattled (on)
19. Small dog's yelp
21. Fireplace residue
22. Part of a dollar
23. "The party's ____ . . ."
24. Behind the times
28. Liquid fat
30. Muscle pain
31. Couple
32. Stopping points
35. Pasta
38. Preceding night
39. Change (a baby)
41. One plus one
44. Love greatly
46. Swans' outstanding features
47. "Begone!"
48. Horseback game
49. Sailing cord
53. Jar cover
55. Torn place
56. Satisfied one's hunger
57. Spot for slumber

96

ACROSS

1. They top i's
5. "Make the ___ of it!"
9. Ocean
12. Tale of heroes
13. Car
14. Footed vase
15. Sidelong look
16. "Star ___," sci-fi show
17. Far from good
18. Offensive remark
20. Shed tears
22. Honey producer
23. Animal traps
26. Fence opening
29. Anger
31. Outer ___
32. Press (clothes)
34. Sorrowful
36. Dull pain
37. Stands up
39. Cloth scrap
41. Singer Jones
42. Scottish beauties
44. Head gesture
46. Skin irritation
47. Golfing area
51. Taxi
53. Gather (leaves)
55. Earth's orbiter
56. Be sick
57. Always
58. ___ eagle, national bird
59. Attempt
60. Sawbucks
61. Chances

DOWN

1. Sandwich shop
2. Unlock
3. Office neckwear
4. Brush vigorously
5. Is important
6. Belonging to us
7. Thick soups
8. Transit coins
9. Deduct
10. Notable period
11. In addition
19. Tropical garland
21. Mama's partner
24. Reverberate
25. Appear (to be)
26. Young woman
27. Opera solo
28. Maybe
30. Corn spike
33. Bird's home
35. The Rockettes, for example
38. Hidden fact
40. Sticky stuff
43. Use a razor
45. Movie elephant
48. 13-Across's thoroughfare
49. Exchanged for cash
50. Concludes
51. Feline
52. Atmosphere
54. Barbie's guy

97

ACROSS

1. Game played on horseback
5. President Lincoln, to pals
8. Thought
12. Eager and enthusiastic
13. Young man
14. "The Long and Winding ____," Beatles hit
15. Transmit
16. Sports shoes
18. 34-Across or 24-Down
19. As well as
20. Wet forecast
23. Obligations to repay
28. Mined metal
31. Horned farm animal
33. Stunt-plane move
34. "Weeping" plant
36. Regard with wonder
38. Misplace
39. Competent
41. Guided
42. Knight mare?
44. Fasting time
46. Hubbub
48. Urban rodents
52. Anxious desire
57. A Great Lake
58. "____ McBeal," TV show
59. Fruit drink
60. Highest point
61. Plumbing tube
62. Allow
63. Next

DOWN

1. Bygone
2. Finished
3. Face wrinkle
4. More unusual
5. Singer Jarreau and actor Pacino
6. Yellow fruit
7. Paradise
8. Annoy
9. Female deer
10. Hearing organ
11. Paid notices
17. Tack on
21. In the past
22. Dubuque's state
24. Shade provider
25. Cook in simmering liquid
26. Ripped apart
27. Moved quickly
28. Night birds
29. Violent disorder
30. Choice word?
32. Story
35. General Robert E.
37. Lion's lair
40. Woman with light-colored hair
43. Newsman Rather
45. Trick alternative
47. Clock face
49. Doorway curve
50. Use a stopwatch
51. Witnessed
52. Sharp bark
53. Cotton gin inventor Whitney
54. High mountain
55. Cereal grass
56. Obtain

98

ACROSS

1. Trousers accessory
5. Make lace
8. Without one's wife
12. At any time
13. Cultivating tool
14. Legend
15. Eat in splendor
16. Eisenhower's nickname
17. "____ upon a time . . ."
18. Sits at an angle
20. Small taste
22. Bit of Morse code
23. Circus height increasers
27. Touchdown-celebrating sound
30. Graceful tree
32. "Saw logs"
33. Royal-flush cards
35. Musical ability
37. Trot or gallop
38. One in charge
40. Unused
42. Negative replies
43. Popcorn beginning
45. Weep mournfully
47. Words at the altar
48. Certain relative
52. Rural skyscraper?
55. "____ Light Up My Life"
57. Greater amount
58. Concluded
59. Reverent fear
60. Conspire
61. Artificial colors
62. Was in the forefront
63. Some offspring

DOWN

1. Mattress sites
2. Far from virtuous
3. Musical Horne
4. Fashion
5. Prickly weed
6. Pilot's "Yes!"
7. Frequent mall visitors
8. Somewhat steep
9. Heavy weight
10. Curving path
11. "Turn right!," to a horse
19. Shoe point
21. Possessive pronoun
24. Bank service
25. Small band
26. Matching collections
27. Oven "shelf"
28. Feel sore
29. One in a will
31. Adult fellow
34. Graduating class
36. Brought a kitten down from a tree, perhaps
39. Gave Fido some kibble
41. Play the suitor to
44. True blue
46. Runs (into)
49. Unaccompanied performance
50. Remove wrinkles from
51. Butterfly catchers
52. Turf
53. Wall climber
54. Peggy or Brenda
56. Be in debt to

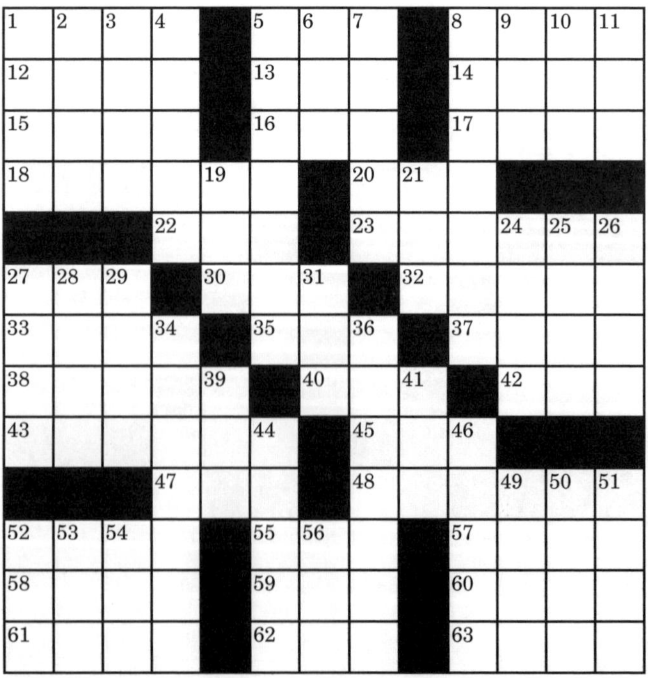

99

ACROSS

1. Destiny
5. Child
8. Electric light source
12. Mr. Trebek
13. Wrath
14. Canal in New York state
15. One's usual foods
16. Complain continually
17. Years and years
18. Trucker's vehicle
20. Least common
22. Julius Caesar's people
25. Conclusion
26. Of Dublin
27. Safety device
28. Man's best friend
31. Is able to
32. Bestirred oneself
34. Screen star Gardner
35. Far from new
36. Headed, as an expedition
37. Long, fictional work
39. Vigor
40. Comes in
41. Live in
44. Cheerleader's cheer
45. "Terrible" czar
46. A Lincoln nickname
48. Otherwise
52. Tepee, for one
53. Tic-toe connector
54. Spool of movie film
55. Flat-bottomed boats
56. Perched (on)
57. Hunt for

DOWN

1. Temporary fashion
2. Legendary boxer
3. Caddy's offer
4. Supplementary actors
5. Queens' royal mates
6. One of the Gershwins
7. Thermometer divisions
8. Facial hair
9. Yen; hankering
10. Untruths
11. Opposite of worst
19. Breathed
21. TV reception improver
22. Puerto follower
23. Spoken
24. Brain
27. Indicate agreement
28. Mr. Letterman, informally
29. Finished
30. "Buffalo ____," song
33. Says again
38. "Do unto ____ . . ."
39. Half quarts
40. Build
41. Hayworth of old films
42. At any time
43. Went under, as the Titanic
47. Sheepish remark?
49. Civil War general
50. Observe
51. Moose

100

ACROSS

1. Chip accompaniment
4. Ill
8. Curve
12. Single
13. "A ____ Grows in Brooklyn"
14. "____ the Rainbow," Judy Garland song
15. Going in
17. Metal strand
18. After all the others
19. Permit
20. Stream of water
23. Inventor Whitney
25. Whistle's noise
26. School formal
27. Deep hole
30. Materialize
32. On land
34. Buzzing insect
35. President Adams
37. "Woe!"
38. Trouble
39. First part
40. Detection device
44. "Which person?"
46. Employs
47. Gratifying
51. Chain segment
52. Actual
53. Brewed drink
54. Dines
55. Chances, to a gambler
56. Pig's home

DOWN

1. Female deer
2. Country hotel
3. Fido or Kitty
4. Unowned 3-Down
5. Showy flower
6. Middle
7. Beer cask
8. Soup vessel
9. Wicked
10. Cruel emperor
11. Sketched
16. Make 50-Down
19. Targets (with "at")
20. Poke with a knife
21. Catholic leader
22. Heavy twine
24. Banking transaction
26. Jab
27. Game on horseback
28. Tehran's land
29. Exam
31. Open
33. Hurts
36. Bayed (at the moon)
39. Young ponies
40. Regulation
41. Largest continent
42. Fender depression
43. Inquires
45. Chief
47. Affirmative vote
48. "____ a boy!"
49. Mesh snare
50. Happy

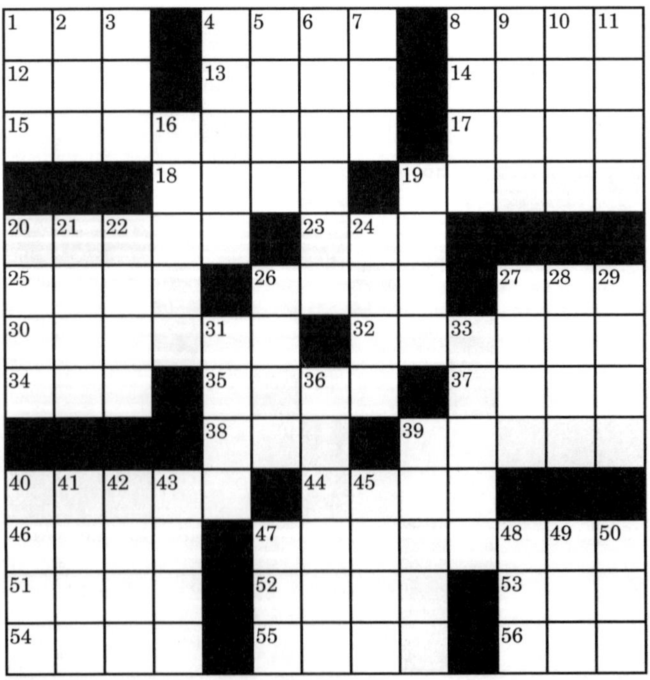

101

ACROSS

1. Opposite of succeed
5. Unacceptable
8. Whirl
12. Hardly working
13. Glamorous Gardner
14. One who saves lives
15. Freed
17. Acorn-bearing trees
18. Corral, perhaps
19. Less good
20. Cereal grain
24. Disgusted exclamation
26. Acquire by labor
27. Insignificant
28. Sound of discovery
31. King's son
33. Stag's horn
35. Golfing gadget
36. Refined woman
38. Eve's mate
39. Boxer Muhammad
40. Lovers' quarrels
41. Colony of bees
45. By way of
47. 2-Down ingredient, sometimes
48. Flying craft
53. Played the copycat
54. Lupino of Hollywood
55. Comply with (orders)
56. Change for a twenty
57. Boys who have grown up
58. Baseball's Rose

DOWN

1. Pine relative
2. Fruit-juice drink
3. Feeling sick
4. Confederate general
5. Foundation
6. Wide thoroughfare
7. Mom's hubby
8. "Beat it!"
9. ". . . and a partridge in a ____ tree"
10. Displeases
11. Snout
16. Likely (to)
19. "At what time?"
20. Cried
21. Loser to a tortoise
22. A Great Lake
23. Tap-dancing Miller
25. Drab color
27. Dinner, for one
28. "M*A*S*H" star
29. Warm (leftovers)
30. Upper appendages
32. Chowder ingredient
34. Pat lightly
37. Split apart
40. Plant fluid
41. Bedspring support
42. Clean (a counter)
43. Prayer ending
44. Scarlet and vermilion
46. Persia, today
48. Point (a gun)
49. Trim (a tree)
50. Actor Vigoda
51. Fishing snare
52. Vision organ

102

ACROSS

1. Violin box
5. Comment from a lamb
8. Farm tower
12. "Woe is me!"
13. Mouth part
14. Like a desert
15. Highlands lassies' caps
16. Tavern brew
17. Locate
18. Moves stealthily
20. Assignments
21. Nevertheless
22. Distant
23. It's between the ribs and the hips
26. Sunscreens and moisturizers
30. Tally up
31. Mariner's map
33. Deep sorrow
34. Arrived at
36. Actress Evans of "Dynasty"
38. Sprint
39. Gymnast's perfect score
40. Long, narrow piece of cloth
43. Counsel
47. Sonnet, for one
48. Horned viper
50. Unemployed
51. Prince Charles's sister
52. Garden implement
53. Work hard
54. Tennis-court dividers
55. In addition to
56. Lane-lining trees

DOWN

1. Purring pets
2. Actor Alda
3. Identical
4. English-class compositions
5. Gust of wind
6. Be unwell
7. Large monkey
8. African wildlife expedition
9. Showy, tall flower
10. Chain unit
11. Ends' partner
19. Hamburger condiment
20. Snitched (on)
22. In favor of
23. Absence of peace
24. Summer drink
25. Movie star Lupino
26. Young fellow
27. Hold, as property
28. Signal with the head
29. Bounding main
32. Feathered female
35. Illegal acts
37. Ask to a party, perhaps
39. Recorded on cassette
40. Stretch across
41. Musical sound
42. Tenant's fee
44. Object of worship
45. Thin
46. Slithery sea-dwellers
48. Villain's cry
49. Daddy's boy

103

ACROSS

1. Vehicle for hire
4. Marksman
8. Cat's "toenail"
12. Malt beverage
13. One in a will
14. Garden watering tube
15. Actress Lupino
16. In a noncommittal way
17. Enthusiastic
18. Giving a moniker to
20. Neighborhoods
21. Sending suggestive looks
24. Young horse
27. Came into
31. Pussycat's companion of rhyme
32. Tent securer
34. "____ Got You Under My Skin"
35. Brought out of danger
37. Prayer-ending word
38. Heeding (commands)
41. Some soft drinks
44. Indispensable
48. Impersonates
49. Boys
51. Hardened H_2O
52. Do an usher's job
53. Correct (copy) for publication
54. The lady in question
55. Terminates
56. Some social gatherings
57. Police officer

DOWN

1. Son of Adam
2. "M*A*S*H" star
3. Radiate
4. See 3-Down
5. Fence made of shrubs
6. Tin Man's request
7. Give it a shot
8. Pay with plastic
9. Abiding affection
10. Giant landmass
11. Says "I do"
19. Sick
20. Begin a poker pot
22. All set
23. Writing liquid
24. In favor of
25. Have bills to pay
26. Pacino and Jolson
28. Basketball-hoop edge
29. Festive night-before
30. Lion's lair
32. Underwater boats
33. Golf-bag find
36. Glides downhill
37. Get older
39. Delhi's land
40. Treetop homes
41. Instance, as of measles
42. Unwrap
43. Be the guide
45. Compact ____, recording
46. Sound reflection
47. Far from shallow
49. Permit
50. Summer beverage

104

ACROSS

1. Fast gait
5. Health facility
8. Slightly open
12. Enthusiastic review
13. Everything
14. Wish
15. Country once called Persia
16. Rubbed sore muscles
18. Turns to liquid, as ice
20. "Ready or ____, here I come!"
21. Lyric poem
23. Large sailboat
28. Mother of chicks
31. Courtroom pledge
33. Cobbler's product
34. Is
36. Take a breath
38. Extremely wealthy
39. Rabbit's relative
41. Five plus five
42. Superman's metal?
44. Observe
45. Not well
47. Mommy's mate
52. Pizza-sauce ingredients
57. Traditional wisdom
58. "Up, up, and ____!"
59. English beverage
60. Level
61. Actor-dancer Kelly
62. Secret agent
63. Stitches (up)

DOWN

1. Cut a bit, as hair
2. Hard to find
3. Shape of a football
4. Canvas shelter
5. Gumshoe Spade
6. Venus or Mars
7. Too
8. "I caught you!"
9. Run for exercise
10. Zoo primate
11. Lipstick color
17. Pig's residence
19. Chimney dirt
22. Go quickly
24. Volcano dust
25. Friendly talk
26. Swiss-cheese cavity
27. High-schooler, usually
28. Word on a towel
29. Way out
30. "Have a ____ day!"
32. Put on the payroll
35. That cow
37. Requirement
40. Taking a nap
43. Ignited
46. Housing divisions
48. Sudsy drinks
49. Peace bird
50. Took (a card)
51. Strong longings
52. Playground game
53. Have unpaid bills
54. Gent
55. Positive vote
56. Utter

105

ACROSS

1. Picnic spoiler
4. Cowboy's boot-heel attachment
8. Those people
12. By way of
13. Imitate
14. Used a loom
15. Sound accompanying a standing ovation
17. Cain's brother
18. Poker stake
19. Force air violently through the nose
20. Missing
23. Tree branch
25. Ms. Bancroft
26. Second-hand
27. Fruit drink
30. One who makes points in a game
32. Bank clerk
34. Fasten with stitches
35. Hen products
37. Inventive thought
38. Pooch pest
39. Brief sleeps
40. Less
43. Thick, strong cord
46. Dry
47. Language of Tokyo
51. Piece of music
52. Matures
53. Mover's vehicle
54. Leg joint
55. Crooked
56. In addition

DOWN

1. Gardner of Hollywood
2. Pinch or bite
3. Strike lightly
4. Glance at quickly
5. Act sullen
6. Disturbs physically
7. Cereal grass
8. String-plucking noise
9. Tramp
10. At all times
11. Thaw
16. Afterward
19. "West ____ Story," musical
20. Young woman
21. At any time
22. Winter forecast
24. Makes damp
26. Strong impulse
27. Actor Alan of "M*A*S*H"
28. "____ Impact," 1998 film
29. Noted periods of time
31. Slippery swimmers
33. Flax fabric
36. Auto shelter
38. Soft candy
40. Face covering
41. Press (clothes) smooth
42. Six plus three
44. Opposite of closed
45. Time gone by
47. Quick punch
48. Actress Gabor
49. ____ Francisco, California
50. Conclude

106

ACROSS

1. Solemn pledge
5. Knife puncture
9. Waterston of "Law and Order"
12. Dull, continual pain
13. Sheltered inlet
14. Wedding-vow words
15. Oak or ash
16. Civil disturbance
17. "____ freedom ring!"
18. Convey
19. Boxing great
20. "Golly!"
21. Shade giver
23. Period of sunlight
25. Baseball move?
28. Wood-eating pest
32. Happy dog's tail movement
33. Out of the way
35. Beam of light
36. Animal that "plays dead"
38. Female relative
40. Chicken's mom
41. ____ Diego, California
42. Address God
45. Cheer syllable
47. Impressive deed
51. Ship's record
52. Sherlock Holmes smoked one
53. Bend (the back)
54. President Lincoln's nickname
55. Employed
56. Ten minus one
57. Word of accord
58. Knight and Koppel
59. Abound

DOWN

1. Cereal grains
2. Land measure
3. At that time
4. Listened to (a warning)
5. "Shoo!": slang
6. Heavy labor
7. Steered clear of
8. Wager (on)
9. Rural tower
10. Citrus drinks
11. Insect that damages woolens
20. School-dance site
22. Rental agreement
24. Boxing site
25. Number for tea?
26. Knock sharply
27. In the past
28. Comic Conway
29. Angry feeling
30. Tic-toe link
31. Storm's core
34. Dawn
37. Like Bashful the Dwarf
39. Baby
41. Loses, as fur
42. Engage in recreation
43. After-bath attire
44. Generations
46. Impersonated
48. One of the Great Lakes
49. Teen's skin woe
50. Those folks
52. Deposit

107

ACROSS

1. Piece of china
5. Cry of discovery
8. Slightly open
12. Contribute to the poker pot
13. ____ rummy, card game
14. Soda flavor
15. Commencing
17. Furnace output
18. Big pig
19. Main dish
21. Fall behind
22. Offend (someone)
26. Large, striped cat
29. Far from new
30. Knight's title
31. Logging product
32. Settle (a bill)
33. Singer Horne
34. Night bird
35. Annoy
36. Like objects in an attic
37. African hunting expedition
39. Suitcase
40. Removed unwanted plants from
42. Lower (the lights)
45. Actor Alan
48. Coast
50. Hinged entryway
51. A Kennedy
52. Nearly circular
53. Had bills
54. Covert agent
55. Departed

DOWN

1. Short race
2. Fascinated by
3. Male deer
4. That cow
5. Maturation process
6. Indirect suggestion
7. With intense irritation
8. Lingering pains
9. Mr. DiMaggio
10. In imitation of: 2 wds.
11. Large rodent
16. Rend
20. Come to a conclusion
21. Was in first
23. Puts in service
24. Pocket fuzz
25. Breakfast-in-bed platter
26. Numbers for Noah
27. Des Moines' state
28. Game with clubs
29. Acorn's tree
32. Catholic clergymen
33. Carry, as a heavy valise
35. Great rage
36. Papas
38. Oscar or Emmy
39. Small and glittering, as eyes
41. Profound
42. Pigeon's cousin
43. Iraq neighbor
44. Turn to liquid
45. Hullabaloo
46. Lie ____, stay hidden
47. 3-Down's mate
49. "In what manner?"

108

ACROSS

1. Tourist's chart
4. Excludes
8. Winter vehicle
12. Make a boo-boo
13. Neglect to include
14. Angler's rod
15. Tall tale
16. Helper
17. Lack of difficulty
18. Narrows gradually to a point
20. Roam
22. States further
23. Common conjunction
24. Poets of old
26. Picasso production
27. Pretending to be shy
30. Follow (orders)
31. Stashed away
32. Tender
33. Marry
34. Mongrel dog
35. Celestial body
36. Existed
37. Hinged fastener
38. Go back (to), as a previous condition
41. Idolized
44. Spoken
45. Earring's spot
47. Adam's mate
48. Constrict
49. Revise (text)
50. Religious misdeed
51. Observes
52. Matching collections
53. Quite clever

DOWN

1. Turn from a solid to a liquid
2. Verdi solo
3. Made ready
4. Wooden planks
5. Improper; wrong
6. Free (of)
7. Ship attendant
8. Use money
9. Burden
10. Otherwise
11. Stag or doe
19. Small whirlpool
21. Social insect
24. Decorative knot
25. President Lincoln's nickname
26. On the ——, broadcasting
27. Make more dense
28. Miner's quest
29. As of now
31. Hurries
32. Just okay: hyph. wd.
34. Auto
35. West Point students
36. Fuses together
37. Customary practice
38. Steals from
39. A Great Lake
40. Wind direction indicator
42. Wicked
43. Declare (a statement) to be untrue
46. Lyric poem

109

ACROSS

1. Three of these make a yard
5. Uncooked
8. Mama's mate
12. Advocate strongly
13. "____ Got You Under My Skin"
14. Worshiped one
15. Intense fury
16. Catch (a crook)
17. Specific knowledge
18. Pester
20. Romantic flowers
21. A holey cheese
24. Relaxed in a chair
25. Encountered
26. Veranda
29. Radio commercials
32. Unrefined mineral
33. Frightening word
34. Margarine square
35. Precious jewel
36. Unpaid bills
38. Inventor Whitney
39. Cook in oil
40. More aged
42. Horrifying
45. Night bird
46. Frilly trim fabric
47. Regulation
49. Biblical boats
53. Actress Bancroft
54. Winter driving hazard
55. Postal delivery
56. Honey makers
57. Newsman Koppel
58. Actor Garcia

DOWN

1. Animal pelt
2. Important time period
3. Omelet ingredient
4. Adolescents
5. Wedding band
6. Hollywood's Gardner
7. Spider's creation
8. Fly (a plane)
9. Troubles
10. Tiny opening
11. Tavern beverages
19. Poisonous snake
20. Cheerleader's exclamation
21. Urban pollution
22. "The Way We ____," song
23. Grocery-list entry
24. Edinburgh native
27. Heed
28. Take another's property
29. Mimicked
30. Valley
31. Mix with a spoon
36. Arid
37. Scatter seeds
39. Releases
41. Woolly animal
42. Hunk of marble
43. Walking stick
44. Possible skin problem for 4-Down
45. Had 36-Across
47. Ignited
48. High card
50. Sprinted
51. Young goat
52. Cunning

110

ACROSS

1. Bassett hound's droopy features
5. Salty expanse
8. Bowlike curves
12. Adhesive substance
13. Asphalting gunk
14. Food store
15. Least rough
17. Cherished
18. Be obliged to pay
19. Shade-giving trees
20. Waved (a bat)
24. Put on (cargo)
27. Singer Turner
28. Inquires
29. Fairyland creature
32. Corrected (copy)
34. Seem
36. Player at Shea Stadium
37. Extremely
39. "Or ____!," a threat
40. Foundation
41. Try a bite of
42. Cobbler's product
45. "Eureka!"
47. Father
48. Newspaper cut-out
53. Ended
54. Outmoded
55. Mental formulation
56. Look after
57. "Farewell!"
58. Young children

DOWN

1. It can be cooked sunny-side-up
2. Tavern beverage
3. Move swiftly
4. Movie backdrop
5. One-dish meal
6. Artists' stands
7. Louvre display
8. Summed up
9. Spool on a fishing rod
10. Shellfish treat
11. Old business-letter greeting
16. Ship's journal
20. Apple-to-branch connector
21. Broad
22. Army grouping
23. Mr. King Cole
25. "All right!"
26. Snake of the Nile
28. Lemon drinks
29. Slippery 5-Across creatures
30. First's opposite
31. Costing nothing
33. Ms. Gabor
35. Split ____ soup
38. In fact
40. Santa's facial hair
41. Touch on the shoulder
42. Blotch
43. Possess
44. Ready to admit customers
46. Put out of sight
48. Corn leftover
49. Fruit stone
50. Wedding words
51. Snaring mesh
52. Cooking or heating fuel

111

ACROSS

1. Baseball's Rose
5. Health resort
8. Storage shack
12. Morally depraved
13. Olive stone
14. Concern
15. Jewelry chain
17. Largest continent
18. Traveler's lodging
19. Different one
20. Eagerly anticipate
24. Actress Lupino
26. Pork fat
27. Native of Glasgow
28. Hit the slopes
31. Nearly
33. It contains salt
35. Cunning
36. Decorative fabric
38. 15-Across loop
39. Expression of disgust
40. Oven gloves
41. Surrounded by
45. In the past
47. Rant
48. Solemn vows
53. Ship's personnel
54. Mature
55. Skater's arena
56. Coop residents
57. "Sure!"
58. TV's Rooney

DOWN

1. Ink holder
2. Holiday precursor
3. ____-tac-toe
4. Large deer
5. Extend over
6. Outdoor meal
7. Enjoyed a 6-Down
8. "Shoo!"
9. Hodge-podge
10. A Great Lake
11. Cherished one
16. Ignited
19. Pledge
20. "Woe is me!"
21. Upright structure
22. Military force
23. Marriage reply: 2 wds.
25. Medicine amount
27. Male 4-Down
28. Short play
29. Superman's alter ego
30. Annoys
32. Hit heavily
34. Famous boxer
37. "To battle!"
40. Dad's mate
41. Bridge support
42. Female horse
43. Baking chamber
44. Current information
46. Departs
48. Recom-pense
49. Mr. Gershwin
50. Offense against heaven
51. Conclude
52. Wild blue yonder

112

ACROSS

1. Kinder-garten rest time
4. Cotton-tipped stick
8. Game for duffers
12. A famous Whitney
13. Tap dancer's prop
14. Role model, often
15. Is able to
16. Military assistant
17. Sniffer
18. Shows reverence, in a way
20. See eye to eye
21. Salad ingredient
24. "____ a loaf is better than none"
27. Savanna sprinter
31. Like: 2 wds.
32. Window sections
34. Dove's murmur
35. Telegram's contents
37. Red-ink situation
38. Part of the workweek
41. Backless chair
44. Chooses democrati-cally
48. One with "pants on fire"?
49. Hit (a fly)
51. City of Brazil, for short
52. Poker stake
53. Marco who explored China
54. Green around the gills
55. Rhythm-section instrument
56. Tiny marchers
57. Slumber site

DOWN

1. Where a tie is worn
2. Alda of "M*A*S*H"
3. Fragrant evergreen
4. Climb up
5. Midsection area
6. Further-more
7. Buzzing insect
8. Pungent root
9. Distinctive smell
10. Misplace
11. Escape
19. Magical being
20. Behaves decisively
22. Musical sounds
23. Purpose
24. Easter meat
25. Pub brew
26. Certain 22-Down
28. Frozen treat
29. Corn discard
30. Boiling
32. Patriot Revere
33. The Ice ____, time of glaciers
36. Mall businesses
37. Coloring agent
39. Delivered, as a blow
40. Some singers
41. Thick slice
42. Turner of rock
43. Granola grains
45. Baby's 57-Across
46. Kitchen floor square
47. Auction announce-ment
49. Posh retreat
50. Took the prize

113

ACROSS

1. Be boastful
5. Lawn starter
8. See 3-Down
12. Full of grease
13. Shed tears
14. Put on ice
15. Herd's out-of-control rush
17. Turns brown in the sun
18. ____ Diego, California
19. Individual
20. Cowboy contest
21. More grim
23. Papa's partner
26. Large body of water
27. Fitting
30. Complied with
33. Scribe
35. Fido or Kitty
36. Ply a shovel
38. Say (an accusation) is untrue
39. Singing great Frank
42. Perspire
45. Rogers or Campanella
46. Tot's toy
49. 1970s sitcom about cabbies
50. Fabric, for one
52. Morally bad
53. "The ____ of Innocence"
54. Division term
55. Makes damp
56. A primary color
57. Historian's interest

DOWN

1. Supervisor
2. Glamorous Hayworth
3. With 8-Across, star of "M*A*S*H"
4. Workout spot
5. Part of a play
6. Commanding officer's directives
7. Coloring agent
8. Laurence Olivier, for one
9. Batch (of laundry)
10. Completed
11. Furthermore
16. Flower planter
20. Back section
21. Utter
22. Unused
23. Clean, as the kitchen floor
24. President Lincoln, familiarly
25. Ran into
27. Had a snack
28. Corral's kin
29. Give it a shot
31. Do a newspaper job
32. Noise
34. Screen star Lupino
37. Auto fix-it shop
39. Goes by ship
40. Hauled
41. Dark bread variety
42. "Irish" dish
43. Ocean breaker
44. Leave the stage
46. Turner of rock
47. Horses' grains
48. Novel's story line
50. Damage slightly
51. Shred

114

ACROSS

1. Not closed
5. Tree fluid
8. Thick slice
12. Got in the saddle
13. Dollar bill
14. "She's a real live ____!"
15. Toe sites
16. Plus
17. Not odd
18. Annoyed
20. Vermin
21. Looks fixedly
24. Illuminated
26. Cavities
27. Mr. Franklin, familiarly
28. Mineral spring
31. Lyricist Gershwin
32. From Dublin
34. Knock softly
35. Animal enclosure
36. Put on (clothes)
37. Where the sky is?
39. Encountered
40. Had a slant
41. Too
44. Fork prongs
46. First course, often
47. Wedding words
48. Towering
52. Tiny skin opening
53. Old's opposite
54. Akron's state
55. Drove too fast
56. Merry
57. Takes a snooze

DOWN

1. Collie's comment
2. Mr. DiMaggio
3. Cooling fruit drink
4. Go to bed
5. Lingers in the tub
6. Ms. Bancroft
7. Sells door to door
8. Used a broom
9. Make one's home (in)
10. God of war
11. Crooked
19. See 9-Down
21. Oceangoing vessel
22. Ripped
23. Actor Alda
25. Draw a breath
27. Storage container
28. Halt
29. Cover (a road)
30. Imitated
33. Giving in to decay
38. Beantown
39. Acted gloomy
40. Bright white
41. Tiny vipers
42. Shoestring circle
43. Certain
45. Mental creation
49. Cry of triumph
50. Mouth part
51. ____ Angeles, California

115

ACROSS

1. Grocery memo
5. Melancholy
8. Reverberate
12. Scent
13. Couple
14. Heap
15. Departed
16. Dine
17. Inspire nothing but yawns
18. Military unit
20. They detect a 12-Across
21. Snapshot
24. Female pig
25. Scientist's room
26. Fancy boat
29. Attempt
32. Consume
33. Baseball's DiMaggio
34. Regret
35. Timid
36. Chinese bear
38. In the manner of: 2 wds.
39. An evergreen tree
40. More joyous
42. Kidnapped
45. Masticate
47. Fermented drink
48. Cow call
49. Trepidation
53. Worshiped one
54. Everything
55. Unattractive
56. Receives
57. Golf prop
58. Fail to win

DOWN

1. ____ cabin, rustic dwelling
2. Wedding vow: 2 wds.
3. Male heir
4. Pay for everyone's dinner
5. Plant stalk
6. "Up, up, and ____!"
7. Round speck
8. Arm joint
9. Pigeon sounds
10. Tortoise's rival
11. Keats' works
19. Singer Orbison
20. Negative word
21. Added to
22. Corned beef go-with
23. Heed
24. Cast off (clothing)
27. Open
28. Opposing vote
29. Serving aid
30. Regulation
31. 365-day span
36. Brooch
37. Mature
39. Experiences
41. Terrible
42. Little branch
43. Helper
44. Half-hitch, for one
45. Songwriter Porter
46. Large gap
48. Wrestling pad
50. Conceit
51. Gore and Pacino
52. Bread with caraway seeds

116

ACROSS

1. Donated
5. Naughty
8. Song for a single singer
12. The largest continent
13. Period in history
14. Eager
15. Prescription-filling store
17. Clark Kent's Lois
18. Perfect score, in gymnastics
19. Rams and roosters
20. "The Arabian ____," collection of children's tales
23. Purpose; goal
24. Anger
25. Looked up to
29. Against
30. Out of the way
32. "____ been thinking . . ."
33. Took a begging position
35. Cozy room
36. Chimp, for one
37. ____ Louis Stevenson, author
40. Fawns' fathers
43. Be in the red
44. Word on a door
45. Dark-haired girl
50. Competent
51. Not in
52. Highway
53. Roll-call votes
54. Tiny
55. Weeps out loud

DOWN

1. Sign of a missing tooth
2. Volcanic dust
3. By way of
4. Our planet
5. Vegetarian staple
6. Curved path
7. "That'll be the ____!"
8. A lunch meat
9. The ____ Office
10. Part of a script
11. Poems by Keats
16. Ran into
19. Street performer, often
20. Shaving accident
21. Steel "ingredient"
22. DNA carrier
23. Recipe verb
25. Help
26. Go by bicycle
27. "Happily ____ after"
28. Can impression
30. European range
31. Understand
34. Winged predators
37. Course of travel
38. Be the proprietor of
39. Products of Bavaria
40. Extent
41. Trumpet's relative
42. One who's on your side
45. Acknowledge applause
46. Feel remorse
47. Also
48. File folder projection
49. McMahon and Sullivan

117

ACROSS

1. Opposite of bright
4. Metal fastener
8. Short note
12. Lyric poem
13. Pulled apart
14. Eager and enthusiastic
15. Flat refusals
16. Bridle strap
17. Watch over
18. Travels by water
20. Stoops (over)
21. Hobo
23. Noted periods of time
25. Intense anger
26. Drawer handle
27. Health resort
30. Wide thoroughfare
32. Pearl-producing mollusk
34. "Affirmative!"
35. Athletic group
37. Make warm
38. Hourglass filler
39. Kinds; classes
40. See 25-Across
43. Cantaloupe, for one
45. Assistant
46. Make donations
47. Preholiday night
50. Strike with the palm
51. A Great Lake
52. Knight's title
53. Garment borders
54. Thaw; liquefy
55. Paving goo

DOWN

1. "Nash Bridges" star Johnson
2. Wedding words
3. Answering-machine recordings
4. Long, narrow piece
5. Christmas carol
6. Resurrected
7. Animal enclosure
8. Spouses
9. Equally balanced
10. Pay attention to
11. Gambler's chances
19. Prayer ending
20. Infant
21. Waiter's platter
22. Talk wildly
24. House chamber
26. See 14-Across
27. Most unyielding
28. Partly decayed plant matter
29. Actor Carney and singer Garfunkel
31. Salt Lake City's state
33. "Go away!"
36. Regard with delight
38. Flight of stairs
39. Frozen rain
40. Clean with soap
41. Irritate
42. Eve's partner
44. Wicked
46. Precious stone
48. By way of
49. Do wrong

118

ACROSS

1. Five minus three
4. Bang (the door)
8. Apiece
12. Tear
13. Winding country road
14. Detective's hint
15. Angry feeling
16. Very bad
17. Loathe
18. Fully grown lads
19. Beavers' structure
20. Played the model
21. Possessive word
23. President Lincoln's nickname
25. "_____ With the Wind," film
27. Thin, wooden strip
28. Doctor's charge
31. Needing immediate action
33. In fact
35. Positive reply
36. Yours and mine
38. Curved roof
39. "_____ for the money . . ."
40. In favor of
41. Gone south, as birds
45. Compete (for)
47. Ms. Lupino
50. Dwell; reside
51. Chanteuse Horne
52. Moral misdeed
53. Prayer ender
54. Feedbag contents
55. Kennedy or Danson
56. Fellow
57. Scheme
58. Home to a pig

DOWN

1. Decorate, as a tree
2. Pipe-cleaner core
3. Introductions
4. Snow vehicles
5. Molten rock
6. Creature
7. Gibson of "Lethal Weapon"
8. Sound reverberation
9. "What a pity!"
10. Precious; adorable
11. Take note of
20. Rose or Sampras
22. Golf-ball prop
24. Soap units
25. Chap
26. Mine extraction
27. Throw for a loop
28. Posy peddlers
29. Shade giver
30. Watch closely
32. Midday hour
34. "Without further _____ . . ."
37. Disclose
40. Rich, elaborate meal
41. Old Glory, for one
42. Green citrus fruit
43. Baker's need
44. Left
46. Fascinated by
48. Food regimen
49. Raggedy Ann's mate
51. Trim (a branch)

119

ACROSS

1. Disorderly crowd
4. True statement
8. Curved lines
12. Nocturnal bird
13. Press (clothing)
14. Pilot's feat
15. Dollar bill
16. Underground plant part
17. Carbonated water
18. Originate (from)
20. Grand slam, for one
21. Otherwise
23. Costar of Swit and Farr
26. Horseback rider's strap
27. Belonging to us
28. Pub drink
31. Columnist Landers
32. Look around secretly
34. Game cube
35. Hang down
36. "How the West ____ Won"
37. Egg-shaped
38. One of Eve's sons
40. Conflicts between nations
41. Beat, as the heart
45. Biblical garden
47. Top part of the body
48. Sharp part of a razor
50. Baseball hat
53. Quite dry
54. Money given temporarily
55. Sight organ
56. Marries
57. Change from solid to liquid
58. Morning mist

DOWN

1. Cow's sound
2. Possess
3. Making holy
4. Burning flames
5. Fragrance
6. Pigeon's cry
7. High explosive: abbr.
8. Additionally
9. Den or kitchen
10. Body of laws
11. Practice punching
19. Six plus four
20. Angel's instrument
21. Historic periods
22. Ms. Horne
24. Far from tight
25. Pair
28. Moved forward
29. Fibber
30. Sea wrigglers
32. Cotton ball
33. Catch (a crook)
37. Have bills
39. Permitted by the state
41. Defrost
42. In this place
43. Sudden invasion
44. Bettors' concerns
46. Fender impression
48. Shade tree
49. Female deer
51. Sailor's affirmative
52. Church seat

120

ACROSS

1. Playground game
4. Do a trial run
8. Plunge a knife through
12. "____ been thinking . . ."
13. Detest
14. Cavity
15. Made a difference
17. Thorny flower
18. Ms. Bancroft
19. Large, sweet fruit
20. Social insects
23. Enjoy the newspaper
25. Strike (a drum)
26. Employed
27. In the manner of: 2 wds.
30. Author Hemingway
32. Diminish
34. Flight record
35. Gal
37. Delicate hue
38. Jacqueline's first husband
39. Rank, as on a top-ten list
40. Clean thoroughly
43. Alan of "M*A*S*H"
46. Tresses
47. Hanging down
51. Concerned with
52. Longings
53. Chinese beverage
54. Autumn fruit
55. Knife's sharp side
56. Pigpen

DOWN

1. Comedian Conway
2. Actress Gardner
3. Receive
4. In those days
5. Work for pay
6. Directs (toward)
7. Newsman Koppel
8. Destroy (documents), in a way
9. Hammer, for one
10. Too
11. Existed
16. Test the flavor of
19. Manufactured
20. Cain's brother
21. Cruel Roman emperor
22. Tartness
24. Slithery swimmers
26. Great Salt Lake's state
27. Thailand's continent
28. Fasting holiday
29. Poker stake
31. Messy person
33. Seat-belt band
36. Trapped
38. One on a courtroom panel
40. Seagoing vessel
41. Walking stick
42. Screen star Hayworth
44. Extended
45. Medicine amount
47. Color (hair)
48. That thing's
49. Fishing mesh
50. Cheery

121

ACROSS

1. Adult pig
4. Garden walkway
8. The one there
12. Reverent respect
13. Reflected sound
14. Angelic glow
15. Japanese money
16. Grind with the teeth
17. Dull routines
18. Snapped, as a photo
20. Songs for one
21. Invoice
23. Female 1-Across
24. Regions
26. Extremely hot place
30. Cry for help
31. Airline vehicle
33. Do a marathon
34. Walked into
36. Tidied (the lawn)
38. Young man
39. Girl-friend of 38-Across
40. Ownerless pet
43. Laundry problem
46. Gait for a 55-Across
47. TV program
48. Hero sandwich, for short
51. Nurse's assistant
52. The Hawkeye State
53. In the past
54. Supervisor
55. Small horse breed
56. Bashful

DOWN

1. Feed for a 55-Across
2. Have debts
3. Least violent
4. Eat like a bird
5. Hurt constantly
6. At that time
7. "_____ are you today?"
8. Pitched
9. Move by truck
10. Woman's vocal range
11. Chuck
19. Like: 2 wds.
20. More painful
21. Naval station
22. Press (pants)
23. Earth's star
25. Use an atomizer
26. Brief trend
27. Little Rock's state
28. Onstage prompts
29. Concludes
32. Showed the way
35. Makes joyful
37. Boxing's Greatest
40. Wound with a knife
41. Crosby, Stills & Nash, for one
42. Metal poles
43. "_____, fly! Don't bother me!"
44. Urban settlement
45. Not at home
47. Drink slowly
49. "Disgusting!"
50. "It's a _____!"

122

ACROSS

1. Beer topping
5. Sneaky
8. Clock sound
12. Paddy grain
13. Excessively
14. Had on
15. Some shade trees
16. Total (up)
17. Not at home
18. Coloring agents
19. Professional's charge
20. Captures (a crook)
21. Helper for 41-Down
23. Hang behind
25. Cowboy's rope
28. That woman's
29. Sauce for chips
32. Swiss mountain
33. Terrify
35. Mr. Gershwin
36. Wide inlet
37. Have brunch
38. Identified
40. Provide with weapons
41. Occupied a sofa
42. "For Whom the ____ Tolls," novel
45. ____ Marie Saint, actress
47. Drags behind
51. Racetrack fence
52. Competed in a footrace
53. Devilish
54. Teen's skin bane
55. Colonial critter
56. Roman fiddler
57. Those folks
58. Black or Aegean
59. Made a pencil sketch

DOWN

1. Mr. Flintstone
2. Slippery
3. Cartoon supply-company
4. States of disorder
5. Group of employees
6. Rich source of minerals
7. One who sings from a 32-Across, perhaps
8. Nasal sound
9. Des Moines' state
10. Grouchy person
11. Piano ivories
22. Also-ran
24. Sports stadium
25. Chemist's workroom
26. In the style of: 2 wds.
27. Be a mole?
28. Head covering
29. Obscure
30. Anger
31. Seat cushion
34. Photographers' equipment
39. Wait on
40. City passageway
41. Yuletide visitor
42. Ill-mannered child
43. Every one
44. Part of an actor's script
46. Wind-direction indicator
48. "____ the Rainbow"
49. Electrical cord
50. Snail-paced

123

ACROSS

1. Annoyingly self-satisfied
5. Lawn starter
8. Rain-cloud color
12. Mama's man
13. Stage signal
14. Get a rise out of
15. Distinctive fragrance
16. Museum offering
17. Unwrap
18. Far from tough
20. Untrained, as recruits
22. Fairy-tale being
23. Made a pig noise
27. Reek
30. The guy over there
31. Vote against
32. Large weights
33. Cry from an ump
34. Medicine portion
35. Rainbow's curve
36. Jacket sleeve
37. Sums owed
38. Late
40. Amusing
41. Dark-grained bread
42. Quit working
46. Couch
49. Spanish watercourse
51. Revered person
52. Single thing
53. McMahon and Bradley
54. Bang (a door)
55. No more than
56. Complete an "i"
57. Koppel and Williams

DOWN

1. Name for a Dalmatian
2. Produced
3. Atop
4. Vegetable patches
5. Neck wrap
6. Plural pronoun
7. Michigan metropolis
8. "My, how you've ____!"
9. Mr. van Winkle
10. Stein drink
11. Desire
19. Mooselike creature
21. Point (an arrow) at
24. Drawer pull
25. Sunup direction
26. Tinting chemicals
27. ____ in the back, betray
28. Pulled (apart)
29. Ruler measure
30. Play a kazoo
33. Requested from a waiter
34. Doctor for teeth
36. Whichever
37. Set to arrive
39. Very angry
40. Decorate (a cake)
43. Without something to do
44. Paved way
45. Tall, shady trees
46. Total
47. Washington's bill
48. An evergreeen
50. Bride and groom's words

124

ACROSS

1. Poke; jab
5. Deep hole
8. Word after "whip" or "eye"
12. Deep affection
13. Adam's mate
14. Teen's skin condition
15. Functions
16. Shipboard assent
17. Little haircut
18. ____ citizen
20. Cries
21. Young woman
22. Automobile
23. Tilt
26. Droop
27. Shout of disapproval
30. Two times five
31. Lobster locale
33. Tack on
34. So far
35. Commit blunders
36. Stormed
38. Gnawing rodent
39. For each
40. Gabriel, for one
43. Dotes on
47. Scorch
48. Fled (from)
50. Simple
51. Prepare (text) for the printer
52. Rink surface
53. China's site
54. Eyeglass glass
55. Actor Gibson
56. Flower stalk

DOWN

1. Math word
2. Fragrant bloom
3. Baking chamber
4. Wallpaper pattern
5. Oyster's gem
6. Clinging vine
7. Golf mound
8. In a while
9. Farmland measure
10. Barbershop sound
11. Shortens (skirts)
19. Hot cereal choice
20. Placed bets
22. Is able to
23. Home for swine
24. Grant's foe
25. Industrious insect
26. Knight's title
27. Grocery sack
28. Poem of praise
29. Strange
32. Picasso creation
37. Delicious smells
38. Leases
39. Comic-strip division
40. A son of Eve
41. Naked
42. Wide smile
44. Remainder
45. A Great Lake
46. Fabric joint
48. Lip of a cup
49. High card

125

ACROSS

1. Had a meal
4. Untidy one
8. Leaf in a book
12. Lion's lair
13. Horseback game
14. Egg-shaped
15. Relaxed in a chair
16. TV star Griffith
17. Does wrong
18. "Home on the ____"
20. Fence made of shrubbery
21. Spoken
23. Storage building
25. Kite propeller?
26. Flower's support
27. Father
30. Flee, as from jail
32. Arctic native
34. Observe
35. Be in front
37. Festive nights before
38. Young dogs
39. Evergreen tree
40. Sweeping implement
43. Puts a stop to
46. Assistant
47. Target for Tiger Woods
48. Holly-wood's Lupino
51. Catalog article
52. Source of Persian rugs
53. Belonging to all of us
54. Girl
55. Take care of
56. "To be, or ____ to be . . ."

DOWN

1. Help-wanted notices
2. Afternoon drink
3. Exit's opposite
4. Reach across
5. Extensive
6. Least young
7. Lad
8. Sat for a painting
9. Enthusi-astic
10. Band of rowdies
11. Otherwise
19. See 44-Down
20. Shortens, as a skirt
21. Is in debt
22. Get out of bed
24. Listen to
26. Ooze out slowly
27. Arithmetic lesson
28. "So be it!"
29. Medicine amount
31. Jack Horner's fruit
33. Held on to
36. On land, to sailors
38. Longfellow's output
40. Prisoner's release money
41. Ms. Moreno
42. Dignified 38-Down
44. With 19-Down, "M*A*S*H" star
45. Give temporarily
47. Connect with (a baseball)
49. Pair
50. Van Gogh's field

126

ACROSS

1. Invoice stamp
5. Automobile
8. Rock's Turner
12. See 54-Across
13. Poem of praise
14. Track shape
15. List entry
16. Picnic drink
17. "____ go!," cheer words
18. Cooks (peanuts)
20. Boy
22. Aquatic mammal
24. Besides
27. Band on a sandal
31. Halloween month
33. Fib source
34. Cave-dwelling flier
35. Existed
36. Zoo residents
38. Permit
39. It's "mightier than the sword"
40. Bottom line
42. Fellows
43. Times of darkness
48. Cover (roads)
51. Use a shovel
53. "The Music Man" state
54. With 12-Across, star of "M*A*S*H"
55. Commit a blunder
56. Toss (a coin)
57. Magician's baton
58. Declare
59. Perfect scores for gymnasts

DOWN

1. Two of a kind
2. Choir voice
3. Thought; notion
4. Water barriers
5. Seashore
6. Find the sum of
7. Keep (a candidate) in office
8. Tattled (on)
9. "____ Got a Secret"
10. ____ King Cole, singer
11. Gore and Pacino
19. Mountain's peak
21. Knack
23. Breakfast item
24. A son of Eve
25. Tyrannical Roman emperor
26. Made a picture
27. Hit with the palm of the hand
28. Fork prong
29. Wet weather
30. Give weapons to
32. Feathered hunter
34. They "have more fun"
37. Had a meal
38. Clay, today
41. Furious
42. Patch up
44. Birthday present
45. Cavity
46. One with a look-alike
47. Undermines
48. Dog's "foot"
49. Similar to: 2 wds.
50. Suburban vehicle
52. Lyricist Gershwin

127

ACROSS

1. Kitchen utensil
4. Book of the New Testament
8. "_____ did you say?"
12. Poetic tribute
13. Urgent appeal
14. Every
15. Like a skyscraper
17. Formation at a teller's window
18. Trims (off)
19. Urban back street
20. Native of The Hawkeye State
23. Shade giver
25. The one over there
26. Factual
27. _____ Marie Saint, actress
30. Word on a movie-theater sign
32. Some traps
34. Broiling
35. Ruler marking
37. Flat, circular object
38. Hit the slopes
39. Songs for a pair
40. Portly
44. Genuine
46. Plays on words
47. Strews about
51. Skilled enough
52. In addition
53. Sticky stuff
54. Sunbeams
55. Football props
56. Possess

DOWN

1. Stew vessel
2. Excitement
3. Never seen before
4. Cook's garment
5. Fastener for papers
6. Less relaxed
7. Lose firmness
8. All better
9. Ice pellets from the sky
10. Teen's skin bane
11. Those people
16. Fill with joy
19. Prayer's last word
20. Poison-ivy sensation
21. Columbus's state
22. Desire
24. Richly abundant
26. Car's gas holder
27. A Great Lake
28. Sleeveless garment
29. Inquires
31. Fine rain
33. Grown-up
36. Geometric shape
39. Sees socially
40. Do some light boxing
41. Big brass horn
42. "I _____ Have Eyes for You"
43. Puts into play
45. Effortlessness
47. Put silverware on (the table)
48. Id's partner
49. Employ oars
50. Male offspring

128

ACROSS

1. Lady of Eden
4. Melt, as frozen food
8. Like an owl?
12. ___ and tonic
13. Garden tube
14. Doing nothing
15. Receive, as a gift
16. Actress's part
17. Bridal accoutrement
18. Run off to wed
20. Diner sign
21. Landscaping purchase
23. Epochs
26. Beneficiary of a will
27. Cowboy's boot-heel attachment
28. Dance like Gregory Hines
31. Writer Hemingway
33. Hard to find
35. Lassie or Fala
36. Every
38. Wind indicator
39. Tortoise's fabled foe
40. The Mississippi, for one
41. Alan of 1970s TV
44. Providence, ___ Island
46. Do the job of a maitre d'
47. Watermelon pit
48. Scale syllables
51. Wan
52. Peel
53. Vanity
54. Went rapidly
55. As well
56. Brick-colored

DOWN

1. Custard ingredient
2. Compete (with)
3. Signing up for (a contest)
4. Pulsate
5. Basketball net's metal rim
6. In dreamland
7. Little
8. Some spouses
9. Lightbulb over one's head?
10. Cut made by a letter opener
11. Snaky sea creatures
19. Angler's bait
21. Shack
22. Submarine sandwich
24. Be in a hurry
25. Circle segment
27. Cast headliner
28. One who gets around
29. Teen skin woe
30. Look (at) curiously
32. The Aegean, for one
34. Enthusiastic
37. Breakfast dish
39. Disliked greatly
40. Cowboy contest
41. Venomous snakes
42. Jump
43. Small valley
45. That woman's
47. Luxury resort
49. Mature
50. Turf

129

ACROSS

1. Small wagon
5. McKuen or Stewart
8. Venetian-blind part
12. Atop
13. Historian's time-division
14. Make exhausted
15. Wavered
17. Horses' grains
18. Bradley and Asner
19. Practical joke
20. "What's the ____ that could happen?"
21. Showed respect for
23. Volcano output
26. Bite lightly
27. Ram's comment
30. Heeded
33. "Do unto ____ . . ."
35. Soggy
36. Cut (off), as branches
38. Skin irritation
39. Got away
42. Isolated
45. Pull along with effort
46. Salty meat
49. Transmit
50. Means of verbal communication
52. Walk to and fro
53. Play a role
54. Giddy joy
55. Raced
56. "You bet!"
57. Party thrower

DOWN

1. Teen-idol adjective
2. Imitated
3. European deer
4. High explosive: abbr.
5. Showed again on TV
6. The Beaver State
7. Mom's partner
8. Rose (up)
9. One who spreads untruths
10. ____ and crafts
11. Examination
16. Self-love
20. Shed tears
21. Certain horse-feed
22. Brazil port, for short
23. Near the ground
24. Lincoln nickname
25. Dog's medico
27. Vegas action
28. Curved path
29. Tough wood
31. Otherwise
32. Physician: slang
34. Concealed
37. Royal dwelling
39. Ceased
40. Football kicks
41. Custard ingredient
42. Poisonous snakes
43. Big jump
44. A single time
46. Saintly symbol
47. Matures
48. Run into
50. Put into place
51. Sound of distaste

130

ACROSS

1. Des Moines' state
5. Commercials on TV
8. Small drink
11. Enjoys some gum
13. Attorney's profession
14. Mr. Gershwin
15. Sing à la Heidi?
16. Applied a wood finish to
18. On a train
20. Anthropologist's subject, maybe
23. Ship's sail support
26. "At what time?"
27. Deeds
30. Mas' mates
32. Dublin's country, poetically
33. A cheer
34. Clean (dishes)
35. Entreat
36. Scandinavian capital
37. Poker stake
38. A deadly 8-Down
40. Full of danger
42. Climb up
45. "The ____ of the Opera"
48. Seeped (out of)
53. Cowboy Rogers
54. Actor Wallach
55. Unbound
56. Have a debt
57. Urban rodent
58. Desire mixed with expectation

DOWN

1. Frozen
2. Exclamation of surprise
3. Marry
4. Inspire wonder in
5. Too
6. Information
7. Hordes of bees
8. Moral fault
9. Wrath
10. Drawing tablet
12. Thick hunk
17. Ms. Lupino
19. Characters in the Goldilocks story
20. One plus two
21. Be a monarch
22. Rural hotel
24. Smack on the rump
25. Flavorful
26. Spider's home
28. Silent ____, U.S. President Coolidge
29. Rose-stem peril
31. Feminine pronoun
34. Existed
36. Mollusk sometimes eaten raw
39. Movers' vehicle
41. Role model, perhaps
43. Soft-drink choice
44. Give forth
45. For
46. "In what manner?"
47. Sailor's "yes"
49. Aah's kin
50. Collection of wild animals
51. Intuitive power
52. Bad grade

131

ACROSS

1. Citrus fruits
6. Upper limb
9. Play a part
12. Idolize
13. Garden tool
14. Bit of nursery babble
15. Eve was the first
16. Shellfish treats
18. ____ sauce, Chinese flavoring
20. Faces of a cube
21. Document duplicating machine
25. Shorten (pants)
26. "Somewhere ____ the rainbow . . ."
27. Looks at
29. "Help!"
32. Country road
33. "Gosh!"
34. Sheep fleece
35. Gore and Jolson
36. Frog's home
37. Light fog; mist
38. Prohibition
39. Fled to wed
41. One in a flight of steps
44. Actress Lupino
45. Oriental
47. Perchance
52. Boxing's Greatest
53. King Cole of song
54. Cook under a flame
55. Steeped drink
56. Number in a pair
57. Odor is its defense

DOWN

1. Perry Mason's field
2. Wedding vow: 2 wds.
3. Dad's spouse
4. The 1960s, for example
5. Touch, for one
6. Nautical cry
7. Cowboy Rogers
8. Sloppy conditions
9. Mellowed, as cheese
10. Apple's center
11. Throw (out)
17. Conway or Robbins
19. The ____ Trail
21. Soft drink
22. Football's shape
23. Ballpoint implements
24. Anger
25. Obeyed (a warning)
28. Strong urge
29. Bathing bar
30. Seep gradually
31. Coasting vehicle
34. "Which person?"
36. Father or mother
38. Bridle part
40. Woolly babies
41. Place to rest
42. Bit of folklore
43. India's site
44. Common preposition
46. Uncooked
48. Noah's boat
49. Solver of this puzzle
50. Storage container
51. Deer's cousin

132

ACROSS

1. Story line
5. Cruel Roman emperor
9. Chest bone
12. Valentine word
13. Moisture-less
14. Historic time span
15. Singletons
16. Egg on
17. Chap
18. Traveled (to)
19. Had a snack
20. Stopping place
21. In a short while
24. Curtain pole
26. Easter symbol
29. Lacking good manners
31. Some hairpieces
34. Less small
36. Slumbering
38. Dog's pest
39. Flour bag
41. Place for pigs
42. Certain snake
44. Lower leg
46. "Little Miss Muffet ____ on a tuffet . . ."
48. Sound of disgust
50. Keats' poems
54. Sudsy brew
55. Emotional state
57. Talk wildly
58. ____ Vegas, Nevada
59. Trim away
60. Pine, for one
61. High explosive: abbr.
62. Simmered meal
63. Mother chickens

DOWN

1. Land-tilling implement
2. The ____ Ranger
3. Cooking chamber
4. Exams
5. Snooze
6. Trip to the store, maybe
7. Mob's action
8. More unusual
9. Cures
10. Iraq's neighbor
11. Musical group
22. Raw metal
23. Belonging to us
25. Nocturnal flier
26. Santa's helper
27. Young woman
28. Ali's nickname (with "The")
30. Every
32. Receive
33. CIA agent, for one
35. Driving fuel
37. Glide down the Alps
40. On dry land
43. Diesel dispensers
45. Opposite of south
46. Pepper's partner
47. Alda or Arkin
49. "Bearded" animal
51. Test of courage
52. Level; flat
53. Witnesses
56. Lawn condensation

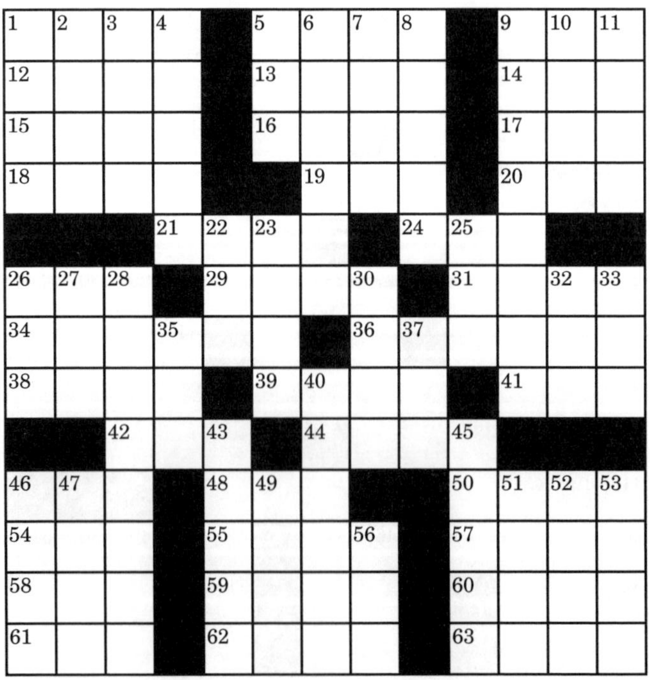

133

ACROSS

1. Shopping vehicle
5. Sunset direction
9. Road chart
12. Scent
13. Strongly dislike
14. High card
15. Recording cassette
16. News bit
17. A Gershwin
18. Makes a smudge
20. Cider fruits
22. Light knock
23. Gibson of "Braveheart"
24. Actress Gardner
27. Skirt edge
29. Assigns an "R" or a "PG" to
33. Cottony fuzz
35. Wheel furrow
37. Affirmative reply
38. Garden trails
40. Gaming cube
42. Desertlike
43. "____ a boy!"
45. Workout room
47. Polish capital
50. Listened to (a warning)
54. "____ been working on the railroad . . ."
55. Come together
57. Ripped (up)
58. Confessor's statement, "I ____ it!"
59. Lacking color
60. Largest continent
61. Sullivan and McMahon
62. Mix (a drink)
63. Evil look

DOWN

1. Portable beds
2. Eve's mate
3. Clothesline, sometimes
4. Halloween handout
5. Speak in an undertone
6. Devour
7. Hot vapor
8. Disposition
9. Postal delivery
10. Farm measure
11. Pod veggies
19. Football cheer
21. Stage production
24. Swiss peak
25. By way of
26. Picnic "pirate"
28. Dirt mixed with water
30. Senator Kennedy
31. Unit of corn
32. Bashful
34. The thing here
36. More constricting
39. Stickers for 9-Down
41. Potato bud
44. Perspire
46. Iron or lead
47. Broad
48. Enthusiastic
49. Cincinnati team
51. Amount of medicine
52. Cleveland's Great Lake
53. Letter-opening word
56. Inventor Whitney

134

ACROSS

1. Lubricates
5. 13-Across fluids
9. Health resort
12. Persia, now
13. Forest plant
14. Prolonged battle
15. Short letter
16. Go by car
17. Point (a rifle) at a target
18. Leg joint
19. Total (up)
20. TV's Rooney
21. Zilch: slang
23. Drag
25. Bird's sound
28. Under
32. "Gotcha!"
33. Separated
35. Actress Arthur
36. Large ape
38. Thoughts
40. Sandwich bread
41. Lawyer's charge
42. Dog's pest
45. Boxing great
47. Use a dagger
51. Small boy
52. Worshiped one
53. New York canal
54. 44-Down resident
55. "Let's Make a ____!"
56. Regulation
57. Football's Marino
58. Ends' partner
59. Pupil's evaluation

DOWN

1. Pig's sound
2. Press (pants)
3. Tardy
4. "Bless you!" preceder
5. Leather band
6. Very dry
7. Bazaar salesperson
8. Observe
9. Long-necked bird
10. Reimbursed
11. Force for a 14-Across
20. Mature
22. Rome's country
24. Loosen (shoelaces)
25. Clothing label
26. "____ is it?," intercom question
27. Hearing organ
28. Sheep call
29. Lincoln, to pals
30. Hot drink
31. Possesses
34. Begged
37. Lyricist Gershwin
39. 6-Down land
41. Satisfies (a need)
42. Ran away
43. Molten rock
44. First garden
46. Heavy burden
48. Factual
49. Is sick
50. Reddish root
52. Altar words

135

ACROSS

1. Prohibit
4. Geographical charts
8. Upper limbs
12. "Car 54, Where ____ You?," old TV show
13. Inventive thought
14. Work hard
15. Was present for
17. Traditional knowledge
18. Nightfall
19. Went out with
20. Grown male deers
23. Noted periods of time
25. Small bay
26. Smell
27. Volcanic dust
30. Gotten up, as from sleeping
32. Horse's home
34. Scarlet
35. Highest point
37. Line of stitches
38. Without cost
39. Withers
40. Month after March
43. Heavy burden
45. McCartney of song
46. Physically fit
50. Otherwise
51. Bride's headdress
52. Mr. Gershwin
53. Feat of courage
54. Fusses
55. Energy

DOWN

1. Sheep's sound
2. Museum attraction
3. Mesh fabric
4. Less
5. Tacks on
6. Sneaked a look
7. Unhappy
8. Book of 4-Across
9. Plant anchor
10. Wet, soggy earth
11. Winter vehicle
16. Borders
19. Move suddenly
20. Wound reminder
21. Ripped apart
22. Eager
24. Sweet-smelling bloom
26. Formerly
27. Cain's brother
28. Venetian-blind strip
29. 16-Down on skirts
31. British nobleman
33. Out of the way
36. Thawed
38. Did an office chore
39. Room dividers
40. Mimicked
41. Ashen
42. Trick
44. Cleveland's state
46. Ms. Gardner
47. Gratuity
48. Anger
49. Baseballer's hat

136

ACROSS

1. Lion or tiger
4. Not at home
8. Poisonous vipers
12. In the past
13. Fence doorway
14. Fiber from sheep
15. Stadium flags
17. Singer's vocal range
18. Helper
19. Take a breather
20. Stubborn spot
23. Require
26. Jack and Jill's climb
27. In a casual way
28. Hog; swine
31. Blackboard cleaning pad
33. Tune
35. Family's cozy retreat
36. Scientists' workplaces
38. Machine for weaving
39. Fermented grape beverage
40. Spheres for bowling
41. Source of cold cuts
44. Beer topping, often
46. Citrus drinks
47. Alternative to glasses
51. Eat out
52. Curve; bend
53. Stately tree
54. Light in the night sky
55. Relatives of wasps
56. Wipe with a towel

DOWN

1. Tam or beret
2. Grow older
3. Freight weight
4. Once more
5. Fairy godmother's stick
6. Show up at (an event)
7. "Certainly!"
8. Hollywood's Oscar, for one
9. Mild-flavored fish
10. Pans' partners
11. Opening for coins
16. Manicure targets
20. Storage shack
21. Become weary
22. An acting Alda
24. Avenue liners
25. Vision organ
27. Persia, now
28. Place for a dip
29. Worshiped object
30. Weight lifters' rooms
32. Cotton gin's Whitney
34. South American beast
37. Previously
39. More knowing
40. Tub soaks
41. Moms' mates
42. Revise (a manuscript)
43. Musical Horne
45. Fairy-tale opener
47. Car for hire
48. Cape ____, Massachusetts peninsula
49. Road-paving goo
50. Blue expanse above us

137

ACROSS

1. Bowlers' targets
5. Light-switch setting
8. Mail-drop opening
12. Eden fellow
13. By way of
14. Detect a sound
15. Tardy
16. Go wrong
17. Poker payment
18. Bancroft of "The Turning Point"
20. Wipe (a blackboard)
21. Coasts
24. Sturdy wood
25. All keyed up
26. Respectful title
27. In the past
30. Rainbow's curve
31. Live (in)
33. Chin bone
34. Hive insect
35. Close to the ground
36. Furious
38. Golf-ball prop
39. Looked at maliciously
40. Celebrities
43. "Angelic" instrument
44. Walk in the shallows
45. Undersea boat, for short
46. Opposite of closed
50. TV actor Alan
51. A tree's rings indicate this
52. Wild anger
53. Nuisance
54. Mr. Torme
55. Jog like a horse

DOWN

1. Close friend
2. Lupino of motion pictures
3. Singer King Cole
4. Disturbs wet paint
5. Baking chambers
6. Flames
7. Distant in space
8. Man-eating fish
9. Horne of "Stormy Weather"
10. Feedbag contents, often
11. Large, woody plant
19. Tailor's implements
20. Previously
21. Wound with a knife
22. In this place
23. Fable beginning
24. Tanker's contents
26. Mend (clothes)
27. Open, as a door
28. Way into a fenced area
29. Had debts
32. Misery
37. Book ____, school assignment
38. "Trick or ____!"
39. Name tag
40. Exchange (items)
41. Yarn; story
42. Finds the sums of
43. Massive
45. Gumshoe Spade
47. Golf standard
48. Sense of self
49. Fish snare

138

ACROSS

1. Sank one's teeth into
4. Eve's mate
8. Sound from a talking doll, often
12. Hockey great Bobby
13. Cheese-loving rodents
14. Opposite of closed
15. "How do ____ do?"
16. Prayer's last word
17. Traveled (to)
18. React to inhaling dust
20. Magazine edition
21. Give up one's position
24. Oscar, Tony, or Emmy
27. Subscription extension
32. Brief memo
33. Cherry center
34. Make angry
35. Pine tree leaves
37. Decreased gradually, as the moon
38. Different ones
40. Bread grain
44. Observed
48. British noble
49. Lemon drinks
51. Tree chopper
52. Stumble (over)
53. Helpful tip
54. ____ and tonic
55. Uses the eyes
56. Aardvark's diet
57. Messy pen

DOWN

1. Laddies
2. Press clothes
3. Actual
4. Filled with sudden wonder
5. Small, silvery coins
6. Perfect serve
7. Grown-up 1-Down
8. Cuts (the lawn)
9. Jungle primates
10. Cafe's bill of fare
11. Poker stake
19. Made a misstep
20. Rural lodging place
22. From the Emerald Isle
23. Obtain
24. Landers of column fame
25. Extreme sorrow
26. Enjoyed doughnuts
28. Rub away
29. Triumph
30. Stein filler
31. Was first
33. Animal pal
36. Builder's site
37. What handcuffs link
39. Happening
40. Saturates with liquid
41. Tortoise's fabled race opponent
42. Ohio's Great Lake
43. Swiss skiing destination
45. Moves like a dog's tail
46. Leave the stage
47. Reject as false
49. "Now I see!"
50. Ruckus

139

ACROSS

1. Unworked metal
4. Coloring agent
7. Made a sketch of
11. Douglas ____, tree species
12. Rowing need
13. Hunger for
14. Baby's drink
16. Employed
17. President Lincoln's nickname
18. Quilts and bedspreads
19. Banana ____, cool treat
22. Make well
23. Roaring cat
24. Part of the weekend
28. Ms. Landers
29. Painful spots
30. Fury
31. One just starting out
33. Touch
34. Badgers
35. Sum
36. Broad boards
39. Vast expanse
40. Weird
41. Soap for hair
45. Puts on (pounds)
46. Skirt edge
47. Plus
48. Pulled thread
49. Asner and McMahon
50. Scarlet

DOWN

1. Switch position
2. ____ de Janeiro
3. Make a misstep
4. Distrust the validity of
5. Ivy League school
6. Distinctive time period
7. Wooden golf club
8. Uncommon
9. At any time
10. Marries
13. Singing group
15. Primary
18. More adorable
19. Thick slice
20. An evergreen
21. Of great duration
22. Shows concern (for)
24. Musical pieces
25. Eating regimen
26. Neighbor-hood
27. Holler
29. Slithering reptiles
32. Baseball-game division
33. Soap froth
35. Red Sox and Yankees
36. Wooden nails
37. Stand at a slant
38. Operatic solo
39. Lose fur
41. That girl
42. Golf norm
43. Six minus five
44. Not even

140

ACROSS

1. Standard cost
5. Flowing, sleeveless garment
9. Sandwich meat
12. Tehran's country
13. Throw hard
14. Cotton-gin inventor Whitney
15. Pub serving of beer
16. Object on a list
17. City creature
18. Rim
19. Angeles lead-in
20. One who throws a party
21. Angler's pole
23. Exercise club
25. Prairie plant
28. Motives
32. Become sickly
33. Shore
35. Romance (someone)
36. Popeye's food
38. Grinds with the teeth
40. Finger-painting, to a tot
41. Reporter's question
42. Say the rosary
45. Indivisible
47. "Excuse me?"
51. Sense organ
52. Cain's victim
53. Certain cocktail garnish
54. Comic actor Conway
55. Resound, as laughter
56. Part of a Steinbeck title
57. Asner and Bradley
58. Goes astray
59. Lairs

DOWN

1. Full-grown
2. Bone-dry
3. Strong taste
4. Gets into (a contest)
5. Offspring
6. Commuting vehicle
7. "Stop the ____!"
8. Lawn tree
9. Someone to emulate
10. "Ah, me!"
11. Kitchen glove
20. Possesses
22. Sesame Street's grouch
24. Mending need
25. Filling-station fuel
26. Tear, as pants
27. Famous boxer
28. Cheering cry
29. Have a debt
30. "It's ____ or never"
31. Morse "Help!"
34. Halloween's month
37. House vote
39. Bayed
41. Oil gushers
42. Baseball great Rose
43. Surprise invasion
44. Weapons of war
46. At hand
48. ____ and seek, child's game
49. Church reply
50. Sawbucks
52. King Kong, for one

141

ACROSS

1. Light-switch position
4. Deal (with)
8. Time in the tub
12. Vegas cube
13. Did an imitation of
14. Sound repetition
15. Bedroom bureaus
17. Half of a sextet
18. Roosters' mates
19. Try out (a theory)
20. The King
23. Acceptable
26. Evil look
27. Make a sweater
28. Mythical forest-dweller
31. ____ Luther King Jr.
33. Intense fear
35. It's sometimes cloudy
36. Valentine flower
38. Facility
39. Sum owed
40. Trash
41. Singer Turner
44. Bellow from a den
46. Prepare for print
47. Completed
51. Zero
52. Poems of praise
53. Actress Gardner
54. Downhill coaster
55. Take a load off
56. Kennedy or Danson

DOWN

1. Peculiar
2. A pine tree
3. Fixed charge, as for admission
4. Instances
5. Ready for customers
6. Human being
7. Asner and Bradley
8. First Lady Ford
9. Land-measurement unit
10. The one here
11. Make an owl's sound
16. Garment worn under a vest
20. Shade providers
21. Pipe problem
22. "Thank you ____ much!"
24. Windy-day flyer
25. Enjoyed a meal
27. Door handle
28. Historic times
29. Misplaced
30. At no charge
32. Great rage
34. Brings up (children)
37. Take long steps
39. Went out with
40. Belt location
41. Perfect gymnastic scores
42. Sacred image
43. "A stitch in time saves ____"
45. Dollar bills
47. Because of
48. Sombrero, for one
49. Eden inhabitant
50. Mom's partner

142

ACROSS

1. Number of a cat's lives?
5. Elderly
9. Elbow's site
12. Aroma
13. Symbol of peace
14. Grant's foe
15. Swift, graceful animal
16. Mournful sound
17. "Sawbuck"
18. Sausage-like meat
20. Keep in hand
21. Singer King Cole
22. Extreme anger
24. Citrus skins
27. Ordinary
31. "Much ____ About Nothing," Shake-speare play
32. Records on audio-cassette
34. Lamb's bleat
35. One under a doctor's care
37. Pirate's treasure container
39. Shed tears
40. Scheduled to arrive
41. Actress Tyler Moore
44. The Great Communi-cator
48. Perfect tennis serve
49. Fabulous review
52. Dressing gown
53. Country lodging
54. China's locale
55. Narrative account
56. Mesh trap
57. Those folks
58. Snow vehicle

DOWN

1. Signals "yes"
2. Mental creation
3. Christmas
4. Messenger's trip
5. Own up to
6. Sticky stuff
7. Ms. Perón
8. Wild animal's lair
9. Choir voice
10. Fishing spool
11. Fix (torn clothes)
19. Become an expert at
20. The girl
22. "If ____ told you once..."
23. Save from danger
24. Strike sharply
25. Lupino of filmdom
26. Word of negation
27. Liable (to)
28. Honest ____ Lincoln
29. Bus fuel
30. Consume (food)
33. Some
36. Like a winter road
38. Valentine shapes
40. Slumber-time vision
41. Principal
42. Teen's skin problem
43. Lease
45. Soccer point
46. Skilled
47. Lack
49. Hamelin pest
50. Bonfire residue
51. Compete (with)

143

ACROSS

1. Hayworth who starred in "Gilda"
5. Equips with weapons
9. Keep time with one's foot
12. De-wrinkling device
13. Owl's sound
14. Rhyming champ
15. Combed hair-line
16. Precious; cute
18. Show scorn
20. ____ and tuck, neck and neck
21. In a short time
24. Fractions of a dollar
28. Dirt, after a rainstorm
31. Act the braggart
33. Grab a bite
34. "To ____ is human . . ."
35. "Zoom!"
36. Log-chopping tool
37. In the past
38. Convey, as a message
40. Cup lip
41. Plains natives' tent
43. Break, as a twig
45. Delivery vehicle
47. Adhesive substance
51. Pullman cars
56. Very slim
57. Settle (a debt)
58. Lake Huron's neighbor
59. Contain
60. Mr. Lincoln
61. Went by train
62. Movie-shooting spots

DOWN

1. Splits apart
2. Persian Gulf country
3. Dashed
4. Poker stakes
5. "So that's the problem!"
6. Curtain-hanging pole
7. Light in the night sky
8. Rigid, as rules
9. Cafe bill
10. The entire amount
11. Coconut cream ____
17. A primate
19. Filch from
22. Percolate
23. Manicurists' targets
25. Close by
26. Car for hire
27. Flower stalk
28. Vegetarian no-no
29. Entreat
30. Go down, as prices
32. Reach across
38. Harvesting machine
39. Bark shrilly
42. Eden dweller
44. Woodland trails
46. Cruel Roman
48. Pump or sandal
49. Pinball foul
50. Completes
51. Mineral bath
52. Scientist's workplace
53. Examine closely
54. Clear (of)
55. Understand

144

ACROSS

1. Expectant belief
5. Fast plane
8. Chunk of concrete
12. Persia, today
13. ____ Baba
14. Slog (through)
15. Fix a tear
16. Poorly lighted
17. Equally matched
18. Preholiday night
20. Smallest amount
21. Evans or Ronstadt
24. Burning
25. Wedding words
26. Bloom from a bulb
29. Common contraction
32. European peak
33. Source of bacon
34. Pair of performers
35. "The Catcher in the ____"
36. They're drawn to a flame
38. Flub up
39. Great weight
40. Woodworking tool
42. Horse's bedding
45. Artificial color
46. Colored part of an eye
47. Sticky stuff
49. Open a crack
53. Pocket fuzz
54. Commercial spots
55. Mild-flavored fish
56. Mining bonanza
57. Martial arts legend Bruce
58. Embraced

DOWN

1. That man
2. 56-Across yield
3. Skillet
4. Cut short; broke off
5. Shade of green
6. Inventor Whitney
7. Tiny ____, Dickens character
8. Sugary
9. Volcano's output
10. Fruit beverages
11. Crooked
19. Industrial tub
20. Cut (off)
21. Dishonest one
22. Without much concern
23. Slangy negative
24. Opposite of low
27. Atop
28. Set ablaze
29. Notion
30. Rotate
31. In need of a rubdown
36. Cut (the grass)
37. Secret agent
39. Try a spoonful of
41. Dog's tether
42. Site for a window box
43. Small singing group
44. Citrus skin
45. Medicine portion
47. Young woman
48. Lyric poem
50. Montana of football
51. Every last one
52. Color for a toy wagon

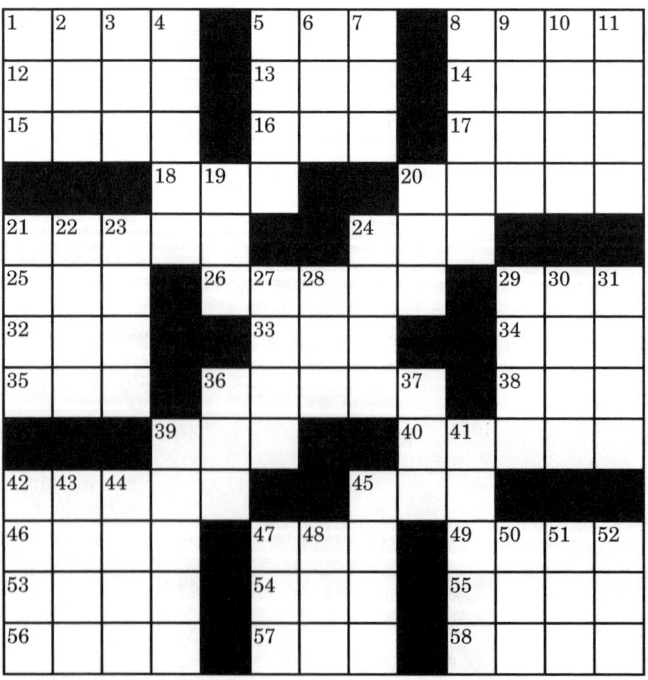

145

ACROSS

1. It's flown in a March wind
5. Cat's "toenail"
9. Playmate
12. Tall flower
13. Irritate
14. In the manner of: 2 wds.
15. Coal weights
16. Pointless, as chatter
17. "____ now or never"
18. Prowls stealthily
20. Horse's gait
21. Puppy's cry
22. Compete, as for affection
24. Native of Geneva
27. Wound covering
31. Hearing organ
32. Song, "The ____ of Silence"
34. Closed rose
35. Pencil parts
37. Separate units
39. Employ
40. Neighbor-hood pub
41. Dress for a ball
44. Beast
48. "There it is!"
49. "Off with you!"
52. Skin opening
53. Be immoral
54. "To ____ his own!"
55. Stretched out in repose
56. Pea shell
57. Orchard plant
58. Partner of odds

DOWN

1. Tool sets
2. Press (pants)
3. Fork prong
4. English composi-tions
5. Crunchy
6. Garbage-can cover
7. Everybody
8. Itsy-bitsy
9. Match up (socks)
10. Male singing voice
11. Go the distance
19. Smooches
20. Slugger Williams
22. Suburban transport
23. One from Calcutta
24. "I told you so!"
25. Lack of peace
26. A Gershwin brother
27. School vehicle
28. Mr. Lincoln's nickname
29. Chewy treat
30. Sullivan and Asner
33. Mineral resource
36. Daylight provider
38. Batter's coup
40. Clean one's body
41. Inhale loudly
42. Akron's site
43. Magician's stick
45. Pained sound
46. Barren
47. Camera's "eye"
49. Fixed
50. Sedan, for one
51. High card

146

ACROSS

1. Easy pace
5. Burning desire
9. Health resort
12. Land measure
13. Fictional account
14. Black goo
15. Sensitive leg part
16. Night-sky twinkler
17. Writing fluid
18. They annoy
20. 30-Across's chirp
22. Inner spirit
24. Behaves
27. Like: 2 wds.
30. Common songbird
32. "Get out!"
33. Paddling (a canoe)
35. Show up
37. Soft cry
38. Border
40. Ocean
41. Barbecue rod
42. Employed
44. Sounds (a horn)
47. Penny-pinching person
51. Inventor Whitney
53. Wheel tracks
55. Cab
56. Moving truck
57. Cain's brother
58. Thunder's boom
59. Hen product
60. Lord's wife
61. Shortens (a skirt)

DOWN

1. Show surprise
2. Dull pain
3. Spring flower
4. Circus "buildings"
5. "____ a boy!"
6. Spill the beans
7. Cat's scratcher
8. At this place
9. Uses a needle and thread
10. Cooking vessel
11. Noah's boat
19. Planted, as seeds
21. Towards the sunrise
23. Impel
25. Musical quality
26. Fizzy drink
27. Upper limbs
28. Aerial stunt
29. Anticipating
31. Reminds excessively
34. Division term
36. Abound (with)
39. Wiped down the furniture
43. Highway trench
45. Spoken
46. Marching-band instrument
48. Bargain event
49. Student's test
50. Tears
51. Holiday precursor
52. Fall behind
54. Clever

147

ACROSS

1. Do some sums
4. Number of sides to every story
7. Cavity
10. "Hi and ____," comic strip
12. Bother; trouble
13. Little rodents
14. Easily carried
16. Atop
17. Enjoy literature
18. Wiggle, as a tooth
20. Ship's company
22. Take to court
23. Morse code bit
25. Cain, to Eve
27. Toothpaste holders
31. Sturdy metal
33. Frequent exclamation at a fireworks display
35. Homework grade
36. Like a haunted house
38. Grandstand shout
40. Put (down), as a pen
41. Prohibit
43. Towering above others
45. Cloth
48. Skin growth
50. Public-opinion report
51. Volume of recipes
54. Ultimatum word
55. Terminate
56. Tender, as muscles
57. Hullabaloo
58. Scarlet or crimson
59. Checkers pieces

DOWN

1. Swiss peak
2. Entranceway
3. Cecil B. De Mille, for one
4. Small flap
5. Humorist Rogers
6. Faux butters
7. Plumbing tube
8. Sacred image
9. "The ____ Commandments," 1956 film
11. Celestial object
13. Dinosaurs' home?
15. Summer beverages
19. Ump's cry
21. Romance
23. Go out, as a fire
24. A raw material
26. Neither's mate
28. Dancing space
29. Geologic period
30. Cloud's site
32. Eat like a bunny
34. Head covering
37. Corn serving
39. Bird of prey
42. More pleasant
44. Science rooms
45. Crease
46. Likewise
47. Traffic-school obstacle
49. Ripped (up)
50. Small, round vegetable
52. Eccentric
53. Slugger Griffey Jr.

148

ACROSS

1. Baseball's DiMaggio
4. Horned viper
7. Give weapons to
10. Classifieds notices
11. Pale purple shade
13. Ghost's shriek
14. Very damp
15. Mrs. Archie Bunker
16. Statute or regulation
17. "If ____ told you once . . ."
19. Likes better
21. Papa's mate
23. Lyricist Gershwin
24. Alda and Ladd
26. Indicated with an index finger
30. Matched group
31. Castle ditches
33. Night before a holiday
34. View out the window
36. Fabled beauty of Troy
38. On in years
39. Lease
40. Rumbled angrily
44. Droop
45. Bone in the chest
46. Standing
48. Gun (an engine)
51. Commotion
52. Put off until later
53. Vote in favor
54. Quilting event
55. Salsa, for one
56. Encountered

DOWN

1. Where teeth are attached
2. Lyric poem
3. More-or-less guess?
4. Assistance
5. ____ of the tongue
6. Nathan Hale, for one
7. Competent
8. Lion's comment
9. Cuts (grass)
11. Grant's foe
12. Hold dear
18. Movers' vehicle
20. Devotee
21. Catholic rite
22. Actor Guinness
25. Sniffed
26. Salary
27. Transatlantic wire, maybe
28. Tied
29. Fender hollow
32. Chose from the menu
35. At this moment
37. Notable period
40. Seize suddenly
41. Take a cab
42. Double-reed instrument
43. Sandwich shop
44. Pigpen
47. Bottle lid
49. Sight organ
50. Fido's doctor

149

ACROSS

1. Genesis mom
4. Carry out (orders)
8. "____ Kind of Fool Am I?"
12. Be under the weather
13. Painfully tender
14. Part for an actor
15. Garment for a showery day
17. Poisonous vipers
18. Has a meal
19. Exterminator target
20. Church singing group
23. Omelet ingredients
26. Jingled
27. Far from busy
28. What a sheep says
31. Pro with a bow
33. Be present for
35. Honey-making insect
36. House's grassy area
38. Set price
39. Jazz legend Horne
40. Sand hills
41. Have (a bath)
44. Oolong and Darjeeling
46. Wedding band
47. Frightened
51. Mental construct
52. Otherwise
53. George Gershwin's brother
54. Use a paring knife
55. Golfer's gadgets
56. Free of moisture

DOWN

1. Sense organ
2. By way of
3. Wallach or Whitney
4. Academy Award
5. Cowboy's footwear
6. Rubbed away
7. Up to now
8. Covers (a gift)
9. Watering tube
10. Swiss peaks
11. School exam
16. Horse sound
20. Sea creature with claws
21. Tortoise's opponent
22. "____ upon a time . . ."
24. Happy
25. Acquire
27. Iraq's neighbor
28. Pea's relative
29. Start a poker pot
30. Cooling drinks
32. Spud bud
34. "In God We ____"
37. Baby's toy
39. Done in accordance with the rules
40. Is brave enough (to)
41. Stumble (over)
42. Certain school worker
43. Joint above the shin
45. Convenience
47. Collection, as of dishes
48. Shoebox cover
49. Goof up
50. Period of sunlight

150

ACROSS

1. Civil War general
4. Rock back and forth
8. Shut noisily
12. _____ roads, winter hazard
13. Fork prong
14. Skin opening
15. That girl
16. Concludes
17. "_____ upon a time . . ."
18. Like a salad, often
20. Period before sunrise
21. Decanter material
24. Mamas' partners
27. How some like it?
28. Ignited
31. Always
32. Give a blow to
33. Drill (a hole)
34. Vacant place
35. Golf score
36. Recorded (a TV show)
37. Big-money raffle
39. Divide equally
42. "From _____ With Love," Bond movie
46. Take a peek
47. Be concerned
49. Fireplace addition
50. Otherwise
51. Fusses
52. Wonder
53. Heroic act
54. Lively
55. Rubber-stamp inker

DOWN

1. Shopper's memo
2. Reverberate
3. Potato buds
4. Controls (a car)
5. Like Chicago's weather
6. In addition to
7. "Absolutely!"
8. Go bad, as food
9. Of great duration
10. Curved doorway
11. Come upon
19. Battle reminder
20. Singer King Cole
22. Sleeved garment
23. Tiny child
24. Wooden pin
25. Ms. Gardner
26. Energy
28. Chop (off)
29. Anger
30. Actor Danson
32. Fedora or sombrero
33. Ocean inlets
35. Cooking vessel
36. Least dishonest
37. Was fond of
38. Mistake
39. Winter glider
40. Fishing rod
41. Fail to win
43. Open-hand strike
44. The Hawkeye State
45. Matured
47. Bottle top
48. Summer drink

151

ACROSS

1. ____ King Cole, singer
4. Exchanged for money
8. Is the right size
12. President Lincoln, casually
13. Cafeteria server
14. Object of worship
15. Sick
16. Alleviate
17. ____ market, place to find bargains
18. Confederate general
19. Gore and Pacino
20. Evaluate
21. Workout site
23. Irritating sensation
26. Traditional knowledge
28. Male protagonist
29. Cat's "foot"
32. Citrus fruit
34. Not out
36. Precious stone
37. Low female voice
39. Towards the sunrise
40. Use a keyboard
41. Soda container
42. A few
45. "Gotcha!"
47. Pen fluid
50. Lean
51. Short voyage
52. Observe
53. Lubricates
54. Existed
55. Attempt
56. Fishing rod
57. Lyrical poems
58. Call for 28-Down

DOWN

1. Use a hammer
2. Competent
3. E-mail's ancestor
4. Water vapor
5. Spoken
6. Famous collie
7. Tint
8. ____ wheel, unnecessary addition
9. Motionless
10. Shoe tips
11. Wooden strip
22. Japanese currency
24. Musical group
25. Negative vote
26. Fireplace wood
27. Miner's find
28. Assistance
29. Ivory ticklers?
30. Commercials
31. Very moist
33. Happy
35. Ocean
38. Watered, as eyes
40. Uptight
41. Sleeveless garments
42. "Cease and desist!"
43. The Buckeye State
44. Grain-grinding machine
46. Employ
48. Roman emperor
49. Lock openers
51. Half of four

152

ACROSS

1. Stared in wonder (at)
6. That doe
9. Maple fluid
12. "Wanted, dead or ____"
13. Foot digit
14. Prospector's find
15. Tablecloth fabric
16. Belonging to you and me
17. Set fire to
18. Show fatigue
20. Cipher system
21. Liable (to)
24. Olympic prize
26. 24-hour span
27. Cooked for
28. Swung (a flag)
32. Parentless child
34. Photographer's tool
35. Slab of beef
36. Operate a jet
37. Feel sick
38. Striped animal seen on safari
40. Dixie general
41. Violent anger
44. Sharp knocks
46. Monkey's kin
47. Chewing treat
48. Pacific or Atlantic
53. Argument against
54. King beater
55. Mexican donkey
56. Blasting compound: abbr.
57. "Sure!"
58. Theater accommodations

DOWN

1. Lass
2. Boxing legend
3. Bowling target
4. New Year's ____
5. Refuse to grant
6. Packed away
7. Hunting dog
8. Always, to poets
9. Unaccompanied performance
10. Dry as dust
11. Tennis star Sampras
19. "So be it!"
20. Common shellfish
21. Major fusses
22. Divide (the hair)
23. Use a word processor
25. On vacation
27. Imitation
29. Calf meat
30. Cleveland's Great Lake
31. Chip and ____, cartoon buddies
33. Somewhat smoky
34. Sound of thunder
36. Picture holders
39. Singer Springsteen
41. True statement
42. Atop
43. Monthly housing expense
45. Weeps aloud
47. Lighthearted
49. Onstage signal
50. Historic time period
51. Sculpture, for instance
52. Flat rejections

153

ACROSS

1. Small taste
4. Dull pain
8. Walk through water
12. Former heavy-weight champ
13. Slimy garden pest
14. Fling
15. Benediction
17. Shopping-list entry
18. Shed tears
19. Tiers, as of seats
20. Helps start a poker pot
23. Wicked
26. Take a risk
27. Onions on the breath, maybe
28. Deplete, as strength
31. Baby's must-have
33. Knock or throw to the ground
35. Wily
36. Behind time
38. What yeast bread dough does
39. Stack
40. 9-Down propeller
41. Wound reminder
44. Largest continent
46. Bowling alley
47. Like a prune
51. Country hotels
52. Cattle group
53. Ms. Perón
54. Army meal
55. Some Keats poems
56. Gymnast's perfect score

DOWN

1. Arrest (a felon)
2. In poor health
3. Diner dessert
4. Horses' relatives
5. Shorten, as toenails
6. Searched (for)
7. What a hen lays
8. Spin rapidly
9. Family car, maybe
10. Made a sketch
11. Shade trees
16. Tidy up with a broom
20. Does sums
21. Hammer's target
22. Cafeteria carrier
24. Cast a ballot
25. A Gershwin
27. Of the mouth
28. Brief comic scene
29. As well
30. Equal
32. Inventor Whitney
34. Frog's sound
37. Became watery, as eyes
39. Use an iron
40. Watches over
41. Thin
42. Sugar source
43. Landers and Miller
45. Foal's dad
47. "Which person?"
48. To ____, for rent
49. Adam's mate
50. Quarter-back Marino

154

ACROSS

1. Golf gadget
4. Small space
7. Skirt bottom
10. Peculiar
11. Work hard
12. Maui dance
13. Sty dweller
14. Abode; residence
15. TV award
16. Write by using a keyboard
18. Had dinner
20. Finish
22. Watchful
26. Celebration
29. Singer Clapton
32. "____ Are My Sunshine"
33. Put into play
34. Parking area
35. ____ and flow
36. Ignited
37. Fir's kin
38. On the ocean
39. Schoolroom 4-Down
41. Grown-up guy
43. Be the possessor of
45. Single entity
48. Practice boxing
51. Persia, nowadays
54. Indicate "yes"
56. Ache
57. "Tune in ____ week!"
58. Neither's partner
59. In addition to
60. 12/24 or 12/31
61. Blue expanse

DOWN

1. Jar lid
2. Correct (copy)
3. Tense
4. Sticky stuff
5. Goal
6. Urgent request
7. Droning sound
8. Lawn tree
9. "Merry" month
11. At that time
12. Foot part
17. Pod veggie
19. Tic- ____ -toe
21. Sandwich store
23. "Peepers"
24. Leisure garment
25. Large brass horn
26. Swallow loudly
27. India's continent
28. Permits
30. Actor Howard
31. News bit
37. Church bench
38. Ms. Landers
40. Ripped
42. Mom's sister
44. Ten minus one
46. Travel stops
47. Captured
48. Place for pampering
49. Frying utensil
50. Help
52. Gun (an engine)
53. Tree chopper
55. Wipe (the dishes)

ACROSS

1. Tiny drink of liquor
4. Strike (flies)
8. Daring deed
12. Mr. Gershwin
13. It "springs eternal"
14. Wild beast's hideout
15. Opposite of pro
16. "So be it!"
17. Body of soldiers
18. Whole
20. Droop
22. One who leases
24. Compete in a downhill race
27. Book of maps
30. Ran away, as from jail
32. "Stay there!"
33. Butter serving
34. Fight in defense of honor
35. Comes into view
37. Musician Bono
38. "Of course!"
39. Lower, as a voice
41. "Help Wanted" listings
42. Looked (at) slyly
46. Cafeteria carrier
49. Line of stitches
51. Wood-chopping tool
52. Grape beverage
53. New York canal
54. Sardine container
55. Chances, in betting
56. Beach surface
57. Place for Porky

DOWN

1. Pleasant
2. Element used in steel
3. Gasp for breath
4. Divides equally with others
5. Grown-up girls
6. Impersonate
7. Least relaxed
8. Old Glory, for one
9. Unit of corn
10. Point (a camera) at
11. Attempt
19. Infuriated
21. Bowlike curve
23. Pester playfully
24. Made yarn
25. Sharp
26. In a nonchalant way
27. Absent
28. Record (music)
29. Pouting features

155

31. Have a crush on
33. Irons (clothes)
36. Say further
37. Appeared
40. Unadorned
41. Affirmative votes
43. City rodents
44. Way out
45. Say it isn't so
46. A pair
47. Relieved (of)
48. Plus
50. Historic time

156

ACROSS

1. Pot covers
5. Paid athlete
8. Trails behind
12. Land measure
13. Dinghy propeller
14. Ms. Fitzgerald
15. "How have you ____?"
16. Singleton
17. Move like liquid
18. Build a tower with (blocks)
20. Kitchen staple
21. Possesses
23. Defraud
25. Tie the knot
26. Vote into office
28. Garden soil
30. Luxury vacation spot
32. Merchant
36. Close by
38. In the heavens
39. Earn a blue ribbon
42. Bite to eat between meals
44. River bottom
45. False gods
47. Reacts like tools left out in the rain
49. Volcano's flow
50. For each
51. Piece of news
54. Those guys
55. Urban trains
56. Fictional detective Wolfe
57. Shoe bottom
58. Sailor's reply
59. Mouse catcher

DOWN

1. Scientist's workplace
2. Frozen H_2O
3. Gets into a costume
4. Dispatched
5. Dog: slang
6. Assigned a rating to
7. Crude metal
8. Remaining
9. Permit
10. Baseball mitt
11. Cut, in a way
19. Leading lady
20. Smears on a window
21. That girl
22. Pub order
24. Offer help
27. Debate position
29. Diner bill
31. Sunbathe
33. Maine treat
34. Night before a festival
35. Crimson
37. Seldom
39. Withers for want of water
40. Boise's state
41. Grisham volume
43. Black-magic spell
46. Weak, as an excuse
48. Color
50. Soup veggie
52. Notable time
53. Wipe (one's brow)

157

ACROSS

1. Cooking vessel
4. Shade providers
8. Electrical cord
12. Commotion
13. Informal affirmative
14. Opera song
15. Newsman Rather
16. Little whirlpool
17. Monthly housing expense
18. Use the nose
20. Slippery swimmers
22. Give assistance to
24. Cooks (a turkey)
28. Nudged
32. Pledged a vow
33. Hearing-aid site
34. Quick sleep
36. Enjoyment
37. Some Middle East natives
40. Bragged
43. Depended (on)
45. Salsa, for one
46. Profound
48. Pancake topping
52. Put into words
55. Dish for mixing
57. Self
58. Unit of land
59. Forest growth
60. Everyone
61. Apparel
62. Movie backdrops
63. Coloring liquid

DOWN

1. Chair cushions
2. First man
3. ". . . and then there were ____"
4. Place to apply shadow
5. Guided
6. Created
7. Less outgoing
8. Capital of Poland
9. Wrath
10. ____ Tin Tin, movie dog
11. Have a meal
19. Young boy
21. Word before "Angeles"
23. Family room
25. Far from hard
26. Not false
27. Transmit; convey
28. Fall fruit
29. Out of the ordinary
30. By mouth
31. Painting stroke
35. Peas holder
38. Auction participant
39. Visualize
41. Theater passage-ways
42. Secret watcher
44. Financial obligations
47. Tiny hole in the skin
49. "You've got to ____ between the lines"
50. Far from good-looking
51. High-jumper's tool
52. Hang down
53. Top card
54. Rhyming Gershwin
56. Soaked

158

ACROSS

1. Puts on (clothing)
5. Go one better than
8. Makes a hole in one
12. "Wrought" metal
13. Color
14. Theatrical part
15. Cruel emperor
16. Make a goof
17. Flower of love
18. Taste victory
20. Unseal
21. 13-Across of grass
24. Melt, as frozen food
27. Commuting routes
28. "As I ____ saying . . ."
29. Perform in a play
32. Classified listings
33. From the Emerald Isle
35. Sticky substance
36. Up to now
37. Quarter-back Marino
38. Deep, blue sea
40. Hackman of the movies
41. Out of practice
42. Fling
45. Group of matching dishes
46. Pakistan's locale
47. Bother
49. Notable times
53. Camera's "eye"
54. Brightest star
55. Pepper's partner
56. Racetrack statistics
57. Wooden fastener
58. Yonder folks

DOWN

1. Great noise
2. Miner's find
3. Neither's companion
4. Came down in flakes
5. At that time
6. "____ Town," Wilder play
7. Apiece
8. Bow missile
9. Chicken's roost
10. Besides
11. Spotted
19. Not outdoors
21. Dreary color
22. Went by donkey
23. Sunrise direction
24. Package cord
25. Holds
26. On land, to sailors
29. Shows one's years
30. Layer (of paint)
31. Mr. Danza
34. High-tailed it
39. Most adorable
40. Pane material
42. Sign of saintliness
43. Exploited
44. Orange peel
45. Ditty
47. Cleopatra's downfall
48. Expected to arrive
50. Grand-stand cheer
51. Frothy beverage
52. Hog's home

159

ACROSS

1. Fork prong
5. Curved doorway
9. Tiny ____, character in "A Christmas Carol"
12. Smell
13. Metal thread
14. Poem of praise
15. Urban settlement
16. Eve's 45-Down
17. In the style of: 2 wds.
18. Went astray
20. Home to 16-Across
21. Pursued
24. Young man
26. Endures
27. Least relaxed
31. Noah's boat
32. Wring
34. ____ de Janeiro, Brazilian city
35. Cowboy movie
37. Find out
39. Summer drink
40. Parts of eyeglasses
41. Mix briskly
44. Clever
46. Fishing pole
47. Use a dagger
48. Outer rim
52. Pub quaff
53. Low female voice
54. Spoil
55. Green veggie
56. Look closely
57. Transmit

DOWN

1. Small child
2. Nuptial vow: 2 wds.
3. At once
4. Actor Borgnine
5. Academy ____, Oscar
6. Go by car
7. Beds for babies
8. Skirt bottom
9. Frog's kin
10. Not in use
11. Cruel
19. Refreshed
20. Asner and Sullivan
21. Cat's "scratcher"
22. Jack rabbit
23. Inquires
25. Deer's horn
27. Can metal
28. Epochs
29. Kingly address
30. Cargo weights
33. Grapple (with)
36. Faucet
38. Goes in
40. Work
41. Cover, as a gift
42. Doughnut center
43. Thought
45. Companion
47. Tree fluid
49. Owed
50. Tonic's partner
51. Cease

160

ACROSS

1. Toot (a whistle)
5. Likely (to)
8. Comparison word
12. Mature
13. Ghost's shriek
14. Traveled by bus
15. ". . . Where the deer and the ____ play"
17. Filled with wonder
18. "Definitely!"
19. In a smooth way
21. Ruby or Sandra
22. Store corridors
26. Underage
29. Baby goat
30. Everyone
31. Musician Clapton
32. Hair goo
33. Ascend
34. Tear
35. Young man
36. Enticed
37. Academic papers
39. Was introduced to
40. Teacher's plan
42. Car fuel
45. Singer Turner
48. Not guilty
50. Smell
51. Crusted dessert
52. Ms. Bancroft
53. Somewhat hot
54. Secret agent
55. Group of players

DOWN

1. Donkey's cry
2. Script excerpt
3. Chooses (with "for")
4. Very small
5. Higher than
6. Catholic VIP
7. Pedicure focus
8. Serving plates
9. "In what way?"
10. Lemon beverage
11. Actor Beatty
16. Ogle (at)
20. Can covering
21. "What's up, ____?"
23. Bear's home
24. Otherwise
25. Winter vehicle
26. Simple
27. Eye part
28. Bites slightly
29. Lock opener
32. Rumor lovers
33. Something folks get stuck in?
35. "See you later!"
36. Late-night's Jay
38. Bell that wakes you up
39. Currency
41. Cut with scissors
42. Mr. Hackman
43. "____ Karenina," novel
44. Plant stalk
45. Drag behind
46. Actress Lupino
47. Neither's partner
49. Feline

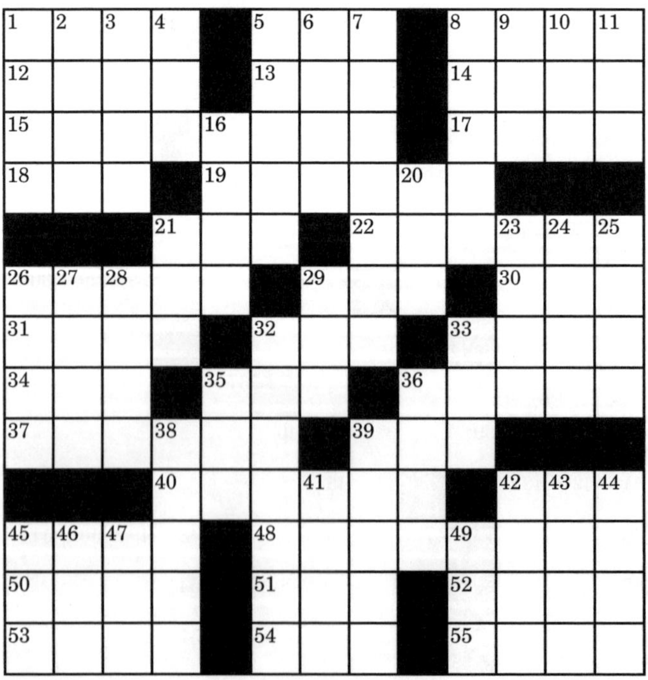

161

ACROSS

1. Comic-book word
4. African serpents
8. Prayer closer, to some
12. Be contrite
13. Not strong at all
14. Barbershop symbol
15. Common; everyday
17. Flower of love
18. Canyon's edge
19. Complained childishly
21. :
24. Be sick
25. Employing
26. Creative work
27. Child's "apron"
30. Backyard trees
31. Do simple math
32. Green Asian gemstone
33. Weep audibly
34. Jolson and Pacino
35. Relates (a story)
36. By means of
37. Walks in water
38. One who lacks courage
41. Coal container
42. Gleeful shouts
43. Threshold
48. Come up
49. Pagan image
50. Self-involvement
51. Goes one better
52. Makes as profit
53. Length of life

DOWN

1. Sports expert
2. Belonging to us
3. Get married
4. Canvas window protection
5. Line of sewing
6. Golf score
7. Up in the air
8. Spring month
9. Night light?
10. Otherwise
11. Required item
16. Presses (clothing)
20. _____ the road
21. Billiards sticks
22. City in Norway
23. Large tree-branch
26. Magazine fillers
27. _____ eagle, magnificent bird
28. Inactive
29. Harry Truman's First Lady
31. Genie-lamp owner
32. Denim pants
34. We breathe it
35. Turns round and round
36. Flower containers
38. Grocery wagon
39. Akron's locale
40. Stinging insect
41. Cowboy's "shoe"
44. Tribute in verse
45. Chinese drink
46. Nest find
47. Great horror writer

162

ACROSS

1. Old, tired horse
4. "I have repaid my ____ to society"
8. Peacock's display
12. Beer's kin
13. Press (clothes)
14. Parcel of land
15. Storage box
16. Baseball glove
17. Lower leg
18. Bird chirp
20. Midterm, for one
21. Lawn-ruining animals
23. Carry out (orders)
26. Mocked
27. Prayer word
28. Oil or oleo
31. Makes untidy (with "up")
33. Dear Abby's specialty
35. Pantry invader
36. Competed (with)
38. Ms. Bancroft
39. Pea's cousin
40. Pigpens
41. Likewise
44. Pasture growth
46. Lion's bellow
47. Tuning knob
48. Bonnet or bowler
51. Arrive
52. Start a poker kitty
53. Self-respect
54. Rushed
55. Hive residents
56. Put on (a 48-Across)

DOWN

1. Catch (a crook)
2. Heavy-weight great
3. Least harsh
4. Small, silvery coins
5. Great Lake near Buffalo
6. Lowest part
7. Blasting compound: abbr.
8. Delicious
9. Dull pain
10. Colored part of the eye
11. Period of fasting
19. Marries
21. Papa's partner
22. Unfasten
24. Necklace orb
25. Last part
27. Largest continent
28. Completed
29. Teen's skin woe
30. Gadgets of Nicklaus
32. Preholiday night
34. Large tanks
37. Car's motor
39. Filled with tedium
40. Retail trans-actions
41. Rainbows' paths
42. Circle (of ribbon)
43. Identical
45. Fixed charge
47. Little bit (of paint)
49. In the past
50. 2,000-pound weight

163

ACROSS

1. "Oh, go fly a ____!"
5. Ready for business
9. Drain (strength) from
12. Press (pants)
13. Challenge
14. Stare at
15. "I ____ believe it's true!"
16. Make a picture
17. Stitch
18. Prepare to be knighted
20. Donkeys' kin
22. Fruit peel
24. Get up
27. Angry
30. Christmas carol
32. The Hawkeye State
33. Important happenings
35. Sports centers
37. Little squeakers
38. Otherwise
40. Messy place
41. Smell
42. Single thing
44. Valentine's Day flowers, usually
47. Rodeo rope
51. Mineral spring
53. Promise
55. Present formally
56. Consume
57. At no charge
58. Ripped (into)
59. Draft drink
60. Raggedy Ann's pal
61. Fixes firmly

DOWN

1. ____ out, forcibly eject
2. Persia, now
3. Atmosphere
4. "Come in!"
5. Unusual
6. Celebratory procession
7. Historic periods
8. Informative TV show, with "the"
9. Appointments
10. Nautical assent
11. Church bench
19. Dryer-filter residue
21. New York canal
23. Smelling organ
25. Bat (at)
26. Simple
27. Office note
28. Fervent
29. Adorn
31. Final
34. Roman emperor
36. Movie spool
39. In the phone book
43. Sail runners
45. Cozy seat
46. Receive (a salary)
48. Sneaker or pump
49. Arrange by type
50. Is indebted to
51. Ocean
52. Chum
54. "Yoo-hoo!"

164

ACROSS

1. Big smile
5. ____ and crafts, camp activity
9. Mouse hunter
12. Folk knowledge
13. Furnace output
14. In the past
15. "Ah, me!"
16. Large continent
17. Fishing trap
18. Fender flaws
20. In poor health
21. TV commercials
22. Performed an aria
24. Baby goat
26. Golfer's peg
29. The ____ Ranger
31. Contended (with)
34. Ask (to a dance)
36. Sea journey
38. Require
39. Sly 1-Across
41. Currently
42. Emulate a crew team
44. Ginger cookie
46. Pig's dwelling
48. Segment of a rainbow
50. Rodeo rope
54. Also
55. Bath bar
57. Broadway production
58. Rustic lodging
59. Bishop of Rome
60. Ceramic square
61. Popular deli bread
62. Crockpot dish
63. Mimicked

DOWN

1. Pleased
2. Part in a 57-Across
3. Persia, nowadays
4. Treetop homes
5. "I caught you!"
6. Leave a job
7. Kite's streamer
8. Corn stem
9. Vancouver native
10. Became older
11. Little children
19. Pretzel coating
23. Christmas carol
25. Climbing plant
26. Food can
27. Compass point
28. All of us
30. Not odd
32. Self-conceit
33. Early-morning condensation
35. Wedding words
37. Expressed in speech
40. Get away
43. Stinging insects
45. Rigatoni or manicotti
46. Mix ingredients
47. Theater award
49. Word before "beer" or "canal"
51. Pirate's vessel
52. Shoe bottom
53. Had a loan to repay
56. Church bench

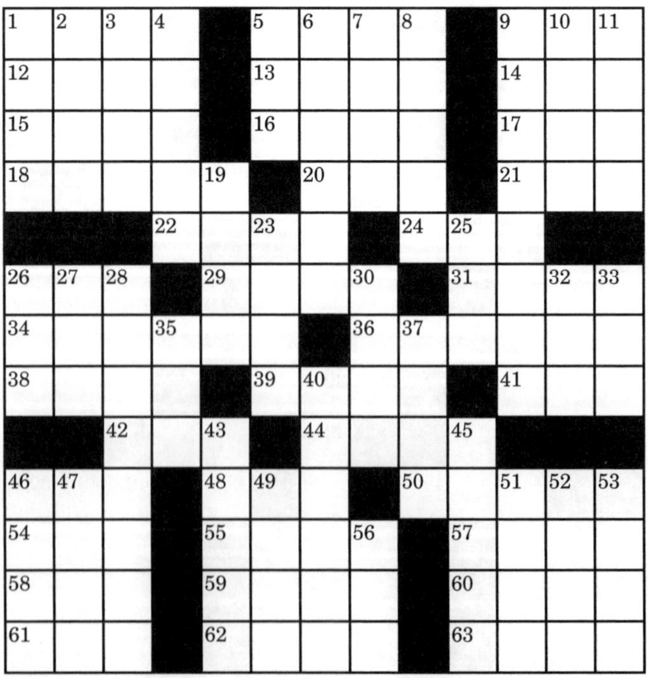

165

ACROSS

1. Wishful expectation
5. Prince, under an enchantment?
9. Ignited
12. "The one that got ____"
13. "Stormy Weather" singer Horne
14. Id's companion
15. Only; no more than
16. Singles
17. In the style of: 2 wds.
18. "Shoo!"
20. Emergency code
21. Lump, as of butter
24. Entry on a list
26. Vaccine injection
27. Audibly
29. Somewhat wet
31. Ski season
33. Worked hard
37. Dry as the desert
39. Naples' country
40. Corned-beef ____
43. Stand-up's jokes
45. Go out, as a flame
46. Grow old
47. New Jersey cagers
49. Civic rule
50. Rats' relatives
52. "Stay there!"
56. Compete (with)
57. Dignified poems
58. Presidential assistant
59. Last bit
60. Walk through water
61. Provoke to action

DOWN

1. Accompaniment for eggs
2. Have debts
3. Golfing standard
4. Organs of vision
5. Parade vehicle
6. Leased (a house)
7. "The loneliest number"
8. Cooking fuel
9. Dog restraint
10. House of ice
11. Browned bread
19. Apple drink
21. Feline "foot"
22. The Greatest
23. 2,000-pound weight
25. Exercise pad
26. Roasting rod
28. 2002 Winter Olympics state
30. Damp
32. Eighteen-wheeler, for one
34. Boy
35. The cotton gin's Whitney
36. Hair coloring
38. Did the Charleston
40. Divide (a grapefruit)
41. "Encore!"
42. Stitched seams
44. "Silly" birds
48. Barter
50. Cut (a lawn)
51. Lovely Lupino
53. Oxygen mix
54. Wedding words
55. Koppel or Turner

166

ACROSS

1. London mist
4. Present formally
8. Shadowbox
12. Important period
13. Wish (for)
14. Singer Nat King
15. Greeted warmly
17. Cry of despair
18. Sidelong glance
19. Back's opposite
20. As well
23. On vacation
25. Cuts (off)
26. Second-hand
27. Lamb's cry
30. Church leader
32. Yellow fruits
34. Grouping of similar items
35. Polish target
37. Sty sound
38. ____ F. Kennedy
39. Bar brews
40. Directional pointer
43. Like some pillows
46. McCartney of The Beatles
47. Arithmetic process
51. Sinful
52. Summer coolers
53. Number to tango
54. Refute
55. Fender ding
56. Use a needle and thread

DOWN

1. The ____ and the proud
2. Raw metal
3. Lass
4. Footwear item
5. Residence
6. Musical dramas
7. Marry
8. Frightening
9. Horseback game
10. Actor Alda
11. Take it easy
16. Shut
19. Lose color
20. Swiss peaks
21. Traditional knowledge
22. Barbecue rod
24. Healthy
26. The Beehive State
27. Heat water, as for pasta
28. Ms. Bancroft
29. Inquires
31. Winter precipitation
33. Castle defenses
36. Not outdoors
38. In good spirits
40. Imitated
41. Rant
42. Utterly destroy
44. Baking chamber
45. Clenched hand
47. Necktie recipient, often
48. "____ a boy!"
49. Have debts
50. Currently

167

ACROSS

1. At this moment
4. Run away
8. An Arnaz
12. "____ You Lonesome Tonight?"
13. Throw (dice)
14. 365 days in a row
15. Sleep chambers
17. Ms. Fitzgerald
18. Inquire
19. Resurrected
20. Gymnast's feat
23. Actor Alda
25. Cargo
26. Using some playground equipment
30. Poetic prize-fighter
31. Wild animal
32. With 36-Across, "Diamond Lil" actress
33. Painting of a person
35. Make a cobweb
36. See 32-Across
37. Church pathway
38. Sulked
41. Accomplished
42. Level
43. They form a body
48. Encounter
49. Stride
50. Flock female
51. "____ You," song
52. Clumsy boats
53. Foot digit

DOWN

1. Seize suddenly
2. Lode yield
3. Tie the knot
4. Sign of autumn
5. Appear
6. Shade tree
7. Overhead trains
8. Adding color to
9. Sea serpents?
10. Shopper's delight
11. Tehran's land
16. Sudden attack
19. ____ and rave
20. Strike with the hand
21. Horseback game
22. Den for a 31-Across
23. Expect
24. Roster
26. Baltic and Caspian
27. Mischievous ones
28. Manicurist's target
29. Mr. Hackman
31. Raised (dogs)
34. Ten plus ten
35. Faction
37. Assistants
38. Short note
39. Cooking chamber
40. Fruit rind
41. Daffy, for one
43. Health resort
44. Paving goo
45. Fishing mesh
46. Half of four
47. View

168

ACROSS

1. Model-building set
4. Daytime drama, for short
8. Salt amount
12. Lyricist Gershwin
13. Communion element
14. Reflected sound
15. Sheer material
16. Frequent Emmy winner
17. Discontinue
18. Blair of Britain
20. Sleeveless sweaters
21. Boast; brag
23. Practice prize-fighting
25. New York Public Library's guardians
27. Walked softly
31. Gorilla, for one
32. Snapshot
34. Beam of light
35. Pushcart salesperson
37. Washer cycle
39. Place for skating
40. Brewery tubs
41. Lurk
44. Appear
46. Function
47. Vietnam's continent
49. Historic period
52. Velvety plant
53. Frees (of)
54. Convent dweller
55. Mailbox opening
56. Arbor Day honoree?
57. "____ Little Indians"

DOWN

1. Family member
2. Temper
3. Like Popeye's arm
4. Ballet bird
5. Full of petroleum
6. Further-more
7. Bean's relative
8. Sandy stretch
9. Behaves
10. Cinematic moment
11. Jumps on one foot
19. Be the proprietor of
20. Clouds, basically
21. Applaud
22. Like a red tomato
23. Fabled baby bringer
24. Where the orchestra sits
26. Break up
28. Decoration
29. Orient
30. Bleaches, maybe
33. Barnyard brooder
36. Least damp
38. "____ Got a Secret"
41. They're for hugging
42. Warm fabric
43. In addition
44. Flank
45. Conve-nience
47. Exhibit at the Louvre
48. Address for a man
50. Regret
51. Tap-dancer Miller

169

ACROSS

1. Book's action
5. A son of Adam
9. Be teary-eyed
12. Rant
13. Actor Alan
14. Color shade
15. Singles
16. Chat
17. Lupino of filmdom
18. Slight depressions
20. Deli bread choice
21. The "p" in "mph"
22. Equip with weapons
24. River blocker
26. Existed
29. Misplaced
31. Sudden increase in wind speed
34. Is ready for
36. Bartender's gadget
38. Raise one's voice
39. English nobleman
41. Ignition insert
42. Roker and Gore
44. Ocean
45. Golfing average
47. "That's disgusting!"
49. Birds' abodes
54. Poetic pummeler
55. House's top
57. An adhesive
58. Avail oneself of
59. Bus passenger
60. Part of "GWTW"
61. Angeles preceder
62. Coast down a snowy slope
63. Did the backstroke

DOWN

1. Nudge; poke
2. Bowling alley
3. Range feature
4. Try out
5. ____ burglar
6. Causes sudden fright
7. In a nonchalant way
8. Without a stitch on
9. Tiny forest mammal
10. Impolite
11. Part of a decade
19. Brine ingredient
23. Deep pink
25. Time of life
26. "My ____," Sinatra song
27. Wonderment
28. Professionals' yearly wages
30. Ripped (apart)
32. Witness
33. Make an effort (to)
35. Under the weather
37. Think ahead
40. On terra firma
43. Rides waves on a board
45. Former Beatle McCartney
46. Too
48. Soccer success
50. Custard base
51. Taking a long time
52. Salad-sandwich fish
53. Appear
56. Provided a meal to

170

ACROSS

1. Touched
5. Appendages for hugging
9. Label
12. Animal's den
13. Jump
14. Bar "rocks"
15. Common skin condition
16. Gave a shriek
18. At that time
19. Slithery swimmers
20. When roosters 58-Across
23. Kindle
27. Gray powder
30. Prepares (the dining table)
32. Closet closer
33. Pipes up
35. Child's "magic word"
37. Harbor city
38. Loyal
40. Martial-arts star Bruce
41. Got to one's feet
43. Poker stake
45. Very fine rain
47. Girl
51. Gifts
55. Canyon effect
56. Belonging to you and me
57. Seaside bird
58. Go "cock-a-doodle-doo!"
59. For each
60. Carry out (an order)
61. Young adult

DOWN

1. Motorist's bane
2. Every one
3. Script scrap
4. Fashion
5. Pacino and Gore
6. New, as an arrival
7. Stable mom?
8. Enchantment
9. "Home Improvement" star Allen
10. Perfect tennis serve
11. Place for sleep
17. Out of the way
21. Voice a request
22. Sunset venue
24. Purpose
25. Hydrant attachment
26. Towering plant
27. Venomous serpents
28. Dog's name
29. Brave person
31. Formed, as a web or a cocoon
34. Mighty particles
36. "____ there be peace on earth..."
39. Baby's toy
42. The San ____ Padres
44. Campaign-poster word
46. Give the cold shoulder to
48. Unit of land measurement
49. Foot's covering
50. Planted, as seeds
51. Burst (a balloon)
52. Be regretful
53. Make a blunder
54. Crafty; calculating

171

ACROSS

1. Science rooms
5. Narrow country byway
9. Shorten (a skirt)
12. All tied up, as a score
13. Worshiped statue
14. Acting Lupino
15. Calendar info
16. Cruel Roman of yore
17. "Tiny" Dickens character
18. Vision organs
20. Starchy dish
22. Unthawed
25. Morning moisture
26. Black bird
27. Commanded
31. Time in history
32. Winged pest
33. Brewery product
34. Postponed
37. Touch or sight
39. Family member
40. More extensive
41. Hurl
44. Expansive
45. Weeding tool
46. Requirement
48. Not doing much
52. "_____ Baba and the Forty Thieves"
53. Sinful
54. Invasion
55. Half of twenty
56. Valley
57. Concludes

DOWN

1. Was in the forefront
2. Filmdom's Gardner
3. Lay odds on
4. Flu symptom
5. Cool fabric
6. Fruity beverages
7. Negative conjunction
8. Got married secretly
9. Goals for batters
10. Prepare (copy) for the printer
11. Baby's first word, often
19. Money of Tokyo
21. Reverent fear
22. Mr. Flintstone
23. Steak order
24. Football shape
25. Wipe (dishes)
27. Aged
28. Pressed (the doorbell)
29. Otherwise
30. Fawn or doe
32. Gave a snack to
35. Major fuss
36. Gaped sleepily
37. Sailor's distress signal
38. Unabridged
40. Soup-serving tool
41. The one yonder
42. Swiss cheese feature
43. Horse's steering wheel?
44. Bride's face covering
47. A Gabor sister
49. Funnyman Aykroyd
50. Flip one's _____, go nuts
51. Sullivan and Asner

172

ACROSS

1. Jaunt; journey
5. That man's
8. Dull-colored
12. Give a job to
13. Cleopatra's slayer
14. Full of fat
15. Inquires (of)
16. Geometric shape
18. Map direction
19. As well as
20. Clothing-tag info
23. Trash-disposal sites
28. Hit the slopes
31. Gift for a tot
33. Word after "billy" or "nanny"
34. Native of Bombay
36. On dry land
38. Move like a bowling ball
39. Apiece
41. Dawn droplets
42. Stick out like a sore thumb?
44. Swerve
46. Intense anger
48. Mountain range in Switzerland
52. Extremely hot, as water
57. Part in a movie
58. Mama's mate
59. Expected, as payment
60. Level (off)
61. ____ and crafts
62. View
63. Enjoy a poem

DOWN

1. Liquefy, as ice
2. Yeast makes bread dough do this
3. Annoys
4. Garden nuisances
5. Head warmer
6. Middle Eastern country
7. Ice skater's motion
8. Put on (apparel)
9. Trucker's vehicle
10. Everyone
11. "Till we meet again!"
17. Do some math
21. Lupino of films
22. City district
24. Exclamation of distaste
25. Frame of mind
26. Cut away the peel from
27. Hearty dish
28. Business-letter greeting
29. Recognize
30. Not operating
32. Dress frill
35. Unhealthy
37. That gal
40. Gracious thoroughfare
43. Box cover
45. More unusual
47. Frees (of)
49. Emotion inspired by Cupid
50. Entreaty
51. Dispatch; convey
52. Healthful retreat
53. Passenger vehicle
54. Likely (to)
55. Scale tones
56. "____ whiz!"

173

ACROSS

1. Sticky stuff
4. Male deer
8. Towards the sunset
12. Chest bone
13. Fork prong
14. Dull pain
15. Pacino and Gore
16. Poker stake
17. Footwear item
18. "See ya!"
19. Lass
20. Cooking vessels
21. Pastrami bread
23. Snakelike fishes
26. Hand over
28. Impulse
29. Church bench
32. Sports sites
34. President Washington
36. Gym mat
37. That girl's
39. Furniture material, often
40. Created
41. Vigor
42. Highest point
45. Normal condition
47. Lode load
50. Performs
51. Piglet of film
52. Unhappy
53. "Woe is me!"
54. Troubles
55. 42-Down's mate
56. Large quantity
57. Summer drinks
58. Cozy room

DOWN

1. Snatch
2. Greasy
3. Witnessed
4. Theater platform
5. Singer Turner
6. 4-Across's horn
7. "Golly!"
8. Stinging insects
9. Reflected noise
10. Discharged (a rifle)
11. Golf pegs
22. Strong desire
24. Hen products
25. Confederate general
26. Small opening
27. Mr. Gershwin
28. Secondhand
29. Put forth (an idea)
30. Self
31. Marry
33. "Gotcha!"
35. Have debts
38. Compensated
40. Far from clean
41. Squeeze
42. First man
43. Soda flavor
44. Nasty
46. Skilled enough
48. Rant
49. Home to 55-Across
51. Lamb's cry

174

ACROSS

1. Exchange one thing for another
5. Curved lines
9. Sullivan and Bradley
12. Arrive
13. Rec-room projectile
14. Go out, as a flame
15. Completely finished
16. Do some light boxing
17. Frost (a cake)
18. In a highly nervous state
20. Add sugar to
22. Acorn tree
24. Produce (eggs)
25. Tilted
29. Intended (to)
33. Hinge lubricant
34. Merry
36. Pursue romantically
37. Use, as money
40. Least messy
43. Annoy; vex
45. Tire filler
46. Hilly
50. Army officer
54. File-folder extension
55. Robert E. and Peggy
57. Superman's cloak
58. "____ got a crush on you . . ."
59. Singer Horne
60. Garden in Genesis
61. Beam of light
62. Snow vehicle
63. Fender depression

DOWN

1. Edinburgh citizen
2. Made cloth
3. "So be it!"
4. Human being
5. Sales announcements
6. Knocks sharply
7. Move like an ant
8. Little river
9. Polish (text)
10. Cut (vegetables) into small cubes
11. Laid eyes on
19. Have a meal
21. Sight organ
23. Small barrel
25. Distress signal
26. Mouth part
27. Beer's cousin
28. Newsman Rather
30. Overpowering wonder
31. Negative replies
32. Tiny child
35. "Three cheers!"
38. Little bite
39. Marching exercises
41. Goal
42. Followed the outline of
44. Prepare to receive a knighthood
46. Recipe instruction
47. Hot, volcanic goo
48. Do as one is told
49. Oscar winner Hackman
51. Asian gemstone
52. "____, sesame!"
53. Tenant's fee
56. Unhappy

175

ACROSS

1. Paradise
5. "____ can play that game!"
8. Barbecue rod
12. Bestowed
13. Slight gleam (of hope)
14. Hercules, for one
15. Got larger
16. Public notices
17. Shopping-list entry
18. Felt
20. Go one better than
22. Take part in a mutiny
24. One of the five W's
27. Iron clothes?
31. Played the general
33. Be in the forefront
34. Sung syllables
35. Underdone, as meat
36. Less punctual
38. Certain recordings
39. Mine's yield
40. Move out of the way of
42. Mass of unruly hair
43. Invaded (the icebox)
48. Apex; summit
51. Tart drink
53. Danny DeVito sitcom
54. Membership fee
55. Caviar, basically
56. Applaud
57. Cozy rooms
58. Lion's cave
59. Dress borders

DOWN

1. Henhouse produce
2. Risk
3. Like a tied score
4. What journalists report
5. Line of business
6. Mouthful, as of gum
7. Shellfish served on the half-shell
8. Large boat
9. Beloved animal
10. Wrath
11. Male turkey
19. Make a gaffe
21. Opposite of new
23. Wooden plank
24. Cover, as a gift
25. In this place
26. Poems by Keats
27. Female vocal range
28. Area in back
29. Stallion's mate
30. Offbeat
32. Historic time period
34. Spotted cat
37. Wedding words
38. Oolong or pekoe
41. Emerald's color
42. Untidy state
44. Skin irritation
45. Valley
46. Midterm, for one
47. Dunks (chips)
48. Total (up)
49. Actor's hint
50. Chaps
52. Fawn's ma

176

ACROSS

1. Untruths
5. European mountain range
9. Bashful
12. First man in the Bible
13. One's usual foods
14. Tiny
15. Zilch
16. Doe or fawn
17. Lyricist Gershwin
18. Newsman Rather
20. Visionary
22. Caught in a trap
25. Lose firmness
26. Firewood unit
27. Bath fixture
29. Concerning good behavior
33. Manipulate
34. Vision organ
36. Cracker-jack pilot
37. Brief breaks
40. Super-natural being
42. Country lodging
43. Picnic invader
45. Iron attractor
47. Sleeping chamber
51. Tic-—-toe
52. Fury
53. Has financial obligations
55. Carbon-ated drink
58. Soft metal
59. Numeral repre-senting 15-Across
60. Couple
61. "On your mark, get ——, go!"
62. Biblical garden
63. Plant stalk

DOWN

1. Sports devotee
2. Groom's words
3. Wound coverings
4. Coat (with) sticky stuff
5. Find a sum
6. Told 1-Across
7. Looks closely (at)
8. Small river
9. Use a pool
10. This place
11. 12 months
19. Gain, as profit
21. In the past
22. Pronounce indistinctly
23. Odor detector
24. Scheduled to arrive
28. "So long!"
30. Foul-weather wear
31. Teenage skin problem
32. Time before Easter
35. Shady tree
38. Rooftop repair goo
39. Nap
41. Calorie-counter's bane
44. Pulled (a car)
46. Pants
47. Small pieces
48. New York canal
49. Fender hollow
50. Nothing other than
54. Male heir, often
56. Fail, as a battery
57. Upper limb

177

ACROSS

1. Air circulators
5. Pro's opposite
8. Location
12. The ____ Office, Bush's headquarters
13. Tint
14. Serving platter
15. Severe anger
16. See 15-Across
17. Part for an actress
18. Graceful shade-giver
20. Swallows some water
22. Grenade, for one
25. Tree fluid
26. Rainbow-shaped curve
27. Itsy-bitsy
29. Pan of fiction
33. Ms. Hayworth
35. Dog's bark
37. Plunged (into the pool)
38. Birds' abodes
40. Golf prop
42. Be under the weather
43. Jar's top
45. With great eagerness
47. African wildlife tour
50. Feline pet
51. Showy flower
52. Volcanic powder
54. Significant time periods
58. Reside (at)
59. Feel regret
60. "Stubborn" beast
61. Poetic tributes
62. "Affirmative!"
63. One-dish meal

DOWN

1. Supportive of
2. Glamorous Gardner
3. Pester incessantly
4. Visit dreamland
5. Fireplace outlet
6. Owned by us
7. Requires
8. Like a zebra
9. Strong metal
10. Speak
11. "I saw it with my own ____!"
19. Deep, as a voice
21. Knock
22. Caution (someone)
23. A Great Lake
24. Performs on-stage
28. Enjoy grapes
30. Warty hopper
31. Sinister
32. Count (on)
34. Books of maps
36. Nectarines' cousins
39. Knight's title
41. Ms. Gabor
44. Journal
46. Newspaper stories
47. Farm tower
48. Dry and barren
49. Lincoln bill
53. Bring civil action against
55. Groove in a dirt road
56. Ginger ____, soft drink
57. Do a tailor's job

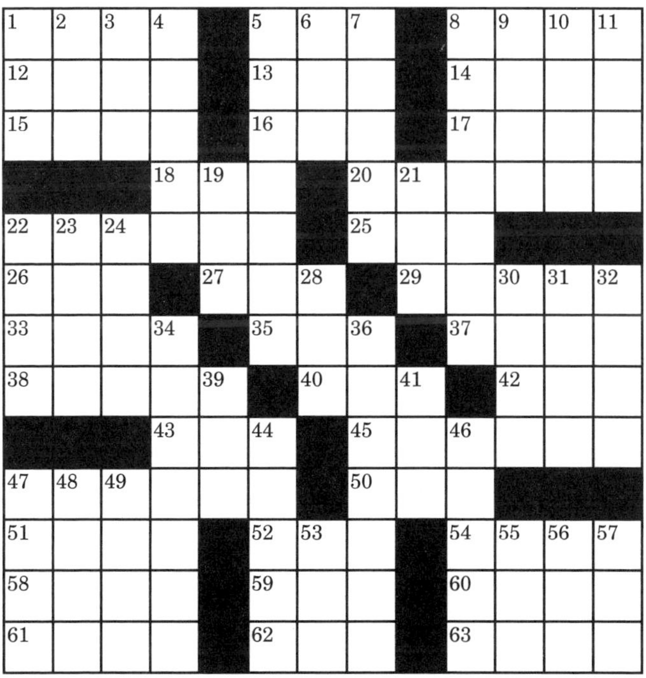

178

ACROSS

1. Fish bait
5. Feedbag morsels
9. Rotten
12. The largest continent
13. Go heels over head?
14. Regret
15. "Sawbucks"
16. Fortune's partner
17. Columnist Landers
18. Brink; margin
19. Perceive visually
20. "____ a Wonderful Life"
21. Flat, round object
24. Family man
26. Jolson and Pacino
29. Genuine
31. Go after a 1-Across
34. Say again
36. No longer sealed
38. Adolescent
39. Silver-screen celebrity
41. Service-station sign
42. Big fuss
44. Smell
46. Annoy
48. Hot spring
50. Sunrise direction
54. Bambi's mother, for one
55. Item's price
57. An eye color
58. Corn unit
59. Female vocal range
60. Adam's garden
61. Classifieds
62. Got up (from)
63. Final

DOWN

1. Tardy
2. Put to work
3. Engagement gift
4. Relieved (a pain)
5. On's opposite
6. Juneau's state
7. "What ____ is it?"
8. Exceed the posted limit
9. Making pigtails
10. Parent's sister
11. Cubs' homes
22. Lyricist Gershwin
23. TV units
25. Mr. Lincoln, familiarly
26. Gallery filler
27. Grant's foe
28. Stereo parts
30. Burden
32. Afternoon social
33. McMahon and Asner
35. Abolish
37. In favor of
40. Raises a glass to
43. Academy Award
45. "____ Without a Cause"
46. Brain flash
47. Highway
49. Horseback sport
51. "M*A*S*H" star
52. Takes to court
53. Shelter for Boy Scouts
56. Sock tip

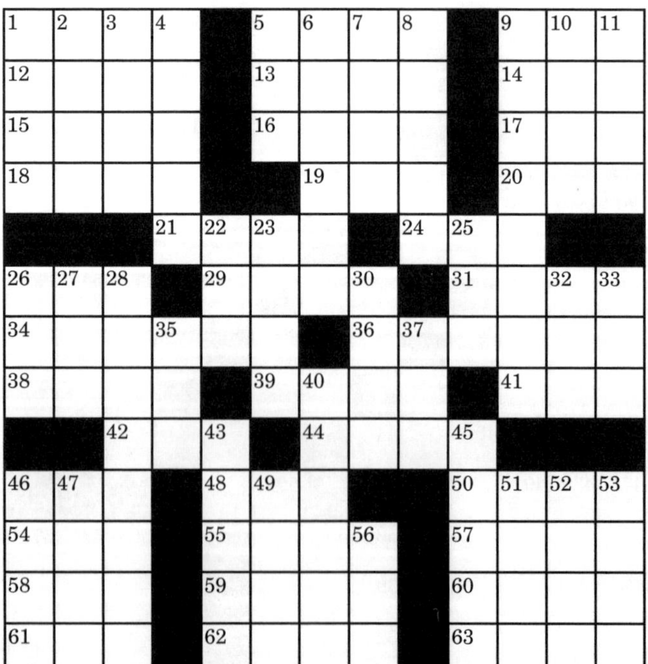

179

ACROSS

1. Young goats
5. Campaign (for office)
8. Poker-pot start
12. Do a publishing job
13. Monkey's relative
14. Show the way
15. Statement in court
16. Disney dwarf
17. Door-slamming sound
18. Exam or quiz
19. Pen filler
20. Encourage strongly
21. Freudian self
23. Male turkey
25. "____ and Prejudice"
28. SOS request
29. Occupation
32. Possessive pronoun
33. Made a blunder
35. Be obligated
36. Garden vegetable
37. Complete collection
38. U.S. national bird
40. Chick's mama
41. Rainbow shape
42. "Get lost!"
45. Cotton-gin inventor Whitney
47. Kennedy and Koppel
51. Listen to
52. Military engagement
53. Involving the mouth
54. Annoys
55. Had a meal
56. Ms. Hayworth
57. Eyeglasses' perch
58. "____ Misérables"
59. Ooze

DOWN

1. Held on to
2. Not doing anything
3. Goes out, as a flame
4. Expressed in words
5. Disc jockey's domain
6. Atop
7. Gift for Dad
8. Book for snapshots
9. Close
10. Distinctive flavor
11. Margin
22. Honking birds
24. More peculiar
25. Burst, as a balloon
26. Be remorseful
27. Lyricist Gershwin
28. Museum exhibit
29. Trot
30. Nocturnal hunter
31. Hive resident
34. Extension, as of a contract
39. Hollywood stars
40. Derby winner
41. Buenos ____, Argentina
42. Lower leg
43. Valiant one
44. Shade trees
46. Far from early
48. A Great Lake
49. Appointment
50. Smacking blow

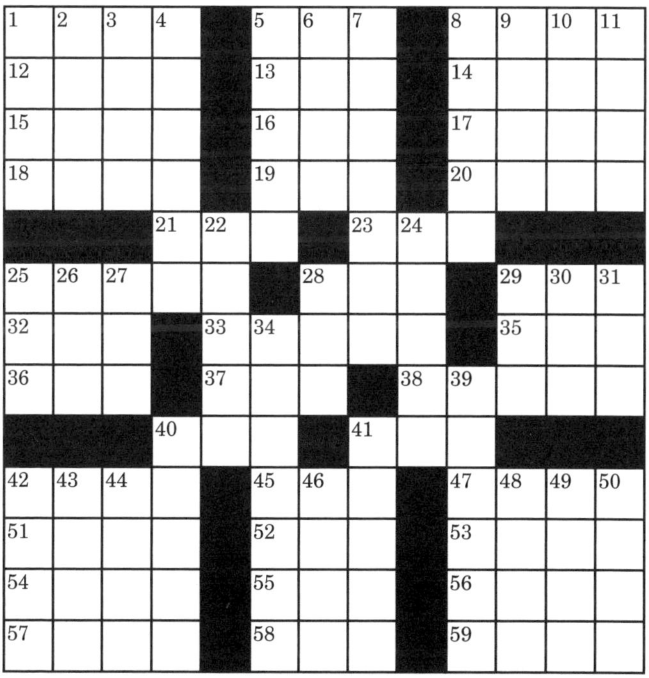

180

ACROSS

1. Entreaty
5. "Busy" insect
8. Egyptian vipers
12. Deserve
13. Long in the tooth
14. Plane stunt
15. Very thin branch
16. Eighteen-wheeler
17. Inland body of water
18. Allergy symptom
20. Wed secretly
22. Free (of)
23. Construct clothing
24. Prohibit
27. Peas' capsule
29. Wicked one
33. Student's perform-ance gauge
35. Angry crowd
37. Test of courage
38. Native American 61-Across
40. Grocery-shelf container
42. Butterfly snare
43. ____ Marie Saint
45. Adding result
47. Certain railroad car
50. Horse-shaped chess piece
54. Dracula's garment
55. Be in debt to
57. Make like a firefly
58. Fruit coolers
59. Little rug
60. Rescuer, for one
61. Portable shelter
62. Classified listings
63. Change for a twenty

DOWN

1. Teachers' favorites
2. Manicured yard
3. One in "HOMES"
4. Ire
5. Tedium
6. Inventor Whitney
7. Outer borders
8. Permitted (to)
9. Cleansing bar
10. Jab, as with an elbow
11. Drove too fast
19. Use a sliding fastener
21. Was winning
24. Make a wager
25. Woodshed tool
26. Pause that refreshes?
28. Disney dwarf
30. Movers' truck
31. Great rage
32. "____ my people go!"
34. Most mild-mannered
36. Easter egg holders
39. Cain's mom
41. Convent inhabitant
44. Cooking smell
46. Power
47. "Go home, kitty!"
48. Fashioned
49. Store sign
51. ____ club, singing group
52. Car's warning signal
53. Couples
56. Ball of paper

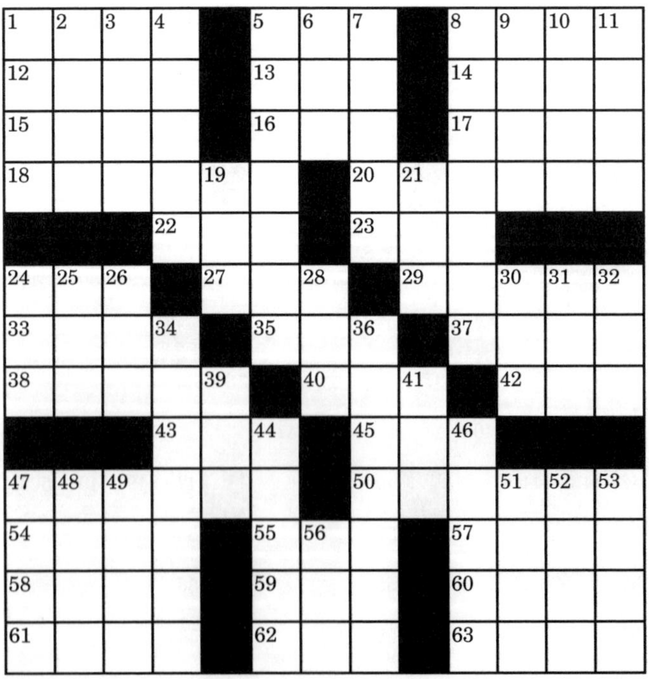

181

ACROSS

1. NYPD employee
4. The thing over there
8. Fail to enunciate
12. Reverent feeling
13. Part for an actress
14. Fragrance detector
15. Mr. Kingsley
16. Sahara-like
17. Pizza cooker
18. Sleeps briefly
20. Remainder
21. Persian Gulf nation
23. Bring joy to
27. Say it ain't so
28. Important period
29. Home for pigs
32. Have breakfast
33. Marshy land
35. Bathwater tester, at times
36. Classified notices
37. Lobe location
38. Baby deer
39. Popular house-plants
41. Bed-and-breakfasts, maybe
42. Practice like Rocky
45. Care for, as a garden
47. Angelic ring of light
48. Play a trick on
50. The Gores, father and son
53. Wallet bills
54. Has in one's possession
55. Pep-rally cheer
56. Midterm or final
57. Delight
58. Tint

DOWN

1. City transport
2. Be in the red
3. Baseball trophies
4. Snare; pitfall
5. Foal, finally
6. "____ Baba and the Forty Thieves"
7. Danson of TV
8. Sleep noisily
9. Tender emotion
10. Employs
11. Monthly expense
19. Some
21. Mental construct
22. Enjoy a novel
24. Gain knowledge
25. Elbow's site
26. Pub spigot
29. Normal
30. Urban center
31. Strong urges
33. Behold
34. "____ and Peace," Tolstoy novel
38. Fish flipper
39. Ice (a cake)
40. Smooth rock
42. Word after "buck" or "sling"
43. Window section
44. Tavern orders
46. In addition
48. London mist
49. Night bird
51. Deposit (eggs)
52. That female

182

ACROSS

1. Plea for assistance
5. Is able to
8. Feel concerned (about)
12. Skunk's defense
13. Individual
14. Of the mouth
15. An evergreen
16. Hill-building insect
17. Sewing fasteners
18. Cooks over hot water
20. Shrubbery fence
21. Snip with scissors
22. Drapes holder
23. Tub soakings
26. Chess piece
27. Lubricate (hinges)
30. Malt beverage
31. Potato-growing state
33. Holly-wood's Gardner
34. Hurried on foot
35. Purring pet
36. Smoothed the sand trap
38. Sweet potato
39. For every
40. Complete amount
43. Worshiped
47. "Once ____ a time . . ."
48. Used to be
50. Tiny rodents
51. Bird's bill
52. Behave
53. Hurt
54. Terminates
55. Positive vote
56. Look for bargains

DOWN

1. Kangaroo moves
2. Revise (text)
3. ____ wolf
4. Emulate a minister
5. Shore
6. Sheridan or Sothern
7. Take, after taxes
8. Dealt (with)
9. Bone-dry
10. Sounded, as a bell
11. Otherwise
19. Broadway show, often
20. Showed respect for
22. Cheer syllable
23. Forbid legally
24. Similar to: 2 wds.
25. Two times five
26. Gymnast's pad
27. Sturdy wood
28. "____ Got a Secret," TV show
29. Young fellow
32. Beaver construc-tion
37. Delicious smells
38. Sudden pulls
39. Macaroni or ziti
40. Hollow cylinder
41. Unsealed
42. Leaping amphibian
44. Wealthy
45. Reflected sound
46. Anything but shallow
48. Procedure
49. Tennis coup

183

ACROSS

1. Repeated sound
5. "_____ are you doing?"
9. Possesses
12. House division
13. Will beneficiary
14. In the manner of: 2 wds.
15. Actor's part
16. Declared firmly
18. Pays out money
20. System of regulations
21. Drink with a straw
22. Chooses (a politician)
26. "_____ a boy!"
29. Mesh snare
31. Broke open
32. Waiter's gratuities
34. Large rodent
36. Food fish
37. Make happy
39. Wide opening
41. Brown-paper sack
42. Olympic-pool lengths
44. Boy
46. Consume
47. Woolly beasts
51. Good-looking
55. Rounded roof
56. Conceit
57. 12/24 and 12/31
58. Sketched
59. Paddle a boat
60. Lease
61. Desires

DOWN

1. Goofs
2. Chicken pen
3. Doughnut's center, maybe
4. Seer's signs
5. Talk in hushed tones
6. Egg layer
7. Supermarket corridor
8. Tests
9. Head covering
10. Tavern offering
11. Gloomy
17. Used a broom
19. Annoying racket
23. Social organization
24. Singer Turner
25. Male elk
26. Grocery-list entry
27. Flooring square
28. Shoe covering
30. Store label
33. Riding horse
35. Most statuesque
38. Mistake-removal device
40. Friend
43. Kitchen appliance
45. Father
48. Additional amount
49. Prayer ending
50. Stitches
51. That woman
52. In the past
53. At this time
54. Chess pieces

184

ACROSS

1. Dislike intensely
5. Frequent letter greeting
9. Health resort
12. At any time
13. A Great Lake
14. Tic-____-toe
15. Twelve-month stretch
16. Vend
17. Boxing great Muhammad
18. Long tale of heroism
20. Ventilated
22. Actress Evans of "Dynasty"
25. Playthings
27. Smallest bill
28. Bee's kin
30. Injured, as a leg
34. Be present for
36. Location of lashes
38. Medication measure
39. Bancroft of "The Graduate"
41. Finish
42. Luxury car
44. Fortunate
46. Browned breakfast bread
49. Light knocks
51. Footed vase
52. The Emerald Isle, to poets
54. Snake's sound
58. Baseball stick
59. Wee rodents
60. Sound reverberation
61. Urban trains
62. Gush forth
63. Marsh grass

DOWN

1. Exclamation of surprise
2. "____ Maria," hymn
3. Afternoon meal
4. Made a mistake
5. Mr. Arnaz
6. Constructs (a building)
7. Be sick
8. Convey (a message)
9. Celestial body
10. Ashen
11. Sour
19. Certain chess piece
21. Capri or Wight
22. Cargo
23. Division word
24. Butterfly traps
26. Unlocked
29. First man in Genesis
31. One of the Baldwins
32. Weasel's cousin
33. Little whirlpool
35. Slippery fishes
37. Sharp bark
40. Observe
43. Articles on a list
45. Theater employee
46. Long pipe
47. Spoken
48. Picnic pests
50. Once more
53. Tear
55. Frozen water
56. That woman
57. Turf

185

ACROSS

1. Do some simple arithmetic
4. Deal (with)
8. Cooking vessel
11. Foot digit
12. Baking chamber
13. Raw mineral
14. One of Santa's helpers
15. Repair
16. Close by
18. Stopwatch, for one
20. Social appointments
22. Negative word
23. Gift topper
26. Model's stances
28. Fishing cord
29. Sidewalk material
32. Wore away
34. Egg shape
35. Thorny blooms
37. Cot, for one
38. Beaver construction
39. Bus station
43. Tall building
45. Shoe bottom
46. Opening for a coin
48. Young man
50. Civil War general
51. Peel
52. A Gabor sister
53. Actor Chaney
54. Grows older
55. Danson of "Cheers"

DOWN

1. Broke a fast
2. Blockhead
3. Give the meaning of (a word)
4. Long-tailed heavenly body
5. Higher than
6. Writer's tool
7. Come to a close
8. Small lake
9. Region
10. Tidy
17. Drive away
19. Red Sea parter
21. Male heir, often
23. Auction offer
24. Individual
25. Marry
27. Sipping tube
28. Misplaces
29. Corn on the ____
30. Preholiday night
31. Angry
33. Stop-sign color
36. Egg dish
38. Bestows love (on)
40. Opinion survey
41. Margarine
42. Adolescent
43. Ripped
44. Rant
46. Health resort
47. Fall behind
49. Mom's mate

186

ACROSS

1. Rate; pace
6. Chum
9. Cut (off)
12. Before the expected time
13. Boxing legend
14. Chopping tool
15. No longer sleeping
16. Drink slowly
17. Moist
18. Early evening
20. Ms. Bancroft
21. Layer of turf
24. Oozes (out)
26. Wedding words
27. Gave a meal to
28. Fibbers
32. Blew, as a whistle
34. President for most of the 1980s
35. Mistake
36. By way of
37. Psyche part
38. Up to the time of
40. Morning mist
41. Harmful remark
44. Causes of sorrow
46. Fall (behind)
47. Feel sick
48. Separated
53. Saudi Arabian export
54. Frozen water
55. Nut used in a pie
56. Attempt
57. Connected with
58. Cleaned (a floor)

DOWN

1. Ocean
2. Dog's "hand"
3. Historic period
4. Moose's relative
5. Changed the color of
6. Threw, as a football
7. Similar
8. External part of the mouth
9. Grassy area in front of a home
10. Beasts of burden
11. Rose of baseball
19. Second-hand, as a car
20. China's continent
21. Location
22. Scent
23. Main entryway
25. Urgent request
27. Popular houseplant
29. Got older
30. Intense anger
31. Winter-weather forecast
33. Guided walk
34. Stir up
36. Bluish-purple hue
39. A couple of times
41. Small opening
42. Animal's den
43. Not pleasing to the eye
45. Drains of energy
47. Intention
49. Church bench
50. Highest card
51. Sharp knock
52. High explosive: abbr.

187

ACROSS

1. Destiny
5. Act the tailor
8. Undermines; weakens
12. Tall tales
13. Nautical "yes"
14. Applaud
15. Summer fruit drinks
16. Word after "hair" or "safety"
17. Steak order
18. Ones who pay 46-Down
20. Dug, as for gold
21. Affirmative vote
22. Narrow mountain pass
23. Not true
26. Restaurant employees
30. In the past
31. Live (at)
33. Sticky substance
34. Answered in writing
36. Makes a cat's sound
38. "The two shall become ____"
39. Writer's tool
40. Object
43. Less rough
47. Lend a ____, help
48. A Gershwin
49. Talk wildly
50. Female voice range
51. Physician: slang
52. Tie (the score)
53. Lunch time, for many
54. Be in debt to
55. Direction of a sunrise

DOWN

1. Motorist's bane
2. Teacher's assistant
3. Adolescent
4. School writing assignments
5. Jolly old Claus
6. Where contact lenses are worn
7. Sodden
8. Source of actors' lines
9. TV's Alda
10. Peel (an apple)
11. Exceeded the limit
19. With a lack
20. Some letter carriers
22. Lass
23. Distant
24. Mature
25. Do a tree surgeon's job
26. Take a spouse
27. Freudian subject
28. Line, as of seats
29. Distress call
32. Extremely little
35. Capital of England
37. Main course
39. What doves symbolize
40. More ____ enough
41. Angelic ring of light
42. Division word
43. Become bigger
44. Molten rock
45. Preholiday nights
46. Money to a landlady
48. Wedding words

188

ACROSS

1. Word after "welcome" or "bath"
4. Silly fight
8. Shut with force
12. Female sheep
13. Hand's "hello"
14. Walking speed
15. In adolescence
17. Points (a camera)
18. Ready for customers
19. Allies oneself (with)
20. Venomous serpents
23. Above
25. Part to play
26. Shed a ——, cry
27. Make clothing
30. Less distant
32. Take off
34. "In what way?"
35. Female relative
37. Had debts
38. Cedar or oak
39. Rustic hotels
40. Simply horrible
43. Phrases exchanged by brides and grooms
46. Horse's strap
47. Building custodians
51. Nothing more than
52. Adam's paradise
53. Anonymous John
54. Made tracks
55. Job to be done
56. Tint

DOWN

1. Came face to face with
2. Reverence
3. Golf peg
4. Trade one thing for another
5. Leaf of a book
6. Gracious thoroughfare
7. Danson of TV
8. Barcelona's location
9. Put down (carpet)
10. Summit
11. Disorderly jumble
16. Face parts
19. Aching
20. Bridge curve
21. Composition for one
22. Farm furrower
24. Fraction of a whole
26. Real; actual
27. Planted, as seeds
28. Level, as land
29. Unites in holy matrimony
31. British nobleman
33. Damp
36. California neighbor
38. Adjusted the pitch of
40. Body limbs
41. Weep aloud
42. Destructive burning
44. Individuals
45. Bat (an eye)
47. Word before "set" or "black"
48. Unconventional
49. Cowboy Rogers
50. Visualize

189

ACROSS

1. Egyptian waterway
5. Snake found near the 1-Across
8. Celestial object
12. Press, as clothes
13. Honey-making insect
14. ____ express, early mail system
15. Is unable to
16. All the people
18. Leg "hinge"
19. Notable time
20. Sound from the pride
23. Cereal grain
28. Billboard messages
31. Became a blonde, perhaps
33. Not in use
34. Make up one's mind
36. Confesses
38. Letter opener?
39. Painful spot
41. Wee child
42. Mist, as from an atomizer
44. Tenant's payment
46. "Eureka!"
48. Jungle creatures
52. Hones, as a pencil
57. Lose brightness
58. The Hawkeye State
59. Long ____, dating back many years
60. Costing nothing
61. Chick's cry
62. Inky implement
63. Strong desires

DOWN

1. Shaving mishap
2. Persia, today
3. Unescorted
4. Go into
5. Mr. Lincoln, familiarly
6. Harsh
7. Social equal
8. CIA agent
9. "____ much of a good thing"
10. Columnist Landers
11. Pastrami partner
17. Uncooked
21. Peculiar
22. Nautical "yeses"
24. That boy
25. Revise (copy)
26. Vocal range
27. School exam
28. Tacks on
29. Hardly shallow
30. Wound memento
32. Be bold
35. Gershwin brother
37. Wolf's home
40. Round citrus fruit
43. Puppy's bark
45. Stretchable candy
47. Mound
49. Remove a rind
50. Idyllic spot
51. Observes
52. Take small swallows
53. Garden tool
54. Fearful wonder
55. Sharp blow
56. Abel, to Adam

190

ACROSS

1. Amend (copy)
5. Sauce for chips
8. Opposite of fast
12. Lacking refinement
13. Poetic tribute
14. Feel concern
15. Freed
17. Matured, as wine
18. Cunning
19. One who governs
21. Classified notices
22. Producing (eggs)
26. Beijing's country
29. After-taxes take
30. Digit that may be stubbed
31. Palm site
32. Pea container
33. Slight surface depression
34. Museum display
35. Jolson and Gore
36. Multiplied by
37. Folks
39. Beatles song, "____ Loves You"
40. Nome's state
42. Pat lightly
45. Emulates De Niro
48. Packed bag
50. Chimney deposit
51. Be human?
52. Peaks in Switzerland
53. Domicile
54. Go down, as the sun
55. Break from work

DOWN

1. Goes awry
2. One-on-one combat
3. In a casual way
4. Caddy gadget
5. Prescribed amounts
6. Mental construct
7. Sold door to door
8. Frightening
9. Drop behind
10. Mine find
11. Join in holy matrimony
16. Actor Robert or Alan
20. Feed oneself
21. Furthermore
23. List article
24. Zero
25. Receives
26. Fellow
27. Jack rabbit
28. Enthralled by
29. Negative replies
32. Is agreeable to
33. Gambling cube
35. Bar none
36. Which
38. School adhesive
39. Women's suit part
41. Unshakably confident
42. "A ____ of Two Cities"
43. Egyptian cobras
44. Annoying person
45. Cigar residue
46. Pigeon's cry
47. ____, Dick, or Harry
49. Automobile

191

ACROSS

1. Glacier material
4. Museum display
7. Leaky-faucet sounds
12. Neither's partner
13. Bring civil action against
14. Cowboy contest
15. Less quiet
17. Oscar or Tony
18. Velocity
19. Road-trip guide
21. Soaking
23. Jumped dramatically
28. Upper limb
31. Mineral wealth
33. Flounder's cousin
34. Distribute (cards)
36. Belonging to us
37. Garden watering tube
38. Challenge
39. Blasting compound: abbr.
40. Fiery color
41. Covering for a 28-Across
43. Calculating
46. Unusual
48. Shouts
52. Soda sipper
56. First
58. A couple of times
59. Fellow
60. "____ Maria," hymn
61. Sing, Swiss style
62. Nest find
63. Seeing red

DOWN

1. Country hotels
2. Henhouse
3. New York canal
4. Out of the way
5. Regret
6. Semester, for one
7. Lay a cloth over
8. Propel a dinghy
9. Actress Lupino
10. For each
11. Turf
16. Use needle and thread
20. Warns
22. Blew (a horn)
24. Fire residue
25. Needy
26. Otherwise
27. Accomplishment
28. Totals (up)
29. Genuine
30. Female horse
32. Operate
35. Robert E. ____
42. A, E, I, O, or U
44. Telling fibs
45. However
47. Ten-cent piece
49. Neeson of Hollywood
50. Volcano output
51. Winter coaster
52. Pigpen
53. A couple
54. Free (of)
55. Fighter pilot
57. Pester

192

ACROSS

1. Money on hand
5. Grass moisture
8. "Whoa!"
12. Irritate
13. Volcano residue
14. Public vehicle
15. Creation-story garden
16. Glide down a snow-covered slope
17. Last word in a prayer
18. Tiny
19. Leg part
20. Fellow
21. Vessel for frying
23. No more than
25. Out of the way
27. Keats poem
28. Lie
31. Kayak's kin
32. Tote
34. Diner breakfast order
35. ____ Code, postman's concern
38. Similar
39. Actor Hackman
40. Fall behind
41. Sage
44. Make well
46. Possesses
49. Wishful expectation
50. Mountain in Switzerland
51. Skin irritation
52. Is indebted
53. Civil War general
54. Infamous Roman ruler
55. Created
56. Asner and McMahon
57. On bended ____, humbly

DOWN

1. Boat's personnel
2. Military assistant
3. Catching some z's
4. Rooster's mate
5. Run swiftly
6. Northern native
7. Complained childishly
8. Playhouse platform
9. Domesticate, as an animal
10. Wagon-pulling animals
11. Two-cup measure
19. Hay-fever symptom
22. Bother
24. Bring to mind
25. Honored pilot
26. Go limp
28. Scare
29. Provoke
30. "So long!"
33. In the style of: 2 wds.
36. Take a breath
37. Prepared (a banana) for eating
39. Birds that honk
41. "To ____ it may concern"
42. Des Moines' state
43. Drove too fast
45. Large primates
47. Land measure
48. Foot protection
51. Pen liquid

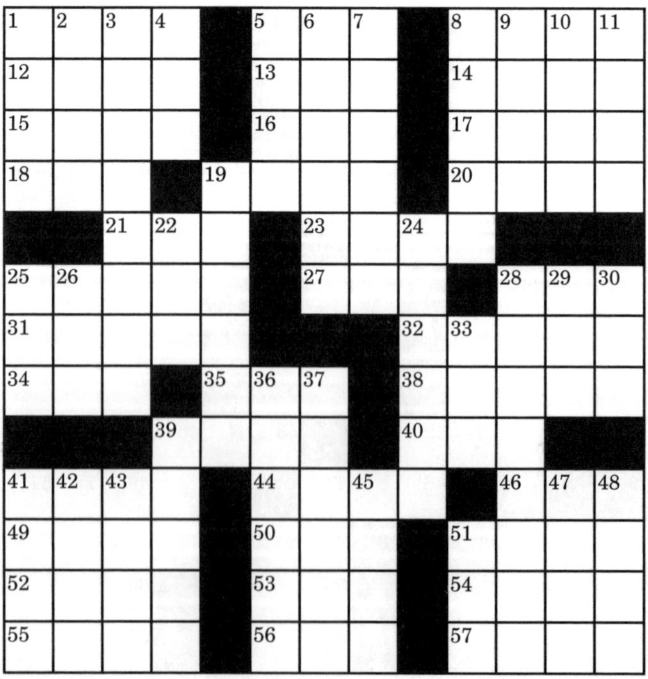

193

ACROSS

1. Official sign (of approval)
5. Tub activity
9. Sibling to a sis, for short
12. Out of action
13. Michigan neighbor
14. Free (of)
15. Moreno of "West Side Story"
16. Knitter's raw material
17. "Much ____ About Nothing"
18. Cooks' appliances
20. More spookily weird
22. Every
24. Japanese monetary unit
25. Exclude
28. Highway
30. Clock face
33. Tavern brew
34. Entices
36. Actress Arden
37. Stare open-mouthed
39. Camp shelter
40. Wharf rodent
41. Little, magical being
43. Adult male deer
45. Adders and boas
48. Tall flowers
52. Humble home
53. Skiers' mecca
55. Folk customs
56. Lofty poem
57. Separate (laundry)
58. Reclined
59. Married
60. Pairs
61. Made tracks

DOWN

1. Old business-letter greeting
2. Blue-pencil
3. Choir voice
4. Furlough
5. "Thrifty, reverent, and clean" one: 2 wds.
6. "So that's your game!"
7. Rubber wheel covering
8. Sweetheart
9. Having more intelligence
10. Go for a gallop
11. Unpleasant smell
19. Nobleman below a marquess
21. Stoplight color
23. Rabbits' relatives
25. Sack for groceries
26. In the style of: 2 wds.
27. Said over again
29. Tooth doctors
31. Glamour-girl Gardner
32. Give permission to
35. Box-office draw
38. Mooselike animal
42. Rich, elaborate meal
44. Fish features
45. Exhibit
46. Undressed
47. Taking a long time
49. Dirt fighter
50. A New York canal
51. Post (mail)
54. Expert

194

ACROSS

1. Tears open
5. Play (a horn)
9. Small sample
12. Spoken
13. Discourteous
14. Fuss and bother
15. Walk in shallow water
16. Secondhand
17. Hot or iced beverage
18. Morse-code signal
20. Possesses
21. _____ for the course
24. At that time
26. Annoying one
27. Precise
29. Pinkish red
31. Fix
33. Not as arid
37. Sing like Ella Fitzgerald
39. Make cloth on a loom
40. Word after "guest" or "shopping"
43. Hollow cylinder
45. Naughty
46. Aardvark tidbit
47. Without clothes
49. Wedding words
50. The thing here
52. In addition
56. Brazilian city, for short
57. Parent's sister
58. Far from imaginary
59. Unhappy
60. Wooden pins
61. Give on credit

DOWN

1. Line (of seats)
2. Lyricist Gershwin
3. Writing tablet
4. Snow-coasting vehicle
5. Smooth (hair)
6. More luxuriant
7. Poetic tribute
8. Tie the knot
9. Use the tub
10. Notions
11. Breakfast bread
19. Housetop room
21. According to
22. Wood chopper
23. Knock (on a door)
25. In the present
26. Folk-singer Seeger
28. Throw (a net)
30. Joined with stitches
32. Unsavory rodent
34. Small flap on a file
35. Certain Gabor
36. Stoplight hue
38. Adjusting (a radio)
40. Dragons' homes
41. Gandhi's land
42. Got to one's feet
44. Bursts or breaks
48. James _____ Jones, actor
50. Touch (on the shoulder)
51. Coloration
53. Civil War general
54. _____ Francisco
55. Far from new

195

ACROSS

1. Frost (a cake)
4. Repeated sound
8. "Out, feline!"
12. 24-hour period
13. Soared
14. Will beneficiary
15. Unrefined metal
16. Blaze
17. Just
18. Student's exercises
20. Guest 53-Across, often
21. Museum display
22. Bread store
25. Publish
28. Distant
29. Regret
30. Endless
31. Coal box
32. Relay a message
33. Likely
34. Wane's opposite
35. Alpine call
36. Required
38. Morning moisture
39. Chest bone
40. Venerable matriarch
44. Summer coolers
46. Fibbing one
47. Small floor covering
48. From ____ till dawn
49. Morally depraved
50. Pub quaff
51. Small specks
52. Refute
53. Sleeping site

DOWN

1. Object of worship
2. Handle with ____
3. Seeing organs
4. Exertion
5. Mr. Eastwood
6. That girl's
7. Have debts
8. Rattled
9. Balanced
10. Be sick
11. Attempt
19. Performed an aria
20. Automobile
22. Bar
23. Regulation
24. Shout
25. Method of proceeding
26. Thick string
27. Attention
28. Repair
31. Naughty, as a child
32. Small city
34. Charlotte's home
35. Annual
37. Flat, circular objects
38. Sewage pipe
40. Donate
41. Dull
42. "Stubborn" animal
43. Matured
44. Total (up)
45. Sonny and Cher were one
46. Showed the way

196

ACROSS

1. Free (of)
4. Identical
8. Use a dagger
12. Lyric poem
13. Pottery material
14. Bridge fee
15. ____ Angeles, California
16. Fixed amount
17. Car
18. Inventor Whitney
19. Social insect
20. Feathered shaft
21. Outer edge
23. Stately tree
25. Rotate
27. A Great Lake
28. Taxi
31. Made a pig's sound
33. Complete
35. Plead
36. Competes
38. "____ upon a time . . ."
39. "____ a Wonderful Life," film
40. Cozy room
41. Tiny
45. Pool stick
47. Feel sick
50. Singer Horne
51. Legal suit
52. Cow's cry
53. Crafts' partner
54. Imitated
55. Possess
56. Golf pegs
57. Danson and Koppel
58. Old horse

DOWN

1. Actor's part
2. Worshiped one
3. Wanting
4. "Shoo!": slang
5. TV's Alda
6. Concern
7. Seeing organ
8. Night-sky twinkler
9. Sight-seeing trip
10. Low female voice
11. Boxing punch
20. Prayer ending
22. Pen liquid
24. Untruths
25. Weep uncontrol-lably
26. Crusted dessert
27. Revise (copy)
28. Baking spice
29. Circle part
30. Hive dweller
32. Morally depraved
34. Foot digit
37. Flee
40. Heroic acts
41. Narrow strip
42. Only
43. Poker stake
44. Young woman
46. Second-hand
48. The Hawkeye State
49. Far from short
51. Feline

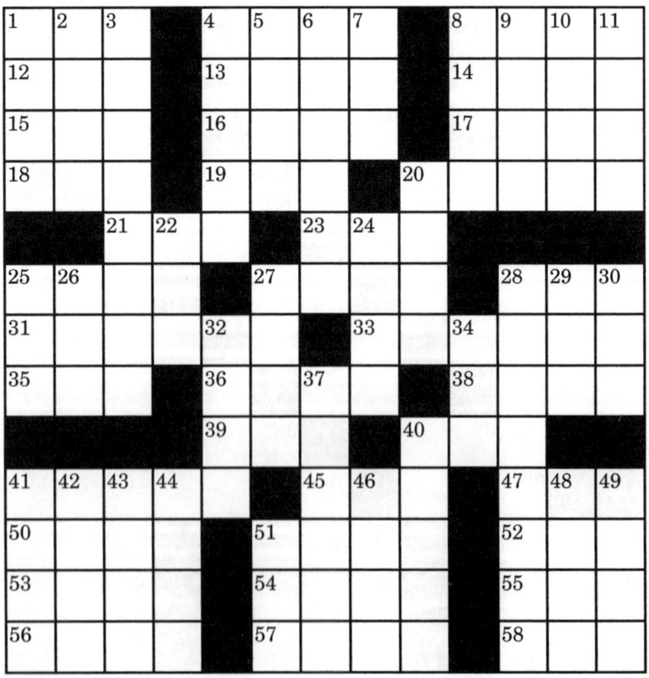

197

ACROSS

1. Clothing labels
5. Hot spring
8. Graceful, white waterfowl
12. Strong cattle
13. Everything
14. Factual
15. With 41-Down, controversial first baseman
16. Parking area
17. Lease
18. Thrill
20. Picnic pests
21. Filled with sudden wonder
24. ". . . and pretty maids all in a ____"
26. Eats in style
27. "Psst!"
28. Passing fashion
31. Long-lived
32. Toboggans, for instance
34. Some
35. Heavens
36. Play it by ____, improvise
37. Packing string
39. Last bit
40. Dreaded
41. Ms. Hayworth
44. Entranceways
46. Lyrical poems
47. Make a blunder
48. Detest
52. Painfully tender
53. City rodent
54. Morally depraved
55. Lawn trees
56. Crafty
57. Display stand

DOWN

1. Highest point
2. Woodshed tool
3. Obtain
4. Common cold symptom
5. Dieter's dish
6. Conspirators' plan
7. Changed
8. Drinking tube
9. Small, brown songbird
10. Mother's sister
11. New Jersey basketball team
19. Diminish
21. Unnecessary fusses
22. Dairy beverage
23. "60 Minutes" commentator Rooney
25. Pearl-bearing shell
27. That girl's
28. County or state exhibition
29. "____ of Green Gables"
30. Colored (one's hair)
33. Portable stairs
38. Laundry machine
39. Relieves, as pain
40. Number of days and nights it rained on Noah
41. See 15-Across
42. Worshiped one
43. School-year division
45. Of the mouth
49. Filmdom's Gardner
50. Muscle twitch
51. Moose kin

198

ACROSS

1. Pieces; sections
6. Dust cloth
9. Mewing creature
12. On the subject of
13. Famous inventor Whitney
14. Volcanic powder
15. Windowsill, for one
16. Against, in a debate
17. Struggle (for)
18. Once in a blue ____
20. Line of stitches
21. Sprite
24. Sleeping vision
26. Dove's murmur
27. Seed container
28. Construct
32. Ship's anchoring spot
34. Thermometer marking
35. More strange
36. Lubricate
37. Tap-dancer Miller
38. A single step
40. Singer King Cole
41. Color
44. Hill insects
46. Fruit drink
47. Boat in the Flood
48. Oyster's prize
53. Vegetable from a 27-Across
54. Great sadness or misery
55. Have a disagreement
56. Hearing organ
57. Finale
58. Current style

DOWN

1. Buddy
2. Nickname for President Lincoln
3. Fishing pole
4. Sudden pull
5. Plant support
6. Use the VCR
7. Unattended
8. Card game
9. Mountain den
10. Pakistan's locale
11. "Let ____ eat cake!"
19. Foul smell
20. Self-satisfied
21. Canyon effect
22. Fill with cargo
23. President Gerald
25. Cain's bro
27. Opposite of starboard
29. Rug-exporting nation
30. Horne of song
31. Fender crease
33. Superior to all others
34. Mud ingredient
36. Made a pig sound
39. Brother of Moses
41. Finish-line strip
42. "I've got a brilliant ____!"
43. Almost
45. Squabble
47. Thunderstruck feeling
49. Go wrong
50. Grow old
51. Sprint
52. Showed (the way)

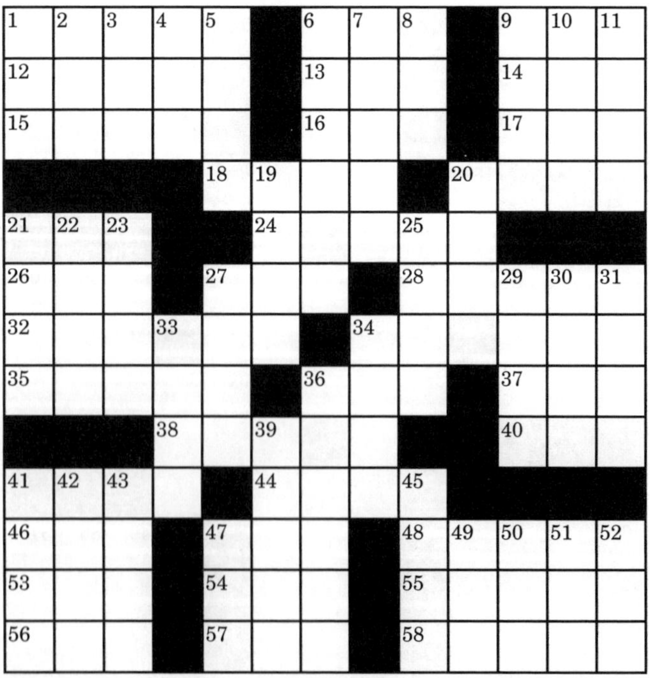

199

ACROSS

1. Settle the bill
4. Not hilly at all
8. Injure with a dagger
12. Brewery product
13. Fully mature, as fruit
14. Spouse to 1-Down
15. Skillet
16. Start a kitty
17. Plow-pulling beasts
18. Have preconceptions
20. Getting older
21. Far from tough
24. Revises, as text
27. Observed
32. Entice; tempt
33. Wager
34. Be in possession of
35. Scared
37. Mature female people
38. In dreamland
40. Fork's partner
44. TV dog
48. Home's grassy expanse
49. Fellow
51. Gift for a child
52. "The Graduate" actress Bancroft
53. Car
54. Worshipful dread
55. Sloppy condition
56. Adult-to-be
57. Vaporous element

DOWN

1. Father
2. "Woe is me!"
3. Strong longings
4. Picture holders
5. Cloth made from flax
6. Liable (to)
7. Golf-ball holder
8. Polluted air
9. "____ Driver," De Niro classic
10. Reply in church
11. Sudden, loud noise
19. Speak
20. Gallery offering
22. Reside (in)
23. Consume food
24. Small, magical being
25. Slated to arrive
26. One of the Gershwins
28. Cuts of lamb, perhaps
29. Sandwich meat
30. Genesis woman
31. Animal lair
33. City vehicle
36. Devotee of a sport
37. Spear or sword
39. Make very happy
40. Bang (the door)
41. Window section
42. Has
43. Small bills
45. Male with antlers
46. Corn Belt state
47. Potato buds
49. Feline companion
50. Tint

200

ACROSS

1. Unengaged
5. Tic-toe bond
8. Impersonated
12. Bright light-gas
13. Tire filler
14. Peace-promoting person
15. Bakery purchase
16. Sneaky
17. Reached (a conclusion)
18. Least new
20. Adder's relative
21. Features of many poems
24. Lubricating liquid
27. "Use your common ____!"
30. Vex
31. Lyricist Gershwin
32. Mineral wealth
33. Mortal conflict
34. ____ Diego
35. Trucker's vehicle
36. Shorten (a skirt)
37. Bolster the economy, in a way
39. Oolong or pekoe
40. Magazine employee
42. Paving goo
44. Living creature
48. Dry as dust
50. Crate's kin
52. Attend
53. Mount Etna's output
54. Summer thirst quencher
55. Equally matched
56. Beanstalk, basically
57. Autumn-leaf color
58. Dispatch; mail

DOWN

1. Common preposition
2. Business transaction
3. English nobleman
4. Walks onstage
5. Delicious
6. Be under the weather
7. Weep
8. Finds the sum of
9. Ocean frolicker
10. Preholiday night
11. Drops on a dawn lawn
19. That filly
20. Inquire
22. Florida city
23. Be mistaken
25. Tehran's locale
26. "____ ho!," crow's-nest cry
27. Divide (laundry)
28. Pennsylvania port
29. Looking on the bleak side
33. Tie the knot
36. See 19-Down
37. Baby boy, to Daddy
38. Smart shoppers compare them
41. Did the work of the IRS
43. First man
45. "Get going!"
46. "So be it!"
47. Give temporarily
48. Gore and Jolson
49. Urban rodent
50. Metal rod
51. Poem of praise

201

ACROSS

1. Round, green veggie
4. Shaker's contents
8. Rotated
12. High mountain in Switzerland
13. Mr. Alda
14. Dracula's cloak
15. Most diminutive
17. Civil uprising
18. Dumbo's "wings"
19. Leafy forest plants
20. Actor Redford
23. View
24. Foe
25. Debuting, as a movie
29. Perform on Broadway
30. Actress Lupino
31. Boot point
32. Answer
35. _____ of drawers
37. Certain lodge member
38. Bells rung by the wind
39. Carrying a weapon
42. Sound of pain
43. Hammer target
44. Building custodians
48. Four plus five
49. Prayer ender
50. Couple
51. Vehicle pulled by huskies
52. Large-mouth fish
53. Conclusion

DOWN

1. Chum
2. Inventor Whitney
3. Inclined (to)
4. Regular pay
5. Vigilant
6. Scottish girl
7. An explosive: abbr.
8. Wire window-mesh
9. Matched set of socks
10. Atop
11. Trawlers' traps
16. Swarm (with)
19. Service charge
20. Area in back
21. Single time
22. Makes a wager
23. Place for a massage
25. Highly unusual
26. Article on a list
27. Eyeglasses perch
28. Receives
30. Pen's fluid
33. Took off the rind
34. Like an antique
35. Winter tire-attachments
36. Helpful suggestion
38. Ice-cream holders
39. Landers and Jillian
40. Fence bar
41. Coal source
42. Papa's mate
44. Poke with a finger
45. Elaborate poem
46. Operate (a machine)
47. Piece of turf

202

ACROSS

1. Attention-getting word
4. Boast
8. Masticate
12. "____ Maria"
13. Molten rock
14. Go by car
15. Brief communications
17. Impel
18. Prayer ending
19. Ooze (out)
20. By oneself
23. Fixed amount
26. Gave temporarily
27. 36-Across, to a horse
28. Mature
31. King's residence
33. Made of oak or pine
35. Wild, blue yonder
36. Cereal grains
38. Magician's scepter
39. The two
40. Small, silvery coins
41. Lowest female voice
44. Wet forecast
46. Glide, as an eagle
47. Least old
51. Prod
52. Actress Bancroft
53. "Golly!"
54. Moved quickly
55. Beloved animals
56. Possess

DOWN

1. Easter meat
2. Night before a holiday
3. "Absolutely!"
4. Find fault with
5. Fury
6. Broad thoroughfare
7. Car fuel
8. Pie top
9. Employ
10. Outer part
11. Sob uncontrollably
16. Mr. Claus
20. Swiss peaks
21. Faucet problem
22. Just
24. Current information
25. Marriage reply: 2 wds.
27. Accomplishment
28. Eden resident
29. Hereditary component
30. Finishes
32. Dove's sound
34. Being in debt
37. Chair in a 31-Across's main hall
39. Drilled (a hole)
40. Has supper
41. Egyptian snakes
42. Ring-shaped object
43. Seize
45. Uncle's wife
47. Shrill bark
48. Self
49. Use a needle and thread
50. One plus nine

203

ACROSS

1. Watering tube
5. Curved doorway
9. Pull along behind
12. Wicked
13. Foot protection
14. Keats poem
15. God of war
16. Medicine tablet
17. Floor-washing tool
18. Icy weather
20. Brief sleep
21. Museum exhibit
22. Freudian self
24. Used a chair
26. Moral failing
29. Final
31. Des Moines' state
34. Hiking paths
36. In dreamland
38. 36-inch unit
39. Attack with the beak
41. TV receiver
42. Cowboy Rogers
44. Hit the slopes
45. Healthful retreat
47. Moose kin
49. Made docile
54. Sizzling
55. 57-Across, to bears
57. Hillside hollow
58. Individual
59. Green citrus fruit
60. Forest growth
61. Strange
62. Superior person
63. Transmit

DOWN

1. Finishes (pants)
2. Egg-shaped
3. Kingly address
4. Otherwise
5. Venomous snake
6. "Armored" African beasts
7. Soda option
8. Gives a hand to
9. Spaghetti-sauce fruits
10. Strong smell
11. Shed tears
19. Tattle (on)
23. Shocked inhalation
25. Be sick
26. Farm enclosure
27. Lyricist Gershwin
28. Spun (a yarn)
30. Bulletin-board pin
32. Little
33. Liable (to)
35. Words at the altar
37. Short, comic play
40. Igloo builder
43. Shouts
45. "Beat it!"
46. Lake's smaller cousin
48. Reclined
50. Performs in a film
51. Stallion's mate
52. Neck and neck
53. Accomplishment
56. Confederate soldier, for short

204

ACROSS

1. Quiche base
5. High card
8. Adult male deer
12. Be bold
13. Candle material
14. Bedtime story, maybe
15. Neck and neck
16. Swiss peak
17. Hard-working cattle
18. 11 o'clock report
19. Unhealthy
20. Ascend, as the sun
21. Break a fast
23. Interrogate
25. Rock singer Ronstadt
28. Use a straw
29. "Long ____ and Far Away"
32. Actress Lupino
33. Horn-nosed beast
35. Bench in a house of worship
36. Child's plaything
37. Possessive pronoun
38. Some do this when they pray
40. Country hotel
41. Saltwater expanse
42. Mouth parts
45. A couple
47. Nudge into action
51. Fruit coolers
52. Important time
53. Mama's partner
54. List at a restaurant
55. Knock sharply
56. At any time
57. Bottom
58. Watch secretly (with "on")
59. Fender impression

DOWN

1. Bible garden
2. Donated
3. Sprouted (up)
4. Felt
5. Be in store for
6. Contact by phone
7. Make clear (to)
8. Baby bringer?
9. Cab
10. Pub brews
11. Hereditary unit
22. Brother of Moses
24. Uttered
25. Illuminated
26. Marriage-vow words
27. Negative vote
28. Title for a gentleman
29. Humanlike animal
30. "Oh, my!"
31. Night-hunting bird
34. Those who shoot deer
39. Took a snooze
40. Magazine edition
41. Full of suds
42. Gentle as a ____
43. Notion
44. Writing tools
46. Envelop
48. Talk deliriously
49. Opposite of closed
50. Missile for a pub game

205

ACROSS

1. Roasting stick
5. Small, poisonous snake
8. Halt
12. Low female voice
13. Pod vegetable
14. Rabbit's relative
15. Sidelong look
16. More succulent, as meat
18. One who domesticates animals
20. Ocean
21. In the style of: 2 wds.
23. Shower alternatives
28. Used a shovel
31. Des Moines' place
33. Fishing spool
34. Short, purposeful journey
36. Photographer's device
38. Got older
39. Work for money
41. "To be or ____ to be . . ."
42. More recent
44. Fido or Fluffy
45. Swiss peak
47. Strike forcefully
52. Spaghetti sauce ingredients
57. Sound repetition
58. Scent
59. Knock sharply
60. The Buckeye State
61. Cried
62. Arid
63. Proceeded

DOWN

1. Sodium chloride
2. Urgent request
3. News bit
4. Ripped apart
5. Likely (to)
6. Teeter-totter
7. Window glass
8. Feminine pronoun
9. Black goo
10. Miner's find
11. Miles ____ hour
17. Pat lightly
19. Droplets from the sky
22. Abundant source of 10-Down
24. Upper-body limb
25. Adolescent
26. Deli sandwich
27. Wooden board
28. College VIP
29. Egg on
30. Got larger
32. Land unit
35. Lemon drink
37. Picnic pests
40. Come into view
43. Mouse relative
46. British nobleman
48. Cat's noise
49. Dull pain
50. Front part of the lower leg
51. Owl's sound
52. Pull (a car)
53. Lyrical poem
54. Floor-cleaning tool
55. Human creativity
56. Secret agent

206

ACROSS

1. Flower of love
5. Skirt's border
8. Barbecue rod
12. Notion
13. Filmdom's Gardner
14. Shredded
15. Wobbled
17. TV's Thicke
18. Inquire
19. Japanese currency
20. Certain golf clubs
21. Tried out
23. Even-handed
26. The 49th state
31. Counsel
34. Gave back
35. Less shallow
36. Finishes
37. Flavors
41. Stinging insects
45. Close friend
46. Bar bill
49. Division word
50. Nail-salon treatment
52. Barber-shop sound
53. Noah's vessel
54. Start a poker pot
55. Towel designation
56. Affirmative reply
57. Remainder

DOWN

1. Ms. Moreno
2. Lyric poems
3. Look for
4. Devour
5. Relatives of rabbits
6. Happening
7. Angry
8. Be a headliner
9. Game played on horseback
10. Persia, now
11. Hamilton bills
16. Vision organ
20. Unengaged
21. Journey
22. Corn unit
23. Temporary trend
24. Fruit drink
25. "____ been thinking..."
27. Gorillas and chimps
28. ____ Diego, California
29. Baby goat
30. Billboard postings
32. Hardens, as cement
33. Definitive time period
38. Extra
39. Army vehicles
40. Inventor Whitney
41. Heart's desire
42. Movie star Bancroft
43. Mix with a spoon
44. Makes a cork's sound
46. Melody
47. Crafts' partner
48. Sweet, red veggie
50. "Merry" month
51. Automobile

207

ACROSS

1. "All's Well That ____ Well"
5. Shop-door sign
9. Easily-shaped metal
12. Violent protest
13. Half of ten
14. Mining yield
15. Common skin disorder
16. At liberty
17. Cow's sound
18. Leak (out) slowly
19. Plus
20. Landers or Miller
21. Bagpipe player, perhaps
24. Occupied a pew
26. Parking section
29. A son of Eve
31. Pieces of fireplace wood
34. France's continent
36. Dozing
38. Emulate an artist
39. Tug at sharply
41. Pig's residence
42. Not healthy
44. Hawaiian necklaces
46. Cooking utensil
48. Exclamation of triumph
50. Brief snoozes
54. Frothy brew
55. Crush (potatoes)
57. Farmland measure
58. Apply, as knowledge
59. Lance Armstrong's "steed"
60. Munch
61. ____ Angeles, California
62. Shut violently, as a door
63. Car starters

DOWN

1. Historic ages
2. Friendly; pleasant
3. Completed
4. Dance moves
5. Switch position
6. Buccaneer
7. On the same level
8. Requirements
9. Summer garden fruits
10. Nutritious mineral
11. Gas in signs
22. Beret or beanie
23. Heed, as orders
25. None's opposite
26. Showed the way
27. Belonging to us
28. Apprentices
30. Rural road
32. Obtain
33. Secret agent
35. Hooting bird
37. Snow runner
40. Largest U.S. state
43. Ewes' offspring
45. Between-meals bite
46. Actor Newman
47. Furthermore
49. "____, Caesar!"
51. Feel sore
52. Mouse, to a 35-Down
53. Mends (clothing)
56. Skirt edge

208

ACROSS

1. Revise (text)
5. Small swallows
9. Deed
12. Bit of dialogue
13. Mare's young
14. Produce (eggs)
15. Wrestling pads
16. The one that got ____
17. Egyptian cobra
18. Coin-bank opening
19. Light beam
20. Poker stake
21. Magical forest-dweller
23. Cease
25. Baseball-card transaction
28. Catholic clergymen
32. Yours and mine
33. Got up
35. Missile for the Three Stooges
36. Signed up for (a race)
38. Hoisting device
40. Ms. Landers
41. Spelling contest
42. Practice boxing
45. One of Zsa Zsa's sisters
47. Aardvark's treats
51. Limo, for one
52. Victor's words
53. Trim (away)
54. Point (a rifle)
55. Plant pest
56. Level
57. Attempt (to)
58. Gamblers' chances
59. Colored (one's hair)

DOWN

1. Stately shade-givers
2. Clock face
3. Absorbed by
4. Tried out
5. Neck wrap
6. The Hawkeye State
7. Contestants
8. Pig's place
9. Alda of TV
10. List of performers
11. Use a keyboard
20. Summertime quencher
22. Gain knowledge
24. Brother's daughter
25. Boot point
26. Flow, as a river
27. Painter's creation
28. Pea case
29. Health resort
30. Toy-soldier material
31. Watch
34. Updated (a subscription)
37. Corn serving
39. Harvested, as wheat
41. Rock groups
42. "Begone!"
43. Couple
44. Military branch
46. Competed (for)
48. See 44-Down
49. Family ____, genealogical chart
50. Transmit
52. ____ Jima

209

ACROSS

1. Wagon's kin
5. Corn center
8. Too
12. Fragrance
13. Have bills to pay
14. Highway
15. Narrative account
16. Plus
17. Unwelcome bread-growth
18. Smudges
20. Ends with the same sound as
22. Draw on the skin
24. Narrow city street
27. "That's amazing!"
28. Dog's yelp
31. Fill with cargo
32. Edge; verge
33. Cold-cuts shop
34. Possessive pronoun
35. Tic-____-toe
36. Sumptuous meal
37. Certain female relatives
39. Bodies' midsections
43. Took (a message) to heart
47. Land measure
48. Wedding words
50. Rant's partner
51. Swig of whiskey
52. Neither's sidekick
53. Woody plant
54. Coop residents
55. Observe
56. Mail

DOWN

1. Folding beds
2. Abel's father
3. Part to play
4. Gave medical attention to
5. Shoreline
6. Possess
7. Sleeping chamber
8. Branch of the military
9. Weaving frame
10. Shopper's event
11. ____ and ends
19. Beam of light
21. "In what way?"
23. A couple of times
24. Boxer Muhammad
25. Building site
26. Vegas intro
28. Affirmative vote
29. Gore and Jolson
30. Quarry hole
32. Bran-cereal fruits
33. Arid environments
35. An explosive: abbr.
36. Doctor's charge
38. Task
39. Cleanse
40. Sore feeling
41. Remove wrinkles from
42. Puts silverware on (the table)
44. Be brave enough
45. Not odd
46. Scout's action
49. Female deer

210

ACROSS

1. Violin-tuning pins
5. Make stitches
8. Melt, as ice
12. Tehran's land
13. Ms. Gardner
14. Tramp
15. Relaxation
16. "____ sleeping dogs lie"
17. Part for an actor
18. Rub out
20. Lyric tributes
21. Flabbergasted
24. Steal from
26. Extend (a subscription)
27. That woman's
28. Common contraction
31. An explosive: abbr.
32. Out of the way
34. Cleaning cloth
35. Take to court
36. Curtain pole
37. Traveling (to)
39. Big fuss
40. "Wild ____ couldn't drag me away!"
41. Air pollution
44. Fashion
46. City conveyance
47. Female chicken
48. Bible garden
52. Prayer ending
53. Sound receiver
54. Reign over
55. Group of workers
56. Wipe (dishes)
57. Like rabbit fur

DOWN

1. Crusted dessert
2. Period in history
3. Car fuel
4. Cold symptom
5. Tossed greens
6. Preholiday nights
7. Tended houseplants, in a way
8. Beat, as a heart
9. Parka's head-covering
10. Skilled
11. Troubles
19. "Lost dog" poster word
21. Crafts' partner
22. Cafe's listing
23. Poker stake
25. Washington's neighbor
27. Kept out of sight
28. Eye's colored part
29. Weather ____, barn topper
30. Easter symbols
33. Comforted
38. Chooses from a 22-Down
39. Getting older
40. Inventor Ford
41. Deer with antlers
42. Papa's mate
43. Plow-pulling cattle
45. Back
49. Pair of performers
50. Sprite
51. Mesh snare

211

ACROSS

1. Model-building sets
5. With 52-Across, “M*A*S*H” star
9. Rainbow’s shape
12. A Great Lake
13. Traveled on Trigger
14. Campus cheer
15. Unit of heredity
16. Necessity
17. “____ got a crush on you . . .”
18. Emotional state
20. Briny deep
21. Mouse with wings?
24. Sailboat’s staff
26. Gracious man
27. Worship
29. Leaf-pickup tool
31. Say once again
33. New York football team
37. Break in two
39. Criminal
40. Wallop (a housefly)
43. Official military position
45. TV cowboy Rogers
46. Cry of surprise
47. One at the end of the line
49. Historic period
50. Shut (the door) loudly
52. See 5-Across
56. Noah’s craft
57. Walk to and fro
58. Close by
59. Seeded bread
60. Grew older
61. Clark ____, Superman’s alter ego

DOWN

1. Beer dispenser
2. Angry feeling
3. Foil metal
4. Appear
5. Knight’s “suit”
6. Cheer-leader’s demand?
7. Billboard messages
8. Tennis-court divider
9. Get up
10. Crow’s cousin
11. Swindle
19. Atlantic or Pacific
21. Soap unit
22. Summer drink
23. Spinning toy
25. Move, as a dog’s tail
26. Toothed wheel
28. Take a break
30. Soccer moves
32. Paving goo
34. Neither’s mate
35. As well
36. Blue expanse
38. Home for royalty
40. Take a vow
41. Mental stress
42. No longer sleeping
44. Given the title of
48. Auto’s gas container
50. Mineral spring
51. Hang back
53. Civil War leader
54. Rather of TV
55. Museum offering

212

ACROSS

1. A pronoun
4. List of actors in a movie
8. Crafts like Noah's
12. Play on words
13. Singing voice
14. Put in prison
15. "I have not ____ begun to fight"
16. Farm building
17. Poker payment
18. Horned safari beast
20. Vexed
21. Word before "letter" or "gang"
23. Young man
25. Telephone sound
26. Paste's cousin
27. Cut (the grass)
30. Pro with a bow
32. Original resident
34. Quilting event
35. Mob uprising
37. Change for a five
38. Rustic hotel
39. Darkroom product
40. Arrange in folds
44. Presses (shirts)
46. The Hawkeye State
47. Cook until bubbling
48. Bar bill
51. Quarrel
52. Film's Bancroft
53. Sight organ
54. Piano ivories
55. Inquires of
56. Tomato color

DOWN

1. Secret watcher
2. Shade
3. Exit's opposite
4. Log cottage
5. Mr. Alda
6. Walk leisurely
7. Coal weight
8. Partially open
9. Military status
10. Flying toy
11. Coasting vehicle
19. "Up above the world so ____ . . ."
20. Concept
21. Clawed crustacean
22. Put on the payroll
24. Uncle's spouse
26. Wide smile
27. Congregation head
28. Baking chamber
29. Direction of the sunset
31. Huron's neighbor
33. Ripped
36. Tear-inducing veggies
39. Vaulting sticks
40. Flat, round object
41. Snag (a steer)
42. Out of the office
43. Taps lightly
45. Skating site
47. Ewe's call
49. Positive vote
50. Sleep locale

213

ACROSS

1. Kids' summer getaway
5. Bit of evidence
9. Plead
12. Scent
13. Not doing much
14. Medieval weapon
15. Signal "hello"
16. Balance ____, gymnastics device
17. ____ Francisco
18. Make indistinct
20. Most excellent
22. Pool stick
24. Knife thrust
25. Every evening
29. Hits (a fly)
32. Flattering poem
33. Sports enthusiast
35. Great deal (of)
36. Cole Porter creations
39. Herbal garnish
42. Bugle "lullabye"
44. Candy alternative
45. Billfolds
48. Shaving mishaps
52. Color shade
53. Come close to
55. Bowling alley
56. Possessive pronoun
57. Pastrami palace
58. Not odd
59. Cooking vessel
60. Snow-day amusement
61. Property document

DOWN

1. Old MacDonald had some
2. Eden dweller
3. Get going
4. Deliver a sermon
5. Lie
6. Lemon drinks
7. Santa ____
8. Lures
9. Babe Ruth's sport
10. Test
11. Unit of heredity
19. Boring routine
21. Uncooked
23. Sprite
25. Negative replies
26. Words at the altar
27. Least harsh
28. Pet-store sound
30. Pedicure target
31. Farm enclosure
34. The old, gray mare, for one
37. Young lady
38. Uses (money)
40. Race, in a way
41. Wore a happy expression
43. The Man of ____, Superman
45. Buggy accessory
46. Japanese import, maybe
47. Retail transaction
49. Prehistoric art gallery?
50. Reflex test-site
51. Convey
54. Free (of)

214

ACROSS

1. Green fruit
5. Paper money
9. Cunning
12. Troubles
13. Pain
14. Confederate general
15. Swabs
16. Calf meat
17. Rural hotel
18. Polite word
20. Woolly creatures
22. Sweet potato
23. Cabin material
24. Talk softly
28. Cleaning substances
32. That woman
33. Scold constantly
35. Mouth part
36. Seer's signs
39. Restaurant plate garnish
42. Likely (to)
44. Fixed course
45. Earnest request
48. Patch of grassland
52. Jar cover
53. Short letter
55. Ore deposit
56. Mimic
57. Elevator button
58. 12/24 and 12/31
59. "Definitely!"
60. Stain
61. Relax

DOWN

1. Light producer
2. Worshiped object
3. Be gloomy
4. College papers
5. Prehistoric guys: 2 wds.
6. High card
7. "____ We Dance?," show tune
8. Happy greetings
9. Thin
10. Ms. Horne
11. Desires
19. Maple fluid
21. In the past
24. "Which person?"
25. Skirt border
26. Wrath
27. Knock sharply
29. Everyone
30. Crusted dessert
31. Secret agent
34. Shirt, for one
37. Senate refusal
38. Uses, as time
40. Regret
41. Less fresh
43. Army group
45. Child's activity
46. Mature
47. Cool drinks
49. Bird of peace
50. Lyric poems
51. Sunset direction
54. A couple

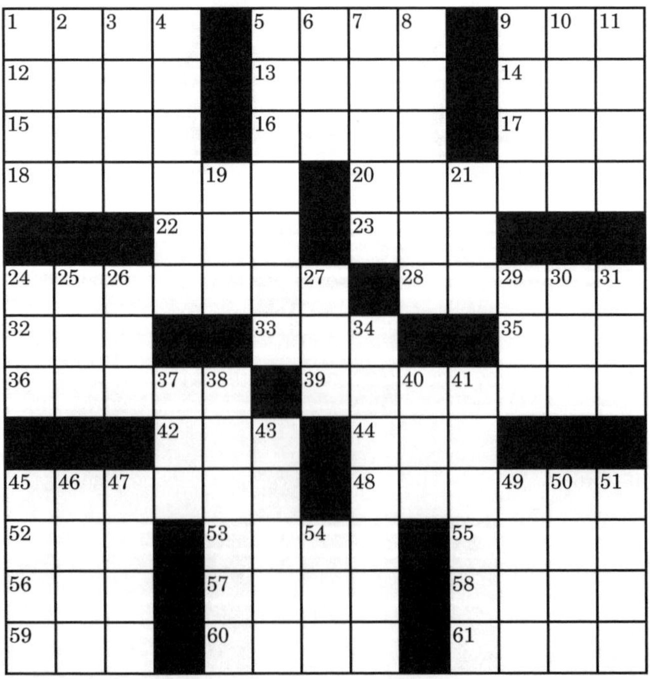

215

ACROSS

1. Moreno or Hayworth
5. Play the copycat
8. Air pollution
12. Like some exams
13. Lass
14. Pirate hangout
15. Tribal knowledge
16. Popular deli bread
17. Actor Alda
18. Main course
20. Wax light
24. Less plentiful
27. Energize, with "up"
28. That man's
31. Was in debt
32. Incon-solable
33. Driver's vehicle
34. Become a spouse
35. Distant
36. Printing machine
37. Costume
39. Takes along
43. Governs, as a monarch
47. School assistant
48. Snacked
50. Hit an oil patch
51. Play (a horn)
52. Mild excla-mation
53. Sandwich fish
54. Slippery swimmers
55. Bring to a conclusion
56. Glimpsed

DOWN

1. Part to play
2. Golf club
3. Small 36-Down
4. Sent a warning to
5. Give consent
6. Shell out money
7. Chosen by voters
8. Read quickly
9. Stale-bread growth
10. Not quite circular
11. Unit of inheritance
19. Commit a blunder
21. Cleopatra's serpent
23. Separately
24. Tier, as of seats
25. Gaping wonder
26. Lipstick shade
28. Color variant
29. "_____ a Wonderful Life"
30. Sailor's distress signal
32. Breakfast link
33. Picasso and Whistler
35. Heavy mist
36. Baked dessert
38. Given one's liberty
39. Talking-pig movie
40. Irritate
41. Object of devotion
42. Journalist's field
44. Certain stickum
45. The whole _____ yards
46. Extend across, as a bridge
49. Six plus four

216

ACROSS

1. Stone in Chinese jewelry
5. Sauna spot
8. Talk to God
12. Heed (a command)
13. Verbal rejections
14. Golfing goal
15. Far from selfish
17. Halloween birds
18. Like a fox, supposedly
19. Picasso or Warhol
21. Successful play
22. Digging tool
26. Make (a bike) go
29. Had some food
30. Lady of Eden
31. Historic time periods
32. That guy's
33. Bridle strap
34. Point (an arrow)
35. Amigo
36. Lassies
37. Fix; mend
39. Unhappy
40. Military decorations
42. "Viva ____ Vegas"
45. Brief note
48. Large mammal with a trunk
50. Not odd
51. Liquid that flows from a tree
52. Division word
53. Sharp taste
54. Blasting compound: abbr.
55. Chick's cry

DOWN

1. Runs for exercise
2. A son of 30-Across
3. Refuse to grant
4. Watch closely
5. Sound from an angry bull
6. Look sulky
7. Gives a hand to
8. Shutter-bug's snapshot
9. Line of chairs
10. "____ That Jazz"
11. "Indeed!"
16. Part of a fence
20. Woman's pronoun
21. Possesses
23. Swerve
24. Satanic
25. Telescope glass
26. Fall fruit
27. Lake by Buffalo
28. Slightly wet
29. Be sick
32. Most difficult
33. Free (of)
35. Filled pastry
36. Labor for breath
38. Sur-rounded by
39. Took a snooze
41. Hawkeye, on "M*A*S*H"
42. Rural route
43. Poker payment
44. Put on the brakes
45. Made the acquain-tance of
46. ____ Marie Saint, actress
47. Fellows
49. Mid-body joint

217

ACROSS

1. One with legal possession
6. Pas' mates
9. Cut (the lawn)
12. "In what place?"
13. Writing liquid
14. Pub brew
15. Less high
16. Mixed with a spoon
18. Not clean
20. Wet, as the weather
23. Sunrise direction
27. Write your name on
28. Ignited
31. A couple
32. Baking chamber
33. Lyric poem
34. Plant stalk
35. Sports enthusiast
36. Short sleep
37. Upper-leg joints
38. Singing voice
40. Vote into political office
42. Tel Aviv's land
46. Inflatable party decoration
49. Second U.S. President John
54. Have debts
55. Wrestler's pad
56. Portrait poser
57. Site for a 36-Across
58. McMahon and Asner
59. Terrible suffering

DOWN

1. Hooting bird
2. "Which person?"
3. Fresh
4. Before, to a bard
5. Televise again
6. Fine spray
7. Opposed to
8. Slip sideways
9. Disfigure
10. Spanish cheer
11. Marry
17. Deli bread
19. Hosiery material
20. Opponent
21. FBI employee
22. Rural hotel
24. Room under the roof
25. Used a broom
26. Male turkeys
27. Couch
29. Ms. Lupino
30. Indian dwelling
34. This woman
39. Lubricate
41. Woolly animal
43. Unspecified amount
44. Car's path
45. Picnic pests
46. Comedian Hope
47. Amazement
48. Guided
50. Barking pet
51. Commotion
52. Chess pieces
53. Cunning

218

ACROSS

1. River float
5. Swiss peaks
9. Noah's boat
12. Skilled
13. Fishing-line device
14. Expected to arrive
15. Swarm (with)
16. Simple to do
17. Beer's kin
18. Open-hand blow
19. Hill-building insect
20. "Grace" ending
21. Pot cover
23. Stir together
25. Donates
28. Continuation, as of a subscription
32. Gardner of Hollywood
33. Audible noise
35. Historic period
36. Salad staple
38. Ledger entries
40. Fishing snare
41. Automobile
42. Barbecue rod
45. Raw mineral
47. Venomous serpents
51. Stenographer's notebook
52. Imitate a top
53. Timepiece face
54. Ingredient in Italian dressing
55. Kick a football
56. Margin; border
57. Take a stab at
58. Poses a question
59. Good turn

DOWN

1. Urban pests
2. Cain's victim
3. Dog's bane
4. House of worship
5. Toward the future
6. Money given temporarily
7. Mail-carrying guys
8. Word before "light" or "scraper"
9. Eden resident
10. Fixed principle
11. Sharp
20. Large hatchet
22. Subject of a debate
24. Land of the rajahs
25. Young lady
26. "____ Been Working on the Railroad"
27. Large tub
28. Feel remorseful about
29. Very small
30. Hugging limb
31. Vegas lead-in
34. Tentacled sea creature
37. Powerful explosive: abbr.
39. Made a swap
41. Pennies
42. Locate
43. Set of socks
44. With no purpose in mind
46. Skating place
48. Faction
49. Book leaf
50. Coasting toy
52. Large whirlpool bath

219

ACROSS

1. Brief sleep
4. Eyelid hair
8. Poems of praise
12. Sense of self
13. Fascinated by
14. Farm tower
15. Annoy
16. Tight-fitting
17. Abel's brother
18. Mild exclamation
19. Five plus five
20. Yosemite ____, cartoon character
21. Shrubbery fence
23. Fragrance
26. In a mess
30. Never seen before
31. School semester
34. Lyricist Gershwin
35. Unemployed
36. Shipboard affirmative
37. Unlocked
39. Oyster's gem
41. Wrangler's rope
45. Peas' casing
46. Paid player
48. Director's shout
49. State next to Kentucky
51. Trampoline stunt
52. Museum display
53. Mother's sister
54. Relaxation
55. General Robert E. ____
56. Beer barrels
57. Artificially colored
58. Be mistaken

DOWN

1. Horse's sound
2. See eye to eye
3. Prodded
4. "Lend me your ears!"
5. Actress Bancroft
6. Shock
7. Sty dweller
8. "Sesame Street" grouch
9. April's birthstone
10. Inventor Whitney
11. Male offspring
20. Declare
22. Confection for chewing
24. Gibson of "Braveheart"
25. Fear and trembling
27. Waiter's bonus
28. Anger
29. Anchorman Rather
31. Dance like Fred Astaire
32. Sight organ
33. Gathering in (wheat)
35. Lupino of Hollywood
37. Ancient
38. Fled to wed
40. Plants' underground parts
42. Pianist's exercise
43. More certain
44. River mammal
46. Join in a game
47. Go up
49. Sturdy tree
50. Color variant
51. Gave meals to

220

ACROSS

1. Comedian Conway
4. "Wise" birds
8. Birthday pastry
12. Gardening implement
13. Tooth anchor
14. Sinister
15. Reverent fear
16. Penniless
17. Name, ____, and serial number
18. Keep vigil (over)
20. Coal source
22. Acorn tree
24. Keyboard instru-ments
28. Title on "M*A*S*H"
32. Lindbergh's vehicle
33. Chopping tool
34. Money of Japan
36. Drink chiller
37. Park seat
40. Told secrets
43. Caught in a trap
45. Jeer at the stadium
46. Examines closely
48. Guitar sound
52. Actual
55. Most excellent
57. Chum
58. Bee's relative
59. Snap (a photo)
60. Bible woman
61. Is indebted to
62. Recipe instruction
63. Hair coloring

DOWN

1. Melt
2. Des Moines' state
3. Encounter
4. "Little ____ Annie," comic strip
5. Court (a sweet-heart)
6. Weaving apparatus
7. Narrow piece, as of cloth
8. Breakfast food
9. Glamorous Gardner
10. Relatives
11. Moose cousin
19. Murmur lovingly
21. Small taste
23. Solution
25. Hammer's target
26. A single time
27. Planter's purchase
28. Cars for hire
29. Strong animals
30. Songstress Horne
31. ____ bygones be bygones
35. Catch, as a suspect
38. Moves stealthily
39. "You there!"
41. Wobble
42. Pull along
44. Unpaid bills
47. Do an usher's job
49. Copied (one's actions)
50. Nation's military sea force
51. Mirth
52. A couple
53. Uncooked
54. Application
56. Hit the slopes

221

ACROSS

1. That boy
4. China's locale
8. Performs a role
12. Crucial period
13. Caution
14. A Corn Belt state
15. Word of negation
16. Copied (actions)
17. Dirty air
18. Creep
20. Mountaineer's destination
21. Diner sign-gas
24. Distributed (cards)
27. Bridge length
30. Haunches
32. Cheerleader's cry
33. Walk in the surf
34. Frost (a cake)
35. Restaurant listing
36. Help
37. Lord Byron, for one
38. Lyric verses
39. Cost
41. Remainder
43. Kids' chasing game
44. Hitchhiker's asset
48. Do the sidestroke
50. Countess's title
53. Chum
54. Circle, as of twine
55. Cameo shape, usually
56. Miner's quest
57. Hankerings
58. ". . . it's how you play the ____!"
59. Never seen before

DOWN

1. Female chickens
2. Sturdy metal
3. Captain's assistant
4. No longer sleeping
5. Tree fluid
6. Extreme anger
7. A conjunction
8. Bride's path
9. Looked at side by side
10. One plus one
11. Droop
19. Bancroft of films
20. Magazine fillers
22. Michigan neighbor
23. More genial
25. Scenic route, often
26. So
27. Trade (with)
28. See 10-Down
29. New wing
31. Mr. Sampras
35. Creature irresistibly drawn to a flame
37. Small, wooden pin
40. Kids' summer resorts
42. Fashion sense
45. Atop
46. Filly's mom
47. Moved, as the wind
48. Scheming
49. Misery
50. Pilot's journal
51. Hollywood's Gardner
52. River barrier

222

ACROSS

1. Border; verge
5. Omelet need
8. "____ Darn Cat!," Disney film
12. Monk's room
13. Cow-pasture sound
14. Every one
15. Brain's locale
16. Houseplant container
17. Tangy fruit
18. Most bizarre
20. Narrow street
21. Poetry features
24. "Jeepers!"
27. Calligraphy liquid
28. Knock sharply
31. Out of town
32. Passing fashion
33. Clock dial
34. *Oui* or *da*
35. Total
36. Striped jungle cat
37. ____ Nations, international body
39. Sketched
43. Crumpled (up)
47. Lounging garment
48. Cool cubes
50. Pay dirt
51. Subjects for Darwin
52. Anonymous John?
53. Neck and neck
54. Waist cincher
55. Fitting
56. Landlord's due

DOWN

1. Canyon effect
2. An act
3. Pleased as punch
4. Aged
5. Vacant
6. Sticky stuff
7. Received
8. Narrate (a story)
9. Summon (a cab)
10. Peak
11. Those folks
19. Hardly outgoing
20. Pose a question
22. Florida city
23. Stop
24. Cheery
25. Have unpaid bills
26. Vegas headliner?
28. Cleanup cloth
29. Skillful pitcher
30. The "p" in "mph"
32. Source of merriment
33. Square-dance violinist
35. Daytime star
36. 4:00 refreshment
38. Chirp
39. Dully colored
40. "I'm at the end of my ____!"
41. One of Eve's sons
42. Utah's region (with "the")
44. Symbol of peace
45. Paradise
46. Fender depression
48. Screen star Lupino
49. Police officer

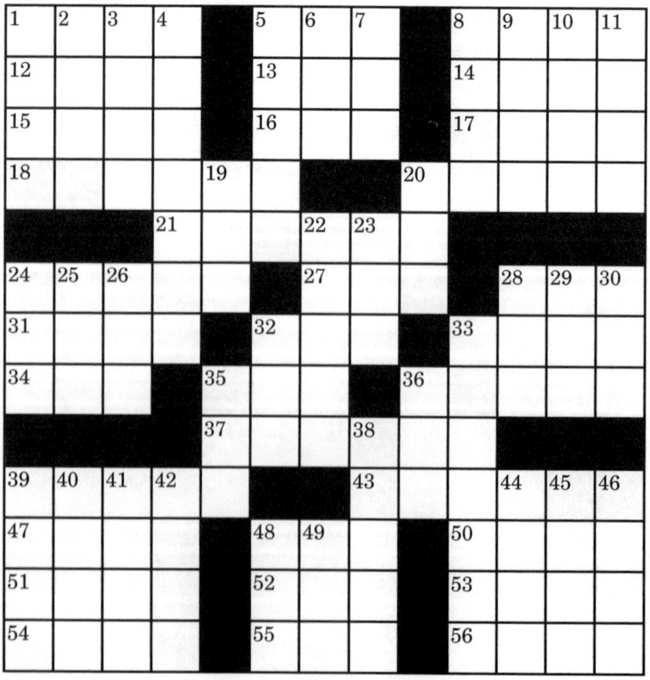

223

ACROSS

1. Songs for one singer
6. Baby's mealtime garment
9. Chest bone
12. Warn
13. Summer fruit drink
14. High card
15. Actor O'Toole
16. Made strong again
18. Tel Aviv's land
20. 1960s flower child: slang
23. "You can say that again!"
26. Achy
27. Level
29. Boy
31. Horse on a chess-board?
33. Shiny plating metal
35. Opposite of no
36. Capital of Norway
38. Not closed
39. Demon-strate
41. Wore away
43. Request boldly
45. Robbers
48. Leaves out
53. Hearing organ
54. Before, to a poet
55. Broad-casting device
56. Inquire of
57. Sunset color
58. Extends across

DOWN

1. Tree fluid
2. Spanish hurrah
3. "____ there be peace on earth . . ."
4. Raw mineral
5. Take off (a covering)
6. Oil container
7. Notion
8. Under
9. Uncooked
10. Frozen water
11. Sleep site
17. Shade tree
19. Removes lumps from (flour)
20. Sharpens, as a knife
21. Like a leprechaun
22. Wooden nail
24. Run off to wed
25. Titled
26. Word after "Vanilla" or "October" in movie titles
28. Oak nut
30. Lion's home
32. Neverthe-less
34. Fishing pole
37. Rented
40. Lyric poem
42. Scents
44. Lowly
45. Steeped beverage
46. Possesses
47. Annoy
49. Atlas feature
50. Lupino of the silver screen
51. Metal can
52. Cry for help

224

ACROSS

1. Fedoras and bowlers
5. Tear apart
8. Bowlike curves
12. Group of troops
13. Lupino of the movies
14. Sliced meats shop
15. Write using a keyboard
16. Quite aged
17. University personage
18. Cast a ballot
20. Graceful trees
21. Pours H_2O on (plants)
24. Conducted (a band)
26. Unaccompanied
27. Wolf's lair
28. Offbeat
31. "____ a girl!," new father's cry
32. Haunting spirit
34. Mournfulness
35. ____ Angeles, California
36. Ump's call
37. Laundry cycle
39. Gracious hotel in the country
40. Felt
41. They pucker up to whistle
44. Rounded roofs
46. Citrus punches
47. Brazilian hotspot, for short
48. The Orient
52. Restaurant's bill of fare
53. Mooselike creature
54. Hint, to Sherlock Holmes
55. Softball bag
56. Tint (fabric)
57. Evened (the score)

DOWN

1. Crude cabin
2. Unspecified one
3. Bit of advice
4. Director Spielberg
5. Public uprisings
6. Pointless
7. Rows, as a canoe
8. Summed (up)
9. Film spool
10. Chowder ingredient
11. Moral transgressions
19. Washington state's neighbor
21. Siren's sound
22. Choir voice
23. Throw lightly
25. Main course
27. Tiny mark
28. Possesses
29. Medicine amount
30. Feat
33. Ten tens
38. Bee or ant
39. Magazine edition
40. Sign of fire
41. Baby sheep
42. Mental creation
43. Writing instruments
45. Full of fat
49. "____ Baba and the Forty Thieves"
50. Take legal action against
51. Newsman Koppel

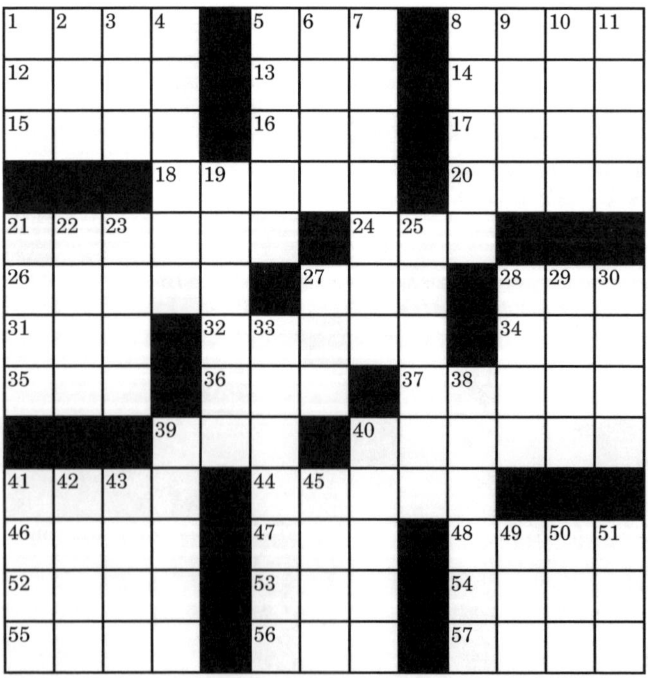

225

ACROSS

1. Lounging garment
5. Performs in a play
9. "Understand?"
12. "____ the Rainbow"
13. Ocean vessel
14. Candle stuff
15. Doe or buck
16. Peel, as an apple
17. Notable time span
18. Go into (a room)
20. Pod veggie
21. Tall shade tree
22. Cooing bird
24. Young fox
26. Swiss crag
29. Is under the weather
31. Enjoyed a letter
34. Holiday march
36. Round citrus fruit
38. Thin, brittle branch
39. Coin worth ten cents
41. Piglets' mom
42. Fido's doctor
44. Close at hand
46. "There you are!"
48. Bonfire remnant
50. Let down
54. Collection of dishes
55. Loud laughter
57. Walk through water
58. Extreme anger
59. Dickens' "A ____ of Two Cities"
60. Preholiday nights
61. Notices in the classifieds
62. Drove too fast
63. Fender hollow

DOWN

1. Went by taxi
2. Food-heating chamber
3. Sweet, edible root
4. Was mistaken
5. Small, poisonous snake
6. Private place of worship
7. Be ready to snooze
8. Talk (to)
9. Adds honey to
10. Noble Brit
11. School test
19. "King of the ____"
23. Contended (for)
25. Lyric writer Gershwin
26. Inclined (to)
27. Legal rule of conduct
28. Low-ranking soldiers
30. Any
32. In the past
33. Condensation on a lawn
35. Mature, as wine
37. Actual
40. Take a breath
43. Little pies
45. Used oars
46. Largest continent
47. Group of cattle
49. Cleansing bar
51. Gesture of greeting
52. Genesis garden
53. Brief sleep
56. Stop-sign color

226

ACROSS

1. Keep out of sight
5. Trucker's vehicle
8. Hunt for bargains
12. Persia, nowadays
13. Perón or Gabor
14. The ____ Star State, Texas
15. Take care of
16. Doctor for dogs
17. Malt beverages
18. Needle opening
20. A Hemingway
22. Web-spinning creature
25. Used a chair
26. Not in
27. Fire residue
29. Divulges
33. Dancer Astaire
35. Take nourishment
37. Distribute (cards)
38. Ready for battle
40. Cow's sound
42. Expert pitcher
43. "Mayday!"
45. Bit playfully
47. Freedom from danger
50. Unwell
51. Completed
52. Cloth scrap
54. Home of the NBA's Jazz
58. Watch one's weight
59. Sound of disgust
60. Cafe list
61. States further
62. Beloved animal
63. Baseball's Rose

DOWN

1. Box-office smash
2. Extreme anger
3. Newsman Rather
4. See 51-Across
5. Turn backward
6. "____ Got a Secret"
7. "Heavenly" doors
8. At an angle
9. Golfer's target
10. Dollar bills
11. Bothersome one
19. Nay's opposite
21. Common rodent
22. Couch
23. Cat's rumble
24. Bit of news
28. Deli meat
30. Broad jump
31. Tie (up), as shoes
32. Snow coaster
34. Very dry habitats
36. This evening
39. Small, round spot
41. Engine lubricant
44. Pancake topping
46. Rounded in form
47. Fizzy drink
48. Eager
49. Give meals to
53. Ripen, as cheese
55. Football prop
56. Aardvark treat
57. Color variation

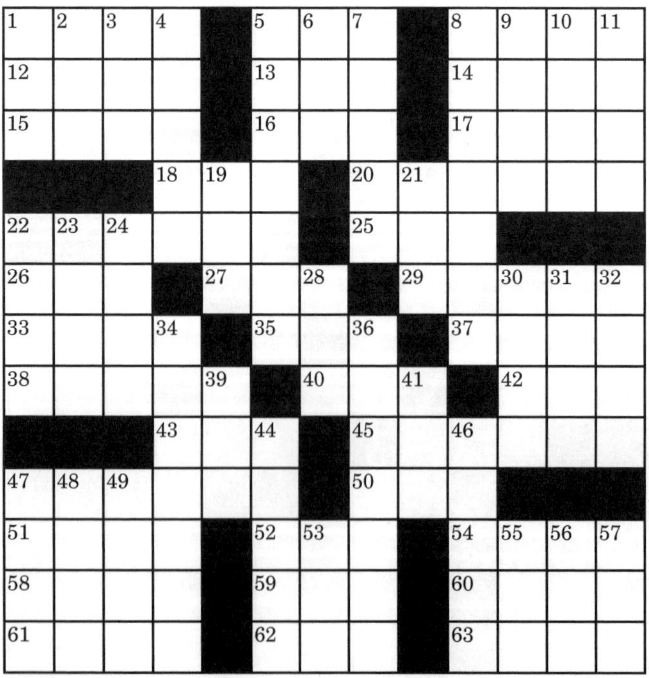

227

ACROSS

1. Summit
5. Utilizes
9. Health resort
12. Shut with force
13. Aim; intention
14. Price label
15. Low-cut shoe
16. Stockings
17. Expert pilot
18. Stool or chair
19. Golf peg
20. Bloodshot
21. "OK!"
24. Caress
26. Bonnet, for one
29. Point of ____, opinion
31. "Woe is me!"
34. Tel Aviv's land
36. Most unusual
38. Slip sideways
39. "Go away!"
41. Bashful
42. Pea container
44. Mimics
46. Close friend
48. Country hotel
50. Was in debt
54. Frozen water
55. Sudsy cleanser
57. Talk loudly
58. High explosive: abbr.
59. Word after "area" or "ZIP"
60. Paradise
61. Opposite of no
62. Metal fastener
63. Lease

DOWN

1. Horned vipers
2. Mystery solving aid
3. Papa's mate
4. Vacant
5. "Yuck!"
6. Make calm
7. Comfort
8. Slumber
9. Surprises
10. Walk to and fro
11. Matured
22. Preholiday night
23. Is sick
25. Hearing organ
26. That man's
27. Inquire
28. Maternity-ward group
30. Shawl, for example
32. Volcanic dust
33. Pig's home
35. "Much ____ About Nothing"
37. Dined
40. Montreal's locale
43. Phonograph records
45. More painful
46. Sympathy
47. Teen's skin problem
49. Midday
51. Walk in water
52. Equally balanced
53. Fender impression
56. Vigor

228

ACROSS

1. Baseball cap, for one
4. Seize
8. Corned-beef mixture
12. Ms. Lupino
13. British noble-woman
14. Dull pain
15. Hare's rival in a fable
17. Sign gas
18. Night bird
19. Biblical beasts of burden
20. Short note
23. Serving of pie
26. Lobby sign
27. Buck's crowning glory?
31. Went on foot swiftly
32. Goldfish aquariums
34. Compete
35. Rich shade of green
37. Superman's alter ego
38. From Dublin
40. Bothers
41. Used a broom
44. "____ a boy!"
46. ____ and go seek, childhood game
47. Taken into police custody
52. Single bills
53. Fabricates a story
54. Time period
55. Canvas shelter
56. Pea coverings
57. Arid

DOWN

1. Strike
2. Trouble
3. Paving goo
4. Radiate
5. Metal bars
6. Radio commer-cials
7. "See you later!"
8. Gretel's brother
9. High cards
10. Sandal or pump
11. Female chickens
16. Whistle sound
19. Performs on stage
20. Simple
21. Test
22. Ore location
24. Guides (a plane) to the runway
25. Writing fluid
28. Always
29. Ice-skating area
30. Television units
32. Sour tasting
33. The Greatest of boxing
36. Most mature
37. Smooch
39. Employed
41. Fired a gun
42. Grape drink
43. Adam's garden
45. Actress Harper
47. Swiss mountain
48. ____ de Janeiro
49. Mogul Turner
50. Make a mistake
51. 24 hours

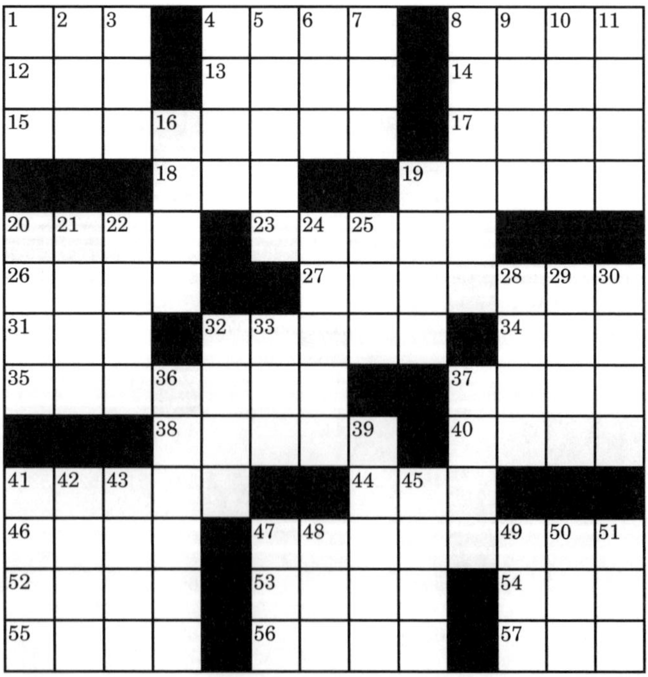

229

ACROSS

1. Owl's sound
5. Pull by rope
8. List of actors
12. Ohio's Great Lake
13. Mr. Lincoln, familiarly
14. Steady pain
15. Freed
17. Gas in some bright lights
18. Rainbow site
19. Stinging insects
20. Rubbish
24. Wicked
26. Irritate
27. Famous garden
28. Short blow from Ali
31. Come into view
33. Safe
35. "That's exactly it!"
36. "Waste not, ____ not"
38. Poker-pot start
39. Comfort
40. Bit of women's wear
41. Madder than a wet hen
44. Like: 2 wds.
46. Fly, eagle style
47. Vows
52. Rose of baseball
53. Antique
54. Storm
55. Arctic vehicle
56. Tint
57. Be sure of

DOWN

1. That woman
2. Mine output
3. Tanker cargo
4. Golf-ball mound
5. Assigned piece of work
6. Complied with
7. Marry
8. Man-made waterway
9. One-spot cards
10. Hit the mall
11. Billfold bills
16. Volcanic dust
19. Grape beverage
20. Serving platter
21. Ready for picking
22. Swiss range
23. "Get it?"
25. Part of a 3-piece suit
27. Note-worthy periods
28. Month after May
29. Partner of crafts
30. Honey makers
32. ". . . in a galaxy far, far ____"
34. Automobile
37. Almost
39. Was mistaken
40. Beavers' structure
41. Egyptian cobras
42. A Christmas carol
43. Door in a fence
45. Major vein of 2-Down
47. Pea's place
48. Pester
49. ____ Diego, California
50. Conceit
51. Fasten with stitches

230

ACROSS

1. Stare, as in surprise
5. Not even
8. Cotton-tipped stick
12. Mental formulation
13. Crusted dessert item
14. Fable; story
15. The _____ Lights, Aurora Borealis
17. Go by bus
18. Single
19. With 10-Down, star of "M*A*S*H"
20. Permit
24. Potter's medium
27. Declared
28. Constellation member
29. That woman
32. Design something new
34. Scott Hamilton is one
36. Fruity drink
37. "Mighty" trees
39. Happy cat's sound
40. Cutting side of a blade
41. Turns (in a river)
42. Practice like Rocky
45. Golf device
47. Papa's sweetheart
48. Benchmark
53. Raw minerals
54. Capone and Pacino
55. Pennsylvania's neighbor
56. Chromosome unit
57. Acquire
58. Mild-mannered

DOWN

1. Barroom order
2. Big fuss
3. Part of "mph"
4. Have supper
5. Unlock
6. Straightforward; to the point
7. Wolf's lair
8. Wander
9. Cry out in mourning
10. See 19-Across
11. Existed
16. "In what way?"
20. Site of China
21. Touch ground, as a plane
22. Not taped
23. Poetic tribute
25. Gal
26. Bible boat
28. Deer with antlers
29. Daze momentarily
30. Cattle group
31. Makes boo-boos
33. Greet silently
35. Gorilla or gibbon
38. Vessel for boiling water
40. Wipe out
41. Mr. Franklin, familiarly
42. City environmental problem
43. Peel
44. Prayer ending
46. Sunup site
48. Droop
49. Small, round speck
50. "I've found it!"
51. Lip of a canyon
52. Fawn's mom

231

ACROSS

1. Steaming
4. Staged drama
8. Practice boxing
12. Geological time span
13. Convenience
14. Basic impulse
15. The Cornhusker State
17. Christmas-card word
18. Fire residue
19. Pal; chum
20. Final
23. Snooze
24. Had body pain
26. It completes an "i"
27. Number it takes to tango
30. Supporting
31. From Dublin's land
33. Free (of)
34. Witness
35. Compete (with)
36. Clear, as a chalkboard
38. Spider-Man's mesh
39. Contact lenses' site
40. Remained upright
43. Lamb's utterance
45. One who fibs
46. Least large
51. Crafts' companion
52. Saucy
53. Syllable from Baby
54. Annoying one
55. Too
56. Be in possession of

DOWN

1. Farm fowl
2. Lode load
3. Bar account
4. Potpie veggies
5. Mascara's target
6. Pose a question
7. Senate floor vote
8. Break of day
9. Poke
10. Very old
11. Depend (on)
16. Velocity
19. Soak in the tub
20. Track circuits
21. Land measure
22. Loafer or moccasin
23. Verbal refusals
25. Jumped off the pool spring-board
26. Metal-cutting tool
27. Waiter's serving platter
28. Like a sage
29. Keatsian poems
32. Chest bone
37. Not fake
38. Opposite of best
40. Hit with an open palm
41. Hubcap hugger
42. Cereal grains
43. Behind ____, in prison
44. Female singer's range
46. Pampering retreat
47. Comedian Brooks
48. Freudian concept
49. Hog mama
50. 2,000 pounds

232

ACROSS

1. Very dry
5. Desk illuminator
9. Child's frequent question
12. Fully cooked
13. Cain's brother
14. Weeding tool
15. Connect the ____
16. DNA carrier
17. In the manner of: 2 wds.
18. Like bacon's flavor
20. Later than
22. Distress signal
24. Ms. Lupino
25. Play a part
28. Atop
30. Overly inquisitive
34. Buck's mate
35. Further-more
36. Minuscule
37. Carbonated beverage
39. Bridle strap
41. Permit
42. Payable, as rent
44. Point (a gun)
46. Frequently
49. Strikes, chicken style
53. Brazil resort, for short
54. Cloak for Count Dracula
58. Bowling alley
59. Actress Gardner
60. Told an untruth
61. Baking enclosure
62. Guided
63. Goes awry
64. Have to have

DOWN

1. Totals
2. Kitchen or den
3. Division term
4. Office work-stations
5. Be a straggler
6. Mr. Lincoln, to friends
7. Boys, all grown up
8. Beg urgently
9. "Excuse me?"
10. Doughnut center
11. 365-day span
19. "____ Are My Sunshine"
21. Air-moving appliance
23. Tire in the trunk
24. Delhi's land
25. Newspaper job notices
26. Dove's cry
27. Mr. Turner of telecom-munications
29. "____, two, buckle my shoe . . ."
31. Wide-eyed bird
32. Observe visually
33. Up to now
38. Summer drink
40. Puppy bite
43. Mom's brother
45. Juicy fruit
46. Like some school reports
47. Half of ten
48. Frog relative
50. Bat dwelling
51. Leg "hinge"
52. Dispatch (a telegram)
55. Scuba-tank filler
56. For each
57. Sullivan and McMahon

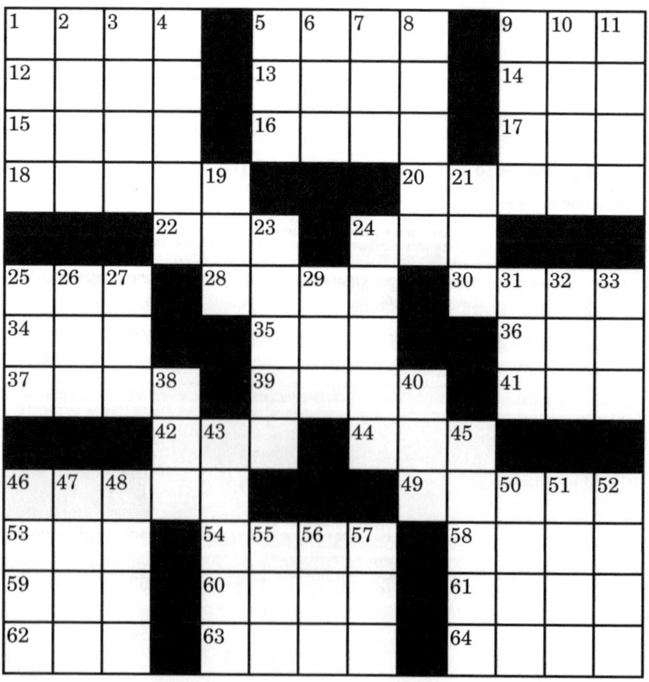

233

ACROSS

1. Person with an identical sibling
5. Golf-ball prop
8. Wineglass support
12. Opposite of all
13. It's for horses!
14. Yours truly's
15. Do, re, or mi
16. Manipulate
17. "ER" guest-star Alan
18. Stadium roof, often
20. Take a breather
21. Unparalleled
24. Singer Cole
26. Baseball move?
27. "____ your best foot forward"
28. Food-storage box
31. It may be served "over easy"
32. Civil War general
34. Juice drink
35. Teensy
36. Lubricate (hinges)
37. Arm joint
39. Furthermore
40. Prepares for knighthood
41. "Woe is me!"
44. Baby goats
45. Big stone
46. Sewing aid
47. Locale
51. "Hi, Mrs. Smith. Can Timmy ____ out to play?"
52. Pen fluid
53. Far from saintly
54. Went fast
55. McMahon and Bradley
56. Giraffe's claim to fame

DOWN

1. Blasting compound: abbr.
2. Play the suitor
3. Rural accommodation
4. Indispensable
5. Hitchhiker's signal
6. Convenience
7. Organ of vision
8. Intelligent
9. Flooring square
10. Winds down
11. Beef or lamb
19. The Beaver State
21. Cook, as prunes
22. Ask earnestly
23. Book leaf
24. "Flying" role for Sally Field
25. Be present for
27. Buddy
28. Movie pig
29. Sacred image
30. Current information
33. Free (of)
38. Decrease
39. Inquired
40. Cricks (in one's back)
41. Curving paths
42. Air-show move
43. Highest peak
44. Goodhearted
46. Diner dessert
48. "____ Got a Crush on You"
49. ____ -tac-toe
50. Large deer

234

ACROSS

1. Be the right size
4. Game fish
8. More ____ enough
12. Mineral resource
13. Dayton's locale
14. Villain's foe
15. Comes in again
17. Hit (the fridge)
18. "I get it!"
19. Shapes (dough)
20. Pastrami shop
23. Flow off
26. Sinister
27. Witness
31. Kingsley of "Gandhi"
32. Helpers
34. Lung filler
35. Quake
37. Docking place
38. Permit
40. Comes to a close
41. Play platform
44. Wordsmith of the Gershwins
46. "One good ____ deserves another"
47. Member of the clergy
52. A single time
53. Mellowed, as fine wine
54. Feel deep regret
55. Exterminator's target
56. Mix, as a salad
57. Ms. Landers

DOWN

1. In favor of
2. Wrath
3. Letter directly following ess
4. The two of them
5. In front (of)
6. Title of respect
7. Cry for help
8. Ruler's chair
9. Mend, as a wound
10. Exceedingly dry
11. ____ off, drifts into sleep
16. Bit of hardware
19. Land wide of the mark
20. Monetary obligation
21. For all time
22. Bit of dialogue
24. Riding and roping show
25. Mr. Lincoln, to most
28. Forecast for Noah?
29. Contended (with)
30. Commits blunders
32. Talented
33. In poor health
36. Attractive object?
37. Fall fruit
39. Married women
41. "Quit it!"
42. Adjust (a piano)
43. Curved lines
45. Cincinnati team
47. Mouse kin
48. Id's companion
49. Notable period in time
50. Cloister resident
51. Home-office room

235

ACROSS

1. Smith who sang "God Bless America"
5. Turf
8. Observed
12. Mental creation
13. Billiards stick
14. Fashioned
15. Small kitchen appliances
17. Pressing impulse
18. Food-can metal
19. Wrote, as an autograph
21. Do De Niro's job
24. Actor Sellers
26. Shoelace circle
28. Fight, as with one's conscience
33. Valley
34. Broadway smash
35. Like some exams
36. Books of maps
38. Takes first prize
39. Mend (jeans)
42. Lyric poem
43. Feline male
47. "You there!"
49. Nearly circular
50. Green gems
55. Musical Horne
56. Use oars
57. Genuine
58. Put crayon to paper
59. Emergency distress code
60. Say it isn't so

DOWN

1. Tool set
2. Commotion
3. Chinese beverage
4. West's opposite
5. Stage setting
6. Possessive pronoun
7. After-dinner treat
8. Annoyingly self-satisfied
9. Gain through hard work
10. Blade's cutting part
11. Require
16. Waiter's reward
20. Wrath
21. "M*A*S*H" star
22. Layer of paint
23. Parkway fee
25. Wind about
27. Tiny veggie
29. Do a farmer's task
30. The Musketeers, for example
31. ____ of the Free
32. Otherwise
34. They warm you in winter
37. Resort for unwinding
40. Works a piece of gum
41. The lady's
43. Narrated
44. "Somewhere ____ the rainbow . . ."
45. Lion's hair
46. Crab's grabber
48. Three-foot measurement
51. Cow's sound
52. General Robert E.
53. Mr. Aykroyd
54. Clever

236

ACROSS

1. Pull by rope
4. Sand sidewalker?
8. Upper limbs
12. "Gadzooks!"
13. Lawn waterer
14. Soccer cry
15. Clear liquor
16. Competent
17. Teen's skin woe
18. Turf
19. Witness
20. Thought highly of
21. Potato bud
23. First garden
25. Roadster's roller
27. Atop
28. Grain container
31. Sports sites
33. Gambling spot
35. Train unit
36. Pack (of cards)
38. Boats like Noah's
39. Poke one's ____ into, snoop
40. Likely (to)
41. Highest points
44. Moved like the wind?
46. Towel set word
49. Feline's "nail"
50. Quick kiss
51. Female deer
52. "Once upon a ____ . . ."
53. British nobleman
54. Wonder
55. Shadowbox
56. Merriment
57. Thanksgiving tuber

DOWN

1. Clothing labels
2. Cleveland's state
3. Vagabond, for one
4. Pursue
5. Judge's uniform
6. Dozing
7. Honey insect
8. Once more
9. Large pebble
10. Lion's pride?
11. Snow skimmer
20. Ms. Horne
22. Strong desire
24. Wharf
25. Word between "tic" and "toe"
26. Lyricist Gershwin
27. Employs
28. "Happy ____ to you . . ."
29. Pen fluid
30. Negative replies
32. Fusses
34. Maple syrup, once
37. Breakfast food
39. Less old
40. Foot joint
41. Play parts
42. Metal fastener
43. Papa's mate
45. Land measure
47. The Hawkeye State
48. Appear (to be)
50. Wooden pin

237

ACROSS

1. Folder flap
4. Drinks slowly
8. Kind; sort
12. Avail oneself of
13. Seth's sire
14. Pay attention to
15. Hit film for Tom Hanks
16. Smelling organ
17. Stool pigeons: slang
18. Alleviated
20. Bedtime story
22. Guy's date
24. Oven-cooks (meat)
28. Circus employee
32. Squirrel away
33. Low note?
34. Excavate
36. Feel regret
37. Goliath, for one
40. Gave to a cause
43. Rivulet
45. Drag
46. "Rock of ——," hymn
48. Distributed, as cards
52. Shadowbox
55. Had loans to repay
57. Honey insect
58. Bucket
59. Ocean swell
60. Discontinue
61. TV's Rooney
62. Hastened
63. Sung syllables

DOWN

1. Hollow cylinder
2. Nepal's continent
3. Panhandles
4. Open-toed summer shoe
5. Marriage words
6. Gone by
7. Make illegible, as a signature
8. Promise of injury
9. Nay's opposite
10. Household animal
11. Bradley and Asner
19. Easter symbol
21. Angeles preceder
23. Headed up
25. Separate (out)
26. Verifiable
27. Word after "sesame" or "poppy"
28. Trots along
29. Single item
30. Toothed wheel
31. Free (oneself of)
35. Received
38. Almost
39. "You're It!" game
41. Signaled "yes"
42. Reverent fear
44. Makes a cat's sound
47. Trade (goods)
49. Child of 56-Down
50. Jazz legend Horne
51. Koppel and Danson
52. Hot spring, maybe
53. Stove utensil
54. Rescue
56. Woman of Eden

238

ACROSS

1. Rub out
6. Watch secretly
9. Filmdom's Lupino
12. Mr. Letterman
13. Historic time
14. "What's up, ____?"
15. "____ up or ship out!"
16. Mug's cousin
17. Shady tree
18. Midday hour
20. Store event
21. Everything
24. Struck a humble pose
26. Fawn's mama
27. Father
28. Our planet
32. Mule's kin
34. ____ eight, skating feat
35. Madrid's land
36. Gore and Jolson
37. Gent's title
38. Ride a bike
40. Gardening tool
41. "Skin" of a 17-Across
44. Bird of prey
46. Put to work
47. "Help!"
48. Mistake
53. Racket
54. Noah's craft
55. Keyboard instrument
56. Used a chair
57. Soup veggie
58. Lugged

DOWN

1. Asner and Sullivan
2. "Go, team!"
3. Gardner of "The Barefoot Contessa"
4. Drink slowly
5. Genesis garden
6. Part of a minute
7. Dried plum
8. Lap dog's "arf"
9. Result of thinking
10. Barbie or Ken
11. Summit
19. "Fine!"
20. Mate for a 26-Across
21. Totals (up)
22. Lasso's noose
23. Singer Horne
25. Oahu garlands
27. Contradict
29. Be in a hurry
30. Small chamber-music group
31. In this place
33. Karate move
34. Went by jet
36. Juneau's state
39. Household job
41. Baby bloomers?
42. South Korea's continent
43. Payment to the landlady
45. Held on to
47. Fir fluid
49. Mexican waterway
50. Wharf rodent
51. Undivided
52. Reel's partner

239

ACROSS

1. Burst, as a balloon
4. Pick (a card)
8. Stair
12. Amazement
13. Preside over
14. Grow weary
15. Ivan the ____
17. Not in use
18. Additionally
19. Athenian one
20. Up to the time of
23. Battle between nations
25. Plant beginning
26. China's continent
27. By way of
30. Chalk-board-cleaning device
32. Making colorful, as an Easter egg
34. Distress code
35. Land measurement unit
37. Teen's skin condition
38. Feminine pronoun
39. Push (a button)
40. Instance of stealing
44. Shopping center
46. Rabbit's kin
47. Slow-pouring syrup
51. Wicked
52. Cooking chamber
53. Sailor's affirmative
54. Encounter
55. Make untidy
56. Fido or Fluffy

DOWN

1. Game-show host Sajak
2. Have debts
3. Miles ____ hour
4. Hole-making tool
5. Buffs with a cloth
6. Permits
7. Very small
8. Mix, as a beverage
9. Ocean motion
10. ____ Stanley Gardner, writer
11. Steal a glance
16. Hostile attacks
19. Blend of black and white
20. Takes advantage of
21. Cruel Roman emperor
22. Pekoe and camomile
24. Assistant
26. Curved doorway
27. Bad habit
28. Country hotels
29. Gets older
31. Opposite of west
33. British noblemen
36. Take off, as a lid
39. Scheduled engagements
40. Everyone else
41. Possess
42. A Great Lake
43. Examined by touching
45. Pub drinks
47. Dad's mate
48. Tree's liquid
49. Sight organ
50. TV receiver

240

ACROSS

1. Acquire
4. Swiss range
8. Miller and Landers
12. Boxing's The Greatest
13. Horseback game
14. Patriot Revere
15. Cooked over a low flame
17. Go by bus
18. Put to work
19. Became sick
20. Radio tuning knob
23. Fish's breathing organ
25. Not busy at all
26. Matched groups
27. Hit the slopes
30. Teeter-totter
32. Whirly-bird, for short
34. Owns
35. ____ out, speak angrily
37. Chain part
38. Celebrity status
39. The National Endowment for the ____
40. Foot encasers
43. Cop's bulletproof garment
46. Horne of popular song
47. Those with auburn locks
51. Rainbow curves
52. Spur (on)
53. Mexican water-course
54. Run into
55. Urgent requirement
56. Gents

DOWN

1. Oven fuel
2. Inventor Whitney
3. Actor Allen
4. Imperson-ates
5. Tribal tradition
6. "I ____ allegiance to the flag . . ."
7. Piece of turf
8. Month of showers
9. Hammer's target
10. Undressed
11. Snow vehicle
16. "Stubborn" beasts
19. Likewise
20. Bit of china
21. Notion
22. Beerlike drinks
24. Reason for scratching
26. Went for a dip
27. Mix with a spoon
28. Clark of "Superman"
29. Annoys
31. Sorrowful word
33. Large, flat 20-Down
36. Harsh, as a winter
38. Thanks-giving meal
40. Shut with a bang
41. In this place
42. A single time
44. Razor's cutting side
45. Storage building
47. Hightail it
48. Upper limb
49. Gambling cube
50. Male heir

241

ACROSS

1. London weather condition
4. Armed combat
7. Possesses
10. President Lincoln's nickname
11. Audio cassette
12. Train track
13. Pro's foe
14. Second-hand
15. TV award
16. Adolescents
18. _____ Diego
20. "All right!"
23. Warm outer garments
27. Motor coach
29. Pleasant; agreeable
31. Mr. DiMaggio
32. Like the Marx Brothers' antics
33. Herbal beverage
34. Shopping area
35. Famous fighter
36. Serpentine sea creatures
37. Coffee server
38. Daisy part
40. Fender scar
42. Baseball referee
44. Say
48. Comparing word
51. Very dry
54. "_____ Got a Secret"
55. Litter's littlest one
56. Challenge
57. "_____ Misérables"
58. Tokyo currency
59. Mineral spring
60. Blasting agent: abbr.

DOWN

1. True statement
2. Clarinet's kin
3. Hackman of Hollywood
4. Existed
5. Large primate
6. Ohio diamond squad
7. Salty pork product
8. Shoot (for)
9. Wily
11. Wart-hog tooth
12. Nevada city
17. Inquisitive
19. Top card
21. Poker stake
22. Give way (to)
24. Slightly open
25. Ripped
26. TV receiver
27. Bundle of hay
28. Troops group
30. Lawyer's focus
32. Ray-gun sound: slang
34. Mongrel dog: slang
36. Shady tree
39. Mom's sister
41. In the buff
43. Writing tablets
45. Slight incline
46. Neck and neck
47. Take a break
48. Attempt
49. Tint
50. Tapper Miller
52. Knock sharply
53. A Gershwin

242

ACROSS

1. Baseball glove
5. Sleeve filler
8. Workplace reminder
12. Smell
13. Senate-floor vote
14. Shaped like a runner's track
15. Part of a skeleton
16. In the direction of the rising sun
18. Have a snooze
20. Enjoy a snow sport
21. Wedding vow: 2 wds.
23. Plays miniature golf
28. Light-switch word
31. Army vehicle
33. Butting barnyard resident
34. Narrow back streets
36. Take a breath
38. Prom attendee, usually
39. Dislike strongly
41. Grass condensation
42. Two are better than one
44. Miles ____ hour
45. "Cleopatra" critter
47. Take place
52. Novels about love
57. The ____ Star State, Texas
58. Persia's modern name
59. Acorn-producing tree
60. Like the Sahara
61. Refined fellow
62. Sample a taste of
63. Beloved animals

DOWN

1. Unruly crowds
2. Revered one
3. Do, re, or mi
4. Birch or willow
5. Sailor's affirmative
6. Logic
7. Facial disguise
8. Cut the lawn
9. TV star Gabor
10. Spoil
11. Ancient
17. Cafe gratuity
19. Sympathetic response
22. Quick, brief run
24. "Yech!"
25. Warty creature
26. Sailor's yarn
27. Hearty meat dish
28. Vow; pledge
29. Make an escape
30. Canine pest
32. Windy-day toy
35. Last part
37. Mean Roman emperor
40. Materialize
43. ____ Diego
46. Highlands native
48. Applaud
49. Apple center
50. Army group
51. Cincinnati team
52. Trailer truck
53. Mine extract
54. Fellow
55. Aardvark tidbit
56. Blue yonder

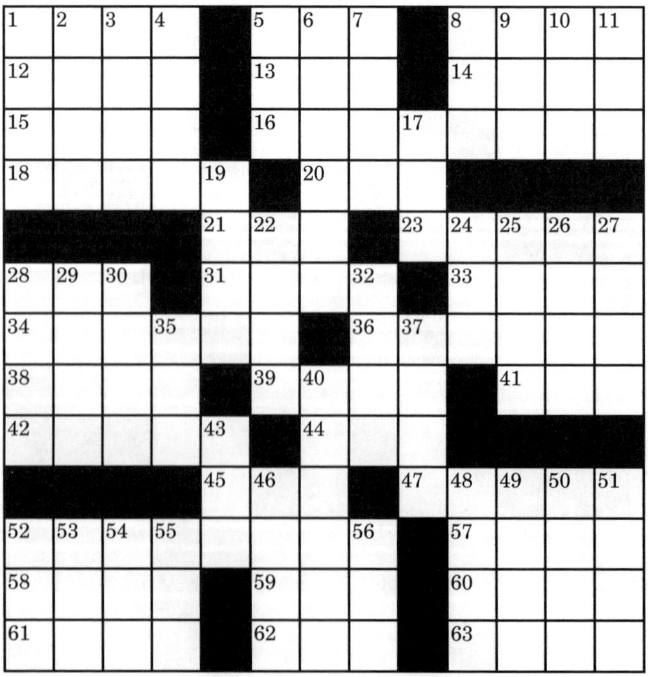

243

ACROSS

1. Bancroft of Hollywood
5. Timid
8. Forehead
12. Abel's brother
13. Chinese export
14. Ready for harvest
15. Slant
16. A shade tree
17. Fruit beverages
18. Poured down frozen rain
20. Clark of "Superman"
21. Sharp knock
22. Top card
24. In complete disorder
27. Cooking fat
28. Butter portion
31. Beer kin
32. Soup-serving utensil
34. Excitement
35. Cherry seed
36. Single object
37. Poem part
39. Use a towel on
40. A Kennedy
41. Mama's mate
44. Becomes smaller
48. Put to work
49. DiMaggio of the Yankees
50. Melody
51. Citrus peel
52. Light-switch word
53. Garden in the book of Genesis
54. Far from difficult
55. Baseball stick
56. Property owner's paper

DOWN

1. Plays a role
2. Bit of hardware
3. Cairo's river
4. Goes into, as a room
5. Like some ski slopes
6. Grasped
7. Sweet potato
8. Car's stopping device
9. Go by bicycle
10. Unlock
11. Sunset direction
19. Pop singer James
22. Feel sick
23. Quick-witted
24. Atlas content
25. Cotton-gin inventor Whitney
26. Group of matching dishes
27. Lyric poem
28. Golfing score
29. Classified notices
30. Sock part
33. "Baa, baa, black sheep, have you ____ wool?"
38. Readied (copy) for printing
39. Mommy's partner
40. Crime of stealing
41. Unblemished
42. India's continent
43. Writing tools
44. Living-room seat
45. Unclothed
46. Leg joint
47. Convey by messenger
49. Employment

244

ACROSS

1. Brief conversation
5. Rebounding sound
9. Derby or bonnet
12. Ms. Horne of song
13. Let slip
14. Conceit
15. Bachelor of ____ degree
16. Department-store employees
18. Frost and Poe
20. Camping shelter
21. Lack of difficulty
23. Carbonated drinks
27. On vacation
30. Trout, for one
32. Govern
33. Slinky mammal
35. Practically, but not quite
37. Every one
38. Molten rock
40. Distress signal
41. Sleeper's vision
43. Uses needle and thread
45. Eyelid hair
47. Shaving mishaps
51. Candy on a stick
55. Soccer score
56. Notable time
57. Traditional learning
58. Musical tone
59. Lawn moisture
60. Simmered dish
61. Drove too fast

DOWN

1. Applaud
2. Leading man
3. Poker payment
4. Sample by eating
5. Sullivan and Asner
6. Packing cases
7. Cavity
8. Tears into (a wrapped gift)
9. Garment edge
10. How old one is
11. Heavy weight
17. Weather forecast, sometimes
19. Unharmed
22. Window ledge
24. Pairs of performers
25. As well
26. Tennis-match divisions
27. Had debts
28. Anxiety
29. Confront boldly
31. Possess
34. "We ____ Overcome"
36. Grass surrounding a home
39. To dry land
42. Sends by post
44. Highway directional aids
46. Stain
48. Chicken enclosure
49. "Kiss Me, ____," musical
50. Vehicle for snowy days
51. Showed (the way)
52. Unrefined mine product
53. Judge's concern
54. Seat for worship, to some

245

ACROSS

1. Volcano output
5. Minor fight
9. Shorten (a skirt)
12. Had debts
13. Woodland trail
14. Señora Perón
15. Speed of travel
16. Finished
17. Atmosphere
18. Change the color of
19. Mr. DiMaggio
20. "The ____ bird gets the worm!"
22. Genuine
24. Golf standard
25. Sudden panic
27. Tomahawk's kin
31. Ms. Horne of song
32. Petroleum product
33. Angel's aura
34. School units
36. Bluejeans material
37. Look at steadily
38. Group of cows
39. Telescope targets
42. Pull with a chain
43. Pine pitch, for example
46. Carry the day
47. Drop of woe
49. Muddle through
50. Industrious insect
51. Nest finds
52. "I'm all for it!"
53. Honey maker
54. Perfumer's prize
55. Mattress locales

DOWN

1. Master
2. Not at one's office
3. November 11 honorees
4. Citrus punch
5. Thread holder
6. Use cobble-stones
7. Took nourish-ment
8. "Promise" of danger
9. Perceive sound
10. Sinister
11. She had a little lamb
19. Fruit preserves
21. Sagittarius of the zodiac
23. Slate-clearing pad
24. Chum
25. Everyone
26. Songstress Peggy
27. That boy's
28. Good-looking in a manly way
29. Whitney of the cotton gin
30. Male cat
32. Dollar bill
35. Clam's colleague
36. Grass moisture
38. Steed or nag
39. Mop (the deck)
40. Fork prong
41. Start a poker kitty
42. Clothes labels
44. Mimicked
45. Animal enclosures
48. Conceit
49. Taxi

246

ACROSS

1. Beach bucket
5. Slender stalk
9. Health club
12. Land unit
13. Broad
14. A lubricant
15. Attempted a free throw
16. Military group
17. Mr. Gibson
18. Circus shelter
19. ____ King Cole
20. To a great degree
21. Poultry product
23. Lyric poem
25. Love madly
28. Inscribed
32. Pledge
33. Wipe (a blackboard)
35. Sailor's assent
36. Books of maps
38. Tossed
40. Tie the knot
41. Apply
42. March flying toy
45. Strike (a ball)
47. Eve's mate
51. Nuptial words
52. Departed
53. Washed-out looking
54. Do the mending
55. Violent emotion
56. Distinctive times
57. ____ Francisco
58. Scent
59. Popular rooms for TVs

DOWN

1. Gone by in time
2. Dull, continual pain
3. What weightlifte rs pump?
4. Long note
5. Waved (a bat)
6. Ms. Turner of rock
7. Newspaper chiefs
8. Introduced oneself to
9. "____ Like It Hot," movie oldie
10. Docking place
11. Supporter
20. Fido's doctor
22. Birds in a gaggle
24. Weight-loss programs
25. Gardner of films
26. It completes an "i"
27. Feathered night-hunter
28. Existed
29. Black roofing goo
30. Needle hole
31. The "N" in "NYC"
34. Person with auburn hair
37. Fear and trembling
39. Made a pile of
41. Speak
42. Peck on the cheek
43. Notion
44. Large village
46. Division term
48. Have the guts (to)
49. Ladd or Alda
50. Disorderly state
52. 27-Down's cry, suppos-edly

1	2	3	4	■	5	6	7	8	■	9	10	11
12				■	13				■	14		
15				■	16				■	17		
18				■	19			■	20			
■	■	■	21	22		■	23	24		■	■	■
25	26	27			■	28				29	30	31
32			■	33	34				■	35		
36			37				■	38	39			
■	■	■	40			■	41			■	■	■
42	43	44		■	45	46		■	47	48	49	50
51			■	52				■	53			
54			■	55				■	56			
57			■	58				■	59			

247

ACROSS

1. Less hazardous
6. Cheer-leader's quality
9. Existed
12. Breathing
13. Brewery product
14. ". . . and to ____ a good night!"
15. Had the guts (to)
16. Near the ground
17. Ms. Lupino
18. Ginger cookie
20. Wound with a dagger
21. Do some sums
24. Sea
26. Regret
27. Bring into play
28. Protect from danger
32. Crisp veggie
34. PhD, for one
35. Attack like a bee
36. Turf
37. Gents
38. Sleeveless garments
40. Conniving
41. Not at home
44. Christmas carol
46. Newsman Rather
47. This minute
48. Dumbfound
53. Antique
54. Raw metal
55. Child's vehicle
56. It may be cloudy
57. Koppel of "Nightline"
58. Got to one's feet

DOWN

1. Melancholy
2. In the style of: 2 wds.
3. An evergreen
4. Eden resident
5. Scarlet and crimson
6. Royal home
7. Run off to wed
8. Church seat
9. Be patient
10. Alan or Robert
11. Thick slice
19. Overly curious
20. ____ as a bug in a rug
21. Circle segments
22. Song for a pair
23. Corned-beef shop
25. Matured
27. Inner drive
29. Upper limbs
30. Rod go-with
31. Contradict
33. A deadly sin
34. Medicine "serving"
36. Packed away neatly
39. Sleep noisily
41. Commotions
42. Stroll; amble
43. Commen-tator Rooney
45. Regulations and statutes
47. Negative word
49. "Welcome" rug
50. In the past
51. Place to see lions, tigers, and bears . . . oh, my!
52. Finale

248

ACROSS

1. Zoo animal from China
6. Thieve from
9. Droop
12. Stay away from
13. Be a debtor
14. Ms. Lupino
15. Went out with
16. Advice columnist Landers
17. Chop (off)
18. Identical
20. Medicine portion
21. Sullivan and McMahon
24. Forgiveness
26. Wheel furrow
27. Turner of communications
28. Jumped like a ballerina
32. President Ronald
34. TV dog
35. Leather band
36. Top for a pen
37. Sick
38. Pavarotti's voice range
40. Everything
41. Birthday pastry
44. Annoys
46. Fighter pilot
47. Chick's ma
48. Noggins
53. Beatles song, "____ Loves You"
54. Hockey playing surface
55. Arctic shelter
56. Half a score
57. The "p" in "mph"
58. Fence uprights

DOWN

1. Drawing tablet
2. Filmdom's Gardner
3. "____ a creature was stirring. . ."
4. Board-game cube
5. Does sums
6. Wandered
7. Dog's mistress
8. Mr. Franklin, familiarly
9. Farm tower
10. Big fusses
11. Stare in amazement
19. "Let it be so!"
20. Coloring chemicals
21. Is mistaken
22. Pair's song
23. One in a constellation
25. Applaud
27. Record (sound)
29. India's locale
30. Medicine capsule
31. Inform
33. Fence's door
34. "Happy" bird
36. Crosswalk site
39. Brother's daughter
41. Broken-arm support
42. Feel painful
43. Sharp, as hearing
45. Sailing vessel
47. Haunch
49. Conceit
50. Gore and Jolson
51. Small, round speck
52. Call for help

249

ACROSS

1. Prisoner's release money
5. Carbonated drink
8. Nile biters
12. Unit of land measure
13. Wonderment
14. Chicken's home
15. City air pollution
16. Never used
17. Narrative account
18. Perceived; felt
20. Inquired
21. Took part in the Indy 500
24. Site for sporting events
28. Baked pasta dish
33. Really big
34. Derby, for one
35. Lunch time, for many
36. One more
38. Covered with white drifts
39. Site of a sprain, sometimes
41. Put off temporarily
45. Ones in possession
50. Afresh
51. Uncooked
53. Spoken
54. Chair or couch
55. Be sick
56. Do a jackknife
57. Ceases
58. Attempt (to)
59. Plant origin

DOWN

1. Male vocal range
2. Highest peak
3. Press
4. Table "limbs"
5. Chinese bear
6. Have a debt
7. Bench in a house of worship
8. Portrays a character
9. Make very wet
10. Warsaw native
11. Went rapidly
19. Historic time
20. Paid notices
22. Mr. Gable
23. Consume a snack
24. "The light has dawned!"
25. Sprint
26. Self-importance
27. Fish trap
29. Miller or Sothern
30. Sticky matter
31. At the present
32. Whichever
34. 14-Across resident
37. Cattle feed
38. Do some tailoring
40. Humble
41. Unit of medicine
42. Uniform; level
43. Be at the head of
44. Crafts' partner
46. Drowses (with "off")
47. One-time canal
48. Talk like a madman
49. Enjoy a winter pastime
51. Wharf pest
52. Atmosphere

250

ACROSS

1. Fuss
4. Pierce with a dagger
8. Chances, in betting
12. "How are ____?"
13. Uncontaminated
14. Sudsy cleanser
15. Onstage arrival
17. Nat King ____
18. Provo's state
19. Removed the peel from
20. Joyful
23. Always
25. Narrow road
26. Tiresome child
27. Brief sleep
30. False
32. Harsh
34. Sullivan and McMahon
35. Fellow
37. Provokes
38. Female choir voice
39. Expense
40. Enraged
43. Record (a TV show)
46. Title for a king
47. Church official
51. Statement in court
52. Skin problem of youth
53. Notable period
54. Stitches together
55. Bambi's kin
56. Wipe with a towel

DOWN

1. Pro vote
2. Put on (clothing)
3. Not in
4. Lovers' quarrel
5. Canned fish
6. Longbow expert
7. Honey maker
8. "Sesame Street" grouch
9. It's on hinges
10. Valley
11. Hurried in a car
16. More impolite
19. Sampras of tennis
20. Adhesive fluid
21. Come ashore
22. Industrious insects
24. Immense
26. Red root veggie
27. Infamous Roman emperor
28. Boats like Noah's
29. Annoying one
31. Very unattractive
33. Unhealthy habits
36. Observe
38. Regions
40. Egyptian snakes
41. Cleopatra's waterway
42. Raised, as crops
44. Bancroft of Hollywood
45. Docking place
47. See 40-Across
48. Baseball great Williams
49. Bungle
50. Beam of sunlight

251

ACROSS

1. Primary
5. Cereal grains
9. That girl
12. Land unit
13. Clock face
14. Give money to
15. Pump or sandal
16. Neatly arrange
18. "Love Me ____," song
20. Short letters
21. Demands
24. Get up
27. Car fuel
28. Drink, as a dog
31. Male monarch
32. Swiss peak
33. Destiny
34. Frozen
35. Self
36. Less sad
37. State-police patrolpers on
39. Chef's coverall
42. One who enjoys books
46. Dark-haired woman
49. Used a loom
50. Fireplace wood
51. Oceans
52. Largest continent
53. Asner and Sullivan
54. Danson and Turner
55. Shout

DOWN

1. Sail's pole
2. Hurt, as a muscle
3. Remove the wrinkles from (clothes)
4. Requiring
5. Smells
6. Atmosphere
7. Clothing label
8. Inclines
9. Barbecue rod
10. Smog's kin
11. Seeing organs
17. Negative replies
19. Conclude
22. Eskimo's abode
23. Tree fluid
24. Hit the slopes
25. ____-tac-toe
26. Every
28. Produce (eggs)
29. Had lunch
30. For each
32. In the past
33. Very distant
35. Actor Borgnine
36. "Golly!"
37. 2,000 pounds
38. See 3-Down
39. Competent
40. Poke
41. Small carpets
43. Medicine unit
44. Morally depraved
45. Genuine
47. Golf peg
48. Small amount

252

ACROSS

1. Peach stone
4. Did the breast stroke, maybe
8. Night-sky twinkler
12. Anger
13. Record (a TV show)
14. Heal
15. Negative replies
16. Level
17. Picnic pests
18. Main course
20. Large explosion
21. Asked for an 18-Across
24. Puts on display
27. Drag
28. Pod vegetable
31. "____ Town," play
32. Golf peg
33. Sick
34. Hive insect
35. "What's up, ____?"
36. Tugs sharply
38. Made calm
40. Sample, as food
43. Least young
47. Friendly country
48. Singer McCartney
50. Had lunch
51. Worshiped one
52. In addition
53. It rises in the east
54. Tardy
55. Unwanted plant
56. Conclude

DOWN

1. Evergreen tree
2. Press (pants)
3. Student evaluation
4. Guides (a ship)
5. Gestured a greeting
6. Mimic
7. Adult boys
8. Burn with water
9. Common food fish
10. Crafts' partner
11. Take it easy
19. Noisy quarrel
20. Plead
22. Vote in
23. Regret
24. Weep
25. Tint
26. Lode load
28. Sewing aid
29. Large deer
30. Pacino and Gore
32. As well
35. Female 29-Down
36. Shouted
37. Total (up)
38. Fashion
39. Full ____, poker hand
40. Dog's wagger
41. Actor Alan
42. Coin opening
44. Alleviate
45. Shock deeply
46. Look after
48. Church bench
49. Pub offering

253

ACROSS

1. Can cover
4. Tiger's 9-Down
7. One who gathers fallen leaves
12. Beethoven's "____ to Joy"
13. Spanish waterway
14. Pimento-stuffed fruit
15. Mobile's site
17. Ate by candlelight, maybe
18. Parachute fabric
19. Board-game cube
21. Hive dweller
23. Wandered
28. Likely (to)
31. Big fuss
33. Apple discard
34. Enjoy a novel
36. Earth's closest star
37. Exact replica
38. Brief note
39. Sock tip
40. Firm up, as gelatin
41. Place to wear one's heart?
43. Football's Marino
46. Goof up
48. Log floats
52. Stinging insects
56. Monogram letter
58. Be in store for
59. ____ Vegas, Nevada
60. By means of
61. Leases
62. Storm's calm center
63. Stately tree

DOWN

1. Banking service
2. In a casual way
3. Give out (cards)
4. Tall bird
5. Shoot (for)
6. Frog's cousin
7. Bronco-busting competition
8. Boxer Muhammad
9. Relatives
10. Woman of Eden
11. Firetruck color
16. Comedian Hope
20. Removed wrinkles from
22. Spring holiday
24. Perform in a play
25. Cuts (the grass)
26. A Great Lake
27. Bumper blemish
28. Limbs for hugging
29. Pare (a fruit)
30. Domesticate
32. Performing pair
35. Stag's mate
42. Three-piece suit parts
44. Wake up
45. Singer King Cole
47. Irritate
49. Three plus two
50. Peacock's pride
51. Close noisily
52. Hostile conflict
53. Stupefied wonder
54. The ____ Antonio Spurs
55. Deep hole
57. A negative

254

ACROSS

1. Perimeter; margin
5. Aladdin's magic vessel
9. Plot of soil for flowers
12. Lustful look
13. Concept or thought
14. Wrath
15. Nasty; cruel
16. Snares for fish
17. Relative
18. Smears a thin layer over
20. Honeyed
22. Hot spring
23. Pod morsel
24. Shipping container
27. Sold door to door
31. Balloon filler
32. Piece of advice
33. Certain Gabor
34. Zero
37. ____ pole, Native American carving
39. Industrious 36-Down
40. Guacamole or salsa
41. Jogs like a horse
44. Salad-dressing ingredient
48. Piece of corn
49. Genesis garden
51. Cleopatra's river
52. Long time-span
53. Adorable
54. Like 2, 4, or 6
55. A Gibson
56. Throw lightly
57. Relax and take it easy

DOWN

1. Lawn trees
2. Far from shallow
3. Toothed wheel
4. Mr. Hemingway
5. Singer Ronstadt
6. Citrus drinks
7. Encountered
8. Went by
9. Ten-speed personal transport
10. Pennsylvania lakeside city
11. Small hollow
19. Gorilla, for one
21. Chunk of gum
23. Zest
24. Is able to
25. Brazil port, for short
26. Gallery offering
27. Sty resident
28. Permit
29. First woman
30. Beaver's structure
32. Dynamite's relative: abbr.
35. Head topper
36. Six-legged critter
37. Sardine holder
38. Kitchen device
40. Eats out
41. Abound (with)
42. Hardly cooked
43. Spoken
44. Former soldiers
45. ____ and take
46. Bubbly drinks
47. Monthly tenant fee
50. The Dynamic ____, Batman and Robin

255

ACROSS

1. Sing without words
4. Window ledge
8. Grain tower
12. Unrefined metal
13. Peter, Paul & Mary, for one
14. Tehran's land
15. Beginning, as a profession
17. Traditional teachings
18. Immense
19. "The ____ justify the means"
20. Hurled
23. Female fowl
25. Harness strap
26. Inhaled and exhaled
31. Be unhealthy
32. More cheerful
33. Anger
34. Ready
36. Body's outer covcring
37. Inquire
38. Bird chirp
39. Heavenly body
42. Urgent request
44. Hankie trim
45. Colorful, after-downpour displays
49. Store window sign
50. Word of sorrow
51. Court (a sweetheart)
52. "Honesty is the ____ policy"
53. Used to be
54. Recently arrived

DOWN

1. Weeding aid
2. Large coffee server
3. Ran into
4. Sipping tube
5. Spring flower
6. Laundry fluff
7. Word before "cabin" or "jam"
8. Speechless
9. Clothes-pressing appliance
10. Bacon grease
11. Single bills
16. Smooth; level
20. Ensnare
21. One in a will
22. Make irritable
23. Listen to
24. Hearing organ
26. Dog's noise
27. Deli bread
28. Wilderness walk
29. New York canal
30. Slight depression, as on a fender
32. Car fuel
35. Father or mother
36. Mop, as a ship's deck
38. Anxious; nervous
39. Untidy one
40. Recording cassette
41. Scores 100% on (a test)
42. With little color
43. Tale-telling one
45. Like the fish in sushi
46. Be in possession of
47. Misery
48. Scatter, as seed

256

ACROSS

1. Distant
4. Out of town
8. "Not guilty," for one
12. Inventor Whitney
13. Rich vein of ore
14. Assistance
15. Deadly viper
16. Profit's opposite
17. Expand, as bread dough
18. Mixed (a salad)
20. Relieved
21. Shellfish served on the half-shell
24. "When it ____, it pours!"
27. "So soon?"
31. See 14-Across
32. Annoy
33. "See you later!"
34. Shield from harm
37. Like sugar
39. Try to pin an opponent to the mat
41. Calcutta's country
44. Broadest
48. Close at hand
49. Careen out of control
51. Boxer Muhammad
52. Highway fee
53. Evergreen tree
54. Free (of)
55. Lowest-denomination bills
56. Refreshing drinks
57. Surveillance expert

DOWN

1. Daring deed
2. In addition
3. Tears, as fabric
4. Narrow back streets
5. Forested area
6. Commercials
7. "Certainly!"
8. Sentence fragment
9. Hawaiian garlands
10. Otherwise
11. Mimicked
19. Male offspring
20. Be incorrect
22. Small pies
23. Moose's kin
24. Knock sharply
25. Scuba-tank filler
26. Vow words
28. President Lincoln's nickname
29. Color-changing agent
30. "I have not ____ begun to fight"
32. Hockey surface
35. Spins
36. Noteworthy period of time
37. Playground fixtures with ladders
38. Get married
40. Strong cord
41. Enthralled by
42. Diner-sign gas
43. Ms. Evans
45. Dumbo's "wings"
46. Lose footing
47. Neat
49. Place for a mud bath
50. Baby goat

257

ACROSS

1. Outer border
5. Fairy-tale beginning word
9. On vacation from work
12. Bun's kin
13. College official
14. Golf standard
15. Brewery products
16. Soil
17. Pastry cut into wedges
18. "To ____, perchance to dream..."
20. Exclamation of wonder
21. ____ Faithful, famous geyser
22. "Disgusting!"
24. Operated (a machine)
26. Tree fluid
29. "Cold, hard" money
31. Be the guide
34. Raps (on a door)
36. Citrus fruit
38. Concerned with
39. Horseback game
41. Number of Biblical Commandments
42. Consumed food
44. Place a wager
45. Swat (a baseball)
47. Perform in a film
49. Skedaddle: slang
54. Fuss and bother
55. Purpose; aim
57. See 36-Across
58. Use your eyes
59. Midwestern lake
60. Perfect tennis serves
61. Owns
62. Tenant's monthly expense
63. Coops and corrals

DOWN

1. Important time periods
2. Raggedy Ann or Barbie
3. Happiness
4. Otherwise
5. Bizarre
6. Horse sounds
7. Show concern
8. Word on a door
9. Adversary
10. Do not pass
11. Dancer Astaire
19. Hockey disk
23. Inhale in surprise
25. Like: 2 wds.
26. Glide down a slope
27. "Dear ____ Landers . . ."
28. Starchy vegetables
30. Swiss-cheese feature
32. Ripen
33. Cozy room
35. Folding bed
37. Decays
40. Get
43. Raring to go
45. Corned-beef concoction
46. Brainstorm outcome
48. Molten center (of the earth)
50. Applaud
51. Chinese grain
52. Prayer end
53. Disorder
56. "Little pig, little pig, ____ me in!"

258

ACROSS

1. Walking aid
5. Grass carpet
8. Oxford or mule
12. Atop
13. "____ on a Grecian Urn"
14. Chess play
15. Most appro-priate
16. Job notices
17. A son of Adam and Eve
18. Pen-filling fluid
20. Slip-ups
22. In that spot
25. Run slowly
26. Less courteous
27. Gabor of "Green Acres"
28. Create clothing
31. Ripen
32. Wind-direction indicators
34. Time in history
35. Craving
36. Not in
37. Rail trans-portation
39. Bustle
40. Relieved
41. Be demanding
44. Find sums
45. Letter opener?
46. Steal from
48. Object on a list
52. Solitary
53. In poor health
54. Bubbly soft-drink
55. Trying to make ____ meet
56. Citrus cooler
57. Party giver

DOWN

1. Baby bear
2. Orang or chimp
3. Negative answers
4. Complete
5. Pretreat laundry, in a way
6. "The ____ Couple"
7. Be worthy of
8. Clever
9. Tramp; vagabond
10. See 12-Across
11. Snaky fishes
19. Anxious
21. Cooked (a turkey)
22. Waiter's platter
23. Jumbo-sized
24. Home, to Eve
25. Campers' shelters
28. Oceans
29. Toledo's Great Lake
30. Fairy god-mother's stick
33. Vienna's land
38. Small, red salad ingredient
39. Lets go of (an employee)
41. Not doing much
42. Vegas strip light-gas
43. Hourglass grit
44. Skilled enough
47. Quite mature
49. Further-more
50. Sullivan and Asner
51. Rug in front of a door

259

ACROSS

1. Pleased as punch
5. "Ladies and gentlemen, children of all ____ . . ."
9. Suitable
12. Frilly dress trim
13. Two-wheeled wagon
14. Negative vote
15. Microwave unit
16. The Muske-teers, for one
17. Clip, as a bud
18. What "haste makes"
20. Drops on a dawn lawn
21. Keats piece
22. Out of harm's way
24. Put into words
26. Chasing game
29. Citrus peel
31. Jar tops
34. Chefs' kitchen wear
36. Wide thorough-fare
38. Shapely fall fruit
39. Golfer's goal
41. Received
42. Freshly made
44. Watch over (a flock of sheep)
46. Long in the tooth
48. Sweltering
50. Makes the sound of a watch
54. Ms. Basinger
55. Preholiday nights
57. Carol word
58. Gardner of films
59. Very unusual
60. Delight
61. "Okay!"
62. Otherwise
63. Post (mail)

DOWN

1. Shine softly
2. Volcanic outpouring
3. King beaters
4. Fender hollows
5. Play a role
6. Flower bed, for one
7. Old New York canal
8. Stores on a ship
9. Pest's action
10. Settled a bill
11. Write using a keyboard
19. Make (a living)
23. Cod or salmon
25. Beer's cousin
26. Knock gently
27. Big monkey
28. Kids' allies, often
30. Valley
32. Batman and Robin, The Dynamic ____
33. All ready
35. Raw mineral
37. Air outlet
40. Playful water animals
43. "This is ____ the action is!"
45. Bell sounds
46. "All right!"
47. Reside (in)
49. Like an elongated circle
51. Songwriter Porter
52. Sharp, as wit
53. Snow vehicle
56. Visualize

260

ACROSS

1. Current events
5. Gore and Roker
8. Grumpy one
12. Eden fellow
13. Outfielder's headwear
14. Covered with grease
15. Present (to)
16. Geometric shape
18. Porter-house or T-bone
20. Country lodging
21. Moreno of movies
23. Swans' notable features
28. Ball (of paper)
31. Young children
33. Alda or King
34. Middle Eastern country
36. Spud
38. Makes (a knot)
39. Put cargo on (a truck)
41. Spider's snare
42. Some birds of prey
44. Forehead
46. Kin of a 13-Across
48. Indy 500 entrant
52. San Francisco treat?: 2 wds.
57. Diva's offering
58. Canton's state
59. Spanish waterway
60. Male alleycats
61. Struggle for breath
62. Upshot
63. Otherwise

DOWN

1. Tired, old horses
2. Revise (text)
3. Signal 11-Down
4. Finger-paint stroke
5. Perform a role
6. Lasso
7. Revolve
8. Opposed
9. Oil derrick
10. Winner takes ____
11. Farewell
17. Raggedy ____, doll
19. Flying toy
22. Parkway fee
24. Consume food
25. Cat's weapon
26. Ms. Hepburn, to pals
27. Snooty one
28. Accompa-nied by
29. India's locale
30. Made a picture with crayons
32. Shadowbox
35. Invite
37. Scent
40. Get
43. That gal
45. Refuse; trash
47. Farm unit
49. Warm's opposite
50. Lawn trees
51. Popular flower
52. Law enforcer
53. "So there you are!"
54. Storage compart-ment
55. Building site
56. Curtain pole

261

ACROSS

1. Little dog's bark
4. Cafe bill
7. Heart; center
8. Ceramic flooring squares
10. Liquor from Russia
11. Warm, knitted garment
13. Serves perfectly, in tennis
14. Surrounded by
15. Number in a pair
16. Singer's tone
17. Like a bug in a rug
18. Toes' locations
19. Sampling (food)
21. Contented kitties' sounds
22. Oft-used contraction
23. ____ Angeles
24. Frontiersman Daniel
27. Pistol case on a belt
31. Land-measurement unit
32. Saw or screwdriver
33. The Greatest
34. Frozen pond's surface
35. Notable camel feature
36. Untidy one
37. Suitcases, collectively
39. Stair units
40. Classic TV miniseries
41. Cone-bearing tree
42. Spoken refusals
43. Picasso's output

DOWN

1. Sings from an Alp
2. Boats like Noah's
3. Soup veggie
4. Like a photo finish
5. In the style of: 2 wds.
6. "For ____ or for worse . . ."
7. Hot drink
8. Thin, brittle stick
9. Seamstress, for one
10. Great in magnitude
11. Self-satisfied
12. Decays slowly
14. Landers and Miller
17. Building location
18. Be cranky
20. Pitchfork prong
21. Survey of public opinion
23. Rollercoaster feature
24. Scoop water out of a boat
25. Happen
26. Washington state's neighbor
27. "There's no place like ____"
28. Native ability
29. Run off to marry
30. Chest bones
32. Hauls
35. Homburgs and sombreros
36. Recipe word
38. Syllable from Baby
39. Health retreat

262

ACROSS

1. Glasgow native
5. Apply (paint) lightly
8. Vocal range
12. Des Moines' site
13. Needle hole
14. Nickel or dime
15. Christmas
16. Southern general
17. Towering
18. Yale graduate
20. Four times five
22. Sports stadiums
25. Young chap
26. Dollars and ____
27. Beloved animal
28. Senator Kennedy
31. Angry
32. Make fun of
34. Beam of sunshine
35. Asner and Bradley
36. Clinging vine
37. Awaken
39. Wallet bill
40. Native American tents
41. Pattern
44. Sweetened lemon drink
45. Egg-shaped
46. Common contraction
48. Water from above
52. Ceramic flooring square
53. Tennis-court barrier
54. Actor Alan
55. Coasting toy
56. Cheery
57. Little quarrel

DOWN

1. Immorality
2. Pigeon's murmur
3. Be in the red, financially
4. Natural ability
5. Pastrami shops
6. Affirmative reply, to Blackbeard
7. Hard-shelled insects
8. Performed in a play
9. Temporary gift
10. Lean to one side
11. And no other
19. Standing the test of time
21. Tended a plant, in a way
22. Highest peak
23. Enjoy a newspaper
24. Extremities
27. "Time to ____ the piper!"
28. Not false
29. Lack of difficulty
30. Colors, as Easter eggs
33. Period between dusk and night
38. "Carmen" and "Aïda"
39. Lubricated
40. Delicious
41. Specks
42. Sinister
43. Bargain event
47. Afternoon refreshment
49. Peak in Switzerland
50. Lupino of film
51. ____ King Cole

263

ACROSS

1. Wrestlers' surface
4. Jogging gait
8. Actor MacMurray
12. Barroom order
13. Freight-yard vagrant
14. Amusement-park attraction
15. In poor health
16. At any ——, nevertheless
17. Not shut
18. Color, as fabric
19. Notable time
20. Took off
21. Solemn pledge
23. Essential nutrient
26. Liquid precipitation
28. Winter flurries
29. Popular pet
32. Bee or cricket
34. Previously
36. "See you later!"
37. Granola grains
39. Poker verb
40. Judge's gown
41. Explosive stuff: abbr.
42. Where one lives
45. In the past
47. "Now I get it!"
50. Bad
51. Slight fight
52. Detroit product
53. Singer Horne
54. Seep (out)
55. Actor Allen
56. Hunter's quarry
57. Flower support
58. Cunning

DOWN

1. One of the help
2. Wartime friend
3. Put on the tube
4. Hurled
5. Crowd sound
6. Get
7. Boot end
8. Disapproving expression
9. Ready to eat, as fruit
10. Unspoiled spot
11. Fender boo-boo
22. Single
24. Burglarizes
25. Be a debtor
26. Chest bone
27. Some
28. Pierce with a dagger
29. People to get in touch with
30. Creative skill
31. Golf-ball holder
33. Turtledove talk
35. Air-circulating device
38. Hot-beverage server
40. Pass along (info)
41. Ancestral symbol
42. Aid
43. Upon
44. Coal source
46. Lingering look
48. Frozen 26-Across
49. Military force
51. Rescue request

264

ACROSS

1. Period of prosperity
5. Derby or bowler
8. Between the devil and the ____ blue sea
12. Helpful one
13. Actress Gabor
14. Useless
15. Dr. Pierce portrayer
16. Fall behind
17. What helium balloons do
18. Siesta
20. Water mammal
21. Droops
24. Milk producer
26. Wedding words
27. Realized
29. Youthful male
32. Fixed; immovable
33. Raw mineral
34. Top gun
35. Owns
36. Small lakes
38. The woman
39. Some
40. Bridal-party guy
42. Plastic drinking tube
46. Tabby or Polly
47. Mortgage, perhaps
48. Sock end
50. A son of Eve
54. Army grouping
55. Lupino of film
56. 33-Across jackpot
57. Nail-polish shades
58. Hollywood's Gibson
59. Misplaced

DOWN

1. Ewe's sound
2. Saudi export
3. Eccentric
4. Intended
5. "SOS!"
6. Gardner of the movies
7. Store's pricing label
8. Mud ingredient
9. Go over (a manuscript) for publication
10. Otherwise
11. British noble
19. Inquire
20. Be in possession of
21. Expectant desire
22. Notion
23. Whole bunch
24. Trite
25. Had monetary obligations
28. 12 o'clock p.m.
29. Whip thong
30. Soreness
31. Doe's family
36. Leopard's "foot"
37. Bring civil action against
41. Horse's condo?
42. Cast aspersions on
43. Vocal pitch
44. Surprise invasion
45. Cooperative insects
46. Resound
48. "Tiny" Cratchit
49. Keatsian work
51. Ghostly yell
52. McMahon and Sullivan
53. "____ me know what you decide!"

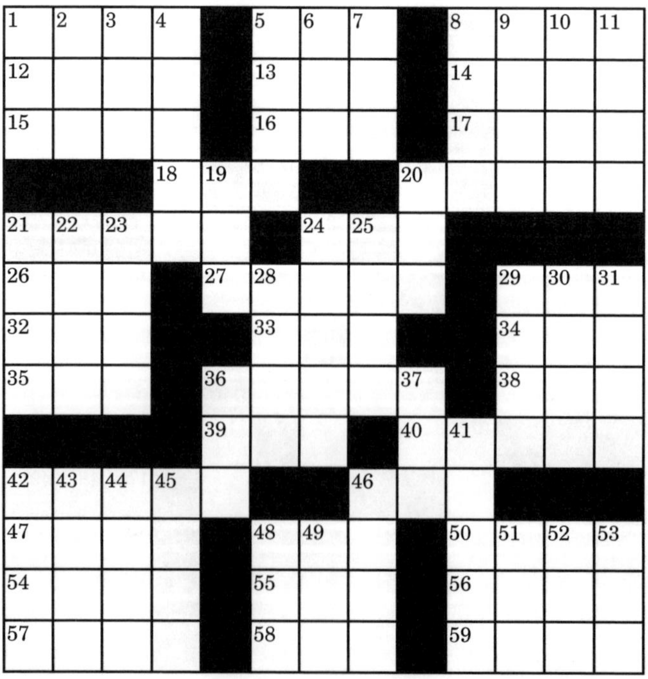

265

ACROSS

1. Crafts' partner
5. Decade number
8. Scottish caps
12. Airplane stunt
13. In the style of: 2 wds.
14. New York canal
15. Object of worship
16. ____ and tuck
17. Evergreen tree
18. Noah's boat
20. First garden
21. Pursue
24. Blaze
27. "Correct!"
28. Summer cooler
29. Common explosive: abbr.
32. Anger
33. Native of Des Moines
35. Garden tool
36. Sleeping site
37. Move quickly
38. Coarse string
40. Places a wager (on)
41. Comforts
42. "Scram!"
45. Peculiar
46. Singer Horne
47. Church bench
49. Compact ____, music purchase
53. Circle parts
54. "Sure, captain!"
55. Canyon feedback
56. Ode author
57. Married
58. 43-Down's act

DOWN

1. Boxing great
2. Fishing pole
3. As well
4. Spatter
5. Fuel container
6. Inventor Whitney
7. Doze
8. Sioux dwelling
9. Very dry
10. Lode location
11. Witnessed
19. Turn in for the night
21. Baby's 36-Across
22. Give a job to
23. Mature
24. Young deer
25. Actress Lupino
26. Leased
29. " ____ Old House," TV show
30. Zilch
31. Golfer's pegs
34. Not indoors
39. Crumpled (paper)
40. Show off
42. Open-handed hit
43. Brave guy
44. In the past
45. Was indebted to
47. Cat's "foot"
48. Seeing organ
50. Frozen water
51. That girl
52. Food fish

266

ACROSS

1. Ms. Moreno
5. Small lie
8. Captain in "Moby-Dick"
12. Showy flower
13. Unrefined mine product
14. Asian grain
15. Performs
16. Comedian's joke
17. Sicilian volcano
18. Conclusion
20. Alleviated (pain)
21. Short, wise expres- sions
24. Festive celebration
27. Floor covering
28. Auction offer
31. Sigh of sorrow
32. Skillet
33. Sandwich fish
34. Dripping
35. Be the right size
36. Musician Bono
37. Person with experience
39. Tossed; flung
42. Worked on (copy)
46. Listen to
47. "I've found it!"
49. Neutral color
50. Rainbows' paths
51. Instant lawn
52. Give a job to
53. Roused
54. Attention-getting cry
55. Related (a story)

DOWN

1. Travel by taxi
2. Sturdy metal
3. Neck and neck
4. Helps
5. Like London's weather, often
6. A Gershwin
7. Ask for alms
8. Regions
9. Top 40 selections
10. Skin affliction
11. Necklace piece
19. A negative
20. Breakfast order
22. Angry
23. Cloistered one
24. Animal's "foot"
25. Bubbly beverage
26. Large city rodent
28. Small bread roll
29. Country lodging
30. Sunrise to sunset
32. Quarry hole
33. This evening
35. Not many
36. Melancholy
37. Poetry
38. Prepared
39. Melt, as ice
40. Valiant man
41. Display stand
43. Small jazz group
44. A British nobleman
45. Colored (hair)
47. Fireplace residue
48. Garden weeder

267

ACROSS

1. Pen liquid
4. Crow's cry
7. "M*A*S*H" star Alan
11. Is able to
12. Spanish cheers
14. Banking service
15. Sense of self
16. Tooted (a horn)
17. Fails to be
18. Made a solemn pledge
20. Colorful Easter item
22. Take care of a bill
23. Person who gives to charity
26. Brief fights
29. Permit
30. Navigator's chart
32. Feeling sick
33. Forbid
34. "____ been thinking . . ."
35. Regret
36. Ungentlemanly fellow
37. Provide food for (parties)
39. Scrub with steel wool
41. Canine companion
42. Doctor for a 41-Across
43. Presses (pants)
46. Farmland measure
49. Genesis garden
51. One of Santa's helpers
53. Conceited
54. Fury
55. Armed conflict
56. Recedes, as the tide
57. Tiny, round speck
58. Observe secretly

DOWN

1. Hockey surface
2. Constantly finds fault
3. Have a clear understanding of
4. Hooded snakes
5. Very narrow street
6. Minuscule
7. Place in a row
8. ____ Angeles
9. Broadcaster Rather
10. Picnic nuisance
13. Nordic nation
19. Choose (with "for")
21. Obtained
24. Leave out
25. Great review
26. Knight's title
27. In addition
28. A Baldwin brother
29. Young man
31. For each
33. Swap goods
36. Actor's prompt
37. Trumpet's kin
38. In the past
40. Pizzeria appliances
41. San ____, site of a famous zoo
44. Nightly world-events show
45. Smack
46. "Hail!"
47. Taxi
48. Torso bone
50. Mom's mate
52. Sizzle in oil

268

ACROSS

1. Also
4. "The Seven Year ____," movie
8. Swiss mountains
12. Possess
13. "Go away!"
14. Fizzy soft drink
15. Agreeable
17. Pull with force
18. Play on words
19. Row of bushes
20. Cone-shaped tent
23. Snow glider
25. Hubbub
26. Tear apart
28. Small bit
31. Bowling target
32. Track in the ground
33. Be in debt
34. Home for a 7-Down
35. More painful
37. Angry
38. Paid notices
39. Follows orders
41. Move rapidly
45. President Lincoln, to pals
46. Volcano output
47. Message sent by Morse code
52. Mine finds
53. Finished
54. In the past
55. Departed
56. Exam
57. Spider's creation

DOWN

1. "____ Gun," Tom Cruise movie
2. "Wise" bird
3. Dollar bill
4. Magazine editions
5. Slender
6. Opposite of pro
7. Adult pig
8. Dull pain
9. Heavy burden
10. Spark ____, car engine device
11. Store event
16. Mimic
19. Successful song
20. Light blows
21. Prepare (copy) for print
22. Small horse
23. Mumbles words
24. Flying toy
27. Jab or poke
28. Covered sports stadium
29. Not present
30. Sleeping spots
35. Unhappy
36. Actor Redford
40. Ask for alms
41. Sluggish
42. Peel
43. Level; steady
44. Sunrise direction
45. Pub brews
47. Young child
48. Adam's mate
49. Uncooked
50. Mature
51. Disorderly crowd

269

ACROSS

1. Vault for valuables
5. Throw in
8. As well
12. Word of woe
13. ____ de Janeiro, Brazil
14. Freight
15. Trapeze artists' safety measures
16. Hollywood's Gibson
17. Bundle of cotton
18. In the past
20. Dried plums
22. Church activity
25. Garment edge
26. Rodeo rope
27. Facial spasm
28. "____ Goes the Weasel"
31. Noah's ship
32. "Armored" African beast
34. Actress Lupino
35. "Of course!"
36. Ruby or sapphire
37. Steam
39. Man's title
40. Harsh; stern
41. Sewing-kit item
44. In favor of
45. Steed-steering strap
46. Drink-cooling cubes
48. Midwest state
52. Lubricates (engines)
53. Convent member
54. Performing pairs
55. Maple or pine
56. Receive
57. Prevent the movement of

DOWN

1. ____ Francisco, California
2. Malt beverage
3. Dieter's bane
4. Student writings
5. Knight's protective gear
6. Gambling cube
7. Marine mammal
8. Book of photos
9. Borrowed money
10. Half-price event
11. Lyric poems
19. Atlanta's state
21. Get well, as from an illness
22. Drama, maybe
23. Underdone, as steak
24. Inquires
27. Funnyman Conway
28. Plumbing tube
29. Aroma
30. Remove the peel from
33. Sheepdog's action
38. Shuns
39. Touch, taste, or smell
40. Used (money)
41. Harness-racing horse's gait
42. One in a will
43. Make irritable
47. Onstage hint
49. Umpire's call
50. Court; romance
51. Cleopatra's snake

270

ACROSS

1. Large rodent
4. Lose one's footing
8. Thin
12. Mature
13. Detest
14. Had on (clothes)
15. Came in first
16. Always
17. Egg-shaped
18. Night visions
20. Lease
21. Go to bed
23. Employ
25. Animal grouping
26. Bay barker
28. Hooting bird
31. Nine minus eight
32. Small and glittering, as eyes
33. Crusted dessert
34. Hearing organ
35. Poker stake
36. Golfer's shout
37. Museum display
38. None the ____, unaware
39. Church chime
42. Mistakes
45. Train track
46. Close
47. "Yuck!"
50. Highest point
51. Food tins
52. Cow's sound
53. Those people
54. Outer part
55. Female pig

DOWN

1. Uncooked
2. In the past
3. Less tough
4. Pasture flock
5. Molten rock
6. Single thing
7. Convince
8. Took an oath
9. Extreme adoration
10. Persia, now
11. Turn to liquid
19. Color of 1-Down meat, often
21. Pump or sandal
22. Singer Horne
24. Clever
26. Paragraph component
27. Have lunch
28. Some marsupials
29. Metal thread
30. Sidelong look
32. Prohibit
36. Common pine tree
37. Bowling lane
38. More unpleasant
39. Impudent child
40. Every
41. Green citrus fruit
43. Peruse (a book)
44. Sounded a 39-Across
48. Sticky stuff
49. "In what way?"

271

ACROSS

1. The thing over there
5. Does sums
9. In addition
12. "Ryan's ____," daytime drama
13. Jump
14. Hooting bird
15. Prayer ending
16. Exclaimed in terror
18. Gets hitched
19. Slippery fishes
20. Smooth
23. Citrus fruits
27. Biblical boat
30. Dines
32. Child's plaything
33. Cooks in an oven
35. Polite word
37. Butterfly's kin
38. The Musketeers, for example
40. Actor Danson
41. Streak (a surface) with grease
43. Poker stake
45. Kitty's sound of contentment
47. Eyelid hair
51. Pastry shops
55. Qualified
56. Employ
57. See 9-Across
58. Rip
59. Bashful
60. Allows
61. Shade trees

DOWN

1. Defrost
2. There's no place like it
3. Mimicked
4. Stressed out
5. Pacino and Gore
6. Proper and fitting
7. Challenge
8. Witch's incantation
9. Newsman Brokaw
10. Have debts
11. Ancient
17. Out of the way
21. Fido's doctor
22. Sunrise direction
24. Castle's protection
25. Otherwise
26. Winter vehicle
27. Sleeves' contents
28. House division
29. Ms. Jackson
31. Rotate
34. Form
36. Parking area
39. Most uncommon
42. Countrified
44. Make (someone) happy
46. Anger
48. He was killed by Cain
49. Noisy impact
50. Belonging to that woman
51. Public transportation
52. Silvery-gray color
53. Locking device
54. Distress call

272

ACROSS

1. "The Tortoise and the ____," fable
5. Cry loudly
8. Unharmed
12. Expression of worry
13. One plus one
14. Food-serving platter
15. Container for gas
16. Stately tree
17. Starchy side dish
18. Car's motor
20. Grooms' mates
22. Geography aid
23. Drink slowly
24. Irritated
28. Vegetarian dish, often
32. Tint of a color
33. Dustcloth, for one
35. Cry of sorrow
36. Begins a poker kitty
39. Sweet dinner course
42. Kindled (a candle)
44. Furrow
45. Queen's seat
48. Field of wildflowers
52. Disorganized pile
53. The Twentieth Century, for one
55. Coal-digging site
56. Primal desire
57. Husband, for one
58. Walk back and forth
59. What a farmer plants
60. Pig's enclosure
61. Snowy day article

DOWN

1. Opposite of love
2. Alda of "M*A*S*H"
3. Played (a bell)
4. Alaska resident
5. Less gradual, as a hill
6. Halloween bird
7. Explosive shells
8. Marking on a zebra
9. Dry and barren
10. Location of 11-Down
11. Sight receptors
19. Negative vote
21. Chest bone
24. "I've got it!"
25. Certain religious female
26. Fish snare
27. Papa
29. Powerful wonder
30. Neither's partner
31. Matched pair
34. Berlin's nation
37. Fled and wed
38. Wrong-doing
40. Take to court
41. Postage stickers
43. Crawls (with)
45. Therefore
46. In this place
47. Intense anger
49. Radio knob
50. ____ and for all
51. Garden intruder
54. Mouse cousin

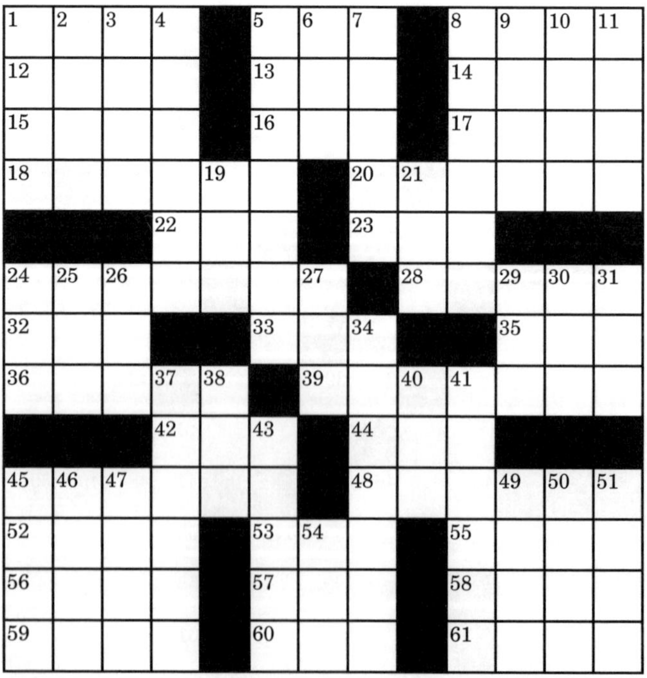

273

ACROSS

1. Govern
5. Plate or saucer
9. Cozy room
12. Not closed
13. Repeated sound
14. "____ Been Working on the Railroad"
15. Beaver's body of water
16. Chair or stool
17. Rodent pest
18. Goes into
20. Sampras of tennis
22. Expected to arrive
23. Chooses democratically
26. Grocery shopper's carrier
29. Historic period
31. Shiny fabric
32. Purposes
34. Tiny ____, Dickens character
36. Office note
37. One who does impressions
39. Mouth part
41. Lawn condensation
42. Uses school stickum
44. Pot cover
46. Narrate (a story)
47. Less shallow
51. Big fuss
53. A citrus fruit
55. Mine location
56. Play on words
57. High cards
58. Was a 37-Across
59. One of Baby's "piggies"
60. Living expense
61. Strong longings

DOWN

1. Clothesline cord
2. Atop
3. Fasting period
4. Came to a close
5. Meal's sweet ending
6. Cooling cubes
7. Form
8. Resort lodgings
9. Did Spielberg's job
10. Ms. Gabor
11. Mesh snare
19. Regret
21. Yoke of oxen
24. Use a stopwatch
25. Winter weather
26. Nudge
27. Largest continent
28. Ring jewel
30. Feel sick
33. Location
35. Least harsh
38. Basement
40. Fruit pastry
43. Portion of a 40-Down
45. Put off
48. Catholic leader
49. Genesis garden
50. Scarlet and crimson
51. Likely (to)
52. Performing pair
54. Gents

274

ACROSS

1. Volcano output
5. Address God
9. Touch affectionately
12. Football-shaped
13. Crop of China
14. In the past
15. Wish for
16. Mental construct
17. Ms. Cole's dad
18. Seep slowly
20. Board-game cube
21. The ____ Antonio Spurs
24. Popular houseplant
26. Fingers' site
27. Grown-up
29. Identical
31. Small horses
33. Smiled brightly?
37. Winter forecast
39. Unit of asparagus
40. Float made of logs
43. Powers of intellect
45. "Don't ____ this at home, folks!"
46. Bungle
47. 24-hour periods
49. "Golly!"
50. Citrus drinks
52. Mouth parts
56. Hard little worker
57. Missing
58. Villainous
59. Scale tones
60. Folksinger Seeger
61. Refuse to accept as truth

DOWN

1. Deep, as a voice
2. Ms. Gardner
3. Delivery vehicle
4. Chorus member
5. Winner's award
6. Equestrians
7. High card
8. Affirmative vote
9. Asian bear
10. One more time
11. Hauled
19. Repeatedly
21. Maple tree fluid
22. Noisy fuss
23. Convent dweller
25. Arrest (a crook)
26. Pile; stack
28. Catalogue
30. In a jumble
32. Hog mama
34. Made the acquaintance of
35. Listening organ
36. Without water
38. Least narrow
40. Fit for a king
41. Stadium for sports
42. Worries
44. Try the flavor of
48. Downhill coaster
50. Swiss peak
51. Female deer
53. "____ Got a Secret"
54. Wrestling victory
55. Cunning

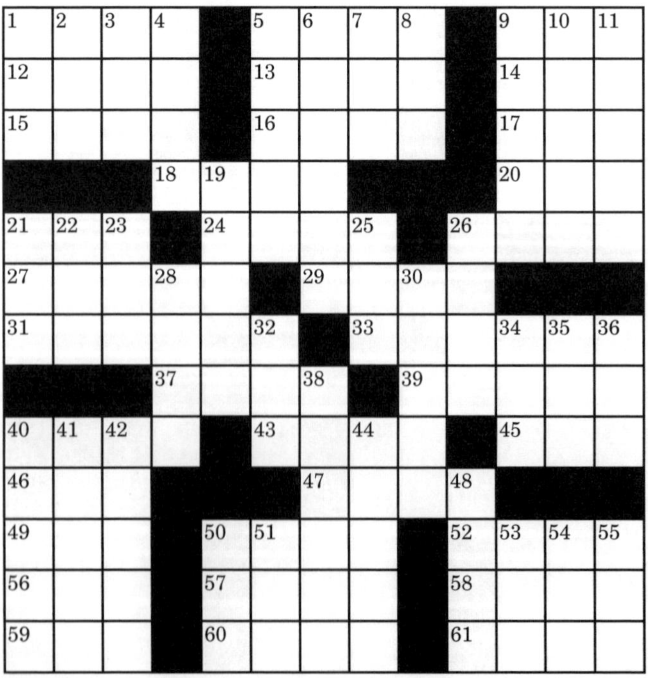

275

ACROSS

1. Guy's partner
4. Beach grit
8. Winter vehicle
12. In the past
13. Urgent request
14. Mineral deposit
15. Boy from Neverland: 2 wds.
17. Desire
18. Expansive
19. Definite arrangement
20. Bowling lane
23. Conclude
25. Borrowed money
26. The Musketeers, for example
27. ____ Jima, Pacific island
30. An apple a day keeps the ____ away
32. Boasted loudly
34. Mimic
35. Existed
37. Competed
38. Actor Majors
39. Has an inclination (to)
40. Stinging insects
44. Elevator direction
46. Repetition of sound
47. Disciplines
51. Horse's gait
52. Experts
53. A Gershwin
54. Does a tailor's job
55. Relax
56. Arid

DOWN

1. Small opening
2. Mature
3. Public parking area
4. Use a gardening hose
5. Swiss mountains
6. More orderly
7. Newscaster Rather
8. Say indistinctly
9. Lady's man?
10. Border
11. Forest creature
16. Occurrence
19. Scent
20. "M*A*S*H" actor
21. Roller-coaster feature
22. Frilly fabric
24. Kind
26. Sycamore or redwood
27. Words from the victor
28. Plant pest
29. Betting advantage
31. Night birds
33. Bakery fixtures
36. Minimize
39. Chubby Checker dance
40. Drenches
41. Farmer's land measurement
42. Performance
43. Flower containers
45. Singles
47. Average score
48. Concealed
49. Make a mistake
50. Express verbally

276

ACROSS

1. Basinger of Hollywood
4. Made (bubbles)
8. Finds the sum of
12. A Gabor
13. Gal or guy Friday
14. Quartet, with one no-show
15. But
16. Short, comic scene
17. One who won't tell the truth
18. Bird's chirp
20. Word before "sugar" or "syrup"
21. Courtroom excuse
23. Some Keats poems
25. Noble Brit
26. Bleak
27. ". . . ____ if by sea . . ."
30. "The ____ Days of Christmas"
32. Sadness
34. Conclusion
35. Part of a foot
37. Acquire by labor
38. Look closely (at)
39. Serves perfectly
40. Drive too 51-Across
43. Wide-awake
46. Expression of 32-Across
47. Object of deep admiration
48. Like Felix and Oscar, as a pair
51. Rapidly
52. Edible shellfish
53. Rogers or Acuff
54. Potato buds
55. Urges
56. Perceive visually

DOWN

1. It opens a lock
2. "____ got an idea!"
3. Made a difference
4. Lamp foundation
5. Prefer
6. One who polishes text
7. Soaking
8. Book of maps
9. Trickle
10. Watch face
11. Tender spot
19. Room's side
20. Office notice
21. Baseball legend Rose
22. Grassy plot
24. Bowl or plate
26. DNA strand
27. Farm vehicles
28. Had on (clothes)
29. Holds the title to
31. Competed (with)
33. Back portion
36. Baby bed on rockers
38. Annoying people
40. Ump's ruling
41. Frolic
42. Make comfortable
44. Bank offering
45. Shade providers
47. Very cold
49. Female deer
50. Color, as hair

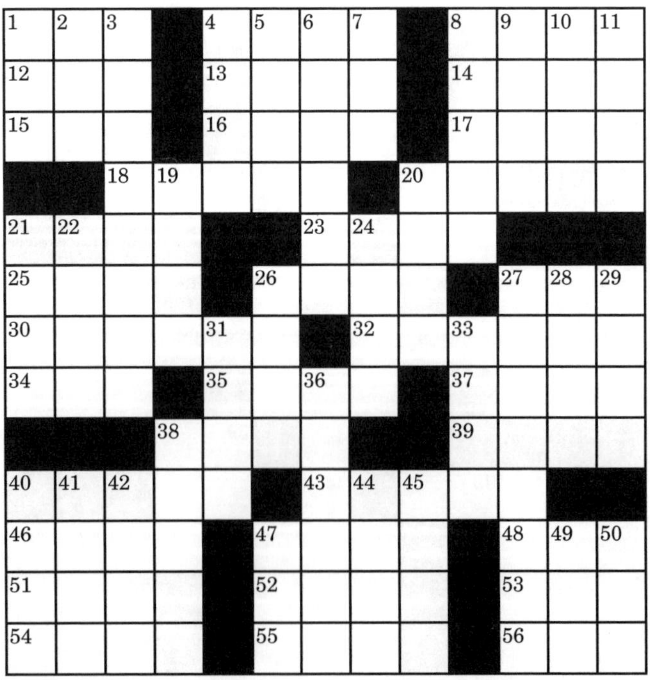

277

ACROSS

1. Light-switch setting
4. European mountain chain
8. Paper to fill out
12. Feel regret
13. Yell, as someone's name
14. Mental construction
15. Period of note
16. Waiter's food holder
17. Bank deal
18. Like the air after a brush fire
20. Lighthearted
21. Water-loving mammal
23. Nights before holidays
25. Destroy
26. Eve's partner
27. Health resort
30. Yearly
32. More downy
34. Dillydally
35. Floating structure
37. Drip, as a faucet
38. Come up
39. Looks for
40. Got to one's feet
43. Machine for cutting grass
45. Mama's mate
46. City car for hire
47. Wedding words
50. Monkeys' uncles?
51. Brewery products
52. In the present
53. Scout's shelter
54. Animal enclosures
55. Exclamation of excitement

DOWN

1. Mine find
2. Cat's hair
3. Eating one's fill
4. Academy Awards category, Best ____
5. A songbird
6. Participated in a sport
7. Crafty
8. Office records
9. Skunk's weapon
10. End of the line
11. Plenty of
19. Restaurant's listing
20. Office reminder
21. Grad student's exam
22. Popular canned fish
24. Expansive
26. "How sad!"
27. Directing (a car)
28. Reach the highest point
29. Boats like Noah's
31. Barren
33. Escape from danger
36. Woman or girl
38. Cook (a turkey)
39. Ham and ____ on rye
40. Little fight
41. VCR insert
42. Opposite of closed
44. Draft animals
46. Knock softly
48. Fawn's mom
49. Have debts

278

ACROSS

1. Prepare (publications) for print
5. Home for hogs
8. Word before "castle" or "crab"
12. Garage occupant
13. Be in the red, financially
14. Opposite of false
15. Refreshing pause
16. Fish flipper
17. Go by bicycle
18. Persian-rug exporting country
20. Lost brightness
21. Tall waterbirds
24. Mouth part
25. Yearns (for)
26. Ship's record
27. Ocean
30. Likely (to)
31. Of the Emerald Isle
33. Tic-____-toe
34. Very small
35. Performed
36. Wring
38. Vigor; energy
39. One of the red suits in cards
40. Oscar or Tony
43. Lass
44. Solo
45. See 12-Across
46. Held on to
50. Gets into (clothes)
51. Monkey's cousin
52. Smooth; level
53. Fruit coolers
54. Mattress site
55. Bumper boo-boo

DOWN

1. Hearing organ
2. Expected, as a baby
3. That thing's
4. Lugging about
5. Cozy seats
6. Identical sibling
7. Japan's money
8. Sandal tie
9. Desert-dry
10. Bare
11. Landowner's document
19. Made one's home (in)
20. Muhammad Ali, for one
21. Cat's scratcher
22. "I'm at the end of my ____!"
23. Poker stake
24. ____ Angeles, California
26. Pot cover
27. Use a spoon
28. Compass direction
29. Play divisions
32. Shred
37. Traveled on foot
38. Iron (clothes)
39. Added to the staff
40. Alan of "The West Wing"
41. Paneling material
42. Bancroft of film
43. Stare open-mouthed
45. Vehicle for hire
47. Abel's mother
48. Writing utensil
49. Blasting compound: abbr.

279

ACROSS

1. Glasses-frames parts
5. Puppy's "foot"
8. Cover (a gift) with paper
12. Mental formulation
13. Movie star Gardner
14. After-bath garment
15. Covers (a wound)
17. Not in use
18. Money in Tokyo
19. Attempt to find
20. Garden tool
24. Subdivision of an army
27. Volcanic molten rock
28. Fall fruit
29. Feminine pronoun
32. Zoo inhabitant
34. Barked like a Yorkie
36. Furniture for sleeping
37. Deprivation
39. Pressed (a doorbell)
40. Catcher's glove
41. Less good
42. Vocal range
45. Brazil resort, for short
47. Air-show maneuver
48. Destructive funnel clouds
53. Ms. Bancroft
54. Wallach or Whitney
55. Impolite
56. Require
57. Pacino and Gore
58. Get together with

DOWN

1. Chest bone
2. Actress Lupino
3. Chaps
4. Downhearted
5. Leaf (of a book)
6. Wide way
7. Used to be
8. Place for a bracelet
9. Traveled by horse
10. Skilled
11. Look shyly
16. "Yes, captain!"
20. Thick slice
21. Window section
22. Enthusiastic
23. River barrier
25. Negative votes
26. Mr. Gershwin
28. Story outline
29. Ship's mast or boom
30. Biddies
31. Knife's sharp side
33. Famous boxer
35. For, in a debate
38. Amble
40. Acted gloomy
41. Scored a victory
42. Arkin or King
43. The ____ Ranger
44. Firm up (muscles)
46. Pigmented eye part
48. Hot drink
49. Sofa limb?
50. Expected
51. Poetic tribute
52. Movie location

280

ACROSS

1. Dress edge
4. Be gloomy
8. Actress Bancroft
12. Lumberjack's cutting device
13. Biblical brother
14. See 13-Across
15. Damage
16. Plumber's problem
17. Orange peel
18. Aromatic
20. Shoe bottoms
21. Helps
24. Arm or leg
27. Cooked in an oven
31. Ms. Gabor
32. Banjo's sound
34. Path
35. Michigan city
37. Make a hole
38. Candor
41. Spring month
44. Attractive
48. Stretched out
49. Angel's headgear
51. A Gershwin
52. Farm building
53. Ready a script
54. Mouth part
55. Singles
56. Mesh snares
57. ____ Angeles, California

DOWN

1. Easter meats
2. Test
3. Only
4. Indoor shopping centers
5. Heeds
6. Pod veggie
7. Moose kin
8. From one side to the other
9. Carpenter's spike
10. Four plus five
11. Concludes
19. Scientist's office
20. Doe's mate
22. Mad
23. Male heir
24. Guided
25. "____ Got a Secret"
26. Floor cloth
28. A couple
29. Jug handle
30. Hair coloring
32. Implement
33. Become victorious
36. Horned beasts
37. Parting word
39. Banana dessert
40. Moves like a horse
41. Too
42. Ache
43. Anger
45. Cultivate (the soil)
46. The Musketeers, for example
47. High-pitched barks
49. Barnyard bird
50. Summer drink

281

ACROSS

1. Raw mineral
4. Alan of 1970s TV
8. Bagpipe player
12. Mink, for one
13. Fastened (shoelaces)
14. Ride to the airport, often
15. Bold and courageous
17. Unseal, as a package
18. Comfort
19. Sports site
20. Profits
23. Towel holder
25. Farm measure
26. Restless desire
27. Self-esteem
30. Delivered some wintry weather
32. Grassy clearing
34. Writing implement
35. Medicine quantity
37. Word before "apple" or "cone"
38. It holds the pants up
39. Detested
40. Cereal utensil
43. ". . . and they lived happily _____ after"
45. Molten rock
46. Most wonderful
50. High playing cards
51. It begins on January 1
52. Currency of Japan
53. Circus shelter
54. Gelatin pan
55. Have supper

DOWN

1. Light-switch setting
2. Be sorrowful
3. Pitcher's stat: abbr.
4. Book of maps
5. Whoppers
6. The Sahara, for one
7. Sales notices
8. Long-legged bird
9. Superhero's cloak
10. Wagon-pulling animals
11. Rock singer Turner
16. Extend a library book's due date
19. Soreness
20. Inhale sharply
21. Skin problem of youth
22. Laundry appliance
24. Summit
26. Worshiped one
27. Use a blue pencil
28. Disappeared
29. Had financial obligations
31. Adam's garden
33. Separated
36. Sound system
38. Brag
39. Got news of
40. Strip of wood
41. Rate of speed
42. Baking chamber
44. Cutlet meat
46. Fitness room
47. Visual organ
48. Baltic or Red
49. An explosive: abbr.

282

ACROSS

1. Civil War general
4. Did the backstroke
8. Shirt stain
12. A Gershwin
13. ____ away, eroded
14. Sheltered inlet
15. Average
16. Pesters
17. Thoroughfare
18. Man of the manor
20. Short periods
22. Flu symptom
24. Anger
25. Told a whopper
26. Least dull, as a knife
30. Commercials
31. Milk farm
33. Rule of conduct
34. Most moist
36. Sandwich shop
37. Stadium cheer
38. Inspired
40. Cereal fruit
43. Go by taxi
44. Very dry
45. Inconsiderate
47. Singer King Cole
50. Teen's skin condition
51. Easter artwork
52. "One, ____, buckle my shoe . . ."
53. Storage shack
54. Medicinal amount
55. Dress edge

DOWN

1. Mouth part
2. Epoch
3. Least late
4. Eddy
5. Sentence units
6. Biblical boat
7. Not as tidy
8. Window insert
9. Game played on a table
10. Shaped like 51-Across
11. Danson and Koppel
19. Antique
21. Hunter's target
22. Lobster's grabber
23. Conceal
26. Tool set
27. At the ____ hour, very late
28. Bargain event
29. Identical sibling
31. College VIP
32. Embarrassed
35. Exchanged (for)
36. Performed
38. Hauls heavily
39. Wash the soap out of
40. Sheep calls
41. Bridge support
42. Baseball-team number
46. Self
48. Wonder
49. Male cat

283

ACROSS

1. Foreman, for example
5. Narrated
9. National Uncle
12. Atop
13. A Great Lake
14. Be indebted to
15. Ram or rooster
16. Tilt
17. Actor Gibson
18. Gratify
20. Most mature
22. Quantities of nails
24. Kitten's cry
25. Become a spouse
28. Singer Clapton
30. Word of comparison
33. Anger
34. Musical toy
36. In the manner of: 2 wds.
37. Chat
39. Fix
40. A little extra for the waitress
41. Help
43. Halt; cease
45. Fine snow
48. It can remove pencil marks
52. Gardner of Hollywood
53. Protein-rich morsel
55. Surface (a road)
56. For each
57. Army group
58. Holiday preceders
59. Exist
60. Mates for turkey hens
61. Tenant's bill

DOWN

1. Run (into)
2. Milky gem
3. Shoe bottom
4. Move furtively
5. Wire
6. Raw metal
7. One who fibs
8. Jeans material
9. To an indefinite degree
10. Amazes
11. Turn to liquid
19. Try to find
21. Cat or dog
23. Small, medium, and large
25. Quick humor
26. Historic age
27. Dover's state
29. Table of ____
31. Boxing champ
32. Catch forty winks
35. Scent
38. Goat's baby
42. Beginning
44. Product of recycling
45. Mama's spouse
46. Finished
47. Nevada city
49. PC command
50. Not odd
51. Remainder
54. Goal

284

ACROSS

1. Quick
5. Paper sacks
9. Deed
12. Smell
13. Way out?
14. Sticky substance
15. Departed
16. Eye drop
17. Actress Gabor
18. Modern
20. Required
22. Baby's sleep spot
25. IRS collection
26. Frying liquid
27. Encountered
29. Shopping centers
33. Fling here and there
35. Scold constantly
37. Castle protector
38. Bar seat
40. Lass
42. Snow runner
43. ____ Vegas, Nevada
45. Skilled craftsman
47. Cosmetics
50. "See ya!"
51. Mine find
52. Intention
54. Marries
58. Sty resident
59. Desire
60. Wicked
61. McMahon and Sullivan
62. Winter vehicle
63. Declare (something) untrue

DOWN

1. Thick, obscuring mist
2. Hubbub
3. Male child
4. Current style
5. In the midst of
6. Tree-chopping tool
7. Goliath, for one
8. Little river
9. Grew old
10. Small inlet
11. Frog's kin
19. Shade tree
21. Test
22. Collapsible beds
23. Public uproar
24. In addition
28. Price label
30. Missing
31. Body of water
32. Twirl a spoon in
34. Foot bottom
36. Wagered
39. Chuckles
41. Produce (eggs)
44. Thread reel
46. Stitched
47. Be dull and spiritless
48. Very dry
49. Beer barrels
53. Mimic
55. Holiday night
56. Confused clamor
57. Cunning

285

ACROSS

1. Physician: slang
4. Inquire
7. Fire residue
12. Groom's words
13. Earn a blue ribbon, maybe
14. The Great Wall's site
15. Female singing voice
17. Toy bear's name
18. Small stream
19. "Which person?"
21. Grass condensation
23. The Beaver State
28. Chest bone
31. Cruel Roman emperor
33. Narrow country road
34. Worshiped statue
36. Road-repair goo
37. Small rodents
38. DNA carrier
39. Comparison word
41. Beatty of the movies
42. Horseback rider's seat
44. Puppy's yelp
46. Noah's boat
48. Walked to and fro anxiously
52. Approximately
56. Get better
58. Stop for a moment
59. Foot digit
60. General Robert E.
61. Sign on a door
62. Instant lawn
63. In addition to

DOWN

1. Round, flat object
2. A skunk's is unpleasant
3. Contend (with)
4. Rouse (from sleep)
5. Break a religious law
6. Be aware of
7. Person in a role
8. That girl
9. Concealed
10. Terminate
11. Declare
16. Bright color
20. "Well done!"
22. Less dry
24. Stately tree
25. Put on (weight)
26. A single time
27. Require
28. Truckers' vehicles
29. Notion
30. Fictional spy James
32. Cheerleader's cry
35. Was in command
40. Bit playfully
43. When some time has passed
45. Golfing average
47. Tool sets
49. Soda flavor
50. Tied, as a score
51. Real-estate title
52. Large primate
53. Forbid
54. Umpire's call
55. ____ up, finish a supply
57. Cow's noise

286

ACROSS

1. Colored part of the eye
5. Desire
9. Weep out loud
12. Pocket fuzz
13. Smell
14. A couple
15. Care deeply for
16. Used to be
17. Ms. Landers
18. Eden dweller
20. Hospital employee
22. Less crazy
24. Figures sums
26. Set of tools
27. Depend (on)
29. Sunrise direction
33. Wedding vow: 2 wds.
34. Bargain events
36. Child's plaything
37. Cruel Roman emperor
39. Relax
40. Slice (off)
41. In a lazy way
43. Extremely angry
45. Point of view
48. Gallop
49. Produce (eggs)
50. Out of town
54. Male deer
57. Not bright at all
58. The ____ Ranger
59. Roof square
60. Gore and Jolson
61. Little ones
62. "Get out of here!"

DOWN

1. Sick
2. ____ de Janeiro
3. Thomas Edison was one
4. Comedian Martin
5. "Holy cow!"
6. Lemon drink
7. Neither's partner
8. Fashion
9. Night-sky light
10. Has possession of
11. Skeletal part
19. Makes mistakes
21. Take advantage of
22. Body's outer covering
23. Helpful person
24. Narrow street
25. Coloring chemicals
28. English nobleman
30. An ocean
31. Chimney dirt
32. Write using a keyboard
35. Mix (ingredients)
38. Frying fluid
42. Gave out cards
44. Corrodes, as iron
45. "M*A*S*H" star Alan
46. Hammer's target
47. Workout rooms
51. Pursue a love
52. Hill insect
53. "Certainly!"
55. In the style of: 2 wds.
56. Obtain

ACROSS

1. Choir voice
5. Corn spike
8. As well
12. Bank offering
13. Ms. Gardner
14. Black _____, oil
15. NASCAR's Earnhardt Jr.
16. Had faith (in)
18. Porch punch
19. Put on the payroll
20. Asner and Sullivan
21. Lunchtime, usually
23. Grouping of similar items
25. Amidst
28. Protective suit
32. Bread-cooking appliance
33. Clothing label
35. Assistant
36. Walked in water
38. Commended
40. Operate (a machine)
42. Landers and Miller
43. Fire residue
46. "I _____ to tell you yesterday . . ."
48. Not home
51. Least expensive
53. Sand hill
54. Ripped
55. Gaming cube
56. Spring bloom
57. Moved quickly
58. Unhappy
59. 32-Across glove

DOWN

1. Actor Alan
2. Trucker's haul
3. Gifted
4. The loneliest number?
5. Kitchen cupboard
6. Above
7. Hay bundles
8. Mature
9. Deep affection
10. Snow glider
11. At _____, in conflict
17. Notion
19. Garden tool
22. Landlord, for one
24. Railway vehicle
25. Fancy knot
26. Ms. Perón
27. Short sleep
29. The Show Me State
30. Flattering poem
31. Common barn color
34. Conceded
37. Place to leave trash
39. Farm resident?
41. Requires
43. Behaves
44. Small store
45. Roll call response
47. China's continent
49. Military troop
50. Exam
52. &
53. Far from bright

287

288

ACROSS

1. Sodium chloride
5. In the style of: 2 wds.
8. "_____ do you mean?"
12. "M*A*S*H" star Alda
13. Silent greeting
14. Apiece
15. Go the _____, endure
17. Sour fruit
18. Ocean
19. Bowling lane
20. Bog; marsh
24. Road goo
26. Wheel covering
27. Quick, casual kiss
28. Lawless crowd
31. Newspaper boss
33. Get away (from)
35. Marry
36. Beer barrels
38. Prayer ending
39. Pirate's "yes"
40. Stately and impressive
41. Use an aerosol can
45. Singleton
47. Knotted together
48. Brass-band horn
53. Too
54. In the past
55. Worshiped statue
56. Obtains
57. Farm enclosure
58. Four years, for a president

DOWN

1. Mournful
2. Heavy-weight champ
3. _____ Vegas
4. Dynamite's cousin: abbr.
5. Actress Bancroft
6. Find
7. Summer refresher
8. Feeling fine
9. Frozen rain
10. Summit
11. Those folks
16. Horned viper
19. Boats like Noah's
20. Meat-and-veggies dish
21. Broad
22. Dry and barren
23. Were introduced
25. High cards
27. Hunter's victim
28. Papa's mate
29. Unlock (a door)
30. Flex, as an elbow
32. "All right!"
34. Station wagon, for one
37. Funnyman Burns
40. Valuable stone
41. Male deer
42. Heap
43. Take a breather
44. Fusses
46. Midday
48. Knock softly
49. Small amount
50. Lyric poem
51. Neither's sidekick
52. Shade tree

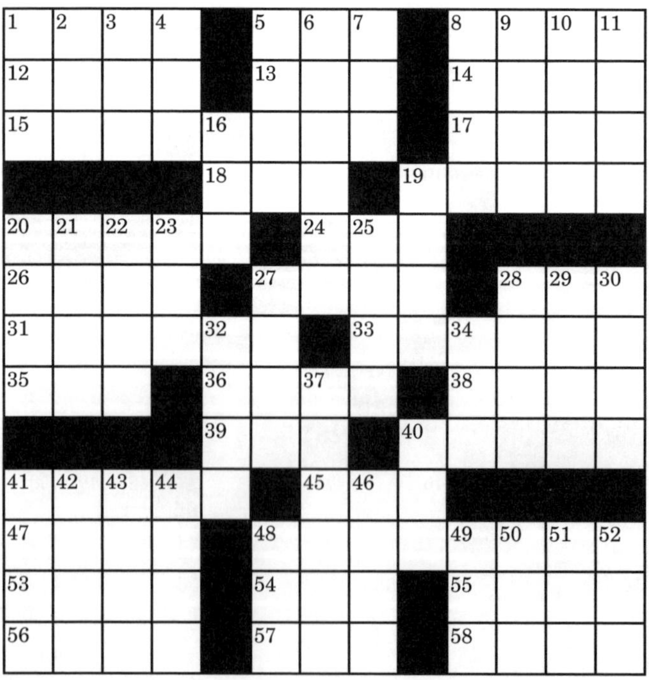

289

ACROSS

1. Tall shade trees
5. Curved lines
9. Pull (a car)
12. Underground plant part
13. Loud, ringing sound
14. Exclamation of surprise
15. Uncommon
16. Domesticated
17. Continuous noise
18. Move quietly, as to avoid being seen
20. Liveliness
21. Flower's home
22. Only
24. Half of four
26. Paid notices
29. Cat's happy sound
31. Sorrowful expression
34. Bread edges
36. Most unusual
38. Push the buttons on a keyboard
39. Serving platter
41. Secret agent
42. Chum
44. Paradise
46. "____ Wants to Be a Millionaire?"
48. That thing's
50. Small trench
54. ____ and hers
55. Appearing stern
57. Feel concern (about)
58. Lemon drink
59. Quite large
60. Classroom test
61. Actor Danson
62. Camping shelter
63. Bones enclosing the chest cavity

DOWN

1. Makes a mistake
2. Money given temporarily
3. A greater amount
4. Water vapor
5. Likely (to)
6. Grain machine
7. Arrived
8. Got some rest
9. Newborn frogs
10. Cleveland's state
11. Desire
19. Fulfilled (a promise)
23. Corrosion on metal
25. Roll of cash
26. Play section
27. Far from wet
28. Assumed (to be true)
30. Vehicle's path
32. Small, poisonous snake
33. Pigpen
35. Ocean
37. Changed the color of
40. Step down (from a job)
43. Illumination
45. More pleasant
46. "Which thing?"
47. Conceal from view
49. Not false
51. Cab
52. Ill-tempered person
53. Skirts' borders
56. Encountered

290

ACROSS

1. Never encountered before
4. Talk to God
8. Imitates a seamstress
12. Ms. Gardner
13. Theatrical part
14. Sapling, for one
15. Nap site
16. Thought
17. Compass direction
18. React to pollen, maybe
20. Takes on a trial run
21. Spotted panther
24. Chore
27. Had life
31. Be on the sick list
32. Slumber
34. A long time ____
35. Wineglass material, often
37. Encourage strongly
38. What teachers teach
41. Drinking tube
44. Changed direction abruptly
48. Browning or Yeats
49. Fruit-juice drinks
51. "____ been meaning to tell you . . ."
52. English princess
53. Football kick
54. Get an eyeful of
55. New Jersey NBA team
56. Mix (a salad)
57. Slip up

DOWN

1. Collars (a crook)
2. Get ____, retaliate
3. Walk in water
4. Winner's award
5. Bronco-busting show
6. Beer cousin
7. "Indeed!"
8. Spirited horses
9. Periods in history
10. See 17-Across
11. TV filming stages
19. Moose kin
20. Voyage; journey
22. Pares
23. Firefighter's chopper
24. Tic-toe go-between
25. Spare-tire filler
26. Clever
28. Paving "gunk"
29. Nest deposit
30. Stag's mate
32. Meat-and-vegetable concoction
33. Spanish article
36. Roof slabs
37. Put to work
39. Baking sites
40. Birds' shelters
41. Reach across
42. Shade
43. Tenant's monthly fee
45. Go up
46. At all times
47. 30-Down, for one
49. Suitable
50. Sonny and Cher were one

291

ACROSS

1. Urban pest
4. Cat's weapon
8. In addition
12. Employ; apply
13. Mascara site
14. Put cargo on board
15. Title for a gentleman
16. Merely
17. No longer wild, as animals
18. Road-repair substance
19. View
20. Postal areas
21. "There's something ____ been meaning to tell you..."
23. Preholiday night
25. Concept or thought
27. Practice, to a prize-fighter
28. Lyricist Gershwin
31. Milk container
33. Like a body temperature of 98.6° F
35. McMahon and Sullivan
36. Affectionate greeting
38. High-pitched puppy barks
39. Suitable
40. Wager
41. Lost pet
45. President Lincoln, familiarly
47. Fire residue
50. Not at home
51. Small bird
52. Kid's plaything
53. Just right
54. Skull site
55. Lane liner
56. Easter finds
57. Racetrack chances
58. Put on (clothes)

DOWN

1. Reddish brown
2. Largest continent on earth
3. Small, feisty dogs
4. Near
5. Country byway
6. Dozing
7. Little child's frequent question
8. Female singing voice
9. Bank offering
10. Identical
11. Poetic tributes
20. Nothing
22. Dyeing tub
24. Delivery trucks
25. Drink cubes
26. Mom's spouse
27. Use scissors
28. Did impressions of
29. Sharp blow
30. Jolson and Gore
32. Acceptable
34. Pastrami on ____
37. Gazed intently
40. Turns (in a river)
41. Umpire's call
42. Small branch
43. Pealed, as a bell
44. Pirates' affirmatives
46. Necklace orb
48. Song for a single singer
49. Church anthem
51. "____ do you think you are?"

292

ACROSS

1. Ready money
5. They can beat kings
9. Happen
11. Came up
12. Needle's partner
14. Permit (someone) to leave
15. View
16. Danish pastry filling, at times
18. Waterlily leaf
19. Beaver's construction
21. Furthermore
22. Flirtatiously shy
23. Florida city
25. 2,000 pounds
26. Rush-hour problem
28. Enjoyed lunch
29. Dairy-aisle finds
31. Paid announcements
32. Con opposite
33. Play a role
35. That guy
36. Unconfirmed story
38. Brazil resort city, for short
40. Light bulb inventor
42. Cartoon duck
44. Previously aired TV show
45. Recorded (a song)
46. Genesis garden
47. Flower plots

DOWN

1. Rollaway sleepers
2. Had sore muscles
3. Frightened yell
4. Shade of a color
5. Curved line
6. Supermarket money saver
7. School paper
8. Flower start
10. Sharp knock
11. Wood chopper
13. Serious play
14. Bring to a close
17. Team outfit
20. Oven ____, kitchen protectors
22. Hot chocolate
24. "We ____ Family"
25. Suit neckwear
27. Deluge
28. Look up to
30. Abrasion
31. Helped out
32. Play on words
34. Did a roofing job
35. In this place
36. Actor Howard
37. Decay; spoil
39. Betting chances
41. Daylight source
43. Seize (a suspect)

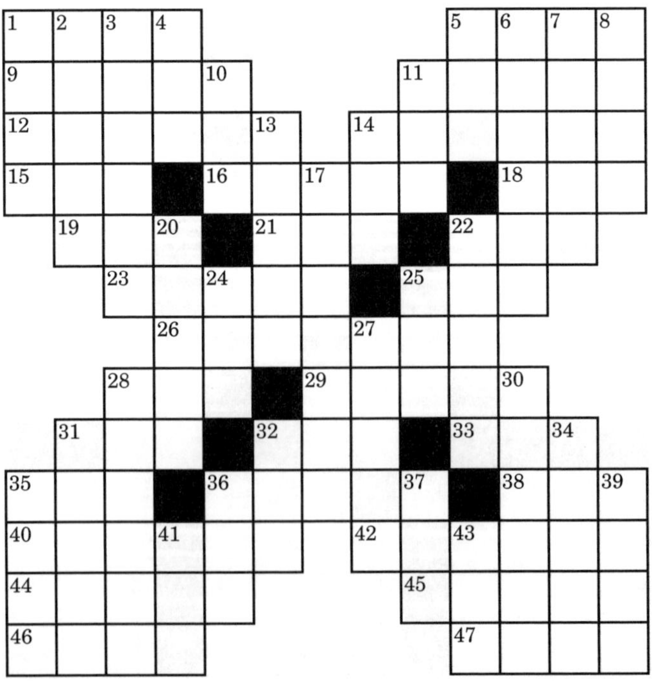

293

ACROSS

1. Mr. Gershwin
4. Coin opening
8. Thought
12. Pilfer
13. Diner listing
14. Aim
15. "I want it ____!"
16. Always
17. Allows
18. Sewing implement
20. Half of four
22. Sick
23. Took a peek
27. Term of endearment
30. Chaps
31. Fruit cooler
32. Exclamation of victory
33. "Sure!"
34. Golf peg
35. Tuck's partner
36. Chum
37. Pay out (money)
39. Grapevine goodies?
41. That girl
42. Vigor
43. Book names
47. Ms. Hayworth
50. Strong metal
52. Unrefined 50-Across
53. Baking chamber
54. Number of a cat's lives?
55. Fish part
56. Diluted
57. Departs
58. Actor Danson

DOWN

1. Persia, now
2. Actress's part
3. Competent
4. Offensive to the nose
5. Even
6. Wallet bill
7. Hares' opponents?
8. Alaskan dwelling
9. Female deer
10. Have lunch
11. Gore and Pacino
19. Expire
21. Was victorious
24. "Kiss Me ____," musical
25. First garden
26. Heroic act
27. Suspend (from)
28. Cleveland's state
29. Takes a snooze
30. Singer Tormé
33. Babbling: slang
36. Crusted dessert
37. Gleams
38. Favorite animal
40. Strike with an open hand
41. Large pebble
44. Artist's studio
45. A Great Lake
46. Transmit
47. Use oars
48. "____ got sunshine on a cloudy day . . ."
49. Oolong, for one
51. Brazilian resort, for short

294

ACROSS

1. Prohibit
4. Cain's brother
8. Petty quarrel
12. Employ
13. Went by car
14. Angelic aura
15. Stir in a circular motion
16. Towards the sunrise
17. In a lazy manner
18. Smooth fabrics
20. Can metal
22. Soap foam
24. Play part
27. Throw forcefully
30. Noah's boat
31. Young man
32. Self
33. With 36-Across, European mountain
35. Mouth feature
36. See 33-Across
37. Atmos-phere
38. Heredity carrier
39. Coloring agent
40. Not outdoors
43. Aged
44. Male feline
48. Cob vegetable
51. Egg-shaped
53. ____ de Janeiro, Brazilian city
54. Spoken
55. Inheritance document
56. Actress Lupino
57. Refuse
58. Declares
59. Sleeping site

DOWN

1. Boxcar inhabitants
2. China's continent
3. Subsequent
4. Sports stadium
5. Show off
6. Sullivan and Asner
7. Written messages
8. Sensitive leg area
9. Gym mat
10. Every bit
11. Child's plaything
19. Sick
21. Annoys
23. 27-Down growths
24. Qualified
25. Dime, for one
26. Use a keyboard
27. Body topper
28. Far from attractive
29. Thick string
33. Boat's wind catcher
34. Skylights, for example
38. Precious stone
41. Rome's country
42. 11-Down figures
43. Mere
45. Baby's 59-Across
46. Assistant
47. Frog's kin
48. Food fish
49. Lode load
50. Sprinted
52. By means of

295

ACROSS

1. _____ back, return
5. Existed
8. "For _____ the Bell Tolls"
12. Mimics
13. Bubbly brew
14. A Corn Belt state
15. Look for
16. Clamor
17. Fasting period
18. Complete
20. Play a role
22. Angry
23. Sampled
27. Archery weapon
30. In favor of
31. Sunbeam
32. Lamb cries
33. Knight's title
34. "Definitely!"
35. Omelet ingredient
36. Combine
37. Help the economy?
38. Decrease
40. Regret
41. Like: 2 wds.
42. Head protection
46. Bread buy
49. Couple
51. Mine amount
52. Border
53. Crimson or scarlet
54. Smooth
55. Bambi, for one
56. Lincoln's nickname
57. Apartment payment

DOWN

1. Violin box
2. Ajar
3. Encounter
4. Igloo dwellers
5. Walked through water
6. Boxing great
7. Government position
8. Droops
9. Garden tool
10. Possess
11. "Welcome" rug
19. Uncooked
21. Automobile
24. Faithful
25. Make money
26. Colored (hair)
27. Cain's sibling
28. Ire
29. Tatters
30. Mend
33. Beloved singer Frank
34. Bee contestant
36. Mr. Tormé
37. Take to court
39. More secure
40. _____ Island, smallest state
43. Dance step
44. Biblical garden
45. Canvas shelter
46. Guided
47. Keats work
48. Grow old
50. Spider's snare

296

ACROSS

1. Wheel edges
5. Hairpiece choice
8. Nail for a bulletin board
12. Oil-rich nation
13. One of the Gabor sisters
14. Kitchen appliance
15. Mama's partner
16. Cheer-leader's quality
17. Ceramic square
18. Dirt-road groove
20. Soup server
21. Lingering pains
24. Get-out-of-jail money
26. Boxing champ Frazier or Louis
27. Vote into office
29. Columnist Landers
32. Similar to: 2 wds.
33. Goal
34. ____ Grande, Mexican border
35. Fiery color
36. Of superior quality
38. Cooling cubes
39. Perform a ditty
40. Swiss warble
42. In pursuit of
45. Singer Torme
46. Look to the future
47. Be in debt
49. Trade (with)
53. Slippery fishes
54. Pay court to
55. Otherwise
56. Mall offering
57. Never seen before
58. Ready to pick

DOWN

1. Tear
2. Gershwin brother
3. Atlas page
4. Capture
5. Cried
6. Common contraction
7. Opening
8. Add up
9. Devoted, as a reader
10. Monk's room
11. Athlete's vulnerable joint
19. Purpose
20. Ignited
21. Not fully closed
22. Old King ____
23. Brain's location
24. Existence
25. Slope's summit
28. Reclined
29. Lacking water
30. Friendly and kind
31. Yuletide carol
36. An evergreen
37. Bread variety
39. Word after "common" or "horse"
41. More mature
42. Zoo favorites
43. Pest for Fido
44. Towering
45. Cat's sound
47. Acknowl-edge
48. "Alas!"
50. Yale alumnus
51. Venomous viper
52. Southern general

297

ACROSS
1. Eat like a bird
5. Sweet potato
8. Move slowly to music
12. Work animals
13. Mr. Lincoln, informally
14. Tardy
15. Bit of dialogue
16. Ink implement
17. They may be beady or shifty
18. Flat-tailed water mammal
20. Piece, as of coal
22. Was in the forefront
24. Space just below the roof
28. Dad's boy
31. Private journal
34. Wedding words
35. Lofty poem
36. The Ice ___, prehistory period
37. Cow's comment
38. On behalf of
39. Parade sight
41. Moose's kin
42. Nice 29-Down
44. Competed in a footrace
46. Detail on a list
49. Pounds, as a drum
53. Nautical yeses
56. Helpful prop
58. Repeated sound
59. Period for fasting
60. Crafty
61. Cheerless; monotonous
62. Rooney of "60 Minutes"
63. Golf-ball holder
64. Adjusts (a clock)

DOWN
1. Game on horseback
2. Door sign
3. Dollar part
4. Bend in prayer
5. Chihuahua's bark
6. Cain's brother
7. List of dishes offered
8. Had a nap
9. Manner
10. Supped
11. "I shall!"
19. Ketchup color
21. June preceder
23. Use an old-fashioned phone
25. Use a stopwatch
26. Role model, maybe
27. Prepare meals
28. Comfy couch
29. Smell
30. Cruel emperor
32. In the past
33. Area in back
39. Frying substance
40. Soda-can ring
43. Shrouded in fog
45. Requirements
47. Dawn's direction
48. Distance measure
50. Farmland unit
51. The thing over there
52. Weeps aloud
53. In the manner of: 2 wds.
54. Craving
55. Conclusion
57. Tinting agent

298

ACROSS

1. Rainy
4. On the summit of
8. Multigenerational story
12. In the past
13. Close by
14. Small, brown songbird
15. Sticky stuff
16. Division word
17. Grew old
18. Alaska native
20. Lima's country
22. Automobile
23. Carpentry tool
26. Heavenly being
29. For each
30. Señora Perón
31. Ms. Lane of "Superman"
32. Gym pad
33. Make a sweater
34. Wooden fastener
35. Give help to
36. Book name
37. Inclines
39. "Wise" bird
40. Negative votes
41. First-place person
45. Darlings
47. Showy flower
49. "____ Maria"
50. A neighbor of Huron
51. Dryer-screen fluff
52. Inky implement
53. Circle parts
54. ____ Benedict
55. Poet's before

DOWN

1. Carry on (war)
2. Selves
3. Captured
4. Living creature
5. Pavarotti, for one
6. Stable morsel
7. Soothsayer
8. Group of bees
9. Quarrel
10. Aitch preceder
11. In addition
19. Does a frosting job
21. Lobed organ
24. Wicked
25. Cost per unit
26. Swiss mountain range
27. Yuletide carol
28. Enormous
29. Writing tablet
32. Guided rocket
33. Pottery oven
35. Had ice cream
36. ____ and turns
38. Smell sensors
39. Deep in debt
42. Back of a neck
43. Always
44. Actress Russo
45. Pod orb
46. Make a mistake
48. Equipment; gear

299

ACROSS

1. Marmalade alternative
4. Like some surgery
8. "Not guilty," for one
12. In the past
13. Treat for a dog
14. Merit
15. Unused
16. Has a meal
17. Detergent target
18. Short nonfiction works
20. Few and far between
22. So far
23. Salad-dressing ingredient
24. Had the rights to
27. Singleton
28. Liable (to)
31. Play the suitor
32. Used to be
33. Gambling cube
34. Showed the way
35. Annoy
36. Fair-haired
38. Citrus beverage
39. Sound from Bossy
40. Fragrances
43. Six-legged creature
47. Vatican VIP
48. Word of comparison
50. Bambi's mom, for one
51. Site of Eve's temptation
52. Sour fruit
53. Barroom order
54. TV rooms, often
55. Cut and paste, perhaps
56. Conclusion

DOWN

1. Tarzan's sweetheart
2. An awfully long time
3. Cuts (hay)
4. Complied with
5. Prepare (peanuts)
6. Crumb seeker
7. Classroom units
8. Propel (a bicycle)
9. Dragon's hideout
10. Blunders
11. Poker stake
19. "Sure, captain!"
21. Apple pastry
24. Wise bird?
25. Sorrow
26. Sign of approval
27. Cask wood
28. Commotion
29. Brooch
30. Newsman Koppel
32. Fight on a mat
35. Lupino of the movies
36. Prairie headgear
37. Angeles leader
38. Church responses
39. Florida metropolis
40. Imitated
41. Took the bus
42. Unseal
44. "The ____ of Night," old soap opera
45. Bit of silver
46. Be inclined (to)
49. Concealed

300

ACROSS

1. Easter meat
4. Shadowbox
8. Crow calls
12. Tavern brew
13. Hired car
14. Medicinal plant
15. Armed conflict
16. Employed
17. A contraction
18. Work (dough)
20. Corn spike
22. Exercise areas
25. Scandinavian
29. TV host Jay
32. Mr. Griffith
34. Sick
35. Trouble
36. Baked dessert
37. ___ Angeles
38. Compete (for)
39. African vipers
40. Baseballer Rose
41. Book of 23-Down
43. Location
45. Timid
47. Severe
51. Leave out
54. Skilled
57. "I found it!"
58. Challenge
59. Courts
60. Neither's mate
61. Forest dweller
62. Neck part
63. Obtain

DOWN

1. Bird of prey
2. Actor Alda
3. Simple
4. Prepare for exams
5. Mas' partners
6. Chopping tool
7. Travel by bicycle
8. Capital of Egypt
9. Gore and Pacino
10. Was victorious
11. Matched pair
19. In the past
21. Some
23. Land charts
24. Cuts quickly
26. Make angry
27. Coin opening
28. Otherwise
29. Molten rock
30. Revise (text)
31. Christmas song
33. Mr. Arnaz
39. Fireplace residue
40. Pod veggie
42. Showy flower
44. The ones here
46. Express exhaustion
48. Sounded a bell
49. Pump or sandal
50. Stag
51. Not even
52. Old Hollywood's West
53. Wrath
55. Crushing snake
56. Sever

301

ACROSS
1. Final
5. Creature with antlers
9. Was introduced to
12. Kentucky neighbor
13. Put on the staff
14. Ms. Gardner
15. Desire
16. A single time
17. Brooks of "The Producers"
18. Bright notion
20. English nobleman
21. Backbone
24. Sick
26. Of considerable size
27. Zoo denizens
31. In the style of: 2 wds.
32. Ice-hockey supply
34. Young dog
35. Least relaxed
37. Over yonder
39. Mine find
40. Lessened (pain)
41. Pleased
44. Totals (up)
46. Wiping cloth
47. Small chamber group
49. Irish instrument
53. High card
54. Walk in water
55. One in "HOMES"
56. Place for sleep
57. Wallet bills
58. Dirty air

DOWN
1. Close to the ground
2. "I caught you!"
3. Moral misdeed
4. Carrying around
5. Foot covering
6. Singer Turner
7. Rainbow's shape
8. "Turn right," to a mule
9. Papa's partner
10. Eternally
11. "That's a ____ order!"
19. More profound
20. Tree species
21. Narrow wooden strip
22. Like a pastel color
23. Persian Gulf republic
24. Printer's material
25. In the phone book
27. Play division
28. Large primates
29. Entice
30. Drove too fast
33. Take advantage of
36. Turf
38. Diner concoctions
41. Seize suddenly
42. Frilly trim
43. Like some cheeses
44. Helper
45. Accomplishes
47. A couple
48. Did a marathon
50. Upper limb
51. Mexican waterway
52. Where to hang one's hat

302

ACROSS

1. Belonging to us
4. Highest point
8. Fastened (shoelaces)
12. Consumed
13. Highway
14. A single time
15. Tic-toe link
16. Boats like Noah's
17. Word after "tooth" or "heart"
18. That gal
19. Hive dweller
20. Little store
21. "____ about time!"
23. Group of troops
26. Volcano outpouring
28. Atop
29. Sty resident
32. Warns
34. Complete
36. Performed
37. Snaky swimmers
39. Interrupt (a sleeper)
40. Walk in water
41. Garnered first place
42. Cola, for one
45. Honest ____ Lincoln
47. Pen fluid
50. Sturdy metal
51. Adored person
52. Witness
53. Be mad (about)
54. Authentic
55. Attempt
56. Winter coaster
57. Makes mistakes
58. Distress signal

DOWN

1. Granola grains
2. Nevada's neighbor
3. Got (a letter)
4. Some Middle East natives
5. Earth's center
6. Lipstick and foundation
7. Asner and Bradley
8. Browned bread
9. Fraction of a foot
10. Reverberation
11. Far from shallow
22. Paving goo
24. Negative replies
25. B and B, maybe
26. Young fellow
27. Boxer Muhammad
28. Employed
29. Certain keyboard players
30. Annoy
31. Mild oath
33. Iced summer drink
35. A pair
38. Person in charge
40. Dwindled
41. Oil sources
42. Business-letter greeting
43. Like some exams
44. Peace symbol
46. Pig with tusks
48. Cruel emperor
49. Door openers
51. Anger

303

ACROSS

1. Villain's scheme
5. Poisonous snakes
9. Tavern
12. Adore
13. Unusual
14. ____ de Janeiro
15. Spoken
16. Melt
17. Combine into a sum
18. Water sources
20. Sailor's reply
21. "Golly!"
22. For each
24. Fido or Rex
26. Scientist's office
29. First man
31. Relieves (of)
34. Lubricating
36. Wide roadway
38. Happy
39. A Great Lake
41. Received
42. Short sleep
44. "Raggedy" doll
45. Inquire
47. Perform on stage
49. This 24-hour period
54. Thespian's clue
55. Small children
57. Enlightened
58. Encountered
59. Angel's headgear
60. Wicked
61. Asner and Sullivan
62. Chunky soup
63. Distribute cards

DOWN

1. Farmer's chore
2. Folk knowledge
3. Egg-shaped
4. Share (a story)
5. Museum exhibit
6. African desert
7. Talk to God
8. Did a tailor's job
9. Boasting
10. Legal assistant
11. Traveled on horseback
19. Extent
23. Border
25. Unrefined mineral
26. Cabin-building material
27. Feel under the weather
28. Bed warmers?
30. Principal
32. Pair
33. Matched collection
35. Hollywood's Lupino
37. Air duct
40. Baby's toy
43. Trails
45. Summit
46. Took to court
48. Winter outergarment
50. Had debts
51. Descend (into the pool)
52. Largest continent
53. Scream
56. Female pig

304

ACROSS

1. Misbehaving youngster
5. Spherical toy
9. Propel a dinghy
12. Lighten (a burden)
13. India's continent
14. One of the Gabor sisters
15. Boats like Noah's
16. Frothy beverages
17. Crooner Torme
18. Birds' abodes
20. McMahon and Asner
21. Pen filler
22. Extremely little
24. Have
26. Waiter's bonus
29. Swiss mountains
31. Eden dweller
34. Narrow city streets
36. Man's dinner jacket
38. Think ahead
39. Important time periods
41. Confederate soldier, for short
42. Marriage words
44. A Lincoln nickname
45. Storage container
47. Perform in a play
49. Records, today
54. Singleton
55. Small children
57. Soon afterward
58. Possessive pronoun
59. Angelic symbol
60. A soft drink
61. Great deal (of)
62. Simmer
63. Lend a hand

DOWN

1. Lima ____, vegetable
2. Red inside, as steak
3. Poses (a question)
4. Exam
5. Lamb's cry
6. Slumbering
7. Spread untruths
8. Cowboy's noose
9. Memo, for one
10. Baking chamber
11. Stroll
19. Move like a palm tree in the breeze
23. Otherwise
25. Candle stuff
26. Touch (on the shoulder)
27. Sick
28. Least elaborate
30. Knife thrust
32. Fruit drink
33. Unruly crowd
35. Finale
37. Put to work
40. Baby's toy
43. Solemn pledges
45. Bubble, as water
46. Absorbed by
48. Winter garment
50. Skin irritation
51. Pump or oxford
52. Prison room
53. Ginger cookie
56. Hog mama

305

ACROSS

1. Soft metal
4. Sink or ____
8. "Stay here a moment"
12. Big fuss
13. Rubber wheel-protector
14. "M*A*S*H" star
15. Acquired
16. Unlock
17. Practice boxing
18. Shirt's arm covering
20. Knock softly
22. Sunset color
23. Not outdoors
27. Major furniture purchase
30. Against
31. Our star
32. Lyricist Gershwin
33. Jet, for one
35. Newsman Koppel
36. Lab animal, often
37. Hearing organ
38. Little children
39. Chooses by ballot
41. Feminine pronoun
43. Allow
44. Rides a bike without pedaling
48. Gemstone from 54-Across
51. Article on a list
53. Feline friend
54. China's locale
55. Zilch
56. Monkey's uncle?
57. "At what time?"
58. Makes tracks
59. Unused

DOWN

1. Gift labels
2. "American ____," popular TV show
3. Pay heed to
4. It may be wood-burning
5. Used a sponge
6. Fury
7. Speak of
8. Stinging insects
9. Swiss peak
10. Lupino of film
11. Paving goo
19. Time to remember
21. Green Gables girl
24. Words in an analogy
25. Song for a pair
26. Concludes
27. Foal's father
28. Of the mouth
29. Destiny
30. Automobile
33. Seeger or Sampras
34. Durable
38. Coffee alternative
40. Spotless
41. Part of a play
42. Domiciles
45. Search, as the horizon
46. Adhesive strip
47. Simmered dinner
48. Stubble site, perhaps
49. Fire residue
50. Go out, as a candle
52. Also

306

ACROSS

1. Quick punches
5. Ring ——, carnival game
9. Avian symbol of wisdom
12. Like some surgery
13. Eve's mate
14. Ms. West
15. Roll-call response
16. Part in a movie
17. Holly-wood's Lupino
18. Unclothed
20. Told
22. Butter square
24. Sneaky
25. Ironed (pants)
29. Time periods
33. Paddle
34. Coarse
37. In the style of: 2 wds.
38. Tinted
40. Wished (for)
42. Peculiar
45. Actor Wallach
46. Positive qualities
50. Fiery gems
54. Summer drink
55. Carpenter's tack
57. Entreaty
58. Ocean
59. First Lady of Song
60. Paradise
61. Faucet
62. Come to a standstill
63. Challenge

DOWN

1. President Kennedy
2. Vicinity
3. Tree-trunk covering
4. Naps
5. Road pitch
6. Fragrance
7. Bargain events
8. Take a sniff
9. Leave out
10. Walk in water
11. Heavy metal
19. 100-meter ——
21. Senate-floor vote
23. Chinese brew
25. Pea container
26. Beam of light
27. Poet's "before"
28. Like a desert
30. Moved swiftly
31. Malt beverage
32. Mournful
35. Under-stand
36. Part of the Anaheim Angels' logo
39. Round speck
41. Torn
43. Sand hills
44. Passed out (the cards)
46. Boundless
47. Notion
48. Harvest
49. Farm tower
51. "M*A*S*H" star
52. Sidelong stare
53. Reasonable
56. Once around the track

307

ACROSS
1. Crazes
5. Lose color
9. Half of four
12. Revise (text)
13. Hydrochloric ____
14. Like food before cooking
15. Photo border
16. Minister to
17. Large coffee server
18. How many years one has lived
20. Objects in catalogs
22. Delicious smell
25. Door unlocker
26. Unused
27. Liquid adhesive
30. Stiffly formal
34. Be abundant
36. Sixth sense
37. Lessen (pain)
38. "Born Free" lioness
39. Dog-catchers' snares
41. In poor health
42. Senator Kennedy
44. Bancroft and Boleyn
46. Oahu greeting
49. "So long!"
50. Hold up (a bank)
51. Thick cord
54. Memorable times
58. Pedicure site
59. Fir, for one
60. Piece of china
61. Secret agent
62. Fire's radiation
63. Oxen's harness

DOWN
1. Doctor's charge
2. Do sums
3. Excavate
4. Kettle output
5. Destiny
6. Expert pilot
7. Constant noise
8. Comedian Murphy
9. Correct
10. Affectionate
11. Possesses
19. Practical joke
21. Use a keyboard
22. Poker stake
23. Film spool
24. Is in debt
25. Retained
28. Give, for now
29. Employ
31. Wet forecast
32. ____ of Capri
33. Torme and Gibson
35. School subject
40. Put into words
43. Our planet
45. Very poor
46. Crafts' partner
47. 6-Down's trick
48. Comply with
49. Borscht veggie
52. Mine find
53. Pod morsel
55. ____ de Janeiro
56. Inquire
57. That woman

308

ACROSS

1. A single time
5. Police officer
8. Edinburgh native
12. Water spring
13. Cutting tool
14. Specific knowledge
15. Inspected
17. Biblical garden
18. Pig's home
19. Disney duck
21. Tavern drink
22. Defeats
26. Indeed
29. Small number
30. Night before a holiday
31. Angel's instrument
32. Writing tablet
33. Hesitate
34. Breakfast food
35. Frying vessel
36. Window ledges
37. More timid
39. Fido, for one
40. Rubbed out
42. Venomous snake
45. Skin disorder
48. Differ in opinion
50. Cleansing agent
51. Moose's kin
52. Prayer ending
53. Jumps on one foot
54. Distress signal
55. Workout areas

DOWN

1. Has debts
2. Following
3. Potter's stuff
4. Shade tree
5. Narrow boat
6. Plow pullers
7. Moved a bike
8. Winter vehicles
9. Food fish
10. Mine find
11. One plus nine
16. In a lazy way
20. Far from high
21. Swiss mountain
23. Arctic beast
24. Wicked
25. Matched collections
26. Those people
27. Fury
28. Implore
29. Air cooler
32. Festive processions
33. Certain hairpiece
35. For each
36. Bubbly beverage
38. Holds on to
39. Students' furniture
41. Farm structure
42. Military group
43. Appear
44. Sketching tools
45. Fire residue
46. Dove's call
47. Short sleep
49. Practical joke

309

ACROSS

1. Nocturnal bird
4. Slide, as a car on ice
8. Old business-letter greeting
12. Great sorrow
13. Very small
14. Like a nonfiction account
15. Put under a spell
17. Leisure
18. ____ and low, everywhere
19. Monthly landlord payments
20. Broadway employee
23. Sinister
25. Lumber
26. Not new
27. Took a load off
30. Become visible
32. Save from peril
34. "Sure thing!"
35. Terribly unappeal-ing
37. Strong dislike
38. Leg joint
39. Majorette's rod
40. Make (wishes) come to pass
43. Not closed all the way
45. Part to play
46. Eating between meals
50. A son of Adam and Eve
51. Little kiss
52. Orbison or Rogers
53. Opposite of worst
54. Boats like Noah's
55. Provide with weapons

DOWN

1. Be obligated to
2. Triumphed
3. Allow
4. Part of a flight of steps
5. Male ruler
6. Parts of a foot
7. Color (hair)
8. Girder metal
9. Persia, today
10. Corrode, as iron
11. Catches a glimpse of
16. Providence, ____ Island
19. Go by taxi
20. On vacation
21. Deal (with)
22. Mountain peaks
24. Extremely
26. Encourage (to act)
27. Sing like Ella Fitzgerald
28. Driver's vehicle
29. Adolescent
31. Female relative
33. "Jaws" terror
36. Having less fat
38. Prepared to be knighted
39. ____ up, goes in reverse
40. Seize suddenly
41. Choir attire
42. Saloon drinks
44. Actor Lemmon
46. Pampering place
47. Lyrical Gershwin
48. Neither's partner
49. Sports room

310

ACROSS

1. Waitress's bonus
4. Borscht ingredient
8. Skier's delight
12. Marriage-vow words
13. Inner drive
14. Singer Horne
15. Neither's mate
16. Stormy anger
17. Elderly
18. Change (plans)
20. Health retreat
21. Far from high
23. Endured
26. Restaurant VIP
29. Master of Eden
31. Climbing vine
32. Grease (hinges)
33. Model of the earth
34. Compete (for)
35. Mine contents
36. Woman's vocal range
37. Grasped
38. Pie nuts
40. Be sorry about
42. Pull (on)
43. Stockings synthetic
47. Bony leg part
49. Copied
52. "I see you!"
53. Owl's sound
54. Adore
55. Scalp coverup
56. Strong longings
57. Hollywood celebrity
58. "Help!"

DOWN

1. Turner of rock
2. Adored statue
3. Sweet, red wine
4. Pack animal
5. Historic epoch
6. Omelet ingredient
7. Golfer's prop
8. Gives a smack to
9. Like a pessimist's attitude
10. Single
11. Handful, as of cotton
19. Santa's helper
20. Identical
22. Room partitions
23. Hard work
24. Wicked
25. Colored, as hair
26. Chicken shelter
27. Take on (a worker)
28. Early-November topic
30. Morse-code symbol
33. Group of friends
37. "You there!"
39. Mother's sisters
41. Beneath
44. Statutes
45. The Buckeye State
46. Annoys
47. Timid
48. Garden cultivator
49. Roker and Gore
50. Pan's kitchen kin
51. Certain Gabor

311

ACROSS

1. Flower beginning
4. Judge's garment
8. First man
12. Mimic
13. Had bills
14. Carbonated water
15. Move up and down
16. Landers and Miller
17. Search (for)
18. Signed up for (a contest)
20. Line of poetry
21. Crimson
22. Baked dessert
23. Pulitzer Prize, for one
26. Leaking
30. Feline
31. Male offspring
32. By way of
33. Arch of hair below the forehead
36. Sheds tears
38. Chest bone
39. Lass
40. Rose up
43. Flawless
47. Mom's sister
48. Birdhouse dweller
49. Solemn pledge
50. Move gradually
51. Freedom from difficulty
52. Yale alum
53. Majors and Remick
54. Changed the color of
55. Jogged

DOWN

1. Ruth of baseball
2. On top of
3. Obligation to pay
4. Made like a lion
5. Possessed
6. Curve (in the road)
7. McMahon and Sullivan
8. Not awake
9. Entrance to a room
10. Fusses
11. Create
19. Goof up
20. Compete
22. Writing stick
23. High card
24. "Where there's a will, there's a ____!"
25. Had a meal
26. "You shall reap what you ____"
27. Common contraction
28. Small bite
29. Car fuel
31. Cry mournfully
34. Clear soups
35. Free (of)
36. Gave notice of coming danger
37. Tiny prankster
39. Ducks' relatives
40. Travel by boat
41. Melody
42. Formerly
43. Recite blessings, as in church
44. At all times
45. Soft-drink option
46. Identical sibling
48. Marry

312

ACROSS

1. Thick mist
4. Slightly open
8. Candle's "fuse"
12. Reverential wonder
13. Prescribed amount
14. Actor's part
15. Lion's lair
16. Salsa option
17. Out of town
18. Twisted cord
20. Shells out
21. Divide equally
23. Noteworthy periods
26. Baby's "little piggies"
27. Atop
28. Filmdom's Gardner
31. Unsettles emotionally
33. Pearl source
35. Fishing snare
36. Departed
38. Informal conversation
39. Be defeated
40. Paper-towel units
41. Mama's partner
44. Make joyful
46. Tall tales
47. Correct (a manuscript)
48. Tic-____-toe, game
51. Summer drinks
52. Oscar winner Hackman
53. Make a blunder
54. Roman emperor
55. Dignified poems
56. Sun's domain

DOWN

1. Passing fashion
2. Be in debt
3. Most kind
4. Confess
5. Unite
6. Napping
7. Stop-sign shade
8. Prepares a gift
9. Des Moines' state
10. Potter's need
11. Piano parts
19. Showing good sense
21. Daze briefly
22. Head of the Roman Catholic Church
24. Plant anchor
25. Some
27. Purposes
28. Sports participants
29. Order for the butcher
30. ____ and crafts
32. "One, ____, buckle my shoe"
34. Kilt wearer, at times
37. Required
39. Cowboy's rope
40. Costs per unit
41. Arrange beforehand
42. Teacher's assistant
43. Social equal
45. Notebook rule
47. Self-love
49. Boat of the Bible
50. Be weepy

313

ACROSS

1. Hollywood's Daniels or Goldblum
5. Huck's pal
8. Inquires
12. Wicked
13. Large primate
14. Poker token
15. Wired message
17. Haul
18. Cruel smile
19. Fireplace item
21. Get married
22. Diner bill
24. Bank vault
26. Green veggie
29. Sack
31. Attracted with bait
34. "M*A*S*H" star
36. Tic-____-toe
38. Infamous Roman ruler
39. Failed to
41. Earth's star
43. Anchorman Rather
44. News article
46. Tavern; pub
48. Matching group
50. Assist
52. Silkworm parents
56. Opera piece
58. "Titanic" prop
60. Mighty beast
61. Long fish
62. Fitzgerald of song
63. Take care of
64. Pig's digs
65. Felix's pal Oscar, for one

DOWN

1. Fast planes
2. Smooth
3. Do some clerical work
4. Naval group
5. La Brea ooze
6. October stone
7. Office notes
8. Play part
9. Rained briefly
10. Flying toy
11. Raced
16. Seize
20. Lass
23. Dracula mascot
25. Enjoyment
26. Notebook
27. Actor Wallach
28. Math topic
30. Neon or oxygen
32. Notable time-span
33. Put on
35. Picnic visitor
37. Baby bear
40. Oolong or pekoe
42. "What's in a ____?"
45. Highway measures
47. Judges' gowns
48. Pepper's mate
49. New York canal
51. Count calories
53. Bridge fee
54. Angelic light
55. Skewer
57. Also
59. Pesky insect

314

ACROSS

1. Blue bird
4. Land measure
8. At ____, in disagreement
12. Mature
13. Pole waver
14. Roman emperor
15. Bragging
17. Lobster's pincer
18. Held on to
19. King's "term"
20. Felix's roomie
23. Inventor Whitney
25. Tree anchor
26. Fusses
27. Arid
30. Changes slightly
32. College diploma
34. ____ Angeles, California
35. Assistant
37. Spring shower
38. Paving goo
39. Shows boredom
40. Got up
44. Expert pilots
46. Pocket change piece
47. Makes waves?
51. Circular opening
52. Juicy fruit
53. Noah's boat
54. Otherwise
55. Nile vipers
56. Attempt

DOWN

1. Prod
2. In another time
3. Affirmative vote
4. Immediately following
5. Movie chunk
6. Talked wildly
7. Omelet ingredient
8. "____ upon a time . . ."
9. Sandwich shop
10. Pull behind
11. Planted, as seeds
16. Play ice hockey
19. Elevate
20. Spoken
21. Song for one
22. Guest beds
24. Ore site
26. Large continent
27. Make a picture
28. Bridle strap
29. Strong desires
31. Appraise
33. Lawn mower's target
36. Window hangings
39. Decade units
40. Dull pain
41. Sheep product
42. Lubricates
43. Leg joint
45. Applaud
47. Health resort
48. Head topper
49. Goof
50. Wild blue yonder

315

ACROSS

1. What model airplanes are built from
5. Pen liquid
8. Large relatives of monkeys
12. Nutritious mineral
13. Stag's mate
14. Great review
15. Tap-dancer's prop
16. Enjoyed a snack
17. Cooking chamber
18. Leg bender
19. Mother chicken
20. Fix by sewing
21. Collection of wild animals
23. Historic period
25. Sky streaker
28. Sign of a fire
29. Touch, as on the shoulder
32. Have bills
33. Flavorsome
35. Ms. Perón
36. High explosive: abbr.
37. Certain lodge member
38. Hero's award
40. Curved path
41. Use one's eyes
42. Relate (a story)
45. Bird that "gives a hoot"
47. Chinese grain
51. Frozen rain
52. Garden implement
53. Revered one
54. Pinnacle
55. Mine extraction
56. Slithery swimmers
57. Those folks
58. "_____ Me Entertain You"
59. Speed of travel

DOWN

1. Propel, as a soccer ball
2. Tehran's country
3. Musical quality
4. Allergy symptom
5. Montana's neighbor
6. Jot down
7. Least dull
8. Tantalizing smell
9. Cover over with asphalt
10. Well-matched
11. Convey
22. Furry sea mammal
24. Mother Goose's specialty
25. Folding bed
26. Have
27. Ran across
28. Seek an answer
29. Newsman Koppel
30. Movie star Gardner
31. Comrade
34. Sterilizing liquid
39. More spookily weird
40. Back street
41. See 51-Across
42. The thing over there
43. Every one
44. Sour, green fruit
46. Had on
48. Concept
49. Stallion-to-be
50. Otherwise

316

ACROSS

1. Perform (a 47-Across)
4. Shut hastily
8. Took a dip
12. "Runaround ——," 1960s song
13. Possess
14. Rate of speed
15. Animal enclosure
16. Bread-maker's cooker
17. Cup lips
18. "—— your room!"
20. Bargain events
21. Great merriment
23. Like a certain duckling?
25. Country path
26. Male protagonist
27. Wallet bill
30. Not factual
32. Arise
34. Asner and Sullivan
35. Recite the rosary
37. Pleased
38. Female deer
39. Hearing organs
40. Skull's contents
43. Grating
46. Exist
47. Movie part
48. Worn, as a coat
51. Revise (copy)
52. Persia, now
53. Cow's sound
54. Marries
55. Lady's beau
56. Likely

DOWN

1. Egyptian viper
2. Pool stick
3. Dime: 2 wds.
4. Foot covering
5. Molten rock
6. Wide thoroughfare
7. Adult boys
8. Jet of liquid
9. Lament loudly
10. Highest point
11. Disorderly heap
19. Malicious look
20. Far from fast
21. Carpenter's adhesive
22. Earth; soil
24. Gloomy color
26. At this place
27. The Sooner State
28. Close by
29. Concludes
31. Atop
33. Matures
36. On 22-Down
38. Eating regimens
40. Was carried by the wind
41. Take a bus
42. Fervent
44. Actor Alda
45. Lease
47. Equip
49. Chop (off)
50. Round speck

317

ACROSS

1. Deal (with)
5. That girl
8. Male deer
12. Completely finished
13. Metal food container
14. Vaulter's tool
15. Grassy area
16. Small carpet
17. Opposite of west
18. Otherwise
19. Boxing great Muhammad
20. Fusses
21. Patriotic Uncle
23. Neither's partner
25. Droops, as a flower
28. Play the odds
29. Figure out a sum
32. Eden woman
33. Of Dublin
35. Pool stick
36. "So long!"
37. Funnyman Rickles
38. _____ away, corroded
40. Allow
41. Sleeve occupant
42. Dismiss from work
45. Appropriate
47. Salt Lake City's state
51. Brainstorm
52. Extremely
53. Performance by one
54. Slide on a banana peel, perhaps
55. Shade tree
56. Winds up
57. Circus structure
58. Distress call at sea
59. Do an usher's job

DOWN

1. Singer Nat or Natalie
2. Football-shaped
3. Church benches
4. Writer Hemingway
5. "Get lost!": slang
6. Transport by truck
7. Motors
8. Lancelike weapon
9. Warty amphibian
10. And
11. Acquires
22. Put _____, save until later
24. Different one
25. Spider's trap
26. _____ League, college group
27. General Robert E.
28. Box for coal
29. Emulate Robert Redford
30. Payable now
31. Lions' lair
34. Switches the positions of (a car's tires)
39. Entertains
40. Sprung
41. Wee particles
42. Clenched hand
43. Inactive
44. Bridle strap
46. Game on horseback
48. Sound quality
49. "M*A*S*H" actor Alan
50. Party giver

318

ACROSS

1. "To ____ is human . . ."
4. Mix, using a spoon
8. Compact ____, recording
12. Compete, as for attention
13. ____ down, demolished
14. Reverberation
15. Skyscraper transport
17. Leak slowly
18. Convey, as a message
19. Convent residents
21. Golf-ball holder
23. Sibling's daughters
27. Air hero
30. Bit of wet paint
32. Demonstrate the truth of
33. Metal bars
35. Oleo container
37. Pine or hemlock
38. Transparent
40. Brief doze
42. Reach the finale
43. Leather-strap footwear
45. Gesture of assent
47. Tinted
49. Stretching will get these out!
53. Bride, after the wedding
56. Opposite of stillness
58. Big fusses
59. Completed
60. Like Willie Winkie
61. Rec-room projectile
62. Butterfly snares
63. Make stitches

DOWN

1. Always
2. Get a rise out of
3. Lively dance
4. Remained
5. Little kid
6. Strong metal
7. Encore performance on TV?
8. Sweet dinner course
9. Frost (cupcakes)
10. Ship's pronoun
11. "NYPD Blue" role
16. Large container
20. Sudden bite
22. Feast on
24. Apple's center
25. Not odd
26. Peach pit or acorn
27. Rainbow shapes
28. Soda flavor
29. Genesis garden
31. Sweet roll
34. Most dejected
36. Forbid
39. Beam of light
41. Certain fireplace tools
44. Tart fruit
46. Low, as light
48. Cooing bird
50. Daily paper's contents
51. Leg joint
52. Simmer
53. Chewing-gum mouthful
54. Lupino of filmdom
55. Gift-tag word
57. Dog's doctor

1	2	3	■	4	5	6	7	■	8	9	10	11
12			■	13				■	14			
15			16					■	17			
18					■	19		20		■	■	■
■	■	■	21		22	■	23			24	25	26
27	28	29	■	30		31	■	32				
33			34	■	35		36	■	37			
38				39	■	40		41	■	42		
43					44	■	45		46	■	■	■
■	■	■	47			48	■	49		50	51	52
53	54	55		■	56		57					
58				■	59				■	60		
61				■	62				■	63		

319

ACROSS

1. Become less distinct
5. Apply appliqués (with "on")
8. Emulate a thrush
12. Alda or King
13. Football prop
14. Bird of ____
15. Bit of ID, often
16. Ancient
17. Chamber
18. Arctic natives
20. Landers and Miller
21. Pause that refreshes?
22. Fishing lure, at times
24. Boasts
27. Visualize
28. Say further
31. Become sick
32. Chirping sound
34. Prosecute
35. Actor Vigoda
36. Consume
37. Spirited away
39. Attempt
40. Decimal base
41. Adore
44. Becomes smaller
48. Kitchen appliance
49. Sticky substance
50. List of cafe offerings
51. Pied Piper's pests
52. Bradley and McMahon
53. Dry and barren
54. Otherwise
55. Actress West
56. Oodles

DOWN

1. Nose's locale
2. "What a shame!"
3. Opposite of light
4. Finishing up
5. Bend down
6. Snakelike swimmers
7. Tie the knot
8. Use air freshener
9. Certain golf club
10. Bright gas
11. Workout rooms
19. Title for a lad
22. Lawyer's charge
23. A, B, or C
24. Wild and woolly greeting?
25. Eve's origin
26. Pub offering
27. "On your mark, get ____ . . ."
28. Question
29. Payable
30. Family room, often
33. Method
38. It may have scales, or perhaps fur
39. Far from relaxed
40. The ones there
41. Folk wisdom
42. Racetrack shape
43. Doctors for pets
44. Baking ____, leavening agent
45. Cruel Roman
46. Make a stocking cap
47. Foam
49. Precious stone

320

ACROSS

1. Nights before holidays
5. See 38-Down
8. Get along
12. Hockey arena
13. Mine deposit
14. Like some medicine
15. Home heating device
17. Camera glass
18. Balanced, as a distribution
19. Small blackboard
20. Gaze steadily
23. Triumphant cry
24. Peach seeds
25. Tricycle path
30. Fuss
31. Made (a cake)
32. Patriot Franklin, familiarly
33. Lizards and snakes
35. Heredity unit
36. "Honest" President
37. Permit
38. Explosive devices
41. Equestrian game
43. False god
44. Not very hot
48. Musical sound
49. A Gershwin
50. Great Lake near Buffalo
51. Epochs
52. Towel off
53. Slight impression

DOWN

1. Goof up
2. By way of
3. Finish
4. Slope devotees
5. Brief letter
6. Press (shirts)
7. ____ diem
8. Be a disciple of
9. Neighborhood
10. Declaim wildly
11. Other
16. "Hail, Caesar!"
19. Storage hut
20. Practice like a boxer
21. Ocean current
22. On the peak of
23. Lyrical poems
25. Auction
26. Eisenhower, informally
27. Cain's brother
28. Carson's successor
29. Recognized
31. Parts of some overalls
34. Meal sites
35. Shone
37. Pub brew
38. Nibble
39. Scent
40. "____ Lisa"
41. Cat sound
42. Approve
44. Box cover
45. Exist
46. ____ Tin Tin
47. Was introduced to

321

ACROSS

1. Fuss
4. Annoying one
8. Hen products
12. Turf
13. Thought
14. Applaud
15. In a position to propose marriage?
17. Fervently wish
18. Decays
19. Pulled by a rope
20. Bright-eyed and bushy-tailed
23. Self
25. Walking stick
26. In a lazy way
27. Sweet potato
30. Concealed
32. Flee
34. Asner and Sullivan
35. Land unit
37. Is indebted to
38. That girl
39. Locates
40. In fact
44. Mend (stockings)
46. Get up
47. Chastises
51. Store sign
52. Teenager's skin condition
53. In the style of: 2 wds.
54. Danson and Turner
55. Require
56. Can metal

DOWN

1. Pose a question
2. Put on (clothes)
3. Flattering poem
4. Airline employee
5. Revise (copy)
6. Perceived
7. Clothing label
8. Sound reflection
9. Radiate
10. Open-mouthed stare
11. Moved quickly
16. Made a mistake
19. Child's playthings
20. Dull pain
21. Put down
22. Finishes
24. Extreme happiness
26. One-twelfth of a foot
27. Show tiredness
28. Imitated
29. Jumbled heap
31. Far from difficult
33. Pocket change
36. Diminish
39. Cooked with oil
40. Horse's gait
41. Ready for picking
42. Second-hand
43. Eyeglass piece
45. "____ of Green Gables"
47. Kitchen vessel
48. Derby or cap
49. Inventor Whitney
50. ____ Diego, California

322

ACROSS

1. Proper
5. Heavy drinking cup
8. Shade providers
12. Rant
13. A Gershwin
14. Metal support
15. Movie premieres
17. Irritate
18. Golf-ball prop
19. Uninterested
20. Lawn growth
24. Close by
26. Large stone
27. Poke with a knife
28. Gardening tool
31. Regard highly
33. Breakfast food
35. Stinging insect
36. Salt Lake City's state
38. Large boats
39. Phonographic record
40. The things there
41. Broadcast again
44. A pair
46. Lyric poems
47. Travel bag
52. Chair, for one
53. Dine
54. Cain's brother
55. Concludes
56. Gore and Pacino
57. Deli meat, roast ____

DOWN

1. Favorable vote
2. Knock sharply
3. "____ Got a Secret"
4. Chess pieces
5. Ore location
6. Pressing
7. Car fuel
8. Mistake
9. Animal den
10. Traveler's measurement
11. Snow vehicle
16. "____ a boy!"
19. Baseballer Ruth
20. Snatch
21. Took a bus
22. Summit
23. Enjoy a winter sport
25. Every
27. Collections
28. Brave man
29. Sturdy trees
30. Otherwise
32. Destroy
34. Cheerleader's word
37. Fact-based
39. Wipes with a cloth
40. Small child
41. Love's bloom
42. Eve's home
43. Peruse a book
45. Smarts
47. Ocean
48. Hired automobile
49. Lincoln, informally
50. Look at
51. Santa's aide

323

ACROSS

1. Make illegal
4. TV program
8. Does some sums
12. Boxing great
13. Wishful feeling
14. Cruel Roman emperor
15. A, B, C, . . .
17. Close by
18. At the top of
19. Window projection
20. Platform
23. Self, to Freud
25. Heap (on)
26. Summer citrus drinks
27. "_____ is it?"
30. A brother of Prince Charles
32. Sister's son
34. Afternoon drink
35. Seemingly endless
37. Authentic
38. Organ of vision
39. Sound-alike of "sense"
40. Less dangerous
44. Sedans and coupes
46. Extract (a tooth)
47. Withholds privileges
51. Article of news
52. Bachelor of _____
53. Furniture wood
54. Drags by a rope
55. Hardly shallow
56. Attempt (to)

DOWN

1. Sheep's bleat
2. Every single one
3. Bite lightly
4. Physical form
5. Freight-train hopper
6. Unlocked
7. Dry's opposite
8. Green Gables girl
9. Property title
10. Go too slowly, as time
11. Tender to the touch
16. More enormous
19. Come in last
20. Tiff
21. Fork prong
22. Robert or Alan of acting fame
24. Mannerly man
26. "Up, up, and _____!"
27. "At what time?"
28. Furnace's output
29. Hooting birds
31. Always
33. Word after "bench" or "printing"
36. Free from peril
39. Light and crunchy
40. Barbecue rod
41. Motorcar
42. Soared
43. Avenue-lining trees
45. Poker stake
47. Steno's notebook
48. Summer weather forecast
49. Lobe locale
50. Blue expanse above

324

ACROSS

1. Relatives
4. Adolescent
8. Eyelid hair
12. A Gershwin
13. Very unattractive
14. A single time
15. Go one better than
16. Sandwich bread option
17. Wound reminder
18. Move quietly
20. Cry loudly
22. Finish
23. Guided
25. Catches (a crook)
27. Postponed
31. Moreno and Hayworth
34. Tall spring flower
35. Come in first
37. Young stallion
38. Halloween costume parts
40. In an avid way
42. Dog's wagger
44. Slangy "sure"
45. Garden tool
47. "Help!," asea
49. Academy Award
53. Possesses
55. Propeller's sound
57. Boxing great
58. Ooze (out)
59. Opposite of short
60. Mama's boy?
61. Rapids swirl
62. Ox harness
63. TV's Danson

DOWN

1. First-aid bags
2. Press (clothes)
3. Back of the neck
4. Thanks-giving fowl
5. Self
6. House additions
7. Elastic fiber
8. ____ Angeles
9. Forebear
10. Scrutinize
11. Cattle group
19. Nome's state
21. Neighbor-hood tavern
24. Morning mist
26. Arm muscles
27. Lower (lights)
28. Historic age
29. Used one's ears
30. Gambling cube
32. ". . . and to ____ a good night!"
33. Pig's home
36. Dissenting vote
39. A sibling, for short
41. See 12-Across
43. Humble
45. Flexible tube
46. Had bills
48. "Go away!"
50. Play's players
51. Lotion plant
52. Citrus skin
54. Secret agent
56. Pen fluid

325

ACROSS

1. Birthday present, for one
5. Flat refusals
8. Baby's bed
12. Smell
13. High playing-card
14. Assistant
15. Ms. Horne
16. Drink-stirring utensil
18. Fathers
19. Boxer Muhammad
20. Brass instrument
23. See 18-Across
28. Inquire
31. Having good judgment
33. Anger
34. Mr. Reagan
36. Most recent
38. Cut short
39. Sunrise direction
41. Distress signal at sea
42. Lodging establishment
44. Swerve suddenly
46. Cover (cake) with frosting
48. "The Seven Year ____," Monroe movie
52. Male choir voice
57. Ashen
58. Way out?
59. Heavy drinking-cup
60. Test
61. Actor Danson and newsman Koppel
62. "Sit up and ____, Fido!"
63. Edges; borders

DOWN

1. Yellow jewelry metal
2. Notion
3. Tender and affectionate
4. Garbage-can contents
5. Singer King Cole
6. Seas
7. Marine animal with flippers
8. Baseballer's hat
9. Brazil city, for short
10. Wedding words
11. Affleck of film
17. Drink a little at a time
21. Wide-eyed bird
22. Travel by car
24. Gallery attraction
25. Crusted baked desserts
26. In addition
27. TV receivers
28. Doorway curve
29. Performance by oneself
30. Work on a sweater
32. Otherwise
35. Mimic
37. Gobbled up
40. Wide thoroughfare
43. Illuminated
45. More mature
47. Hair-parting item
49. Car for hire
50. Chowder seafood
51. Garment borders
52. Wager
53. Tree-chopping tool
54. Free (of)
55. Part of "TGIF"
56. Hen product

326

ACROSS

1. Inhales suddenly
6. Fellow
9. Columnist Landers
12. Expect
13. Singer Yoko
14. General Robert E.
15. Window shelf
16. Transgression
17. "What's up, ____?"
18. Mae of Hollywood
20. Went beneath the surface
21. Citrus drink
24. Passageway between seats
26. Performed
27. Egyptian viper
28. Due; unpaid
32. In an eager manner
34. Dorm room decoration
35. Iron or aluminum
36. Drink slowly
37. Period of time
38. Pancake topping
40. Disorderly crowd
41. Two together
44. Dollar bills
46. Ms. Gardner
47. Public transport
48. Ronstadt or Evans
53. Forbid
54. Utilize
55. Keep away from
56. European moose
57. Mesh trap
58. Made cat sounds

DOWN

1. Lass
2. Wonder
3. Unhappy
4. Sty resident
5. Hearty dish
6. Spread rumors
7. Military groups
8. Over there
9. Actor Alan
10. Gas found in signs
11. Choker site
19. Simple
20. Uses needle and thread
21. Eve's mate
22. Plunge headfirst into water
23. Prepare (copy) for print
25. Stunt plane maneuver
27. TV character McBeal
29. Bit of news
30. Cruel Roman emperor
31. Seize suddenly
33. Short, fast race
34. Plumbing tube
36. "____ Boulevard," Gloria Swanson film
39. Wake
41. Infant
42. Egg-shaped
43. Container for liquid
45. Shut with force
47. Small roll
49. "____ Got a Secret," old TV show
50. "ASAP!"
51. Gaming cube
52. Tack on

327

ACROSS

1. Repeated sound
5. Against
8. Concert selection
12. Snatch
13. Have debts
14. Higher than
15. Obtains
16. Picnic crasher?
17. Female horse
18. Dessert offerings
20. Underneath
21. Spin
24. Cumbersome
27. Old cloth
28. Cheerleader's yell
31. A Great Lake
32. Tiny bark
33. Superman's accessory
34. Sweet potato
35. Spider's home
36. Authority
37. Spring holiday
39. Inquired
43. Forest official
47. Singer Horne
48. Lincoln, to friends
50. Small inlet
51. Buck or doe
52. Newsman Rather
53. Singles
54. Summer drinks
55. Father
56. Most excellent

DOWN

1. Omelet ingredients
2. Ship's staff
3. Despise
4. See
5. Shore
6. Possess
7. Mesh snare
8. Any
9. President's room in the White House, the _____ Office
10. Roman emperor
11. Thrived
19. Child's plaything
20. Implore
22. Some Middle East natives
23. Strike lightly
24. Greeting word
25. Time period
26. Intention
28. Uncooked
29. Mimic
30. That woman
32. Affirmative vote
33. Yellow vegetable's center
35. Marry
36. Pod morsel
38. Current style
39. Actor Alan
40. Plant beginning
41. Leg joint
42. Jug handles
44. Away
45. 12/24 and 12/31
46. Relax
48. Sum (up)
49. Lamb's call

328

ACROSS

1. Got bigger
5. Military conflict
8. Hugged
12. Not recorded, as a musical performance
13. Lofty poem
14. Lake near Cleveland
15. Jungle primates
16. Bizarre
17. Leaf-roundup tool
18. Bent in
20. Struck a stance
21. Out of the way
24. Single step
28. Regular
33. Wolf's 38-Down
34. Top pilot
35. "Over hill, over ____ . . ."
36. Tiny hair
38. Pay-TV service
39. Less outgoing
41. Ebony-hued
45. Yours truly
50. Apiece
51. Deadly viper
53. Creative thought
54. Square of three
55. Butterfly catcher
56. Peruse (a book)
57. Doodled, perhaps
58. Night's opposite
59. "Do the ____ justify the means?"

DOWN

1. Joyful
2. Fit for picking
3. Neck and neck
4. Left, on a map
5. Certain golf clubs
6. Find a total
7. Ketchup color
8. Epic character
9. Historic stretches
10. Be fond of
11. Feat
19. Play by ____, make up as you go along
20. Vigor
22. In need of a scratch
23. Tinting agent
24. Pronoun for a ship
25. Doll or wagon
26. Reverent fear
27. Sick
29. Ms. Lupino
30. Trucker's perch
31. Every one
32. A Confederate general
34. Fire residue
37. Interrogate
38. Loud call
40. Holding nothing
41. Flex, as an elbow
42. Bear's cave, for one
43. Teenager's skin bane
44. Enjoy gum
46. Paddock papa
47. Garden of paradise
48. Guide (an expedition)
49. Passing fancies
51. Common connecting word
52. Saltwater body

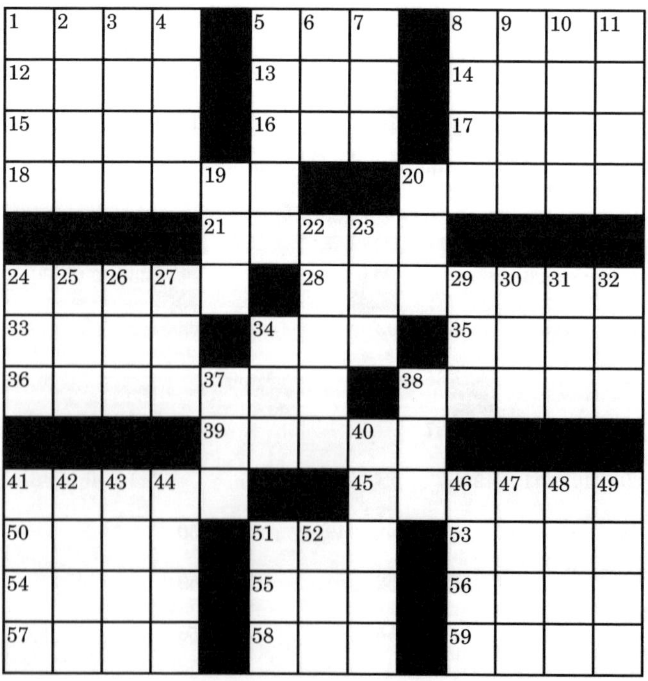

329

ACROSS

1. Significant times
5. ____ up, robbed
9. Syllable from Baby?
12. Bowling alley
13. Region
14. Take part in a marathon
15. Locale
16. Sports ally
18. Adversary
20. Home-owner's document
21. Listening organ
23. First-course choices, often
26. Clothes closet
31. The Great ____ of China
32. Lyricist Gershwin
33. Entrance-ways
35. Golf-ball peg
36. Go by horse
38. Brow
40. Corrects (a manu-script)
42. Place for pigs
43. Sour substance
45. Slight quarrels
49. Early-morning wrap
53. Take on
54. Self-esteem
55. 12/24 and 12/31
56. Garden in the Bible
57. Neither's partner
58. Acrobats' safety measures
59. Require-ment

DOWN

1. Otherwise
2. Water from above
3. Poker payment
4. Appeared to be
5. Derby or stovepipe
6. Before: poetic
7. Be ahead of all others
8. Titled English-women
9. Receive a degree
10. On the town
11. "____, two, buckle my shoe . . ."
17. Cat's sound
19. Three-foot measure-ment
22. House's top
24. Urgent request
25. Vehicle pulled by huskies
26. Electri-cian's supply
27. Sahara-like
28. Hissing heater
29. Jeer for the umpire
30. Makes a mistake
34. Places silverware on (the table)
37. Draw on glass
39. Typograph-ical mark
41. Loud warning whistle
44. Cooing bird
46. Assistant, as to a teacher
47. Forest growth
48. Post (a letter)
49. Patriot Franklin
50. In the past
51. Casino wager
52. Snaky letter

330

ACROSS

1. Cereal grains
5. Poisonous snake
8. First man
12. Turn (over)
13. Actor's hint
14. Shoestring
15. Ended
17. Makes mistakes
18. Female deer
19. Concurs (with)
21. Escorts to a seat
24. "____ me introduce myself"
25. Extra
26. Playground attractions
30. Corn spike
31. Father
32. Chip accompaniment
33. Had visions while sleeping
36. Slumber sound
38. Competed in a marathon
39. Shut, as a door
40. Pressing
43. Ignited (a fire)
44. Ripped
45. Monogrammed letters
50. China's continent
51. Earth's star
52. Mince
53. Egg layers
54. High explosive: abbr.
55. Effortless

DOWN

1. Away from work
2. The Greatest of boxing
3. Can material
4. It climbed up the water spout in a song
5. Discomforts
6. Take to court
7. Propelled a bike
8. Warnings
9. Challenge
10. Farmer's land measurement
11. Untidy sight
16. Painful
20. "Golly!"
21. Employed
22. Shadowbox
23. Rabbit's kin
26. Woeful
27. Troubles
28. Metal strand
29. Hurried (away)
31. Tooth doctor
34. Sports centers
35. Fellow
36. Small cut
37. Formal announcement
39. Mr. Eastwood
40. Salt Lake City's state
41. Scented bloom
42. Smile broadly
46. She may wear a habit
47. "I found it!"
48. ____ Angeles
49. Secret agent

331

ACROSS

1. Egg-shaped
5. Travel by yacht
9. "Murder, ____ Wrote," old TV show
12. Sandwich shop
13. Long African river
14. Pod vegetable
15. Gobbles up
16. Inactive
17. Pacino and Jolson
18. Vending-machine opening
19. Doctor's rate
20. Mr. Rooney
21. Tiny, magical being
23. Young woman
25. Sports stadium
28. Filled with tears, as a 27-Down
32. Light beam
33. Petite
35. Anger
36. Cheddar and mozzarella
38. Oak nut
40. ____ Angeles, California
41. Volcanic dust
42. Candle cord
45. Adult female pig
47. Sound repetition
51. A Gershwin
52. Turner of music
53. Display; exhibit
54. In favor of
55. Choker site
56. Domesticated
57. Conclude
58. Shade provider
59. Moved quickly

DOWN

1. Lyric poems
2. Calf meat
3. Lowest female choir voice
4. Be all ears
5. Nose noise
6. Assistant
7. Forbidden by statute
8. General Robert E.
9. Reach across
10. Clutched
11. Simple
20. Sudsy brew
22. Rancher's rope
24. Book of maps
25. Circle curve
26. Cheerleader's cry
27. Organ of sight
28. Existed
29. Brazilian city, for short
30. Do wrong
31. Lion's lair
34. More cluttered
37. European moose
39. Storage boxes
41. Rouse from sleep
42. Husband's mate
43. Numbered golf club
44. Word after "credit" or "green"
46. Formerly
48. Fellow
49. "____ Alone," 1990 movie
50. Was in debt
52. High explosive: abbr.

332

ACROSS

1. Impudent child
5. Pairs
9. Mud-bath site
12. Alleviate
13. Cleveland's state
14. Kitchen faucet
15. River boats
16. Source of water
17. Mature
18. Birds' roosts
20. Storm's center
21. Lipstick shade, often
22. Night flier
24. Used (a chair)
26. Prolonged battle
29. Water vapor
31. Untruths
34. Weds secretly
36. Citrus fruit
38. 45-Across color?
39. At this place
41. Received
42. Arrest
44. Ocean
45. Unhappy
47. Large deer
49. Mommy's mate
54. Tint
55. Trot or canter
57. Folk knowledge
58. "____ about time!"
59. Highest point
60. Level
61. Word of negation
62. Casino lighting
63. Stitches

DOWN

1. Green legume
2. Unusual
3. Inquires
4. Student evaluation
5. Pull by rope
6. Skateboard rollers
7. Greasy
8. Shoe bottoms
9. ____ gate, horse track feature
10. Sheet of paper
11. Mimicked
19. A few
23. Hope fervently
25. In the style of: 2 wds.
26. Spider's trap
27. Every last bit
28. Most rotund
30. Ripped
32. Self
33. Fix firmly
35. Pod veggie
37. Peruse (a book)
40. Northern native
43. Commenced
45. Sensitive leg area
46. Car
48. Meshed fabric
50. Pub quaffs
51. Symbol of peace
52. Made a picture
53. Strong desires
56. Sawbuck

333

ACROSS

1. "I found it!"
4. Region
8. Is right for
12. Small amount
13. Pub missile
14. Correct (text)
15. Frothy brew
16. Toledo's state
17. Inquisitive
18. Grinding tooth
20. Long poem
22. Plead
24. Prepared
28. Distribute (the cards)
31. A single time
34. Briny deep
35. Border
36. Neither's partner
37. One who avoids the truth
38. Actor Majors
39. Rose of baseball
40. Make money
41. Gandhi's land
43. Was victorious
45. Hosiery defect
48. Express (an opinion)
52. Zoo primates
55. Goad
57. Comic Rickles
58. South American republic
59. Adolescent
60. Ancient
61. Oak or maple
62. Has debts
63. ____ Vegas

DOWN

1. First man
2. Angelic aura
3. A son of 1-Down
4. Worship
5. "Go, team!"
6. One in "HOMES"
7. On
8. Picket barrier
9. Bride's words
10. "____ the season . . ."
11. Pigpen
19. Competent
21. Angry feeling
23. Departed
25. Big continent
26. Letter start
27. Knitter's supply
28. Food shop
29. 1-Down's home
30. See 60-Across
32. Negative word
33. Ship's workers
37. Comedian Jay
39. Skillet
42. Topic for a political debate
44. Hot appliances
46. Car
47. Became big
49. Beloved one
50. Soft-drink flavor
51. Finishes
52. Liable
53. For each
54. Poet's before
56. "Golly!"

334

ACROSS

1. Corn core
4. Give off light
8. Accompanied by
12. President Lincoln, to pals
13. Dubuque's state
14. Inventive thought
15. Guided
16. Pealed, as a bell
17. Dinner bread
18. Personal pronoun
20. Telephone greeting
21. Takes for granted
24. Headliner
27. Neither's partner
28. Helpful hint
31. Bodily discomfort
32. Wedding words
33. Skin opening
34. Upper limb
35. Dollar bill
36. Bank transaction
37. Daybreak
40. Incline
43. More orderly
47. Agreeable
48. Soft drink
50. Fruit beverage
51. Actress Bancroft
52. Prepare (copy) for print
53. Pod veggie
54. Look closely
55. Afternoon socials
56. Finish

DOWN

1. Peaceful
2. Follow orders
3. River bottoms
4. Young women
5. Goofs off
6. Possess
7. Move from side to side, as a tail
8. Electrical cables
9. Object of worship
10. Reveal
11. Angel's headdress
19. Gain through hard work
20. That girl
22. Below
23. Cow's cry
24. Health resort
25. Paving material
26. Intention
28. In addition
29. Lyricist Gershwin
30. Writing implement
32. Country hotel
33. Urgent request
35. "Three strikes and you're ____!"
37. Contemptuous smile
38. Bombay's country
39. Stools and chairs
40. Metal fastener
41. Face wrinkle
42. Common teen skin problem
44. Record (sound)
45. Paradise
46. Enjoy a book
48. Harden, as cement
49. Lyric poem

335

ACROSS

1. Soccer move
5. Truckers' radios
8. Field furrower
12. Lazy
13. Surprised cry
14. Rural road
15. Next-door ____
17. Matured
18. Narrow opening
19. Dali, for one
21. By means of
22. Austrian city
26. Person who plays Romeo
29. For each
30. Broadcast
31. Like a snail
32. Goop for 16-Down
33. Jagger of the Rolling Stones
34. Touch lightly
35. Marsh
36. Strolls or ambles
37. Person who sleeps loudly
39. Facial twitch
40. Revised (copy)
42. Dog or cat
45. Pond croaker
48. More solitary
50. Corn Belt state
51. Permit
52. Capital of Norway
53. Rod's mate
54. Fire remnant
55. Gone by

DOWN

1. His Majesty
2. Thought; concept
3. Cut out, as newspaper articles
4. Beer barrel
5. Hooded snake
6. Cowboy's footwear
7. Wither
8. Dinner dish
9. Linger behind
10. Individual
11. Marry
16. Crowning glory
20. Knightly title
21. Solemn oath
23. Finger's "claw"
24. Tiny notch
25. Boats like Noah's
26. Small vipers
27. Family group
28. Oz dog
29. Wooden pin
32. Rain-forest ape
33. Slangy term for a man
35. Slumber spot
36. Broad
38. Like a 1-Down
39. A dime, to a dollar
41. Foot digits
42. Leaning-tower city
43. Slippery fishes
44. Jogging gait
45. Douglas ____, an evergreen
46. Fish eggs
47. Be in debt
49. Cut (off)

336

ACROSS

1. Smell; aroma
5. European peak
8. Price
12. Do a jackknife
13. Dove call
14. A neighbor of Pennsylvania
15. Profound
16. Instrument with a slide
18. Sandal feature
20. Sketch
21. Under the weather
23. Birds' homes
27. Falls back, as an army
32. Reveal
33. Lupino of the movies
34. Shun
36. Untruth
37. Tip
39. Forefather
41. Book of maps
43. Barbie's beau
44. Superman's girlfriend
47. Waltz or twist
51. In need of companionship
55. Thick string
56. Persia, nowadays
57. "That's great!"
58. Leg joint
59. Financial obligation
60. Mature
61. Stitched

DOWN

1. Bettor's chances
2. Count calories
3. Above
4. Fix
5. Play a role
6. A nobleman
7. Unsatisfactory
8. Spider's trap
9. Surprised expression
10. Moral transgression
11. Foot digit
17. Guy
19. Sincere, urgent request
22. Molten rock
24. Table seasoning
25. Small musical group
26. Prophet
27. Ms. Hayworth
28. Revise (copy)
29. Statuesque
30. Freight weight
31. See 21-Across
35. Heroic act
38. Natural skill
40. Midnight raids on the fridge
42. Distress call
45. Des Moines' locale
46. Air pollution
48. Zilch
49. Work team
50. First garden
51. Shoe-box cover
52. Mine find
53. Arrest
54. Female sheep

337

ACROSS

1. Overcast
5. Nile vipers
9. Sick
12. Assess
13. Christmas song
14. Brazilian resort, for short
15. Crafts' partner
16. Job preparation
18. "Busy" insect
19. Wager
20. Sleeveless garments
21. Vote against
23. Church seat
24. Soup spoon
26. For each
27. Uncle ——, American figure
30. Complimentary poems
31. Use a shovel
32. Food fish
33. Marry
34. Cooking vessel
35. Holy person
36. Candied-apple color
37. Perform a role
38. Word after "Boy" or "Girl"
41. Small wound
43. Feline
46. Violent windstorms
48. Grotto
49. In the style of: 2 wds.
50. Citrus fruit
51. Big continent
52. Lass
53. Moved quickly
54. River bottoms

DOWN

1. Snatch
2. Unusual
3. Showed up
4. "Absolutely!"
5. Poker stake
6. Classify by kind
7. Pod veggie
8. Thin slice (of cake)
9. Spring bloom
10. Pocket fluff
11. Ships' records
17. Just out
19. "See ya!"
22. Pacino and Gore
23. Wooden coat hanger
24. Near the ground
25. Fruity refresher
26. Sewing tool
27. Travel bag
28. Columnist Landers
29. Welcoming rug?
31. Mom's man
32. It's between "tic" and "toe"
34. Flower leaves
35. Used a chair
36. Operate (a machine)
38. Male deer
39. Soda flavor
40. Spoken
41. Arrive
42. Employed
44. Fervent
45. Hot beverages
47. Chips' partner
48. Taxi

338

ACROSS

1. Flying mammal
4. Cease
8. "Go on home!"
12. Honest ____ Lincoln
13. Factual
14. Flag holder
15. Pub beverage
16. Make money
17. Feedbag bits
18. Felt
20. Airline pro
21. Twisted snack
24. Bistro listing
27. Terrier's bark
28. Used to be
31. Kitchen appliance
32. Tear
33. Bucket
34. Soaked to the skin
35. Play on words
36. Repulsive
37. Most enormous
40. Copy of a magazine
43. Small
47. Bridge fee
48. Cain's brother
50. Metal bar
51. Seafood delicacy
52. Wharf
53. "____ been thinking . . ."
54. Dress edges
55. Finishes (an "i")
56. Gents

DOWN

1. Sheepish cries?
2. Skilled
3. Adolescent
4. Cowboy's concern
5. Barter
6. Belonging to us
7. Writing implement
8. Go bad
9. Furnace fuel
10. Female vocal range
11. Exam
19. Twirled
20. Energy
22. Sailor's skill with knots
23. See 20-Down
24. Cut the grass
25. Festive night before
26. Tennis-court divider
28. Move like a dog's tail
29. Become sick
30. Crafty
32. Small carpet
33. Miniature-golf move
35. ____ in the sky
37. Electric lamp inserts
38. Vote into office
39. Fabrics from China
40. Skin irritation
41. Achy
42. Bang (the door)
44. Remove, as fat
45. Abiding affection
46. Paradise
48. Throw in
49. Ghost's shout

339

ACROSS

1. Hit (a drum)
5. Hole stopper
9. Small swallow
12. Mountain's highest peak
13. Actress Hayworth
14. Neither's mate
15. Now and ____
16. Horse feed
17. Have obligations
18. Male children
19. Raw mineral
20. Not on the home field
21. Magical being
23. Chest bone
25. Prolonged look
28. Be worthy of
32. Possesses
33. Butlers' coworkers
35. Ventilate (a room)
36. Investigate new areas
38. Escort others to their seats
40. Hill-building insect
41. Cheer-leader's quality
42. Do origami
45. Freezer-tray cubes
47. Team's defeat
51. Zoo primate
52. Native of Glasgow
53. Poker-pot starter
54. Chaps
55. Alan of TV
56. Look over hastily
57. Finish
58. Fruit skin
59. Cattle group

DOWN

1. Cavern fliers
2. Repeated sound
3. Prayer ending
4. Less relaxed
5. Conclu-sive evidence
6. Person who fibs
7. Said
8. Service-station purchase
9. Winter flakes
10. Des Moines' state
11. Hunter's quarry
20. Lincoln, to friends
22. A citrus fruit
24. Political topic
25. That cow
26. Impose a levy
27. Dangerous snake
28. Gaming cube
29. Stadium shout
30. Enter into competi-tion (for)
31. Misjudge
34. Magazine piece
37. Young man
39. Sound from the swimming pool
41. Flower part
42. Celebrity status
43. Unwrapped
44. Give temporarily
46. Set of secret symbols
48. Fairy-tale beginning
49. One with 42-Down
50. Transmit (a message)
52. Plant juice

340

ACROSS

1. Beer barrels
5. Roasting rod
9. Far from bright
12. Smooth wrinkles
13. Ocean current
14. Wrath
15. Social engagement
16. Had debts
17. Point (a weapon)
18. Makes a mistake
20. In addition to
21. Like a 31-Across
24. Likely (to)
26. Dwells
27. Hailed, in a way
31. Skating surface
32. Picked
34. Farm fodder
35. Flightless bird
37. Rental agreement
39. "Definitely!"
40. Turned (a solid) into a liquid
41. First man
44. Green gemstone
45. Original
46. Shadowbox
48. Black bird
52. Steeped beverage
53. Couple
54. Canned fish
55. Secret agent
56. Wartime friend
57. Plant origin

DOWN

1. Baby goat
2. Time period
3. Received
4. Allergy symptom, maybe
5. Bound by an oath
6. Fido's "feet"
7. "____ Got a Crush on You," song
8. Newsman Koppel
9. Watch face
10. Showy flower
11. Short letter
19. Save
20. Dined
21. Turn (pancakes)
22. Chinese food staple
23. Baking vessel
24. Gore and Pacino
25. Skinned (a fruit)
27. Male heir
28. Yonder thing
29. Comfort
30. Used a coloring agent
33. This gentleman's
36. Sports building
38. Votes into office
40. Wed
41. Colonial insects
42. Shallow's opposite
43. Not present
44. Place of confinement
46. Mineral spring
47. Buddy
49. Regret
50. Washington's bill
51. Lump of gum

341

ACROSS

1. Loses firmness
5. Possesses
8. "Whose _____ are you on, anyway?"
12. Get _____, square accounts
13. Historic period
14. Spoken
15. Domesticated
16. Emulate De Niro
17. Certain evergreens
18. Figure out a sum
20. Use up foolishly
21. Penniless
24. Health resort
26. Government regulation
27. More modern
29. Picnic intruder
32. Miner's quest
33. A voice vote
34. Compete (for)
35. Tie the knot
36. Experiences emotion
38. Rural hotel
39. Nile viper
40. Gave help to
42. Pep-rally chant
46. Strange
47. Volcano's flow
48. Half a dozen
50. Swiss range
54. Pub options
55. One-spot card
56. Crop-ruining weather
57. A larger amount
58. Adult lads
59. Heed, as orders

DOWN

1. Put into place
2. Filmdom's Gardner
3. Ruby or topaz
4. Move furtively
5. Skull's site
6. Rainbow shape
7. Rested one's feet
8. Major furniture purchase
9. Tall flower
10. Toy missile
11. Otherwise
19. Bear's home
20. Child's card game
21. Make (a bubble)
22. Seldom seen
23. Had financial obligations
24. Use a broom
25. Ring out, as a bell
28. Sight organs
29. Eager, as a puzzles fan
30. Three-fourths of a dozen
31. Have an inclination (to)
36. Not near at all
37. Downhearted
41. Boise's state
42. Certain mollusk
43. Heavenly headpiece
44. For all time
45. Relief
46. Teamed beasts
48. Detective Spade
49. Sherbet's cousin
51. Chemist's workplace
52. Dessert to be divided
53. Crafty

342

ACROSS

1. Beavers' constructions
5. Young guys
9. Papa
12. Article on a checklist
13. Run amok
14. Application
15. Hereditary unit
16. TV actor Griffith
17. Religion's bane
18. Resembling one another
20. "All right!"
21. Slumbered noisily
24. Headed (an expedition)
26. Shoreline
27. Library patrons
31. Put a question to
32. Sightseers' outings
34. Chihuahua's bark
35. Honor
37. In that place
39. Picasso's output
40. Made fun of
41. Connecting corridor
44. Scents
46. "____ Got a Secret"
47. Child of Eve
48. Strongly dislike
52. Gambler's cube
53. Hand out (cards)
54. Wickedness
55. Bradley and Sullivan
56. Makes blunders
57. Went down, as a ship

DOWN

1. Use a shovel
2. Had supper
3. Former 5-Across
4. Spreads (on) messily
5. Interweave, as strands of hair
6. Squeal from the 8-Down
7. One who sings, Swiss style
8. Pigpen
9. Nightfall
10. Largest continent on earth
11. Contradict
19. Alphabet component
20. Weird
21. Permanently disfigure
22. On the ____, exactly
23. Squirrel supermarkets?
25. Holiday after Lent
27. Fixed, dull procedure
28. Some facial features
29. Infrequent
30. Went swiftly
33. Halloween month
36. Buddy
38. Diner dishes
40. Highway fees
41. Take cover
42. Keenly interested
43. Peggy and Spike
45. Precious
47. Fruit drink
49. Filmdom's Gardner
50. Sardine container
51. Large deer

343

ACROSS

1. Mom's sister
5. Creative skills
9. Weep noisily
12. Mix (a drink)
13. College head
14. Solemn wonder
15. Washed-out
16. Guys in retail
18. Piece, as of paper
20. Profound
21. Playmate for young Tarzan
23. Angered
27. Bowlike curved line
30. Infamous Roman emperor
32. Secret symbol-system
33. Auto-repair shop
35. Sea journey
37. Far from saintly
38. Urgent appeal
40. Served a meal to
41. Monetary obligations
43. Colony insect
44. Shady lane-liners
46. "Out of the park" hit
51. Least bald
55. Went by horse
56. Figure out a sum
57. Half of a sextet
58. Parched
59. Afternoon social
60. Viewed
61. "____ have a party!"

DOWN

1. African vipers
2. Provo's state
3. Egyptian river
4. Sequoia, for one
5. Classified listings
6. Novel enthusiast
7. "A ____ of Two Cities," Dickens work
8. Look of contempt
9. Detective Spade
10. Have 41-Across
11. Big ____, London clock
17. Full of zest
19. Tartness
22. Chick's chirp
24. Unit of bread
25. Outer border
26. Title to a piece of property
27. On in years
28. Speak wildly
29. Bed for baby
31. Pizza-baking chamber
34. Revise, as plans
36. Sworn promise
39. Heroic collie of TV
42. Long, narrow openings
45. Only
47. Spoken
48. Opposite of less
49. Revise text
50. Cincinnati's baseball team
51. Fedora, for one
52. Summer drink
53. Ms. Lupino
54. 2,000-pound measure

344

ACROSS

1. Increase in size
5. Tam or beret
8. Graph paper's pattern
12. Assistant
13. Color variant
14. Fit
15. Loch Lomond's locale
17. Hooting birds
18. For each
19. Sacred stands
21. Noah's vessel
22. Soap (up)
26. Farmer's spread
29. Mild oath
30. Tree-felling tool
31. Adoration
32. Cape ____, Massachusetts
33. Pleased as punch
34. Reverent fear
35. Stayed in one place
36. Makes tranquil
37. Takes a sip of
39. Pup's tail motion
40. Muffin morsel
42. Your and my
45. Speak incoherently
48. "Don't be silly!"
50. Comedian King
51. Peculiar
52. Superb tennis serves
53. Pinkie's location
54. Declare
55. Try out

DOWN

1. Sudden inhalation
2. Asian grain
3. Smell
4. Like rainy weather
5. Blackboard stick
6. Female relation
7. Propelled (a bicycle)
8. Spook
9. Unrefined
10. Green around the gills
11. ____ Moines
16. Hog fat
20. "Norma ____," Sally Field movie
21. Mug filler
23. School corridor
24. Final or midterm
25. Lipstick shades
26. Like a prairie
27. Davenport's state
28. December 24 and December 31
29. Acquired
32. Reno attractions
33. Practical joke
35. Large body of water
36. Supermarket display
38. Fashion
39. Characterized by breezes
41. Pop
42. A single time
43. Purposes
44. Take a breather
45. Word of cheer?
46. In the style of: 2 wds.
47. Moving vehicle
49. Have a snack

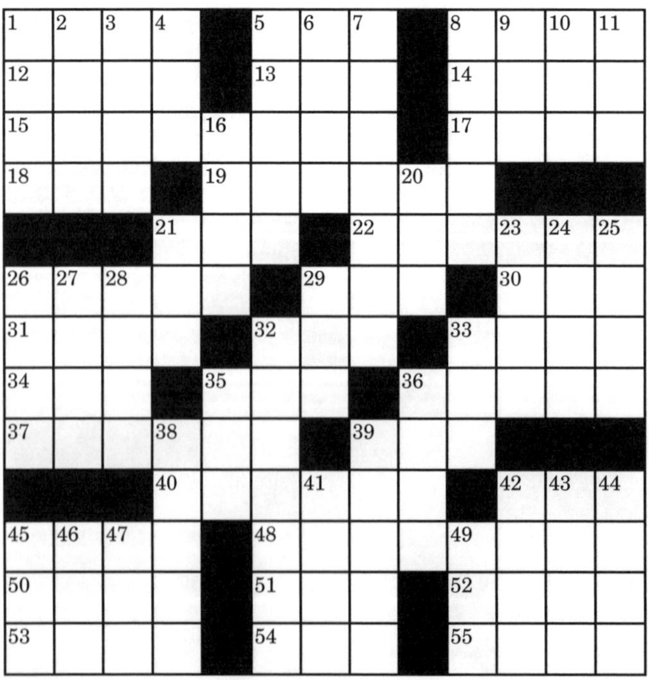

345

ACROSS

1. Deep affection
5. Moral misdeed
8. Opening for a coin
12. Roasting chamber
13. Refreshing beverage
14. Record on a VCR
15. Small fruit pie
16. "This minute!"
17. Equal; fair
18. Most cunning
20. Denim trousers
21. Cooked, as a turkey
24. Horse tamer's rope
27. Cat's "foot"
28. ____ Vegas, Nevada
31. Like: 2 wds.
32. A couple of times
34. Swiss peak
35. Nevertheless
36. Bowler or derby
37. Humble
39. Less neat
41. Had pains
44. Steps heavily
48. Broadway attraction
49. Become mature
51. Fiddler of ancient Rome
52. Ashen
53. Popular Easter meat
54. Profit
55. Went at high velocity
56. Pacino and Roker
57. Some shade trees

DOWN

1. Building sites
2. The ____ Office
3. To an extreme degree
4. Takes part in (a contest)
5. Mr. Claus
6. Wedding vow: 2 wds.
7. Recent
8. Spirited mount
9. Volcano outpouring
10. Shop sign, "Come in, we're ____"
11. Hamilton bills
19. Comforted
20. One who sells engagement rings
22. Barbecue rods
23. Tic-toe link
24. Deposit (eggs)
25. Beer's cousin
26. Used a sofa
28. Attorney's profession
29. Everything
30. Emulate James Bond
33. Existed
38. Juicy source of vitamin C
39. Cried, as a kitten
40. Articles on a list
41. Cleopatra's vipers
42. Fellow
43. Golfer's goal
45. Dinner is one
46. Prudish
47. Male heirs
49. Exclamation of discovery
50. Lass

346

ACROSS

1. Mouser, maybe
4. Bingo or poker
8. Zoo primates
12. Color shade
13. Cart-pulling cattle
14. Old TV knob
15. Enjoyed salad
16. Allow to borrow
17. "Thank you ____ much!"
18. Sat for a portrait
20. Sandwich shop
22. Was ahead of
24. Pediatrician, for one
28. Santa's entryway
32. Create cloth on a loom
33. Boy
34. Annoy
36. Pig's home
37. Geographical reference book
40. Able to wait
43. Removed the rind from
45. Place to park a 2-Down
46. Cleaning woman
48. Inquired (about)
52. Soprano's duet partner, perhaps
55. Soap bubbles
57. Like treacherous winter roads
58. Tells a whopper
59. Make a stocking cap
60. Yonder lass
61. Petty fight
62. Observes
63. Distress call

DOWN

1. Fellow
2. Car
3. Printed shirts
4. ____ retriever, yellow dog
5. Hatchet's kin
6. Repair, as pants
7. Terminated
8. Words to the wise
9. Boston cream ____
10. Corn-on-the-cob serving
11. Clever; crafty
19. Suburban tree
21. Far from high
23. Family room
25. VCR insert
26. Baking appliance
27. Tenant fee
28. Sound of thunder
29. Despise
30. Not doing anything
31. Puppy's bark
35. Young lady
38. Close, but not quite
39. Salt-water body
41. Browns bread
42. That thing's
44. Computer floppies
47. Huge sand mound
49. Affectionate greeting
50. Repeat sound
51. Tinting chemicals
52. Capone and Pacino
53. Pouting facial part
54. British drink
56. Perish

ACROSS

1. Droops
5. Make a request (for)
8. Jogger's gait
12. Eve's partner
13. Frozen water
14. Ready to be picked
15. Smelling organ
16. Gymnastics surface
17. Second-hand, as a car
18. Ready for action
20. Glass part of a camera
21. Gazed steadily
24. Place (bricks)
26. Secretariat, for one
27. Mr. Gibson
28. Annoy
31. Hardy tree
32. Cook over an open fire
34. Feel remorse for
35. Asner and McMahon
36. Mess up
37. Getting older
39. Not even
40. Bread edges
41. Short argument
44. Rub out
46. Desire
47. Steal from
48. Oceans
52. Teen's skin condition
53. Yale alum
54. Adhesive strip
55. One of equal rank
56. Family room
57. Dish of meat and vegetables

DOWN

1. ____ Francisco, California
2. Fuss
3. Car fuel
4. Slanders
5. Pointed (a weapon)
6. Wound reminder
7. Vessels for boiling water
8. Yours ____, letter closing
9. Stand up
10. Ready for business
11. Koppel and Danson
19. Looked (at) maliciously
21. Wingtip or sneaker
22. Frog relative
23. Large riverboats
25. Sacred platforms
27. Make imperfect
28. Colored part of the eye
29. Smallest animal in a litter
30. Metal beer-barrels
33. Gave a command
38. Party attendees
39. Flat-tailed mammal
40. Shipboard bedroom
41. Trade
42. Walk back and forth
43. Actress Bancroft
45. Part in a play
49. Have a meal
50. Mimic
51. Stitch (clothing)

347

1	2	3	4	■	5	6	7	■	8	9	10	11
12				■	13			■	14			
15				■	16			■	17			
■	■	■	18	19				■	20			
21	22	23				■	24	25		■	■	■
26					■	27			■	28	29	30
31			■	32	33				■	34		
35			■	36			■	37	38			
■	■	■	39			■	40					
41	42	43		■	44	45				■	■	■
46				■	47			■	48	49	50	51
52				■	53			■	54			
55				■	56			■	57			

348

ACROSS

1. Canoe, for one
5. Burden to carry
9. Beaver's creation
12. Division word
13. Inner impulse
14. Important time
15. Abound
16. Fishing-rod spool
17. Luau wreath
18. Affirmative votes
20. China native
22. Glued
25. "See you later!"
26. Bread spreads
27. Medieval fortresses
31. Function
32. Lose firmness
33. Pub brew
34. This evening
37. Sight or smell
39. Hint for an actor
40. Conducted; led
41. Bed covering
44. Uncle's wife
45. Baby goat
46. VCR insertion
48. Possess
52. Anger
53. Flock females
54. One of the Great Lakes
55. Lair
56. Remainder
57. Not imaginary

DOWN

1. Nibbled, perhaps
2. Dollar bill
3. Had lunch
4. The "T" in "BLT"
5. Attracted
6. Unrefined metals
7. How old one is
8. Postpones
9. Sliced-meats market
10. Region
11. Primary
19. Word of approval
21. Matched pair, perhaps
22. Sulk
23. In addition
24. Viewed
25. Grocery sack
27. Feline creature
28. Come ashore
29. Ultimatum ender
30. Plant start
32. That woman
35. Frozen water
36. Roadside channel
37. Earth's heater
38. Or's partner
40. Visitor
41. Lose traction
42. Employ
43. Genesis garden
44. Mimics
47. Reverence
49. Exist
50. By way of
51. Moray, for one

349

ACROSS

1. Smooth (one's nails)
5. Used a bench
8. Night birds
12. First man
13. Overwhelm
14. "_____ is your favorite color?"
15. Step on a banana peel, perhaps
16. Possesses
17. Three times three
18. Canvas shelter
19. Crafts' partner
21. Be a tailor
22. Three-foot length
24. Butter serving
26. Certain musical tones
29. Fuel for a Ferrari
30. Agitates
33. Movie star's statuette
35. Vigilant
36. Fictional detective Sam
37. Boxing legend
39. No longer wet
40. One of Baby's "piggies"
41. Wind-direction gauge
43. Play a 54-Across
45. Feat
47. Ski-vacation destination
51. Verbal refusals
53. Connecting word
54. Part on TV
55. Ripped (open)
56. Billiards stick
57. Shade giver
58. Otherwise
59. Belonging to the girl
60. Big pile

DOWN

1. Abstain from food
2. Pointless
3. Stretched out in repose
4. Hollow
5. North African desert
6. Bestows, as a prize
7. Exam
8. Be the proprietor of
9. Hailed a taxi, in a way
10. Highway divider
11. Hearty meal
20. Injure (an ankle)
23. Reached the same conclusion
25. Become sick
26. Angeles preceder
27. Nile viper
28. Disperses
31. Go astray
32. Place for pigs
34. Bustle
37. Boulevard's kin
38. Jacob's _____
42. Our planet
43. Start the kitty
44. Warm's opposite
46. Every
48. Folk learning
49. Entreaty
50. Leak out slowly
52. Get a glimpse of

350

ACROSS

1. Relatives
4. Expense
8. Prepare a field for planting
12. Wedding words
13. Green Gables gal
14. Seldom seen
15. Male heir
16. Arctic mammal
17. Grew older
18. Slumbered
20. Frolic
22. Inventor Whitney
24. Perfumes
28. Aretha Franklin song
32. Girl Scout unit
33. Acorn tree
34. Pup's yelp
36. Steeped beverage
37. Like Chinese food
40. Least distant
43. Tenant
45. Some
46. Slim, brittle branch
48. Flu causes
52. Despise
55. Heap
57. Have lunch
58. Atop
59. Wicked
60. Fruit drink
61. Repair (a rip)
62. Cincinnati team
63. Morning moisture

DOWN

1. Smooch
2. Object of worship
3. Nary a soul
4. Coastal construction project?
5. Individual
6. "____ to it!"
7. Shares, as a secret
8. Religious recitation
9. Linger behind
10. Raw mineral
11. Get hitched
19. Vim and vigor
21. Perform a part
23. Like hazardous winter weather
25. Marking on a musical score
26. Bath-water testers
27. Minor argument
28. Crowd sound
29. Relaxation
30. Body's covering
31. Moldable metal
35. Pod morsel
38. Show up at (a party)
39. Brand, spanking ____
41. Winged messengers
42. Hearty bread choice
44. Less green
47. Donate
49. Enjoy a novel
50. Manufactured
51. One-pot meal
52. Purr like an engine
53. King Kong, for one
54. 2,000-pound weight
56. Shoebox cover

1	2	3	■	4	5	6	7	■	8	9	10	11
12			■	13				■	14			
15			■	16				■	17			
18			19		■	20		21		■	■	■
■	■	■	22		23	■	24			25	26	27
28	29	30				31	■	32				
33			■	■	34		35	■	■	36		
37			38	39	■	40		41	42			
43					44	■	45			■	■	■
■	■	■	46			47	■	48		49	50	51
52	53	54		■	55		56		■	57		
58				■	59				■	60		
61				■	62				■	63		

351

ACROSS

1. Marching bug?
4. A pair
7. Autumn
11. Very tiny
12. Part in a movie
14. Concept
15. Looked at closely
17. Cincinnati's baseball team
18. Mouse snare
19. Locale
21. Graceful tree
23. Domesticated (a wild beast)
26. The "p" in "mph"
29. Corn serving
31. Used a peeler
33. Notable times
35. Grass droplets
37. Number of a cat's lives?
38. Knight's "suit"
40. In favor of
42. Potato bud
43. Jack who could eat no fat
45. The World Wide ____
47. Close friend
49. Exercise facilities
52. Indefinite amount
55. Seminar centers
58. Dock
59. Run away
60. Tree juice
61. Partner nation
62. An explosive: abbr.
63. Give it a go

DOWN

1. Wonder
2. Call from a bank teller
3. Rip (apart)
4. One base short of a homer
5. Triumphed
6. Spanish cheers
7. Hook-and-ladder crew member
8. Lemon drink
9. Conducted (an orchestra)
10. ____ Vegas
13. Prepare (copy) for publication
16. Actress West
20. Keg spigot
22. Furious
24. Ohio's Great Lake
25. Declare to be untrue
26. Small, round vegetable
27. Blunders
28. Inclined walkway
30. Ump's basketball counterpart
32. Billy ____ Williams
34. Wizard's craft
36. "That's extraordinary!"
39. Stadium yell
41. Be sorry about
44. Sod
46. "So long!"
48. Thaw, as ice
50. Pole for sails
51. Heavenly twinkler
52. Luxury resort
53. Lubricate (hinges)
54. Gibson or Torme
56. The Roman numeral X, to us
57. CIA operative

352

ACROSS

1. Badger constantly
4. Shady trees
8. Deep-voiced man
12. Be in debt
13. Word before "year" or "frog"
14. Pennsylvania port
15. Family room
16. To a great extent
17. Assistant
18. Wring
20. Tacked on
21. Cotton bundles
23. Without much commitment
25. Puts to work
26. Make a sweater
27. Paid athlete
30. "Hark!"
32. Flew aloft
34. Flying mammal
35. Pack (of cards)
37. ". . . ____ me your ears!"
38. Wharf
39. Termites or rats
40. Divide evenly
43. Entertain with humor
45. Mourn loudly
46. Mate for Eve
47. Loud knock
50. Teen's skin problem
51. Paper ____, fastener
52. By way of
53. Require
54. Kennedy and Danson
55. Blunder

DOWN

1. Signal "yes"
2. Amazement
3. Least rough
4. Mr. Presley
5. Brenda and Bruce
6. Comedian Short
7. Intelligence agent
8. Small and glittering, as eyes
9. Extremely dry
10. Flank
11. Plant's beginning
19. Sunset direction
20. Choir colleague of 8-Across
21. Tulip root
22. Big continent
24. Flat, round object
26. Leg "hinge"
27. Can (fruits)
28. Landlady's due
29. Racetrack statistics
31. Revise (copy)
33. Tavern brews
36. ". . .when the wind blows, the ____ will rock . . ."
38. Heaped
39. Women's dress shoes
40. Graceful bird
41. Walk the floor
42. Script scrap
44. Housekeeper
46. Play division
48. Atmosphere
49. Golfing norm

SOLUTIONS

CROSSWORD 1

S	O	F	A		W	A	G		T	A	S	K
O	V	E	N		I	C	E		A	L	A	N
D	E	A	N		L	E	E		I	D	L	E
A	R	R	E	S	T			E	L	A	T	E
				U	S	I	N	G				
A	I	S	L	E		R	O	O	S	T	E	R
I	D	E	A		B	A	T		H	E	R	E
R	O	W	B	O	A	T		B	E	A	R	D
				A	R	E	N	A				
S	P	A	N	K			E	D	I	T	E	D
T	O	N	E		M	O	W		T	A	X	I
A	L	T	O		A	D	E		C	L	A	P
B	E	E	N		P	E	R		H	E	M	S

CROSSWORD 2

A	P	E	D		A	P	T		F	L	A	T
R	E	L	Y		I	R	A		L	A	C	E
M	A	K	E		R	O	B		A	G	E	D
			D	I	P		S	A	M			
S	P	A		V	O	W		W	E	E	D	S
H	E	R		E	R	A	S	E		L	E	T
O	D	E			T	I	P			A	L	A
P	A	N		A	S	S	E	S		T	A	R
S	L	A	S	H		T	E	E		E	Y	E
			P	A	L		D	E	W			
C	A	R	E		A	L	I		A	N	T	S
A	L	A	N		M	E	N		I	O	W	A
B	E	N	D		P	E	G		T	R	O	T

CROSSWORD 3

O	R	A	L		T	O	N		C	R	I	B
L	O	D	E		R	U	E		H	A	T	E
D	Y	E	S		A	R	C		O	N	C	E
			S	K	Y		K	N	I	G	H	T
A	G	R	E	E	S		T	A	R			
C	L	I	N	T		F	I	R		P	E	A
M	A	P		C	H	E	E	R		L	A	G
E	D	S		H	O	E		A	R	O	S	E
			R	U	N		S	T	O	W	E	D
S	T	R	I	P	E		L	E	T			
H	A	U	L		S	P	A		A	D	A	M
E	L	S	E		T	I	N		T	I	L	E
D	E	E	D		Y	E	T		E	D	E	N

CROSSWORD 4

E	V	E	R		A	L	A	N		S	P	A
N	I	L	E		L	A	C	E		H	U	G
D	A	M	P		T	R	E	A	S	U	R	E
			L	O	O	K		R	A	T	E	D
P	L	A	I	D	S		M	E	T			
A	I	L	E	D		F	O	R		B	U	S
N	E	E	D		A	R	M		H	U	R	L
E	D	S		T	R	Y		F	U	D	G	E
			D	O	C		R	I	N	S	E	D
S	T	R	A	P		M	I	N	D			
P	R	O	M	I	S	E	S		R	O	B	S
A	I	D		C	U	R	E		E	D	I	T
N	O	S		S	E	E	N		D	E	N	Y

CROSSWORD 5

D	R	I	P		M	E	L		A	R	T	S
A	I	D	E		O	R	E		L	U	R	E
M	O	A	T		V	I	A		B	E	E	N
			T	W	E	E	T		U	S	E	D
A	G	R	E	E	D		H	I	M			
B	L	A	D	E		B	E	N		A	C	T
L	A	Y		D	E	A	R	S		B	O	O
E	D	S		E	N	D		I	D	E	A	S
			A	D	E		A	D	U	L	T	S
S	H	O	P		M	A	L	E	S			
P	A	P	A		I	C	E		T	I	N	A
E	V	E	R		E	R	R		E	D	E	N
D	E	N	T		S	E	T		D	O	W	N

CROSSWORD 6

C	O	P	S		J	E	T	S		L	O	G
A	L	E	C		I	R	O	N		E	W	E
N	E	R	O		M	E	D	I	C	I	N	E
T	O	T	O			C	A	P	E			
			T	A	S	T	Y		L	Y	E	S
A	L	E		B	U	S		G	L	O	V	E
D	E	G	R	E	E		C	O	O	K	I	E
A	N	G	E	L		M	A	N		E	L	M
M	A	S	S		J	U	D	G	E			
			T	I	E	S			A	P	E	D
W	R	E	S	T	L	E	D		T	A	P	E
H	A	Y		C	L	U	E		E	R	I	C
O	N	E		H	Y	M	N		N	E	C	K

CROSSWORD 7

H	E	N		S	H	O	P		S	T	A	R
I	R	E		T	U	B	A		H	U	G	E
M	A	T	T	E	R	E	D		O	N	E	S
			R	E	L	Y		T	O	A	S	T
G	R	O	U	P		E	G	O				
O	A	K	S		I	D	L	Y		S	T	Y
S	K	A	T	E	D		A	S	H	O	R	E
H	E	Y		N	E	E	D		A	L	A	N
				V	A	N		D	R	O	P	S
A	L	L	E	Y		T	H	U	S			
J	O	A	N		I	R	I	S	H	M	A	N
A	V	I	D		T	E	N	T		E	V	A
R	E	D	S		S	E	T	S		T	A	P

CROSSWORD 8

L	O	C	K		S	A	T		E	D	I	T
I	R	A	N		P	I	E		L	I	V	E
P	A	N	E		A	L	A		O	P	E	N
S	L	E	E	P			R	A	P			
				I	C	Y		L	E	A	S	H
W	I	G		G	O	A	L	S		J	O	E
A	T	E			A	C	E			A	L	L
Y	E	N		O	T	H	E	R		R	O	D
S	M	E	L	L		T	R	Y				
			O	D	D			E	A	R	T	H
E	C	H	O		I	T	S		L	U	R	E
N	O	E	S		G	O	T		D	E	A	R
D	O	M	E		S	P	Y		A	S	P	S

CROSSWORD 9

K	I	T		T	A	P	S		S	N	U	B
I	D	O		E	D	I	T		H	O	S	E
N	E	W		P	O	N	Y		O	V	E	N
D	A	N	C	E	R			O	W	E		
			H	E	E	D	E	D		M	O	O
F	L	E	A			W	A	D		B	I	N
L	A	M	P		P	E	R		G	E	N	E
E	V	E		G	A	L			A	R	K	S
W	A	R		A	L	L	O	W	S			
		A	S	P			M	A	P	L	E	S
A	B	L	E		A	P	E	S		I	C	E
R	O	D	E		R	E	N	T		S	H	E
T	O	S	S		C	A	S	E		T	O	P

CROSSWORD 10

T	O	W		P	I	P	E		O	P	E	N
O	R	E		I	R	A	N		U	R	G	E
M	A	R		S	A	L	T		T	O	O	T
S	L	E	E	T			E	L	F			
			N	O	R		R	A	I	S	E	D
T	O	D	D	L	E	R		S	T	O	V	E
A	H	A			D	I	G			M	E	N
L	I	M	E	S		P	A	Y	M	E	N	T
L	O	S	S	E	S		G	E	E			
			S	A	T			A	L	A	R	M
S	O	D	A		A	J	A	R		D	O	E
A	W	A	Y		B	A	L	L		A	V	A
D	E	N	S		S	W	A	Y		M	E	T

CROSSWORD 11

F	I	R	S		A	R	C	H		A	L	S
I	D	O	L		C	O	R	E		L	O	W
B	A	B	Y		M	O	A	N		S	P	A
			E	N	E	M	Y		N	O	S	Y
A	R	I	S	E	S		O	R	E			
S	A	N	T	A		S	N	O	W	I	N	G
K	I	T		T	O	A	S	T		R	I	O
S	L	O	W	E	S	T		T	W	I	C	E
			A	R	T		L	E	A	S	E	S
L	O	N	G		R	A	I	N	S			
A	H	A		L	I	N	K		T	A	P	S
Y	I	P		A	C	N	E		E	X	I	T
S	O	S		S	H	E	D		D	E	N	Y

CROSSWORD 12

L	A	D		P	I	E	R		S	T	E	W
A	B	E		U	R	G	E		P	O	L	E
B	E	N		R	A	G	S		E	A	S	E
S	L	Y	E	S	T		T	R	A	D	E	D
			D	U	E		O	A	K			
S	T	A	G	E		T	R	Y		P	O	T
H	E	R	E		S	U	E		B	O	N	E
Y	E	T		B	I	G		G	A	P	E	D
			T	A	X		P	U	N			
T	H	R	O	A	T		A	I	S	L	E	S
R	O	O	T		E	A	R	L		I	D	A
A	L	D	A		E	D	I	T		M	E	N
P	E	E	L		N	O	S	Y		E	N	D

CROSSWORD 13

A	L	A	N		T	W	O		A	C	T	S
R	I	S	E		W	O	W		C	L	I	P
K	N	I	T		A	N	N		M	A	N	E
S	E	A	S	O	N			M	E	W	E	D
				I	G	L	O	O				
M	E	T	A	L		A	D	M	I	R	A	L
O	V	E	N		E	N	D		L	U	R	E
B	A	N	D	A	G	E		E	L	E	C	T
				L	O	S	E	R				
D	R	I	L	L			M	A	T	T	E	R
R	O	D	E		T	O	P		R	A	V	E
O	P	E	N		O	U	T		A	P	E	S
P	E	A	S		T	R	Y		P	E	S	T

CROSSWORD 14

M	A	P		O	V	A	L		A	D	A	M
A	L	A		L	I	F	E		C	O	L	A
S	O	S		D	A	R	E		T	E	S	T
T	N	T				A	R	T	S			
S	E	A	L		D	I	S	H		N	A	T
			A	V	I	D		R	H	O	D	E
L	A	S	S	I	E		T	E	A	R	E	D
E	D	I	T	S		T	E	E	N			
T	O	P		I	R	O	N		K	N	O	W
			I	T	E	M				A	L	I
P	R	O	D		S	C	A	R		K	I	D
R	A	I	L		T	A	X	I		E	V	E
O	N	L	Y		S	T	E	M		D	E	N

CROSSWORD 15

J	U	S	T		A	C	T	S		S	O	N
A	S	I	A		R	O	O	T		T	W	O
N	E	C	K		R	O	P	E		A	N	T
E	S	K	I	M	O	S		V	E	R	S	E
			N	O	W		P	E	G			
B	I	N	G	O		S	I	N	G	I	N	G
A	C	E			V	A	T			D	U	E
D	E	T	R	O	I	T		F	R	O	N	T
			A	P	E		R	I	O			
L	A	R	G	E		P	I	R	A	T	E	S
A	L	I		N	E	O	N		S	O	D	A
I	L	L		E	V	E	S		T	R	I	P
D	Y	E		R	A	T	E		S	E	T	S

CROSSWORD 16

T	A	P	E		S	E	A		W	I	N	D
A	B	E	L		H	A	T		O	D	O	R
G	L	E	E		A	R	T		M	A	R	Y
S	E	R	V	E	D		E	V	A			
			A	D	E		M	I	N	D	E	D
F	R	E	T	S		A	P	E		R	A	Y
L	O	V	E		T	N	T		M	E	R	E
A	L	E		L	A	Y		F	A	W	N	S
G	E	R	M	A	N		B	U	N			
			E	G	G		E	R	A	S	E	S
W	I	T	S		L	O	T		G	O	A	T
O	N	E	S		E	A	T		E	L	S	E
O	K	A	Y		S	K	Y		S	E	E	M

CROSSWORD 17

S	O	N	G		O	F	F		R	O	B	E
O	V	E	R		C	O	O		E	V	E	R
L	A	T	E		E	A	R		L	E	E	R
E	L	S	E		A	L	E		A	N	N	S
			C	A	N		M	I	X			
A	D	D	E	D		H	A	S		T	A	M
G	A	Y		O	P	E	N	S		A	V	A
O	N	E		R	A	N		U	P	P	E	R
			H	E	R		T	E	A			
S	I	L	O		S	P	A		L	A	V	A
O	R	A	L		L	A	S		A	B	E	L
F	O	I	L		E	L	K		C	L	I	P
A	N	D	Y		Y	E	S		E	E	L	S

CROSSWORD 18

B	E	D		P	R	A	Y		S	C	A	N
A	W	E		H	O	L	E		L	E	N	O
B	E	N		O	W	E	S		E	N	D	S
E	S	T	A	T	E	S		J	E	T		
			R	O	D		T	O	K	E	N	S
W	I	C	K	S		F	A	T		R	I	O
E	R	A			M	U	G			E	L	F
R	A	P		F	A	N		C	A	D	E	T
E	N	T	R	E	E		S	O	L			
		A	I	D		T	A	I	L	O	R	S
S	P	I	N		S	O	U	L		V	A	T
H	E	N	S		O	N	C	E		E	V	E
E	A	S	E		W	E	E	D		N	E	W

CROSSWORD 19

S	E	A		P	A	P	A		S	L	O	T
A	L	P		O	W	E	D		C	A	P	E
T	I	P		T	A	P	S		O	V	E	N
			E	A	S	Y		S	T	A	N	D
S	P	A	R			B	E	T				
W	O	R	M	S		A	V	A		T	N	T
A	L	E		T	O	D	A	Y		R	I	O
N	O	D		A	I	L		S	C	A	L	P
				F	L	Y			A	C	E	S
S	T	U	F	F			D	E	B	T		
T	O	N	E		F	L	E	A		O	D	D
E	R	I	E		R	E	A	R		R	U	E
W	E	T	S		Y	E	L	L		S	E	W

CROSSWORD 20

K	I	D		T	O	O			B	R	E	W
I	R	A		R	I	B		G	O	O	S	E
T	A	R		A	L	E		E	G	Y	P	T
E	N	T	R	Y		Y	E	N				
			A	S	S	E	R	T		S	P	A
	P	E	T		I	D	O	L		L	I	P
T	A	V	E	R	N		D	E	D	U	C	T
A	P	E		O	G	L	E		I	R	K	
P	A	R		B	L	A	D	E	S			
				B	E	T		A	C	T	O	R
A	R	O	S	E		E	D	S		A	X	E
D	O	N	O	R		S	U	E		P	E	A
O	W	E	S			T	E	D		E	N	D

CROSSWORD 21

F	R	O	M		P	A	D		C	A	S	H
R	A	V	E		A	W	E		R	I	L	E
E	R	A	S		N	A	P		O	D	O	R
E	E	L	S		D	Y	E		W	E	T	S
			E	V	A		N	U	N			
L	A	S	S	O		A	D	S		W	A	D
A	L	P		I	R	I	S	H		A	I	R
G	A	Y		C	O	D		E	A	R	L	Y
			N	E	W		A	R	T			
S	W	A	Y		B	A	G		T	O	W	S
H	I	L	L		O	U	R		E	V	E	N
I	N	T	O		A	T	E		N	E	R	O
N	E	O	N		T	O	E		D	R	E	W

CROSSWORD 22

N	E	E	D	S	■	D	A	N	■	P	E	P
I	G	L	O	O	■	R	I	O	■	A	D	E
P	O	K	E	R	■	A	D	D	■	P	I	T
■	■	■	■	E	D	G	E	■	G	A	T	E
P	A	L	■	■	Y	O	D	E	L	■	■	■
A	C	E	■	P	E	N	■	N	E	S	T	S
S	H	A	D	E	D	■	A	V	E	N	U	E
T	E	P	E	E	■	C	R	Y	■	A	N	N
■	■	■	A	L	A	R	M	■	■	P	A	D
P	L	A	N	■	R	A	Y	S	■	■	■	■
L	O	P	■	T	R	Y	■	L	A	M	B	S
O	D	E	■	W	O	O	■	A	W	A	I	T
W	E	D	■	O	W	N	■	B	E	T	T	Y

CROSSWORD 23

S	O	R	T	■	D	I	S	C	■	C	A	P
I	D	E	A	■	O	R	A	L	■	A	B	E
P	E	A	K	■	N	I	L	E	■	N	E	T
■	■	D	E	W	■	S	T	A	R	T	L	E
F	L	A	S	H	■	■	I	R	A	■	■	■
L	A	B	■	O	P	E	N	■	P	A	P	A
A	I	L	■	M	O	L	E	S	■	T	I	P
G	R	E	W	■	R	I	S	E	■	L	E	E
■	■	■	A	N	T	■	■	A	W	A	R	D
L	A	W	Y	E	R	S	■	M	A	N	■	■
A	V	A	■	C	A	I	N	■	S	T	A	B
K	I	D	■	K	I	T	E	■	P	I	L	E
E	D	S	■	S	T	E	W	■	S	C	A	N

CROSSWORD 24

R	E	A	R	■	O	A	T	S	■	A	S	K
I	D	L	E	■	F	L	E	A	■	S	E	A
P	I	L	E	■	F	I	N	N	■	P	A	T
S	T	Y	L	E	■	■	■	T	A	S	T	E
■	■	■	S	A	Y	■	M	A	N	■	■	■
R	A	G	■	R	O	P	E	■	Y	A	W	N
I	C	E	■	N	U	R	S	E	■	D	O	E
M	E	M	O	■	N	O	S	Y	■	D	E	W
■	■	■	W	A	G	■	Y	E	A	■	■	■
C	H	I	N	A	■	■	■	S	W	A	T	S
L	O	T	■	R	A	G	E	■	A	C	H	E
A	B	E	■	O	X	E	N	■	I	R	A	N
M	O	M	■	N	E	E	D	■	T	E	N	D

CROSSWORD 25

O	N	C	E	■	R	A	H	■	S	P	I	T
R	O	A	R	■	A	G	O	■	T	O	R	E
A	S	I	A	■	D	E	N	■	A	L	A	N
L	E	N	S	■	A	D	O	■	M	E	N	D
■	■	■	E	R	R	■	R	A	P	■	■	■
S	P	A	R	E	■	P	E	R	■	O	D	D
H	E	N	■	P	R	I	D	E	■	W	A	R
E	A	T	■	L	O	G	■	N	A	N	N	Y
■	■	■	G	Y	M	■	M	A	R	■	■	■
F	L	E	E	■	A	L	I	■	I	T	C	H
R	O	D	E	■	N	E	T	■	S	A	L	E
O	D	E	S	■	C	A	T	■	E	X	A	M
G	E	N	E	■	E	D	S	■	N	I	P	S

CROSSWORD 26

A	L	D	A	■	E	L	F	■	W	I	S	E
R	E	I	N	■	A	I	L	■	I	D	L	E
K	E	N	T	U	C	K	Y	■	V	E	A	L
■	■	■	■	S	H	E	■	■	E	A	T	S
T	R	I	B	E	■	L	O	T	S	■	■	■
H	I	R	E	■	T	Y	P	E	■	L	I	P
E	D	I	T	O	R	■	E	N	T	I	R	E
Y	E	S	■	W	O	R	N	■	O	A	K	S
■	■	■	A	N	T	E	■	W	O	R	S	T
D	E	L	I	■	■	A	L	A	■	■	■	■
A	V	I	D	■	P	L	A	Y	M	A	T	E
M	I	M	E	■	E	L	K	■	O	X	E	N
S	L	E	D	■	R	Y	E	■	W	E	E	D

CROSSWORD 27

T	O	R	E	■	S	O	S	■	B	U	S	H
A	D	O	S	■	T	W	O	■	A	S	I	A
N	O	D	S	■	E	N	D	■	L	E	N	T
G	R	E	A	S	E	■	A	I	L	■	■	■
■	■	■	Y	I	P	■	S	T	O	W	E	D
W	H	I	S	P	E	R	■	S	T	A	R	E
A	I	R	■	■	R	A	T	■	■	D	A	B
I	D	A	H	O	■	P	O	O	R	E	S	T
T	E	N	O	R	S	■	R	I	O	■	■	■
■	■	■	M	E	N	■	P	L	A	N	T	S
A	C	R	E	■	A	B	E	■	M	A	R	E
H	O	U	R	■	K	I	D	■	E	V	E	N
A	N	T	S	■	E	G	O	■	D	Y	E	D

CROSSWORD 28

B	O	B	■	S	C	O	T	■	S	H	U	T
A	W	E	■	H	A	L	O	■	P	A	N	E
S	E	A	■	A	N	D	Y	■	A	R	I	D
E	S	K	I	M	O	■	■	F	R	E	T	S
■	■	■	D	E	E	P	E	R	■	■	■	■
M	A	M	A	■	■	A	Y	E	■	A	D	D
A	G	E	■	T	H	R	E	E	■	R	A	Y
T	O	N	■	E	A	T	■	■	A	C	M	E
■	■	■	■	S	T	Y	L	E	S	■	■	■
C	R	E	P	T	■	■	L	A	P	P	E	D
L	O	V	E	■	E	R	A	S	■	A	D	O
A	P	E	S	■	L	I	M	E	■	P	E	W
W	E	S	T	■	F	O	A	L	■	A	N	N

CROSSWORD 29

M	O	W	■	A	L	E	S	■	A	D	D	S
A	W	E	■	S	O	R	E	■	N	E	R	O
P	L	E	A	S	A	N	T	■	T	E	A	M
■	■	■	G	E	N	E	■	H	E	D	G	E
S	P	A	R	S	■	S	K	Y	■	■	■	■
T	I	L	E	■	S	T	E	M	■	V	I	A
O	L	D	E	S	T	■	E	N	D	I	N	G
P	E	A	■	L	A	M	P	■	A	C	N	E
■	■	■	■	I	R	A	■	P	R	E	S	S
S	T	O	R	M	■	T	R	U	E	■	■	■
C	A	P	E	■	S	T	A	N	D	A	R	D
A	P	E	S	■	K	E	N	T	■	S	U	E
T	E	N	T	■	I	R	K	S	■	P	E	N

CROSSWORD 30

E	D	I	T	■	S	I	P	■	C	H	E	W
L	I	N	E	■	N	O	R	■	L	O	V	E
M	A	T	S	■	O	W	E	■	A	M	E	N
S	L	O	T	■	R	A	P	■	R	E	S	T
■	■	■	E	A	T	■	A	S	K	■	■	■
P	A	N	D	A	■	A	R	T	■	B	I	D
E	G	O	■	R	I	P	E	R	■	A	N	Y
P	O	W	■	O	N	E	■	A	W	A	K	E
■	■	■	A	N	N	■	R	Y	E	■	■	■
P	E	A	R	■	I	R	E	■	A	L	A	S
A	C	R	E	■	N	O	D	■	L	U	S	H
T	H	I	N	■	G	O	D	■	T	R	I	O
S	O	D	A	■	S	T	Y	■	H	E	A	T

CROSSWORD 31

E	A	S	E	■	T	O	M	■	S	H	O	T
A	G	E	S	■	I	V	E	■	T	A	X	I
T	O	W	S	■	M	E	N	■	O	V	E	N
■	■	■	A	L	E	R	T	■	R	E	N	T
S	T	A	Y	E	D	■	I	R	K	■	■	■
W	A	I	S	T	■	J	O	E	■	I	C	E
A	L	L	■	T	W	A	N	G	■	N	A	Y
Y	E	S	■	E	R	R	■	R	I	N	S	E
■	■	■	I	R	E	■	S	E	N	S	E	S
M	O	W	S	■	S	P	A	T	S	■	■	■
A	P	E	S	■	T	O	N	■	E	A	S	T
M	E	N	U	■	L	O	T	■	C	L	U	E
A	N	T	E	■	E	R	A	■	T	A	M	E

CROSSWORD 32

T	I	L	T	■	S	T	Y	■	S	W	A	B
O	D	O	R	■	H	O	E	■	T	I	M	E
T	A	P	E	■	A	N	T	■	U	S	E	S
■	■	■	N	A	P	■	■	■	D	E	N	T
P	E	D	D	L	E	■	C	R	Y	■	■	■
L	E	A	S	T	■	D	U	E	■	S	P	A
E	L	M	■	E	R	R	E	D	■	K	E	Y
A	S	P	■	R	A	Y	■	U	N	I	T	E
■	■	■	A	S	H	■	S	C	E	N	E	S
W	E	L	L	■	■	■	T	E	A	■	■	■
H	A	I	L	■	F	E	E	■	T	A	K	E
A	C	N	E	■	A	L	E	■	E	V	I	L
T	H	E	Y	■	N	I	P	■	R	A	N	K

CROSSWORD 33

P	A	R	■	S	L	A	B	■	R	A	T	E
A	C	E	■	W	O	V	E	■	O	V	A	L
T	N	T	■	E	D	E	N	■	W	I	N	S
H	E	R	■	P	E	N	■	■	E	D	G	E
■	■	E	A	T	■	U	S	E	D	■	■	■
S	W	A	P	■	T	E	A	R	■	A	G	E
H	O	T	T	E	R	■	L	A	P	P	E	D
Y	E	S	■	V	I	C	E	■	A	P	E	S
■	■	■	M	E	M	O	■	A	L	E	■	■
H	E	R	O	■	■	M	A	N	■	A	S	H
A	R	I	D	■	D	E	B	T	■	R	O	Y
S	I	D	E	■	I	D	L	E	■	E	L	M
H	E	E	L	■	D	Y	E	S	■	D	O	N

CROSSWORD 34

```
NEW■TOAD■BABE
AXE■ABLE■OWED
BAR■LEIS■DENS
SMELLY■SAY■■■
■■■OYSTER■DAM
SLOT■■IRK■ELI
OAK■MITTS■LAS
AVA■ALL■■PINT
PAY■PLEASE■■■
■■■USE■GIANTS
SNAP■GAIT■AIL
HOBO■ACNE■IRE
EDEN■LEGS■LED
```

CROSSWORD 35

```
GROW■SOS■HURL
AIDE■TWO■ASIA
SCOTLAND■LENT
PER■IRE■DODGE
■■■STEREO■■■■
COOL■■■GOSSIP
UNLESS■GREECE
PEDDLE■■■TEEN
■■■■AWARDS■■■
SCALP■BAY■TNT
POLO■LOVELIER
ALAS■IVE■ALTO
TENT■DEN■WEST
```

CROSSWORD 36

```
PILE■OATS■MAD
ARID■FLAT■ALI
RANG■FAME■CAR
KNEEL■SEE■ANT
■■■SINK■PER■■
CUT■FOAM■ROPE
AGREES■EARNED
THEY■YARD■ITS
■■MEL■PEAL■■■
DAB■ASP■MATCH
OIL■TILT■SHOE
ODE■EDEN■TILL
RED■REST■SNAP
```

CROSSWORD 37

```
BRAG■ADD■SOFA
LACE■HOE■TRAP
OVEN■ELF■RARE
WEST■ALI■ALES
■■■LID■NEW■■■
SPIED■MEL■FAD
TIN■AMUSE■ELI
YEN■HOG■CREAM
■■■LOT■ATE■■■
SODA■HER■NAGS
THUS■ERR■TIRE
OILS■RIO■EDIT
POLO■SEW■DENS
```

CROSSWORD 38

```
ALAS■CATS■WAD
TAXI■HIRE■ACE
EDEN■AMEN■SHE
■■■CAP■EITHER
PRIEST■SOW■■■
ROD■HEN■ROAST
ADO■■RIP■■BOO
MELTS■PAT■EDS
■■■ITS■DALLAS
COMMON■DRY■■■
AHA■MEAL■IRIS
LIT■PALE■NINE
LOS■SKID■GONE
```

CROSSWORD 39

```
LAB■THAW■PURE
ICE■ROBE■ASIA
ANT■APED■REST
RESIDE■■CASES
■■■REDHEAD■■■
DESKS■ARRESTS
OAK■■FUR■■KIT
CRYSTAL■RAINY
■■■WORSHIP■■■
ALLOW■■ENTERS
LEER■ACES■RAT
SAND■COLE■AGE
ODDS■TOSS■SEW
```

CROSSWORD 40

```
SNOB■PEP■BLOW
PIPE■AGE■RARE
ACES■NOR■OWED
RENTED■FEW■■■
■■■■AARON■EVA
APART■ORDERED
LANE■GUM■LAND
PUDDLES■MISTS
SLY■ARENA■■■■
■■■GYM■ERNEST
JAIL■ADS■OVER
ALDA■NOT■SITE
READ■YES■ELSE
```

CROSSWORD 41

```
FIR■WOVE■SHOP
IDO■IRAN■TINA
BOB■LEND■EDEN
SLEET■■■GEESE
■■■ASP■ALP■■■
HALT■URGE■OWN
ELI■SNARE■DOE
RIP■ACHE■BENT
■■■UGH■ERA■■■
SPATS■■■ANGRY
WANT■OVER■RUE
ACNE■FIVE■ILL
PEER■FEAR■MEL
```

CROSSWORD 42

```
HOST■GEMS■SKY
ODOR■EVEN■ONE
GENE■NERO■WIN
■■■NOT■CRUSTS
SANDAL■YET■■■
PRO■KEG■DARED
ACTS■RAP■HIDE
THEIR■POT■PIN
■■■LET■SAFETY
DOLLAR■SPA■■■
AXE■GAME■KISS
TEN■ADOS■ECHO
END■NEWS■DYED
```

CROSSWORD 43

```
FATE■BAA■TINA
ALAN■RID■ONES
REST■OLD■WITH
ESKIMOS■LET■■
■■■RIM■HOLIER
UTTER■RIB■AXE
NOR■ATOMS■LID
IRE■COD■TESTS
TEMPLE■HER■■■
■■BEE■FARAWAY
BALE■RIP■SAME
OVER■ALP■EVEN
WADS■HEY■DENS
```

CROSSWORD 44

```
PAPA■CAP■SITE
OVAL■ALL■ARIA
WANT■RIO■TINT
■■■EYE■TEASES
SNORED■TAN■■■
HIVES■HER■WON
ICED■POD■CAVE
PEN■CAW■CADET
■■■DUD■WATERS
SCARED■ARE■■■
LACE■LAG■RATE
ANTS■EGO■EDEN
MESS■SON■DEED
```

CROSSWORD 45

```
GIVE■LASS■POP
ADES■ARCH■ADO
SEEK■DIRECTED
PARIS■DULL■■■
■■■MOW■BLASTS
ACROBAT■SPEAK
BOO■■YIP■■ELI
LIARS■POSTMEN
ENDING■TEA■■■
■■■SOUP■WIDER
MATERIAL■LIVE
ONE■EDGE■OVEN
ODD■DEED■REST
```

CROSSWORD 46

D	R	U	M		E	R	R		S	E	E	P
R	O	S	E		Y	E	A		A	L	D	A
I	D	E	A		E	G	G		P	E	G	S
P	E	S	T	S		A	S	H		V	E	T
			S	T	A	R		O	W	E		
H	A	T		A	D	D		L	A	N	D	S
I	N	H	A	L	E		P	I	S	T	O	L
S	T	A	G	E		R	E	D		H	E	Y
		N	O	S		E	R	A	S			
A	S	K		T	I	C		Y	A	C	H	T
S	O	F	A		R	I	P		F	L	E	E
P	L	U	G		A	P	E		E	A	R	N
S	O	L	E		N	E	W		S	P	O	T

CROSSWORD 47

S	O	D		T	U	R	F		W	I	F	E
P	I	E		A	S	I	A		I	R	O	N
I	L	L		N	E	C	K		L	A	R	D
T	Y	I	N	G		H	E	L	D			
			O	L	D		S	E	E	S	A	W
R	E	T	R	E	A	T		D	R	O	V	E
A	X	E			M	A	Y			A	I	D
P	I	A	N	O		R	E	W	A	R	D	S
S	T	R	A	W	S		T	A	C			
			I	N	T	O		I	T	E	M	S
O	R	A	L		E	V	I	L		R	I	O
D	A	T	E		W	A	V	E		A	N	D
D	Y	E	D		S	L	E	D		S	E	A

CROSSWORD 48

I	R	A		A	C	T		E	L	A	T	E
D	O	C		S	H	Y		L	O	V	E	D
E	L	M		H	I	P		S	W	A	N	S
A	L	E	S		N	I	N	E				
			P	I	A	N	O			S	P	A
G	R	E	A	T		G	O	T		P	A	Y
R	O	A	R	E	D		N	A	T	I	V	E
A	P	T		M	A	D		K	I	T	E	S
Y	E	S			R	I	P	E	R			
				S	T	A	R		E	A	C	H
A	P	A	R	T		P	O	T		J	O	E
R	A	D	I	O		E	V	E		A	L	A
T	R	O	O	P		R	E	D		R	A	P

CROSSWORD 49

H	A	Y		A	B	L	E		S	K	I	D
E	G	O		D	E	A	L		A	N	D	Y
N	O	D		M	A	S	K		F	I	L	E
		E	D	I	T	S		H	A	T	E	D
S	P	L	I	T	S		A	I	R			
T	R	E	E	S		A	S	S	I	S	T	S
E	A	R			I	N	K			P	O	P
M	Y	S	T	E	R	Y		V	A	L	U	E
			A	R	K		R	E	G	A	R	D
S	C	O	U	R		B	O	R	E	S		
L	U	N	G		P	L	U	S		H	A	M
A	R	C	H		R	O	S	E		E	Y	E
B	E	E	T		O	W	E	S		S	E	T

CROSSWORD 50

D	A	B		A	P	E	D		F	R	E	D
I	C	E		C	O	R	E		L	I	A	R
P	E	T	E	R	P	A	N		A	L	S	O
			L	E	E				K	E	E	P
C	L	A	M		S	P	O	K	E			
R	U	G	S			A	W	E		L	O	G
I	R	E		E	A	R	L	Y		A	D	E
B	E	D		V	I	E			O	V	E	N
			Y	A	R	D	S		V	A	S	T
S	I	L	O				O	R	E			
I	D	O	L		S	A	L	A	R	I	E	S
L	E	A	K		E	N	V	Y		T	A	P
L	A	D	S		E	Y	E	S		S	T	Y

CROSSWORD 51

M	E	R	E		A	D	O		S	L	O	W
I	R	A	N		R	A	N		P	A	V	E
L	A	N	D		R	Y	E		O	W	E	D
E	S	K	I	M	O	S			I	N	N	S
			N	O	W		G	A	L			
B	R	A	G	S		F	A	N		F	I	B
A	I	R		C	R	U	S	T		O	R	E
T	O	T		O	U	R		L	U	R	E	D
			A	W	E		B	E	N			
S	N	A	P			G	O	R	I	L	L	A
H	O	U	R		T	A	X		T	O	A	D
I	N	T	O		I	V	E		E	R	I	E
N	E	O	N		P	E	R		D	E	N	S

CROSSWORD 52

A	C	N	E		P	O	T		C	R	A	B
S	H	I	N		R	I	O		H	O	B	O
K	I	N	G		E	L	M		I	D	L	Y
S	P	E	L	L	S			K	N	E	E	S
			A	U	S	T	R	I	A			
A	M	O	N	G		W	O	N		A	G	O
L	E	A	D		R	I	D		I	R	A	N
I	N	K		N	O	R		U	N	C	L	E
			P	U	B	L	I	S	H			
S	P	A	I	N			R	E	A	P	E	D
W	A	R	N		E	V	A		L	A	V	A
A	C	M	E		L	I	T		E	V	E	R
M	E	S	S		F	E	E		D	E	N	T

CROSSWORD 53

B	E	E	P		T	E	A	S		O	F	F
O	R	A	L		A	R	C	H		M	A	E
B	A	R	E		P	I	E	R		I	R	A
			A	M	E	N		A	F	T	E	R
C	H	A	S	E	D		O	N	E			
L	I	N	E	N		A	W	K	W	A	R	D
U	R	N			I	L	L			J	A	Y
B	E	E	H	I	V	E		A	W	A	R	E
			A	N	Y		F	L	A	R	E	S
P	R	A	Y	S		O	I	L	S			
O	U	R		E	G	G	S		T	I	E	D
E	L	I		C	O	L	T		E	D	G	E
T	E	D		T	O	E	S		S	O	O	N

CROSSWORD 54

N	A	P		A	R	C	S		G	R	E	W
A	G	E		P	A	L	E		L	O	N	E
T	O	N		R	I	O	T		O	D	D	S
		N	A	I	L	S			V	E	S	T
S	T	A	L	L		E	L	S	E			
H	A	N	D		U	T	A	H		B	A	A
A	L	T	A	R	S		S	E	C	O	N	D
D	E	S		Y	E	A	H		L	A	N	D
			P	E	S	T		B	U	S	E	S
S	H	O	O			T	W	E	E	T		
T	A	X	I		S	E	A	T		I	D	A
E	V	E	N		K	N	I	T		N	I	P
W	E	N	T		I	D	L	Y		G	E	T

CROSSWORD 55

O	N	C	E		S	E	T		M	A	M	A
W	O	O	L		T	A	R		O	V	A	L
L	O	R	D		E	R	A		P	A	D	S
S	N	E	E	Z	E		I	V	E			
			R	I	P	P	L	E		A	D	O
S	C	A	L	P		L	E	T		M	E	N
T	O	N	Y		B	A	R		R	E	E	L
A	P	T		A	R	C		H	E	N	R	Y
G	E	E		T	E	E	M	E	D			
			S	E	A		A	M	U	S	E	D
P	A	P	A		T	N	T		C	O	V	E
E	X	A	M		H	O	E		E	D	E	N
G	E	N	E		E	D	S		D	A	R	T

CROSSWORD 56

P	A	R		A	C	T	S		S	T	O	P
I	D	O		L	O	O	M		I	O	W	A
L	O	P		S	O	L	E		D	E	E	D
O	R	E				L	A	T	E			
T	E	S	T		W	E	R	E		A	H	A
			U	S	E	D		N	Y	L	O	N
P	L	A	N	E	T		F	O	O	L	E	D
E	A	G	E	R		E	A	R	L			
R	Y	E		V	E	N	T		K	I	S	S
			B	E	A	T				N	O	T
T	I	L	E		R	I	T	A		D	U	O
I	D	O	L		T	R	A	P		I	N	N
M	A	S	T		H	E	R	E		A	D	E

CROSSWORD 57

A	G	E	D		S	I	T		S	C	A	N
W	I	P	E		C	R	Y		T	A	L	E
E	V	I	L		H	A	P	P	E	N	E	D
D	E	C	I	D	E		E	A	R			
			S	U	D	S		D	E	A	L	T
H	E	N		M	U	L	E		O	B	O	E
I	D	O		B	L	A	M	E		L	A	D
S	I	N	S		E	V	E	R		E	D	S
S	T	E	A	M		E	R	I	E			
			M	O	P		A	N	G	L	E	S
C	O	R	P	O	R	A	L		Y	A	L	E
O	R	A	L		O	L	D		P	I	L	E
P	E	T	E		S	I	S		T	R	A	P

CROSSWORD 58

K	I	D		D	I	S	H		C	H	A	P
I	R	E		I	N	T	O		H	I	D	E
T	A	C		S	C	A	T		A	L	A	N
		I	T	C	H	Y		F	I	L	M	S
A	S	S	E	S		E	A	R	N			
R	A	I	N		I	D	L	E		S	H	E
C	L	O	S	E	T		L	E	T	T	E	R
H	E	N		V	E	R	Y		H	E	A	R
			M	E	M	O		W	E	E	D	S
C	A	B	I	N		T	R	A	M	P		
O	R	A	L		S	T	U	N		L	A	S
L	I	K	E		P	E	S	T		E	L	K
A	D	E	S		A	N	T	S		S	P	Y

CROSSWORD 59

J	E	T	S		S	P	A		S	C	A	T
A	C	H	E		L	I	T		C	L	U	E
W	H	E	N		A	L	L		R	A	T	E
S	O	N	S		T	E	A		U	P	O	N
			E	Y	E		S	O	B			
T	R	A	D	E		P	E	P		C	R	Y
N	U	N		A	R	O	S	E		A	Y	E
T	E	N		R	O	D		N	O	T	E	S
			A	N	T		A	S	P			
I	R	K	S		A	P	T		E	N	D	S
T	O	E	S		T	O	T		R	I	O	T
E	D	G	E		E	L	I		A	C	M	E
M	E	S	S		D	O	C		S	E	E	M

CROSSWORD 60

G	R	I	N		F	A	T		A	C	N	E
A	U	T	O		I	V	E		C	O	A	L
L	E	S	S	E	N	E	D		T	R	I	M
				A	N	N			E	E	L	S
S	H	O	R	T		U	S	E	D			
L	E	N	A		L	E	E	R		P	O	P
A	R	C	H	I	E		A	R	R	I	V	E
T	E	E		C	A	R	T		A	L	A	S
			T	Y	P	E		K	N	E	L	T
S	O	L	E			S	K	I				
T	H	A	N		C	I	N	N	A	M	O	N
A	I	M	S		A	D	O		I	O	W	A
R	O	B	E		P	E	W		L	O	N	G

CROSSWORD 61

A	B	E	L		S	A	T		C	R	A	B
H	A	V	E		E	L	I		L	A	C	E
E	R	A	S		N	A	G		A	N	T	E
M	E	S	S	E	S		H	A	Y			
			E	L	E	C	T	S		P	A	T
T	H	A	N	K		A	L	P		O	U	R
R	A	M	S		F	L	Y		T	U	N	A
I	R	E		A	R	M		F	O	R	T	Y
M	E	N		L	I	S	T	E	N			
			U	S	E		E	D	I	T	E	D
C	H	A	P		N	O	D		G	R	A	Y
A	U	T	O		D	A	D		H	I	R	E
T	E	E	N		S	K	Y		T	O	L	D

CROSSWORD 62

J	U	G		A	C	M	E		S	L	A	P
O	N	E		I	R	A	N		T	O	N	E
G	I	N		D	O	N	E		R	A	T	E
S	T	E	R	E	O		M	E	A	N	E	R
			A	S	K		I	V	Y			
G	A	N	G			S	E	E	S	A	W	S
A	G	O		C	R	O	S	S		T	E	E
P	E	D	D	L	E	D			D	E	B	T
			R	A	N		S	K	I			
R	E	C	I	P	E		T	I	N	S	E	L
O	V	A	L		W	A	R	N		O	R	E
B	I	L	L		A	V	I	D		W	I	N
E	L	M	S		L	A	P	S		S	E	A

CROSSWORD 63

F	O	A	L		S	P	A		E	C	H	O
I	D	L	E		H	I	D		F	O	O	D
S	O	D	A		E	N	D		F	A	M	E
T	R	A	V	E	L	S		M	O	L	E	S
			E	L	F		F	O	R			
F	A	L	S	E		G	E	N	T	L	E	R
I	D	O		V	I	E	W	S		I	V	Y
R	E	P	L	A	C	E		T	E	P	E	E
			A	T	E		P	E	R			
P	L	A	T	E		F	A	R	A	W	A	Y
E	A	C	H		H	I	S		S	O	M	E
A	N	N	E		A	N	T		E	V	E	N
L	E	E	R		T	E	A		D	E	N	S

CROSSWORD 64

T	O	Y		S	L	I	M		T	W	I	G
A	W	E		P	I	N	E		H	I	R	E
G	E	N	T	L	E	S	T		U	N	I	T
			W	I	D	E			M	E	S	S
A	D	M	I	T		C	L	U	B			
J	O	I	N		S	T	A	G		T	E	A
A	S	L	E	E	P		S	H	A	R	E	S
R	E	D		V	E	S	T		S	U	L	K
			M	A	D	E		C	H	E	S	S
D	E	L	I			C	O	R	E			
O	X	E	N		P	U	N	I	S	H	E	S
T	I	N	E		A	R	C	S		A	L	A
S	T	A	R		W	E	E	P		S	K	Y

CROSSWORD 65

L	I	C	K		G	E	M		M	E	N	U
I	R	A	N		I	R	E		A	G	E	S
P	O	P	E		V	A	N		N	O	T	E
S	N	E	E	Z	E		D	R	Y			
				I	N	D	I	A		B	A	A
S	H	E	E	P		E	N	G	L	A	N	D
W	I	L	L		T	A	G		I	N	T	O
A	D	M	I	R	A	L		E	D	G	E	S
Y	E	S		U	N	T	I	L				
			K	E	G		O	F	F	I	C	E
A	C	N	E		L	A	W		I	D	O	L
S	O	O	N		E	V	A		S	E	A	S
P	O	S	T		S	A	N		T	A	L	E

CROSSWORD 66

I	R	K	S		A	S	K		P	A	T	H
N	A	I	L		D	I	E		A	C	R	E
T	I	N	Y		D	R	Y		S	H	I	N
O	L	D		U	S	E		S	T	E	P	S
		N	A	T		N	O	T	E			
S	P	E	N	T		S	U	E		S	A	P
E	A	S	T	E	R		R	E	D	U	C	E
E	D	S		R	U	G		P	U	R	E	R
			P	E	T	E		L	O	P		
S	A	L	A	D		O	R	E		R	A	T
L	I	A	R		P	R	O		L	I	V	E
E	D	I	T		E	G	O		A	S	I	A
D	E	N	Y		P	E	T		W	E	D	S

CROSSWORD 67

D	A	M	E		L	A	Y		B	R	A	G
O	D	O	R		I	V	E		R	A	G	E
T	O	M	A	T	O	E	S		O	V	E	N
				I	N	N			W	E	S	T
S	W	A	R	M		U	P	O	N			
I	O	W	A		D	E	L	I		E	V	A
P	R	A	Y	E	R		O	L	I	V	E	S
S	K	Y		V	A	S	T		D	I	S	K
			D	E	B	T		H	A	L	T	S
H	A	L	O			A	L	I				
U	S	E	S		S	L	I	P	P	E	R	S
M	I	N	E		P	E	N		E	R	I	E
P	A	T	S		A	R	K		G	R	O	W

CROSSWORD 68

F	L	I	P		B	U	S		S	H	O	P
A	I	D	E		A	S	P		I	O	W	A
N	O	E	S		T	E	E		R	E	N	T
S	N	A	T	C	H		E	Y	E			
				A	S	I	D	E		M	O	O
C	L	E	A	R		R	E	S	P	O	N	D
R	O	L	L		A	I	R		A	P	E	D
A	S	S	I	S	T	S		D	R	E	S	S
B	E	E		O	T	H	E	R				
			O	W	E		M	Y	S	E	L	F
I	R	O	N		M	O	P		O	V	A	L
D	U	L	L		P	U	T		N	I	C	E
A	N	D	Y		T	R	Y		G	L	E	E

CROSSWORD 69

B	A	R	S		T	A	P	E		P	O	P
U	N	I	T		O	P	E	N		O	W	L
T	Y	P	E		T	E	N	D		L	E	E
			R	Y	E				A	L	D	A
S	T	R	E	A	M		S	I	R			
T	R	O	O	P		G	A	R	M	E	N	T
A	I	L		P	I	A	N	O		V	I	E
G	O	L	F	E	R	S		N	I	E	C	E
			O	D	E		L	E	N	S	E	S
S	P	U	R				A	D	S			
T	A	P		W	A	I	T		U	T	A	H
A	G	O		H	I	D	E		L	O	N	E
B	E	N		O	D	O	R		T	O	N	Y

CROSSWORD 70

F	A	N	G		T	R	Y		C	A	M	P
I	D	O	L		A	Y	E		E	R	I	E
N	E	R	O		L	E	T		L	I	M	E
			V	I	E			O	L	D	E	R
O	F	F	E	R		S	K	I				
A	L	I		K	N	E	E	L		S	H	E
T	E	N			O	W	N			W	A	Y
S	A	D		P	O	E	T	S		A	W	E
				A	N	D		O	I	N	K	S
E	L	B	O	W			A	D	D			
R	E	A	D		M	E	L		A	J	A	R
A	N	N	E		A	L	A		H	O	B	O
S	A	G	S		D	I	N		O	B	E	Y

CROSSWORD 71

N	E	D			A	S	H			W	A	S
A	R	I	D		V	I	A		R	A	I	L
P	A	V	E	M	E	N	T		U	G	L	Y
	S	I	L	O		S	E	N	S	E	S	
		S	I	L	K		S	O	S			
A	L	I		D	E	W		R	I	S	E	S
D	O	O	R		N	O	T		A	C	R	E
O	W	N	E	R		W	H	O		I	R	E
			C	U	P		E	O	N	S		
	A	N	I	M	A	L		P	O	S	T	
F	L	I	P		P	A	S	S	P	O	R	T
R	A	C	E		E	V	E		E	R	I	E
O	N	E			R	A	T			S	O	D

CROSSWORD 72

B	U	R	N		P	A	R		A	G	E	D
A	S	I	A		I	D	O		R	O	L	E
K	E	N	T		L	E	T		C	A	S	E
E	S	K	I	M	O		T	A	S	T	E	D
			O	U	T	F	I	T				
G	R	A	N	D		O	N	E		L	I	T
A	I	L	S		H	U	G		P	A	C	E
S	P	A		V	A	N		A	I	D	E	D
			O	R	D	E	R	S				
T	H	R	O	W	N		A	T	T	E	N	D
R	E	A	D		E	D	S		O	D	O	R
A	R	I	D		S	U	E		L	I	M	E
P	O	D	S		S	O	D		S	T	E	W

CROSSWORD 73

U	P	O	N		S	H	E		M	O	P	E
S	A	M	E		T	A	R		I	R	O	N
E	V	E	R		E	Y	E		L	A	N	D
D	E	N	V	E	R			A	L	L	Y	
			O	W	N	E	R	S				
V	A	L	U	E		G	A	P		E	A	R
A	G	E	S		G	Y	M		A	L	T	O
N	O	D		H	O	P		A	S	K	E	D
				U	T	T	E	R	S			
	K	N	I	T			S	K	E	T	C	H
S	E	E	D		W	A	S		R	O	L	E
P	E	E	L		A	L	E		T	O	U	R
A	N	D	Y		G	A	S		S	L	E	D

CROSSWORD 74

P	A	L		H	A	M	S		S	T	A	B
A	G	O		I	T	E	M		T	I	N	Y
P	E	A		D	E	L	I		A	C	N	E
A	D	D	E	D			L	A	Y			
			V	E	T		E	V	E	N	T	S
B	A	N	A	N	A	S		A	D	O	R	E
A	C	E			P	A	D			N	O	W
T	R	A	C	K		M	A	R	K	E	T	S
H	E	R	O	E	S		D	I	E			
			U	G	H			N	Y	L	O	N
S	T	I	R		A	P	E	S		A	H	A
O	W	N	S		R	A	G	E		D	I	P
W	O	K	E		P	R	O	D		S	O	S

CROSSWORD 75

M	A	D	E		S	O	D		T	A	L	L
A	B	E	L		C	U	E		O	H	I	O
S	L	A	M		A	T	E		L	A	P	S
T	E	N	S	E	R		P	A	D			
				A	F	T	E	R		S	H	E
S	M	E	A	R		E	S	C	A	P	E	D
T	A	X	I		S	A	T		G	A	N	G
A	N	I	M	A	L	S		H	O	R	S	E
G	E	T		N	I	E	C	E				
			A	N	T		O	Y	S	T	E	R
S	N	I	P		H	E	M		W	I	D	E
P	A	R	E		E	V	E		A	M	E	N
A	G	E	D		R	A	T		T	E	N	T

CROSSWORD 76

C	A	R	T		S	P	A		R	I	T	A
O	D	O	R		A	I	L		U	N	I	T
P	A	L	E		P	R	E	S	E	N	C	E
S	M	E	A	R		A	S	K				
			T	I	L	T		Y	A	C	H	T
H	O	T		C	U	E	D		P	L	E	A
A	R	I	S	E	S		R	E	T	U	R	N
R	A	N	K		H	A	I	R		B	E	G
P	L	A	I	T		S	P	A	T			
				O	W	L		S	O	W	E	D
N	I	N	E	T	E	E	N		W	A	V	E
E	V	E	L		T	E	A		E	D	E	N
W	E	E	K		S	P	Y		L	E	N	S

CROSSWORD 77

A	R	K		S	C	O	T		S	T	A	Y
H	O	E		C	L	U	E		L	I	V	E
O	D	E		H	O	R	N		A	P	E	S
Y	E	L	L	O	W		D	A	M			
			E	O	N		I	N	S	E	C	T
P	E	T	A	L		E	N	D		D	O	E
I	R	O	N		W	A	G		F	I	L	E
L	I	T		B	A	T		S	A	T	A	N
L	E	E	R	E	D		R	A	N			
			O	D	D		A	N	G	E	L	S
A	L	A	S		L	A	N	D		D	O	T
R	I	C	E		E	D	G	E		E	V	E
T	E	E	S		S	E	E	D		N	E	W

CROSSWORD 78

M	O	P		S	L	U	R		B	I	D	S
O	W	L		T	O	N	Y		E	R	I	E
O	N	E		A	N	T	E		G	I	V	E
		A	N	G	E	R		B	A	S	E	S
E	L	S	E			U	P	O	N			
R	O	A	R		E	E	L	S		S	A	T
A	R	N	O	L	D		A	S	S	U	M	E
S	E	T		U	G	L	Y		A	P	E	D
			F	R	E	E			L	E	N	S
S	M	I	L	E		E	N	T	E	R		
L	I	N	E		T	R	I	O		M	A	P
A	N	N	E		W	E	N	T		A	L	A
M	E	S	S		O	D	E	S		N	E	T

CROSSWORD 79

B	E	G		A	H	A	S		S	C	A	T
L	E	O		C	O	I	L		T	R	I	O
E	R	A		R	U	D	Y		R	A	R	E
A	I	L		O	R	E		L	I	T		
T	E	S	T	S				O	P	E	N	S
			A	S	S	O	R	T		R	I	O
M	A	R	X		I	D	O		A	S	P	S
E	G	O		G	R	E	E	T	S			
W	E	A	R	Y				W	H	O	S	E
		S	U	M		D	I	E		P	A	N
A	N	T	S		G	I	R	L		R	U	T
D	U	E	T		A	V	I	V		A	C	E
E	N	D	S		B	A	S	E		H	E	R

CROSSWORD 80

A	L	T	O		S	A	L	T		W	E	B
B	O	A	R		P	L	E	A		A	L	E
L	A	N	D		Y	A	N	K		G	I	N
E	D	G	E			S	T	E	V	E		
			R	A	C	K		N	O	R	T	H
A	S	H		S	O	A	R		T	I	R	E
S	T	O	C	K	S		O	P	E	N	E	R
P	O	L	O		T	U	B	A		G	E	E
S	P	I	L	L		N	E	R	O			
		D	E	A	L	T			C	H	A	P
I	D	A		B	A	I	T		C	O	P	E
R	A	Y		E	V	E	R		U	S	E	S
E	D	S		L	A	D	Y		R	E	S	T

CROSSWORD 81

B	A	Y		A	D	D	S		P	A	W	S
A	C	E		C	O	A	T		E	R	I	E
A	H	A		T	I	N	E		A	C	R	E
S	E	R	M	O	N		R	U	S	H	E	D
			O	R	G	A	N	S				
A	L	T	O	S		G	E	E		H	E	Y
L	I	E	D		F	I	R		C	O	V	E
S	P	A		P	E	N		I	O	W	A	N
				R	E	G	A	R	D			
S	C	H	O	O	L		N	I	E	C	E	S
C	A	I	N		I	R	K	S		A	V	A
A	N	N	E		N	I	L	E		S	I	N
N	E	T	S		G	O	E	S		E	L	K

CROSSWORD 82

T	A	P	E		F	L	A	T		C	O	P
W	I	L	D		L	U	R	E		A	V	A
O	D	E	S		O	N	C	E		M	A	N
S	E	A		G	A	G		M	A	P	L	E
		S	C	O	T		G	E	M			
A	P	A	R	T		R	E	D	U	C	E	S
D	I	N	E		H	O	E		S	E	A	T
E	N	T	E	R	E	D		H	E	N	R	Y
			P	A	R		F	A	S	T		
C	R	I	S	P		S	A	Y		E	R	A
R	I	D		P	A	I	D		W	R	E	N
I	L	L		E	D	G	E		H	E	A	T
B	E	E		D	O	N	S		O	D	D	S

CROSSWORD 83

T	H	A	T		E	D	S		C	O	L	A
W	I	D	E		G	I	N		O	W	E	D
I	R	O	N		G	R	U	M	B	L	E	D
N	E	S	T	S		E	G	O				
				A	R	C		B	I	R	T	H
T	E	A		M	O	T	H		N	E	R	O
H	A	N	S	E	L		A	N	K	L	E	S
A	C	N	E		L	O	V	E		Y	E	T
W	H	E	A	T		P	E	T				
				O	R	E		S	W	E	A	T
S	T	A	R	T	I	N	G		R	A	R	E
I	O	W	A		T	E	E		A	S	K	S
P	O	E	T		A	D	E		P	E	S	T

CROSSWORD 84

R	E	N	O		S	W	A	M		P	U	P
O	V	E	R		C	O	L	A		E	R	R
D	A	T	A		E	V	E	R		E	G	O
			T	U	N	E		T	Y	P	E	D
O	D	D	E	S	T		R	I	O			
V	E	R	S	E		J	A	N	U	A	R	Y
A	L	A			G	A	G			L	E	E
L	I	G	H	T	E	R		M	E	D	A	L
			A	R	E		R	E	C	A	L	L
G	L	I	D	E		M	O	T	H			
E	A	T		A	R	E	A		O	O	P	S
A	V	E		T	A	N	S		E	R	I	E
R	A	M		S	H	U	T		D	E	N	T

CROSSWORD 85

A	I	D	E		A	L	P	S		S	P	A
I	R	O	N		D	E	E	P		N	A	G
R	E	N	T		V	E	E	R		I	C	E
			E	L	I		R	E	A	P	E	D
O	P	E	R	A	S		S	A	T			
D	A	D		W	E	T		D	E	N	I	M
D	I	G			R	A	N			I	D	A
S	L	E	D	S		P	E	P		C	O	D
			Y	E	S		P	I	C	K	L	E
T	H	R	E	A	T		H	E	R			
H	O	E		R	O	B	E		E	A	S	E
A	L	I		C	R	E	W		P	L	A	Y
T	E	N		H	E	N	S		T	A	M	E

CROSSWORD 86

N	A	I	L		S	L	I	M		W	A	S
A	C	N	E		L	A	V	A		R	A	H
G	E	N	E		O	B	E	Y		I	R	E
			R	I	P	E				T	O	E
A	I	R		R	E	L	Y		C	E	N	T
B	R	I	C	K		S	I	L	O			
E	A	G	L	E	S		P	A	L	A	C	E
			I	D	L	Y		C	A	R	O	L
D	R	I	P		Y	A	N	K		T	O	M
E	A	T				W	E	S	T			
A	D	E		O	W	N	S		U	S	E	S
R	I	M		D	I	E	T		C	O	L	E
S	O	S		E	N	D	S		K	N	I	T

CROSSWORD 87

K	N	O	B		S	P	A		S	L	A	P
I	O	W	A		T	A	X		P	A	C	E
T	R	E	A	S	U	R	E		E	V	E	R
				A	N	T			L	A	S	T
T	H	I	N	G		E	A	R	L			
H	I	R	E		I	D	L	Y		A	H	A
E	D	I	T	O	R		L	E	A	D	E	R
Y	E	S		N	O	S	Y		L	A	R	K
			D	E	N	T		M	E	M	O	S
D	E	L	I			E	R	A				
O	X	E	N		R	A	I	N	I	E	S	T
T	I	N	E		O	D	D		R	A	K	E
S	T	A	R		B	Y	E		E	R	I	E

CROSSWORD 88

C	O	P	E		S	P	I	T		P	O	P
A	R	I	D		A	L	D	A		R	U	E
T	A	N	G		T	E	L	L		E	R	R
S	L	E	E	P		D	E	L	I	S		
			S	O	N	G			N	E	T	S
C	A	R		L	E	E	S		T	R	I	O
O	P	E	N	E	R		P	R	O	V	E	N
M	E	M	O		O	H	I	O		E	D	S
E	D	I	T			O	N	L	Y			
		N	E	V	E	R		L	O	A	F	S
F	A	D		A	C	N	E		L	U	R	E
E	V	E		T	H	E	Y		K	N	E	E
W	A	R		S	O	R	E		S	T	E	M

CROSSWORD 89

E	L	I		S	A	M		T	A	S	T	E
G	I	N		I	R	A		A	V	O	I	D
G	O	T		R	O	Y		G	A	S	P	S
S	N	O	W		M	O	S	S				
			A	P	A	R	T			A	C	T
T	R	A	I	L		S	E	T		B	O	O
R	U	S	T	E	D		W	A	T	E	R	S
A	L	I		A	I	L		P	I	L	E	S
P	E	A			S	O	W	E	D			
				S	H	O	E		Y	E	L	L
L	A	P	E	L		S	A	P		V	I	E
O	L	I	V	E		E	V	A		I	N	N
S	P	E	E	D		N	E	W		L	E	T

CROSSWORD 90

H	A	I	R		S	A	N	D		S	E	A
A	L	D	A		P	L	E	A		L	A	D
W	A	L	K		Y	A	R	D		E	R	A
K	N	E	E	L		S	O	D		E	L	M
			I	R	K		Y	A	P			
L	O	S		N	E	A	R		G	I	R	L
A	D	M	I	T	S		A	V	E	N	U	E
B	E	A	D		T	I	R	E		G	E	T
		R	O	Y		N	E	T				
A	C	T		A	S	H		S	T	R	A	W
W	O	E		W	H	A	T		R	O	P	E
A	D	S		N	I	L	E		A	L	E	S
Y	E	T		S	P	E	D		P	E	S	T

CROSSWORD 91

N	A	G		S	L	O	B		A	S	P	S
A	L	A		T	A	P	E		C	O	L	A
B	E	L	I	E	V	E	D		H	A	U	L
			R	E	A	R		V	E	R	S	E
C	L	E	A	R		A	W	E				
R	E	N	T		U	S	E	S		B	A	A
I	N	V	E	N	T		S	T	R	A	N	D
B	A	Y		E	A	S	T		A	L	T	O
				W	H	O		F	I	L	E	S
W	R	A	P	S		I	R	O	N			
A	I	D	E		P	L	E	A	S	I	N	G
S	P	A	N		R	E	A	L		R	I	O
H	E	M	S		O	D	D	S		A	P	T

CROSSWORD 92

L	O	D	E		B	R	A	T		I	R	A
A	D	O	S		R	A	R	E		N	O	D
Y	E	N	S		A	I	M	S		T	O	E
			A	V	I	D		T	R	O	T	S
S	T	A	Y	E	D		F	E	E			
W	O	R	S	T		T	O	D	D	L	E	R
I	R	K			J	A	R			A	V	A
M	E	S	S	I	E	R		W	O	V	E	N
			A	R	T		S	H	R	A	N	K
P	I	A	N	O		M	O	O	D			
O	D	D		N	E	A	R		E	V	E	S
P	E	A		E	R	I	E		R	I	L	E
S	A	M		D	A	D	S		S	A	F	E

CROSSWORD 93

M	O	P	E		S	A	P		W	A	S	H
E	A	R	L		P	I	E		O	H	I	O
S	T	A	M	P	E	D	E		R	A	N	G
S	H	Y		L	E	E	R	E	D			
			M	A	D	D	E	R		T	W	O
A	L	L	E	Y	S		D	A	S	H	E	D
L	A	I	N						P	I	P	E
A	N	N	U	A	L		P	L	A	N	T	S
S	E	E		T	I	D	I	E	R			
			D	E	S	I	G	N		I	R	A
R	I	T	A		T	E	E	T	E	R	E	D
O	V	E	R		E	G	O		V	A	N	E
B	E	A	N		D	O	N		A	N	T	S

CROSSWORD 94

PLOT■SKID■COT
LOVE■ANNE■ORE
USED■NOTE■MAR
MEND■■COD■ELM
■■■YOLK■SOD■■
GEM■LASH■WITS
AVOIDS■ASLEEP
YARN■SOLO■SAY
■■TNT■BOWL■■■
HOG■APT■■AWAY
AHA■ROAR■RARE
RIG■TRIO■GRIN
DOE■SEND■ENDS

CROSSWORD 95

PINK■CASH■APT
IRAN■ABLE■WOO
TAPE■REAL■ALL
■■■EYE■PLAYED
COLLIE■SOS■■■
EVA■PRO■SHAPE
NET■■SIN■■CAN
TREED■LOT■HID
■■■VIA■OWNERS
SPREAD■DOE■■■
COO■POLL■CRAB
ALP■ERIE■KITE
TOE■REDS■SPED

CROSSWORD 96

DOTS■MOST■SEA
EPIC■AUTO■URN
LEER■TREK■BAD
INSULT■WEPT■■
■■■BEE■SNARES
GAP■IRE■SPACE
IRON■SAD■ACHE
RISES■RAG■TOM
LASSES■NOD■■■
■■ITCH■COURSE
CAB■RAKE■MOON
AIL■EVER■BALD
TRY■TENS■ODDS

CROSSWORD 97

POLO■ABE■IDEA
AVID■LAD■ROAD
SEND■SNEAKERS
TREE■■AND■■■■
■■■RAIN■DEBTS
ORE■GOAT■LOOP
WILLOW■ADMIRE
LOSE■ABLE■LED
STEED■LENT■■■
■■■■ADO■■RATS
YEARNING■ERIE
ALLY■ADE■ACME
PIPE■LET■THEN

CROSSWORD 98

BELT■TAT■STAG
EVER■HOE■LORE
DINE■IKE■ONCE
SLANTS■NIP■■■
■■■DOT■STILTS
RAH■ELM■SNORE
ACES■EAR■GAIT
CHIEF■NEW■NOS
KERNEL■SOB■■■
■■■IDO■COUSIN
SILO■YOU■MORE
OVER■AWE■PLOT
DYES■LED■SONS

CROSSWORD 99

FATE■KID■BULB
ALEX■IRE■ERIE
DIET■NAG■AGES
■■■RIG■RAREST
ROMANS■END■■■
IRISH■NET■DOG
CAN■AROSE■AVA
OLD■LED■NOVEL
■■■PEP■ENTERS
RESIDE■RAH■■■
IVAN■ABE■ELSE
TENT■TAC■REEL
ARKS■SAT■SEEK

CROSSWORD 100

DIP■SICK■BEND
ONE■TREE■OVER
ENTERING■WIRE
■■■LAST■ALLOW
SPRAY■ELI■■■■
TOOT■PROM■PIT
APPEAR■ASHORE
BEE■JOHN■ALAS
■■■■ADO■FRONT
RADAR■WHOM■■■
USES■PLEASING
LINK■REAL■TEA
EATS■ODDS■STY

CROSSWORD 101

FAIL■BAD■SPIN
IDLE■AVA■HERO
RELEASED■OAKS
■■■■PEN■WORSE
WHEAT■UGH■■■■
EARN■MERE■AHA
PRINCE■ANTLER
TEE■LADY■ADAM
■■■■ALI■SPATS
SWARM■VIA■■■■
LIME■AIRPLANE
APED■IDA■OBEY
TENS■MEN■PETE

CROSSWORD 102

CASE■BAA■SILO
ALAS■LIP■ARID
TAMS■ALE■FIND
SNEAKS■■TASKS
■■■YET■FAR■■■
WAIST■LOTIONS
ADD■CHART■WOE
REACHED■LINDA
■■■RUN■TEN■■■
STRIP■■ADVISE
POEM■ASP■IDLE
ANNE■HOE■TOIL
NETS■AND■ELMS

CROSSWORD 103

CAB■SHOT■CLAW
ALE■HEIR■HOSE
IDA■IDLY■AVID
NAMING■■AREAS
■■■LEERING■■■
FOAL■■ENTERED
OWL■STAKE■IVE
RESCUED■■AMEN
■■■OBEYING■■■
COLAS■■NEEDED
APES■LADS■ICE
SEAT■EDIT■SHE
ENDS■TEAS■COP

CROSSWORD 104

TROT■SPA■AJAR
RAVE■ALL■HOPE
IRAN■MASSAGED
MELTS■NOT■■■■
■■■■ODE■YACHT
HEN■OATH■SHOE
EXISTS■INHALE
RICH■HARE■TEN
STEEL■SEE■■■■
■■■■ILL■DADDY
TOMATOES■LORE
AWAY■TEA■EVEN
GENE■SPY■SEWS

CROSSWORD 105

ANT■SPUR■THEM
VIA■COPY■WOVE
APPLAUSE■ABEL
■■■ANTE■SNORT
LOST■■TWIG■■■
ANNE■USED■ADE
SCORER■TELLER
SEW■EGGS■IDEA
■■■FLEA■■NAPS
MINUS■ROPE■■■
ARID■JAPANESE
SONG■AGES■VAN
KNEE■BENT■AND

CROSSWORD 106

O	A	T	H		S	T	A	B		S	A	M
A	C	H	E		C	O	V	E		I	D	O
T	R	E	E		R	I	O	T		L	E	T
S	E	N	D		A	L	I		G	O	S	H
			E	L	M		D	A	Y			
T	R	A	D	E		T	E	R	M	I	T	E
W	A	G		A	S	I	D	E		R	A	Y
O	P	O	S	S	U	M		N	I	E	C	E
			H	E	N		S	A	N			
P	R	A	Y		R	A	H		F	E	A	T
L	O	G		P	I	P	E		A	R	C	H
A	B	E		U	S	E	D		N	I	N	E
Y	E	S		T	E	D	S		T	E	E	M

CROSSWORD 107

D	I	S	H		A	H	A		A	J	A	R
A	N	T	E		G	I	N		C	O	L	A
S	T	A	R	T	I	N	G		H	E	A	T
H	O	G		E	N	T	R	E	E			
			L	A	G		I	N	S	U	L	T
T	I	G	E	R		O	L	D		S	I	R
W	O	O	D		P	A	Y		L	E	N	A
O	W	L		I	R	K		D	U	S	T	Y
S	A	F	A	R	I		B	A	G			
			W	E	E	D	E	D		D	I	M
A	L	D	A		S	E	A	S	H	O	R	E
D	O	O	R		T	E	D		O	V	A	L
O	W	E	D		S	P	Y		W	E	N	T

CROSSWORD 108

M	A	P		B	A	R	S		S	L	E	D
E	R	R		O	M	I	T		P	O	L	E
L	I	E		A	I	D	E		E	A	S	E
T	A	P	E	R	S		W	A	N	D	E	R
		A	D	D	S		A	N	D			
B	A	R	D	S		A	R	T		C	O	Y
O	B	E	Y		H	I	D		S	O	R	E
W	E	D		C	U	R		C	O	M	E	T
			W	A	S		H	A	S	P		
R	E	V	E	R	T		A	D	O	R	E	D
O	R	A	L		L	O	B	E		E	V	E
B	I	N	D		E	D	I	T		S	I	N
S	E	E	S		S	E	T	S		S	L	Y

CROSSWORD 109

F	E	E	T		R	A	W		P	A	P	A
U	R	G	E		I	V	E		I	D	O	L
R	A	G	E		N	A	B		L	O	R	E
			N	A	G			R	O	S	E	S
S	W	I	S	S			S	A	T			
M	E	T		P	O	R	C	H		A	D	S
O	R	E			B	O	O			P	A	T
G	E	M		D	E	B	T	S		E	L	I
			F	R	Y			O	L	D	E	R
S	C	A	R	Y			O	W	L			
L	A	C	E		L	A	W		A	R	K	S
A	N	N	E		I	C	E		M	A	I	L
B	E	E	S		T	E	D		A	N	D	Y

CROSSWORD 110

E	A	R	S		S	E	A		A	R	C	S
G	L	U	E		T	A	R		D	E	L	I
G	E	N	T	L	E	S	T		D	E	A	R
				O	W	E			E	L	M	S
S	W	U	N	G		L	O	A	D			
T	I	N	A		A	S	K	S		E	L	F
E	D	I	T	E	D		A	P	P	E	A	R
M	E	T		V	E	R	Y		E	L	S	E
			B	A	S	E		T	A	S	T	E
S	H	O	E			A	H	A				
P	A	P	A		C	L	I	P	P	I	N	G
O	V	E	R		O	L	D		I	D	E	A
T	E	N	D		B	Y	E		T	O	T	S

CROSSWORD 111

P	E	T	E		S	P	A		S	H	E	D
E	V	I	L		P	I	T		C	A	R	E
N	E	C	K	L	A	C	E		A	S	I	A
				I	N	N		O	T	H	E	R
A	W	A	I	T		I	D	A				
L	A	R	D		S	C	O	T		S	K	I
A	L	M	O	S	T		S	H	A	K	E	R
S	L	Y		L	A	C	E		L	I	N	K
				U	G	H		M	I	T	T	S
A	M	O	N	G		A	G	O				
R	A	V	E		P	R	O	M	I	S	E	S
C	R	E	W		A	G	E		R	I	N	K
H	E	N	S		Y	E	S		A	N	D	Y

CROSSWORD 112

N	A	P		S	W	A	B		G	O	L	F
E	L	I		C	A	N	E		I	D	O	L
C	A	N		A	I	D	E		N	O	S	E
K	N	E	E	L	S			A	G	R	E	E
			L	E	T	T	U	C	E			
H	A	L	F			O	S	T	R	I	C	H
A	L	A		P	A	N	E	S		C	O	O
M	E	S	S	A	G	E			D	E	B	T
			T	U	E	S	D	A	Y			
S	T	O	O	L			E	L	E	C	T	S
L	I	A	R		S	W	A	T		R	I	O
A	N	T	E		P	O	L	O		I	L	L
B	A	S	S		A	N	T	S		B	E	D

CROSSWORD 113

B	R	A	G		S	O	D		A	L	D	A
O	I	L	Y		C	R	Y		C	O	O	L
S	T	A	M	P	E	D	E		T	A	N	S
S	A	N		O	N	E		R	O	D	E	O
			S	T	E	R	N	E	R			
M	A	M	A			S	E	A		A	P	T
O	B	E	Y	E	D		W	R	I	T	E	R
P	E	T		D	I	G			D	E	N	Y
			S	I	N	A	T	R	A			
S	W	E	A	T		R	O	Y		T	O	P
T	A	X	I		M	A	T	E	R	I	A	L
E	V	I	L		A	G	E		I	N	T	O
W	E	T	S		R	E	D		P	A	S	T

CROSSWORD 114

A	J	A	R		S	A	P		S	L	A	B
R	O	D	E		O	N	E		W	I	R	E
F	E	E	T		A	N	D		E	V	E	N
			I	R	K	E	D		P	E	S	T
S	T	A	R	E	S		L	I	T			
H	O	L	E	S		B	E	N		S	P	A
I	R	A		I	R	I	S	H		T	A	P
P	E	N		D	O	N		A	B	O	V	E
			M	E	T		S	L	O	P	E	D
A	L	S	O		T	I	N	E	S			
S	O	U	P		I	D	O		T	A	L	L
P	O	R	E		N	E	W		O	H	I	O
S	P	E	D		G	A	Y		N	A	P	S

CROSSWORD 115

L	I	S	T		S	A	D		E	C	H	O
O	D	O	R		T	W	O		L	O	A	D
G	O	N	E		E	A	T		B	O	R	E
			A	R	M	Y		N	O	S	E	S
P	H	O	T	O			S	O	W			
L	A	B		Y	A	C	H	T		T	R	Y
U	S	E			J	O	E			R	U	E
S	H	Y		P	A	N	D	A		A	L	A
			F	I	R			G	A	Y	E	R
T	A	K	E	N		C	H	E	W			
W	I	N	E		M	O	O		F	E	A	R
I	D	O	L		A	L	L		U	G	L	Y
G	E	T	S		T	E	E		L	O	S	E

CROSSWORD 116

G	A	V	E		B	A	D		S	O	L	O
A	S	I	A		E	R	A		A	V	I	D
P	H	A	R	M	A	C	Y		L	A	N	E
			T	E	N			M	A	L	E	S
N	I	G	H	T	S		A	I	M			
I	R	E				A	D	M	I	R	E	D
C	O	N		A	S	I	D	E		I	V	E
K	N	E	E	L	E	D				D	E	N
			A	P	E		R	O	B	E	R	T
S	T	A	G	S			O	W	E			
P	U	L	L		B	R	U	N	E	T	T	E
A	B	L	E		O	U	T		R	O	A	D
N	A	Y	S		W	E	E		S	O	B	S

CROSSWORD 117

D	I	M		S	N	A	P		M	E	M	O
O	D	E		T	O	R	E		A	V	I	D
N	O	S		R	E	I	N		T	E	N	D
		S	A	I	L	S		B	E	N	D	S
T	R	A	M	P		E	R	A	S			
R	A	G	E		K	N	O	B		S	P	A
A	V	E	N	U	E		O	Y	S	T	E	R
Y	E	S		T	E	A	M		H	E	A	T
			S	A	N	D		S	O	R	T	S
W	R	A	T	H		M	E	L	O	N		
A	I	D	E		G	I	V	E		E	V	E
S	L	A	P		E	R	I	E		S	I	R
H	E	M	S		M	E	L	T		T	A	R

CROSSWORD 118

T	W	O		S	L	A	M		E	A	C	H
R	I	P		L	A	N	E		C	L	U	E
I	R	E		E	V	I	L		H	A	T	E
M	E	N		D	A	M		P	O	S	E	D
		I	T	S		A	B	E				
G	O	N	E		S	L	A	T		F	E	E
U	R	G	E	N	T		R	E	A	L	L	Y
Y	E	S		O	U	R	S		D	O	M	E
				O	N	E		F	O	R		
F	L	O	W	N		V	I	E		I	D	A
L	I	V	E		L	E	N	A		S	I	N
A	M	E	N		O	A	T	S		T	E	D
G	E	N	T		P	L	O	T		S	T	Y

CROSSWORD 119

M	O	B		F	A	C	T		A	R	C	S
O	W	L		I	R	O	N		L	O	O	P
O	N	E		R	O	O	T		S	O	D	A
		S	T	E	M			H	O	M	E	R
E	L	S	E		A	L	D	A				
R	E	I	N			O	U	R		A	L	E
A	N	N		S	N	O	O	P		D	I	E
S	A	G		W	A	S			O	V	A	L
				A	B	E	L		W	A	R	S
T	H	R	O	B			E	D	E	N		
H	E	A	D		E	D	G	E		C	A	P
A	R	I	D		L	O	A	N		E	Y	E
W	E	D	S		M	E	L	T		D	E	W

CROSSWORD 120

T	A	G		T	E	S	T		S	T	A	B
I	V	E		H	A	T	E		H	O	L	E
M	A	T	T	E	R	E	D		R	O	S	E
			A	N	N	E		M	E	L	O	N
A	N	T	S			R	E	A	D			
B	E	A	T		U	S	E	D		A	L	A
E	R	N	E	S	T		L	E	S	S	E	N
L	O	G		L	A	S	S		T	I	N	T
			J	O	H	N			R	A	T	E
S	C	R	U	B		A	L	D	A			
H	A	I	R		D	R	O	O	P	I	N	G
I	N	T	O		Y	E	N	S		T	E	A
P	E	A	R		E	D	G	E		S	T	Y

CROSSWORD 121

H	O	G		P	A	T	H		T	H	A	T
A	W	E		E	C	H	O		H	A	L	O
Y	E	N		C	H	E	W		R	U	T	S
		T	A	K	E	N		S	O	L	O	S
B	I	L	L				S	O	W			
A	R	E	A	S		F	U	R	N	A	C	E
S	O	S		P	L	A	N	E		R	U	N
E	N	T	E	R	E	D		R	A	K	E	D
			L	A	D				L	A	S	S
S	T	R	A	Y		S	T	A	I	N		
T	R	O	T		S	H	O	W		S	U	B
A	I	D	E		I	O	W	A		A	G	O
B	O	S	S		P	O	N	Y		S	H	Y

CROSSWORD 122

F	O	A	M		S	L	Y		T	I	C	K
R	I	C	E		T	O	O		W	O	R	E
E	L	M	S		A	D	D		A	W	A	Y
D	Y	E	S		F	E	E		N	A	B	S
			E	L	F		L	A	G			
L	A	S	S	O		H	E	R		D	I	P
A	L	P		S	C	A	R	E		I	R	A
B	A	Y		E	A	T		N	A	M	E	D
			A	R	M		S	A	T			
B	E	L	L		E	V	A		T	O	W	S
R	A	I	L		R	A	N		E	V	I	L
A	C	N	E		A	N	T		N	E	R	O
T	H	E	Y		S	E	A		D	R	E	W

CROSSWORD 123

S	M	U	G		S	O	D		G	R	A	Y
P	A	P	A		C	U	E		R	I	L	E
O	D	O	R		A	R	T		O	P	E	N
T	E	N	D	E	R		R	A	W			
			E	L	F		O	I	N	K	E	D
S	T	I	N	K		H	I	M		N	A	Y
T	O	N	S		O	U	T		D	O	S	E
A	R	C		A	R	M		D	E	B	T	S
B	E	H	I	N	D		F	U	N			
			R	Y	E		R	E	T	I	R	E
S	O	F	A		R	I	O		I	D	O	L
U	N	I	T		E	D	S		S	L	A	M
M	E	R	E		D	O	T		T	E	D	S

CROSSWORD 124

P	R	O	D		P	I	T		L	A	S	H
L	O	V	E		E	V	E		A	C	N	E
U	S	E	S		A	Y	E		T	R	I	M
S	E	N	I	O	R			W	E	E	P	S
			G	A	L		C	A	R			
S	L	A	N	T		S	A	G		B	O	O
T	E	N		M	A	I	N	E		A	D	D
Y	E	T		E	R	R		R	A	G	E	D
			R	A	T		P	E	R			
A	N	G	E	L			A	D	O	R	E	S
B	U	R	N		R	A	N		M	E	R	E
E	D	I	T		I	C	E		A	S	I	A
L	E	N	S		M	E	L		S	T	E	M

CROSSWORD 125

A	T	E		S	L	O	B		P	A	G	E
D	E	N		P	O	L	O		O	V	A	L
S	A	T		A	N	D	Y		S	I	N	S
		R	A	N	G	E		H	E	D	G	E
O	R	A	L			S	H	E	D			
W	I	N	D		S	T	E	M		D	A	D
E	S	C	A	P	E		E	S	K	I	M	O
S	E	E		L	E	A	D		E	V	E	S
			P	U	P	S			P	I	N	E
B	R	O	O	M		H	A	L	T	S		
A	I	D	E		H	O	L	E		I	D	A
I	T	E	M		I	R	A	N		O	U	R
L	A	S	S		T	E	N	D		N	O	T

CROSSWORD 126

P	A	I	D		C	A	R		T	I	N	A
A	L	D	A		O	D	E		O	V	A	L
I	T	E	M		A	D	E		L	E	T	S
R	O	A	S	T	S		L	A	D			
				O	T	T	E	R		A	N	D
S	T	R	A	P		O	C	T	O	B	E	R
L	I	A	R		B	A	T		W	E	R	E
A	N	I	M	A	L	S		A	L	L	O	W
P	E	N		T	O	T	A	L				
			M	E	N		N	I	G	H	T	S
P	A	V	E		D	I	G		I	O	W	A
A	L	A	N		E	R	R		F	L	I	P
W	A	N	D		S	A	Y		T	E	N	S

CROSSWORD 127

P	A	N		A	C	T	S		W	H	A	T
O	D	E		P	L	E	A		E	A	C	H
T	O	W	E	R	I	N	G		L	I	N	E
			L	O	P	S		A	L	L	E	Y
I	O	W	A	N		E	L	M				
T	H	A	T		T	R	U	E		E	V	A
C	I	N	E	M	A		S	N	A	R	E	S
H	O	T		I	N	C	H		D	I	S	K
				S	K	I		D	U	E	T	S
S	T	O	U	T		R	E	A	L			
P	U	N	S		S	C	A	T	T	E	R	S
A	B	L	E		E	L	S	E		G	O	O
R	A	Y	S		T	E	E	S		O	W	N

CROSSWORD 128

E	V	E		T	H	A	W		W	I	S	E
G	I	N		H	O	S	E		I	D	L	E
G	E	T		R	O	L	E		V	E	I	L
		E	L	O	P	E			E	A	T	S
S	H	R	U	B		E	R	A	S			
H	E	I	R		S	P	U	R		T	A	P
E	R	N	E	S	T		S	C	A	R	C	E
D	O	G		E	A	C	H		V	A	N	E
			H	A	R	E		R	I	V	E	R
A	L	D	A			R	H	O	D	E		
S	E	A	T		S	E	E	D		L	A	S
P	A	L	E		P	A	R	E		E	G	O
S	P	E	D		A	L	S	O		R	E	D

CROSSWORD 129

C	A	R	T		R	O	D		S	L	A	T
U	P	O	N		E	R	A		T	I	R	E
T	E	E	T	E	R	E	D		O	A	T	S
E	D	S		G	A	G		W	O	R	S	T
			H	O	N	O	R	E	D			
L	A	V	A			N	I	P		B	A	A
O	B	E	Y	E	D		O	T	H	E	R	S
W	E	T		L	O	P			I	T	C	H
			E	S	C	A	P	E	D			
A	L	O	N	E		L	U	G		H	A	M
S	E	N	D		L	A	N	G	U	A	G	E
P	A	C	E		A	C	T		G	L	E	E
S	P	E	D		Y	E	S		H	O	S	T

CROSSWORD 130

I	O	W	A			A	D	S		S	I	P
C	H	E	W	S		L	A	W		I	R	A
Y	O	D	E	L		S	T	A	I	N	E	D
				A	B	O	A	R	D			
	T	R	I	B	E			M	A	S	T	
W	H	E	N		A	C	T	S		P	A	S
E	R	I	N		R	A	H		W	A	S	H
B	E	G		O	S	L	O		A	N	T	E
	E	N	V	Y			R	I	S	K	Y	
			A	S	C	E	N	D				
P	H	A	N	T	O	M		O	O	Z	E	D
R	O	Y		E	L	I		L	O	O	S	E
O	W	E		R	A	T			H	O	P	E

CROSSWORD 131

L	I	M	E	S		A	R	M		A	C	T
A	D	O	R	E		H	O	E		G	O	O
W	O	M	A	N		O	Y	S	T	E	R	S
				S	O	Y		S	I	D	E	S
C	O	P	I	E	R		H	E	M			
O	V	E	R		E	Y	E	S		S	O	S
L	A	N	E		G	E	E		W	O	O	L
A	L	S		P	O	N	D		H	A	Z	E
			B	A	N		E	L	O	P	E	D
S	T	A	I	R		I	D	A				
E	A	S	T	E	R	N		M	A	Y	B	E
A	L	I		N	A	T		B	R	O	I	L
T	E	A		T	W	O		S	K	U	N	K

CROSSWORD 132

P	L	O	T		N	E	R	O		R	I	B
L	O	V	E		A	R	I	D		E	R	A
O	N	E	S		P	R	O	D		M	A	N
W	E	N	T			A	T	E		E	N	D
			S	O	O	N		R	O	D		
E	G	G		R	U	D	E		W	I	G	S
L	A	R	G	E	R		A	S	L	E	E	P
F	L	E	A		S	A	C	K		S	T	Y
		A	S	P		S	H	I	N			
S	A	T		U	G	H			O	D	E	S
A	L	E		M	O	O	D		R	A	V	E
L	A	S		P	A	R	E		T	R	E	E
T	N	T		S	T	E	W		H	E	N	S

CROSSWORD 133

C	A	R	T		W	E	S	T		M	A	P
O	D	O	R		H	A	T	E		A	C	E
T	A	P	E		I	T	E	M		I	R	A
S	M	E	A	R	S		A	P	P	L	E	S
			T	A	P		M	E	L			
A	V	A		H	E	M		R	A	T	E	S
L	I	N	T		R	U	T		Y	E	A	H
P	A	T	H	S		D	I	E		D	R	Y
			I	T	S		G	Y	M			
W	A	R	S	A	W		H	E	E	D	E	D
I	V	E		M	E	E	T		T	O	R	E
D	I	D		P	A	L	E		A	S	I	A
E	D	S		S	T	I	R		L	E	E	R

CROSSWORD 134

O	I	L	S		S	A	P	S		S	P	A
I	R	A	N		T	R	E	E		W	A	R
N	O	T	E		R	I	D	E		A	I	M
K	N	E	E		A	D	D		A	N	D	Y
			Z	I	P		L	U	G			
T	W	E	E	T		B	E	N	E	A	T	H
A	H	A		A	P	A	R	T		B	E	A
G	O	R	I	L	L	A		I	D	E	A	S
			R	Y	E		F	E	E			
F	L	E	A		A	L	I		S	T	A	B
L	A	D		I	D	O	L		E	R	I	E
E	V	E		D	E	A	L		R	U	L	E
D	A	N		O	D	D	S		T	E	S	T

CROSSWORD 135

B	A	N		M	A	P	S		A	R	M	S
A	R	E		I	D	E	A		T	O	I	L
A	T	T	E	N	D	E	D		L	O	R	E
			D	U	S	K		D	A	T	E	D
S	T	A	G	S		E	R	A	S			
C	O	V	E		O	D	O	R		A	S	H
A	R	I	S	E	N		S	T	A	B	L	E
R	E	D		A	C	M	E		S	E	A	M
			F	R	E	E		W	I	L	T	S
A	P	R	I	L		L	O	A	D			
P	A	U	L		A	T	H	L	E	T	I	C
E	L	S	E		V	E	I	L		I	R	A
D	E	E	D		A	D	O	S		P	E	P

CROSSWORD 136

C	A	T		A	W	A	Y		A	S	P	S
A	G	O		G	A	T	E		W	O	O	L
P	E	N	N	A	N	T	S		A	L	T	O
			A	I	D	E			R	E	S	T
S	T	A	I	N		N	E	E	D			
H	I	L	L		I	D	L	Y		P	I	G
E	R	A	S	E	R		M	E	L	O	D	Y
D	E	N		L	A	B	S		L	O	O	M
			W	I	N	E		B	A	L	L	S
D	E	L	I			F	O	A	M			
A	D	E	S		C	O	N	T	A	C	T	S
D	I	N	E		A	R	C	H		O	A	K
S	T	A	R		B	E	E	S		D	R	Y

CROSSWORD 137

P	I	N	S		O	F	F		S	L	O	T
A	D	A	M		V	I	A		H	E	A	R
L	A	T	E		E	R	R		A	N	T	E
			A	N	N	E		E	R	A	S	E
S	H	O	R	E	S		O	A	K			
T	E	N	S	E		S	I	R		A	G	O
A	R	C		D	W	E	L	L		J	A	W
B	E	E		L	O	W		I	R	A	T	E
			T	E	E		L	E	E	R	E	D
S	T	A	R	S		H	A	R	P			
W	A	D	E		S	U	B		O	P	E	N
A	L	D	A		A	G	E		R	A	G	E
P	E	S	T		M	E	L		T	R	O	T

CROSSWORD 138

B	I	T		A	D	A	M		M	A	M	A
O	R	R		M	I	C	E		O	P	E	N
Y	O	U		A	M	E	N		W	E	N	T
S	N	E	E	Z	E			I	S	S	U	E
			R	E	S	I	G	N				
A	W	A	R	D		R	E	N	E	W	A	L
N	O	T	E		P	I	T		R	I	L	E
N	E	E	D	L	E	S		W	A	N	E	D
				O	T	H	E	R	S			
W	H	E	A	T			V	I	E	W	E	D
E	A	R	L		A	D	E	S		A	X	E
T	R	I	P		H	I	N	T		G	I	N
S	E	E	S		A	N	T	S		S	T	Y

CROSSWORD 139

O	R	E		D	Y	E			D	R	E	W
F	I	R		O	A	R		C	R	A	V	E
F	O	R	M	U	L	A		H	I	R	E	D
			A	B	E		C	O	V	E	R	S
S	P	L	I	T		C	U	R	E			
L	I	O	N		S	A	T	U	R	D	A	Y
A	N	N		S	O	R	E	S		I	R	E
B	E	G	I	N	N	E	R		F	E	E	L
			N	A	G	S		T	O	T	A	L
P	L	A	N	K	S		S	E	A			
E	E	R	I	E		S	H	A	M	P	O	O
G	A	I	N	S		H	E	M		A	N	D
S	N	A	G			E	D	S		R	E	D

CROSSWORD 140

R	A	T	E		C	A	P	E		H	A	M
I	R	A	N		H	U	R	L		E	L	I
P	I	N	T		I	T	E	M		R	A	T
E	D	G	E		L	O	S		H	O	S	T
			R	O	D		S	P	A			
G	R	A	S	S		R	E	A	S	O	N	S
A	I	L		C	O	A	S	T		W	O	O
S	P	I	N	A	C	H		C	H	E	W	S
			A	R	T		W	H	O			
P	R	A	Y		O	N	E		W	H	A	T
E	A	R		A	B	E	L		L	I	M	E
T	I	M		P	E	A	L		E	D	E	N
E	D	S		E	R	R	S		D	E	N	S

CROSSWORD 141

O	F	F		C	O	P	E		B	A	T	H
D	I	E		A	P	E	D		E	C	H	O
D	R	E	S	S	E	R	S		T	R	I	O
			H	E	N	S			T	E	S	T
E	L	V	I	S		O	K	A	Y			
L	E	E	R		K	N	I	T		E	L	F
M	A	R	T	I	N		T	E	R	R	O	R
S	K	Y		R	O	S	E		E	A	S	E
			D	E	B	T		W	A	S	T	E
T	I	N	A			R	O	A	R			
E	D	I	T		F	I	N	I	S	H	E	D
N	O	N	E		O	D	E	S		A	V	A
S	L	E	D		R	E	S	T		T	E	D

CROSSWORD 142

N	I	N	E		A	G	E	D		A	R	M
O	D	O	R		D	O	V	E		L	E	E
D	E	E	R		M	O	A	N		T	E	N
S	A	L	A	M	I				H	O	L	D
			N	A	T		I	R	E			
R	I	N	D	S		A	V	E	R	A	G	E
A	D	O		T	A	P	E	S		B	A	A
P	A	T	I	E	N	T		C	H	E	S	T
			C	R	Y		D	U	E			
M	A	R	Y				R	E	A	G	A	N
A	C	E		R	A	V	E		R	O	B	E
I	N	N		A	S	I	A		T	A	L	E
N	E	T		T	H	E	M		S	L	E	D

CROSSWORD 143

R	I	T	A		A	R	M	S		T	A	P
I	R	O	N		H	O	O	T		A	L	I
P	A	R	T		A	D	O	R	A	B	L	E
S	N	E	E	R			N	I	P			
			S	O	O	N		C	E	N	T	S
M	U	D		B	O	A	S	T		E	A	T
E	R	R			Z	I	P			A	X	E
A	G	O		R	E	L	A	Y		R	I	M
T	E	P	E	E		S	N	A	P			
			V	A	N			P	A	S	T	E
S	L	E	E	P	E	R	S		T	H	I	N
P	A	Y		E	R	I	E		H	O	L	D
A	B	E		R	O	D	E		S	E	T	S

CROSSWORD 144

H	O	P	E		J	E	T		S	L	A	B
I	R	A	N		A	L	I		W	A	D	E
M	E	N	D		D	I	M		E	V	E	N
			E	V	E			L	E	A	S	T
L	I	N	D	A			H	O	T			
I	D	O		T	U	L	I	P		I	T	S
A	L	P			P	I	G			D	U	O
R	Y	E		M	O	T	H	S		E	R	R
			T	O	N			P	L	A	N	E
S	T	R	A	W			D	Y	E			
I	R	I	S		G	O	O		A	J	A	R
L	I	N	T		A	D	S		S	O	L	E
L	O	D	E		L	E	E		H	E	L	D

CROSSWORD 145

K	I	T	E		C	L	A	W		P	A	L
I	R	I	S		R	I	L	E		A	L	A
T	O	N	S		I	D	L	E		I	T	S
S	N	E	A	K	S				T	R	O	T
			Y	I	P		V	I	E			
S	W	I	S	S		B	A	N	D	A	G	E
E	A	R		S	O	U	N	D		B	U	D
E	R	A	S	E	R	S		I	T	E	M	S
			U	S	E		B	A	R			
G	O	W	N				A	N	I	M	A	L
A	H	A		S	C	A	T		P	O	R	E
S	I	N		E	A	C	H		L	A	I	N
P	O	D		T	R	E	E		E	N	D	S

CROSSWORD 146

G	A	I	T		I	T	C	H		S	P	A
A	C	R	E		T	A	L	E		T	A	R
S	H	I	N		S	T	A	R		I	N	K
P	E	S	T	S		T	W	E	E	T		
			S	O	U	L			A	C	T	S
A	L	A		W	R	E	N		S	H	O	O
R	O	W	I	N	G		A	T	T	E	N	D
M	O	A	N		E	D	G	E		S	E	A
S	P	I	T			U	S	E	D			
		T	O	O	T	S		M	I	S	E	R
E	L	I		R	U	T	S		T	A	X	I
V	A	N		A	B	E	L		C	L	A	P
E	G	G		L	A	D	Y		H	E	M	S

CROSSWORD 147

A	D	D			T	W	O			P	I	T
L	O	I	S		A	I	L		M	I	C	E
P	O	R	T	A	B	L	E		U	P	O	N
	R	E	A	D		L	O	O	S	E	N	
		C	R	E	W		S	U	E			
D	O	T		S	O	N		T	U	B	E	S
I	R	O	N		O	O	H		M	A	R	K
E	E	R	I	E		R	A	H		L	A	Y
			B	A	N		T	A	L	L		
	F	A	B	R	I	C		W	A	R	T	
P	O	L	L		C	O	O	K	B	O	O	K
E	L	S	E		E	N	D		S	O	R	E
A	D	O			R	E	D			M	E	N

CROSSWORD 148

J	O	E			A	S	P			A	R	M
A	D	S		L	I	L	A	C		B	O	O
W	E	T		E	D	I	T	H		L	A	W
		I	V	E		P	R	E	F	E	R	S
M	A	M	A				I	R	A			
A	L	A	N	S		P	O	I	N	T	E	D
S	E	T		M	O	A	T	S		E	V	E
S	C	E	N	E	R	Y		H	E	L	E	N
			O	L	D				R	E	N	T
G	R	O	W	L	E	D		S	A	G		
R	I	B		E	R	E	C	T		R	E	V
A	D	O		D	E	L	A	Y		A	Y	E
B	E	E			D	I	P			M	E	T

CROSSWORD 149

E	V	E		O	B	E	Y		W	H	A	T
A	I	L		S	O	R	E		R	O	L	E
R	A	I	N	C	O	A	T		A	S	P	S
			E	A	T	S			P	E	S	T
C	H	O	I	R		E	G	G	S			
R	A	N	G		I	D	L	E		B	A	A
A	R	C	H	E	R		A	T	T	E	N	D
B	E	E		Y	A	R	D		R	A	T	E
			L	E	N	A		D	U	N	E	S
T	A	K	E			T	E	A	S			
R	I	N	G		S	T	A	R	T	L	E	D
I	D	E	A		E	L	S	E		I	R	A
P	E	E	L		T	E	E	S		D	R	Y

CROSSWORD 150

L	E	E		S	W	A	Y		S	L	A	M
I	C	Y		T	I	N	E		P	O	R	E
S	H	E		E	N	D	S		O	N	C	E
T	O	S	S	E	D			N	I	G	H	T
			C	R	Y	S	T	A	L			
P	A	P	A	S		H	O	T		L	I	T
E	V	E	R		H	I	T		B	O	R	E
G	A	P		P	A	R		T	A	P	E	D
			L	O	T	T	E	R	Y			
S	P	L	I	T			R	U	S	S	I	A
L	O	O	K		C	A	R	E		L	O	G
E	L	S	E		A	D	O	S		A	W	E
D	E	E	D		P	E	R	T		P	A	D

CROSSWORD 151

N	A	T		S	O	L	D		F	I	T	S
A	B	E		T	R	A	Y		I	D	O	L
I	L	L		E	A	S	E		F	L	E	A
L	E	E		A	L	S			T	E	S	T
		G	Y	M		I	T	C	H			
L	O	R	E		H	E	R	O		P	A	W
O	R	A	N	G	E		I	N	S	I	D	E
G	E	M		A	L	T	O		E	A	S	T
			T	Y	P	E		C	A	N		
S	O	M	E			A	H	A		I	N	K
T	H	I	N		T	R	I	P		S	E	E
O	I	L	S		W	E	R	E		T	R	Y
P	O	L	E		O	D	E	S		S	O	S

CROSSWORD 152

G	A	P	E	D		S	H	E		S	A	P
A	L	I	V	E		T	O	E		O	R	E
L	I	N	E	N		O	U	R		L	I	T
				Y	A	W	N		C	O	D	E
A	P	T			M	E	D	A	L			
D	A	Y		F	E	D		W	A	V	E	D
O	R	P	H	A	N		C	A	M	E	R	A
S	T	E	A	K		F	L	Y		A	I	L
			Z	E	B	R	A			L	E	E
F	U	R	Y		R	A	P	S				
A	P	E		G	U	M		O	C	E	A	N
C	O	N		A	C	E		B	U	R	R	O
T	N	T		Y	E	S		S	E	A	T	S

CROSSWORD 153

N	I	P		A	C	H	E		W	A	D	E
A	L	I		S	L	U	G		H	U	R	L
B	L	E	S	S	I	N	G		I	T	E	M
			W	E	P	T			R	O	W	S
A	N	T	E	S		E	V	I	L			
D	A	R	E		O	D	O	R		S	A	P
D	I	A	P	E	R		T	A	C	K	L	E
S	L	Y		L	A	T	E		R	I	S	E
			P	I	L	E		M	O	T	O	R
S	C	A	R			A	S	I	A			
L	A	N	E		W	R	I	N	K	L	E	D
I	N	N	S		H	E	R	D		E	V	A
M	E	S	S		O	D	E	S		T	E	N

CROSSWORD 154

T	E	E			G	A	P			H	E	M
O	D	D		T	O	I	L		H	U	L	A
P	I	G		H	O	M	E		E	M	M	Y
	T	Y	P	E			A	T	E			
			E	N	D			A	L	E	R	T
G	A	L	A		E	R	I	C		Y	O	U
U	S	E			L	O	T			E	B	B
L	I	T		P	I	N	E		A	S	E	A
P	A	S	T	E			M	A	N			
			O	W	N			U	N	I	T	
S	P	A	R		I	R	A	N		N	O	D
P	A	I	N		N	E	X	T		N	O	R
A	N	D			E	V	E			S	K	Y

CROSSWORD 155

N	I	P		S	W	A	T		F	E	A	T
I	R	A		H	O	P	E		L	A	I	R
C	O	N		A	M	E	N		A	R	M	Y
E	N	T	I	R	E		S	A	G			
			R	E	N	T	E	R		S	K	I
A	T	L	A	S		E	S	C	A	P	E	D
W	A	I	T		P	A	T		D	U	E	L
A	P	P	E	A	R	S		S	O	N	N	Y
Y	E	S		D	E	E	P	E	R			
			A	D	S		L	E	E	R	E	D
T	R	A	Y		S	E	A	M		A	X	E
W	I	N	E		E	R	I	E		T	I	N
O	D	D	S		S	A	N	D		S	T	Y

CROSSWORD 156

L	I	D	S		P	R	O		L	A	G	S
A	C	R	E		O	A	R		E	L	L	A
B	E	E	N		O	N	E		F	L	O	W
		S	T	A	C	K		S	T	O	V	E
H	A	S		C	H	E	A	T		W	E	D
E	L	E	C	T		D	I	R	T			
R	E	S	O	R	T		D	E	A	L	E	R
			N	E	A	R		A	B	O	V	E
W	I	N		S	N	A	C	K		B	E	D
I	D	O	L	S		R	U	S	T	S		
L	A	V	A		P	E	R		I	T	E	M
T	H	E	M		E	L	S		N	E	R	O
S	O	L	E		A	Y	E		T	R	A	P

CROSSWORD 157

P	A	N		E	L	M	S		W	I	R	E
A	D	O		Y	E	A	H		A	R	I	A
D	A	N		E	D	D	Y		R	E	N	T
S	M	E	L	L		E	E	L	S			
			A	I	D		R	O	A	S	T	S
P	R	O	D	D	E	D		S	W	O	R	E
E	A	R			N	A	P			F	U	N
A	R	A	B	S		B	O	A	S	T	E	D
R	E	L	I	E	D		D	I	P			
			D	E	E	P		S	Y	R	U	P
S	A	I	D		B	O	W	L		E	G	O
A	C	R	E		T	R	E	E		A	L	L
G	E	A	R		S	E	T	S		D	Y	E

CROSSWORD 158

D	O	N	S		T	O	P		A	C	E	S
I	R	O	N		H	U	E		R	O	L	E
N	E	R	O		E	R	R		R	O	S	E
			W	I	N				O	P	E	N
G	R	E	E	N		T	H	A	W			
R	O	A	D	S		W	A	S		A	C	T
A	D	S		I	R	I	S	H		G	O	O
Y	E	T		D	A	N		O	C	E	A	N
			G	E	N	E		R	U	S	T	Y
H	U	R	L				S	E	T			
A	S	I	A		A	D	O		E	R	A	S
L	E	N	S		S	U	N		S	A	L	T
O	D	D	S		P	E	G		T	H	E	Y

CROSSWORD 159

T	I	N	E		A	R	C	H		T	I	M
O	D	O	R		W	I	R	E		O	D	E
T	O	W	N		A	D	A	M		A	L	A
			E	R	R	E	D		E	D	E	N
C	H	A	S	E	D		L	A	D			
L	A	S	T	S		T	E	N	S	E	S	T
A	R	K		T	W	I	S	T		R	I	O
W	E	S	T	E	R	N		L	E	A	R	N
			A	D	E		L	E	N	S	E	S
W	H	I	P		S	M	A	R	T			
R	O	D		S	T	A	B		E	D	G	E
A	L	E		A	L	T	O		R	U	I	N
P	E	A		P	E	E	R		S	E	N	D

CROSSWORD 160

B	L	O	W		A	P	T		T	H	A	N
R	I	P	E		B	O	O		R	O	D	E
A	N	T	E	L	O	P	E		A	W	E	D
Y	E	S		E	V	E	N	L	Y			
			D	E	E		A	I	S	L	E	S
M	I	N	O	R		K	I	D		A	L	L
E	R	I	C		G	E	L		R	I	S	E
R	I	P		B	O	Y		L	U	R	E	D
E	S	S	A	Y	S		M	E	T			
			L	E	S	S	O	N		G	A	S
T	I	N	A		I	N	N	O	C	E	N	T
O	D	O	R		P	I	E		A	N	N	E
W	A	R	M		S	P	Y		T	E	A	M

CROSSWORD 161

P	O	W		A	S	P	S		A	M	E	N
R	U	E		W	E	A	K		P	O	L	E
O	R	D	I	N	A	R	Y		R	O	S	E
			R	I	M		W	H	I	N	E	D
C	O	L	O	N			A	I	L			
U	S	I	N	G		A	R	T		B	I	B
E	L	M	S		A	D	D		J	A	D	E
S	O	B		A	L	S		T	E	L	L	S
			V	I	A			W	A	D	E	S
C	O	W	A	R	D		B	I	N			
A	H	A	S		D	O	O	R	S	T	E	P
R	I	S	E		I	D	O	L		E	G	O
T	O	P	S		N	E	T	S		A	G	E

CROSSWORD 162

N	A	G		D	E	B	T		T	A	I	L
A	L	E		I	R	O	N		A	C	R	E
B	I	N		M	I	T	T		S	H	I	N
		T	W	E	E	T			T	E	S	T
M	O	L	E	S		O	B	E	Y			
A	P	E	D		A	M	E	N		F	A	T
M	E	S	S	E	S		A	D	V	I	C	E
A	N	T		V	I	E	D		A	N	N	E
			B	E	A	N		S	T	I	E	S
A	L	S	O			G	R	A	S	S		
R	O	A	R		D	I	A	L		H	A	T
C	O	M	E		A	N	T	E		E	G	O
S	P	E	D		B	E	E	S		D	O	N

CROSSWORD 163

K	I	T	E		O	P	E	N		S	A	P
I	R	O	N		D	A	R	E		E	Y	E
C	A	N	T		D	R	A	W		S	E	W
K	N	E	E	L		A	S	S	E	S		
			R	I	N	D			R	I	S	E
M	A	D		N	O	E	L		I	O	W	A
E	V	E	N	T	S		A	R	E	N	A	S
M	I	C	E		E	L	S	E		S	T	Y
O	D	O	R			I	T	E	M			
		R	O	S	E	S		L	A	S	S	O
S	P	A		O	A	T	H		S	H	O	W
E	A	T		F	R	E	E		T	O	R	E
A	L	E		A	N	D	Y		S	E	T	S

CROSSWORD 164

G	R	I	N		A	R	T	S		C	A	T
L	O	R	E		H	E	A	T		A	G	O
A	L	A	S		A	S	I	A		N	E	T
D	E	N	T	S		I	L	L		A	D	S
			S	A	N	G		K	I	D		
T	E	E		L	O	N	E		V	I	E	D
I	N	V	I	T	E		V	O	Y	A	G	E
N	E	E	D		L	E	E	R		N	O	W
		R	O	W		S	N	A	P			
S	T	Y		A	R	C		L	A	S	S	O
T	O	O		S	O	A	P		S	H	O	W
I	N	N		P	O	P	E		T	I	L	E
R	Y	E		S	T	E	W		A	P	E	D

CROSSWORD 165

H	O	P	E		F	R	O	G		L	I	T
A	W	A	Y		L	E	N	A		E	G	O
M	E	R	E		O	N	E	S		A	L	A
			S	C	A	T				S	O	S
P	A	T		I	T	E	M		S	H	O	T
A	L	O	U	D		D	A	M	P			
W	I	N	T	E	R		T	O	I	L	E	D
			A	R	I	D		I	T	A	L	Y
H	A	S	H		G	A	G	S		D	I	E
A	G	E				N	E	T	S			
L	A	W		M	I	C	E		W	A	I	T
V	I	E		O	D	E	S		A	I	D	E
E	N	D		W	A	D	E		P	R	O	D

CROSSWORD 166

F	O	G		S	H	O	W		S	P	A	R
E	R	A		H	O	P	E		C	O	L	E
W	E	L	C	O	M	E	D		A	L	A	S
			L	E	E	R		F	R	O	N	T
A	L	S	O			A	W	A	Y			
L	O	P	S		U	S	E	D		B	A	A
P	R	I	E	S	T		L	E	M	O	N	S
S	E	T		N	A	I	L		O	I	N	K
			J	O	H	N			A	L	E	S
A	R	R	O	W		S	O	F	T			
P	A	U	L		D	I	V	I	S	I	O	N
E	V	I	L		A	D	E	S		T	W	O
D	E	N	Y		D	E	N	T		S	E	W

CROSSWORD 167

N	O	W		F	L	E	E		D	E	S	I
A	R	E		R	O	L	L		Y	E	A	R
B	E	D	R	O	O	M	S		E	L	L	A
			A	S	K			R	I	S	E	N
S	P	L	I	T		A	L	A	N			
L	O	A	D		S	W	I	N	G	I	N	G
A	L	I		B	E	A	S	T		M	A	E
P	O	R	T	R	A	I	T		S	P	I	N
			W	E	S	T		A	I	S	L	E
M	O	P	E	D			D	I	D			
E	V	E	N		S	T	U	D	E	N	T	S
M	E	E	T		P	A	C	E		E	W	E
O	N	L	Y		A	R	K	S		T	O	E

CROSSWORD 168

K	I	T		S	O	A	P		D	A	S	H
I	R	A		W	I	N	E		E	C	H	O
N	E	T		A	L	D	A		S	T	O	P
		T	O	N	Y			V	E	S	T	S
C	R	O	W			S	P	A	R			
L	I	O	N	S		T	I	P	T	O	E	D
A	P	E		P	H	O	T	O		R	A	Y
P	E	D	D	L	E	R		R	I	N	S	E
			R	I	N	K			V	A	T	S
A	W	A	I	T			S	E	E	M		
R	O	L	E		A	S	I	A		E	R	A
M	O	S	S		R	I	D	S		N	U	N
S	L	O	T		T	R	E	E		T	E	N

CROSSWORD 169

P	L	O	T		C	A	I	N		C	R	Y
R	A	V	E		A	L	D	A		H	U	E
O	N	E	S		T	A	L	K		I	D	A
D	E	N	T	S		R	Y	E		P	E	R
				A	R	M		D	A	M		
W	A	S		L	O	S	T		G	U	S	T
A	W	A	I	T	S		O	P	E	N	E	R
Y	E	L	L		E	A	R	L		K	E	Y
		A	L	S		S	E	A				
P	A	R		U	G	H		N	E	S	T	S
A	L	I		R	O	O	F		G	L	U	E
U	S	E		F	A	R	E		G	O	N	E
L	O	S		S	L	E	D		S	W	A	M

CROSSWORD 170

F	E	L	T		A	R	M	S		T	A	B
L	A	I	R		L	E	A	P		I	C	E
A	C	N	E		S	C	R	E	A	M	E	D
T	H	E	N			E	E	L	S			
			D	A	W	N		L	I	G	H	T
A	S	H		S	E	T	S		D	O	O	R
S	P	E	A	K	S		P	L	E	A	S	E
P	O	R	T		T	R	U	E		L	E	E
S	T	O	O	D		A	N	T	E			
			M	I	S	T			L	A	S	S
P	R	E	S	E	N	T	S		E	C	H	O
O	U	R		G	U	L	L		C	R	O	W
P	E	R		O	B	E	Y		T	E	E	N

CROSSWORD 171

L	A	B	S		L	A	N	E		H	E	M
E	V	E	N		I	D	O	L		I	D	A
D	A	T	E		N	E	R	O		T	I	M
			E	Y	E	S		P	A	S	T	A
F	R	O	Z	E	N		D	E	W			
R	A	V	E	N		O	R	D	E	R	E	D
E	R	A			F	L	Y			A	L	E
D	E	L	A	Y	E	D		S	E	N	S	E
			D	A	D		L	O	N	G	E	R
T	H	R	O	W		V	A	S	T			
H	O	E		N	E	E	D		I	D	L	E
A	L	I		E	V	I	L		R	A	I	D
T	E	N		D	A	L	E		E	N	D	S

CROSSWORD 172

T	R	I	P		H	I	S		D	R	A	B
H	I	R	E		A	S	P		O	I	L	Y
A	S	K	S		T	R	I	A	N	G	L	E
W	E	S	T			A	N	D				
			S	I	Z	E		D	U	M	P	S
S	K	I		D	O	L	L		G	O	A	T
I	N	D	I	A	N		A	S	H	O	R	E
R	O	L	L		E	A	C	H		D	E	W
S	W	E	L	L		V	E	E	R			
				I	R	E			A	L	P	S
S	C	A	L	D	I	N	G		R	O	L	E
P	A	P	A		D	U	E		E	V	E	N
A	R	T	S		S	E	E		R	E	A	D

CROSSWORD 173

G	O	O		S	T	A	G		W	E	S	T
R	I	B		T	I	N	E		A	C	H	E
A	L	S		A	N	T	E		S	H	O	E
B	Y	E		G	A	L			P	O	T	S
		R	Y	E		E	E	L	S			
G	I	V	E		U	R	G	E		P	E	W
A	R	E	N	A	S		G	E	O	R	G	E
P	A	D		H	E	R	S		W	O	O	D
			M	A	D	E		P	E	P		
A	C	M	E			P	A	R		O	R	E
D	O	E	S		B	A	B	E		S	A	D
A	L	A	S		A	I	L	S		E	V	E
M	A	N	Y		A	D	E	S		D	E	N

CROSSWORD 174

S	W	A	P		A	R	C	S		E	D	S
C	O	M	E		D	A	R	T		D	I	E
O	V	E	R		S	P	A	R		I	C	E
T	E	N	S	E		S	W	E	E	T	E	N
			O	A	K		L	A	Y			
S	L	A	N	T	E	D		M	E	A	N	T
O	I	L			G	A	Y			W	O	O
S	P	E	N	D		N	E	A	T	E	S	T
			I	R	K		A	I	R			
S	L	O	P	I	N	G		M	A	J	O	R
T	A	B		L	E	E	S		C	A	P	E
I	V	E		L	E	N	A		E	D	E	N
R	A	Y		S	L	E	D		D	E	N	T

CROSSWORD 175

E	D	E	N		T	W	O		S	P	I	T
G	A	V	E		R	A	Y		H	E	R	O
G	R	E	W		A	D	S		I	T	E	M
S	E	N	S	E	D		T	O	P			
				R	E	B	E	L		W	H	O
A	R	M	O	R		O	R	D	E	R	E	D
L	E	A	D		L	A	S		R	A	R	E
T	A	R	D	I	E	R		T	A	P	E	S
O	R	E		D	O	D	G	E				
			M	O	P		R	A	I	D	E	D
A	C	M	E		A	D	E		T	A	X	I
D	U	E	S		R	O	E		C	L	A	P
D	E	N	S		D	E	N		H	E	M	S

CROSSWORD 176

F	I	B	S		A	L	P	S		S	H	Y
A	D	A	M		D	I	E	T		W	E	E
N	O	N	E		D	E	E	R		I	R	A
		D	A	N		D	R	E	A	M	E	R
S	N	A	R	E	D		S	A	G			
L	O	G		T	U	B		M	O	R	A	L
U	S	E			E	Y	E			A	C	E
R	E	S	T	S		E	L	F		I	N	N
			A	N	T		M	A	G	N	E	T
B	E	D	R	O	O	M		T	A	C		
I	R	E		O	W	E	S		S	O	D	A
T	I	N		Z	E	R	O		P	A	I	R
S	E	T		E	D	E	N		S	T	E	M

CROSSWORD 177

F	A	N	S		C	O	N		S	I	T	E
O	V	A	L		H	U	E		T	R	A	Y
R	A	G	E		I	R	E		R	O	L	E
			E	L	M		D	R	I	N	K	S
W	E	A	P	O	N		S	A	P			
A	R	C		W	E	E		P	E	T	E	R
R	I	T	A		Y	A	P		D	O	V	E
N	E	S	T	S		T	E	E		A	I	L
			L	I	D		A	V	I	D	L	Y
S	A	F	A	R	I		C	A	T			
I	R	I	S		A	S	H		E	R	A	S
L	I	V	E		R	U	E		M	U	L	E
O	D	E	S		Y	E	S		S	T	E	W

CROSSWORD 178

L	U	R	E	■	O	A	T	S	■	B	A	D
A	S	I	A	■	F	L	I	P	■	R	U	E
T	E	N	S	■	F	A	M	E	■	A	N	N
E	D	G	E	■	■	S	E	E	■	I	T	S
■	■	■	D	I	S	K	■	D	A	D	■	■
A	L	S	■	R	E	A	L	■	B	I	T	E
R	E	P	E	A	T	■	O	P	E	N	E	D
T	E	E	N	■	S	T	A	R	■	G	A	S
■	■	A	D	O	■	O	D	O	R	■	■	■
I	R	K	■	S	P	A	■	■	E	A	S	T
D	O	E	■	C	O	S	T	■	B	L	U	E
E	A	R	■	A	L	T	O	■	E	D	E	N
A	D	S	■	R	O	S	E	■	L	A	S	T

CROSSWORD 179

K	I	D	S	■	R	U	N	■	A	N	T	E
E	D	I	T	■	A	P	E	■	L	E	A	D
P	L	E	A	■	D	O	C	■	B	A	N	G
T	E	S	T	■	I	N	K	■	U	R	G	E
■	■	■	E	G	O	■	T	O	M	■	■	■
P	R	I	D	E	■	A	I	D	■	J	O	B
O	U	R	■	E	R	R	E	D	■	O	W	E
P	E	A	■	S	E	T	■	E	A	G	L	E
■	■	■	■	H	E	N	■	A	R	C	■	■
S	H	O	O	■	E	L	I	■	T	E	D	S
H	E	A	R	■	W	A	R	■	O	R	A	L
I	R	K	S	■	A	T	E	■	R	I	T	A
N	O	S	E	■	L	E	S	■	S	E	E	P

CROSSWORD 180

P	L	E	A	■	B	E	E	■	A	S	P	S
E	A	R	N	■	O	L	D	■	L	O	O	P
T	W	I	G	■	R	I	G	■	L	A	K	E
S	N	E	E	Z	E	■	E	L	O	P	E	D
■	■	■	R	I	D	■	S	E	W	■	■	■
B	A	N	■	P	O	D	■	D	E	V	I	L
E	X	A	M	■	M	O	B	■	D	A	R	E
T	E	P	E	E	■	C	A	N	■	N	E	T
■	■	■	E	V	A	■	S	U	M	■	■	■
S	M	O	K	E	R	■	K	N	I	G	H	T
C	A	P	E	■	O	W	E	■	G	L	O	W
A	D	E	S	■	M	A	T	■	H	E	R	O
T	E	N	T	■	A	D	S	■	T	E	N	S

CROSSWORD 181

C	O	P	■	T	H	A	T	■	S	L	U	R
A	W	E	■	R	O	L	E	■	N	O	S	E
B	E	N	■	A	R	I	D	■	O	V	E	N
■	■	N	A	P	S	■	■	■	R	E	S	T
I	R	A	N	■	E	L	A	T	E	■	■	■
D	E	N	Y	■	■	E	R	A	■	S	T	Y
E	A	T	■	S	W	A	M	P	■	T	O	E
A	D	S	■	E	A	R	■	■	F	A	W	N
■	■	■	F	E	R	N	S	■	I	N	N	S
S	P	A	R	■	■	■	T	E	N	D	■	■
H	A	L	O	■	F	O	O	L	■	A	L	S
O	N	E	S	■	O	W	N	S	■	R	A	H
T	E	S	T	■	G	L	E	E	■	D	Y	E

CROSSWORD 182

H	E	L	P	■	C	A	N	■	C	A	R	E
O	D	O	R	■	O	N	E	■	O	R	A	L
P	I	N	E	■	A	N	T	■	P	I	N	S
S	T	E	A	M	S	■	■	H	E	D	G	E
■	■	■	C	U	T	■	R	O	D	■	■	■
B	A	T	H	S	■	M	A	N	■	O	I	L
A	L	E	■	I	D	A	H	O	■	A	V	A
R	A	N	■	C	A	T	■	R	A	K	E	D
■	■	■	Y	A	M	■	P	E	R	■	■	■
T	O	T	A	L	■	■	A	D	O	R	E	D
U	P	O	N	■	W	A	S	■	M	I	C	E
B	E	A	K	■	A	C	T	■	A	C	H	E
E	N	D	S	■	Y	E	A	■	S	H	O	P

CROSSWORD 183

E	C	H	O	■	W	H	A	T	■	H	A	S
R	O	O	M	■	H	E	I	R	■	A	L	A
R	O	L	E	■	I	N	S	I	S	T	E	D
S	P	E	N	D	S	■	L	A	W	■	■	■
■	■	■	S	I	P	■	E	L	E	C	T	S
I	T	S	■	N	E	T	■	S	P	L	I	T
T	I	P	S	■	R	A	T	■	T	U	N	A
E	L	A	T	E	■	G	A	P	■	B	A	G
M	E	T	E	R	S	■	L	A	D	■	■	■
■	■	■	E	A	T	■	L	L	A	M	A	S
H	A	N	D	S	O	M	E	■	D	O	M	E
E	G	O	■	E	V	E	S	■	D	R	E	W
R	O	W	■	R	E	N	T	■	Y	E	N	S

CROSSWORD 184

H	A	T	E	■	D	E	A	R	■	S	P	A
E	V	E	R	■	E	R	I	E	■	T	A	C
Y	E	A	R	■	S	E	L	L	■	A	L	I
■	■	■	E	P	I	C	■	A	I	R	E	D
L	I	N	D	A	■	T	O	Y	S	■	■	■
O	N	E	■	W	A	S	P	■	L	A	M	E
A	T	T	E	N	D	■	E	Y	E	L	I	D
D	O	S	E	■	A	N	N	E	■	E	N	D
■	■	■	L	I	M	O	■	L	U	C	K	Y
T	O	A	S	T	■	T	A	P	S	■	■	■
U	R	N	■	E	R	I	N	■	H	I	S	S
B	A	T	■	M	I	C	E	■	E	C	H	O
E	L	S	■	S	P	E	W	■	R	E	E	D

CROSSWORD 185

				A	D	D		C	O	P	E	
P	A	N		T	O	E		O	V	E	N	
O	R	E		E	L	F		M	E	N	D	
N	E	A	R	■	T	I	M	E	R			
D	A	T	E	S	■	N	O	T	■	B	O	W
			P	O	S	E	S	■	L	I	N	E
C	E	M	E	N	T	■	E	R	O	D	E	D
O	V	A	L	■	R	O	S	E	S			
B	E	D	■	D	A	M	■	D	E	P	O	T
			T	O	W	E	R	■	S	O	L	E
	S	L	O	T		L	A	D		L	E	E
	P	A	R	E		E	V	A		L	O	N
	A	G	E	S		T	E	D				

CROSSWORD 186

S	P	E	E	D	■	P	A	L	■	L	O	P
E	A	R	L	Y	■	A	L	I	■	A	X	E
A	W	A	K	E	■	S	I	P	■	W	E	T
■	■	■	■	D	U	S	K	■	A	N	N	E
S	O	D	■	■	S	E	E	P	S	■	■	■
I	D	O	■	F	E	D	■	L	I	A	R	S
T	O	O	T	E	D	■	R	E	A	G	A	N
E	R	R	O	R	■	V	I	A	■	E	G	O
■	■	■	U	N	T	I	L	■	■	D	E	W
S	L	U	R	■	W	O	E	S	■	■	■	■
L	A	G	■	A	I	L	■	A	P	A	R	T
O	I	L	■	I	C	E	■	P	E	C	A	N
T	R	Y	■	M	E	T	■	S	W	E	P	T

CROSSWORD 187

F	A	T	E	■	S	E	W	■	S	A	P	S
L	I	E	S	■	A	Y	E	■	C	L	A	P
A	D	E	S	■	N	E	T	■	R	A	R	E
T	E	N	A	N	T	S	■	M	I	N	E	D
■	■	■	Y	E	A	■	G	A	P	■	■	■
F	A	L	S	E	■	W	A	I	T	E	R	S
A	G	O	■	D	W	E	L	L	■	G	O	O
R	E	P	L	I	E	D	■	M	E	O	W	S
■	■	■	O	N	E	■	P	E	N	■	■	■
T	H	I	N	G	■	G	E	N	T	L	E	R
H	A	N	D	■	I	R	A	■	R	A	V	E
A	L	T	O	■	D	O	C	■	E	V	E	N
N	O	O	N	■	O	W	E	■	E	A	S	T

CROSSWORD 188

M	A	T	■	S	P	A	T	■	S	L	A	M
E	W	E	■	W	A	V	E	■	P	A	C	E
T	E	E	N	A	G	E	D	■	A	I	M	S
■	■	■	O	P	E	N	■	S	I	D	E	S
A	S	P	S	■	■	U	P	O	N	■	■	■
R	O	L	E	■	T	E	A	R	■	S	E	W
C	L	O	S	E	R	■	R	E	M	O	V	E
H	O	W	■	A	U	N	T	■	O	W	E	D
■	■	■	T	R	E	E	■	■	I	N	N	S
A	W	F	U	L	■	V	O	W	S	■	■	■
R	E	I	N	■	J	A	N	I	T	O	R	S
M	E	R	E	■	E	D	E	N	■	D	O	E
S	P	E	D	■	T	A	S	K	■	D	Y	E

CROSSWORD 189

N	I	L	E	■	A	S	P	■	S	T	A	R
I	R	O	N	■	B	E	E	■	P	O	N	Y
C	A	N	T	■	E	V	E	R	Y	O	N	E
K	N	E	E	■	■	E	R	A	■	■	■	■
■	■	■	R	O	A	R	■	W	H	E	A	T
A	D	S	■	D	Y	E	D	■	I	D	L	E
D	E	C	I	D	E	■	A	D	M	I	T	S
D	E	A	R	■	S	O	R	E	■	T	O	T
S	P	R	A	Y	■	R	E	N	T	■	■	■
■	■	■	■	A	H	A	■	■	A	P	E	S
S	H	A	R	P	E	N	S	■	F	A	D	E
I	O	W	A	■	A	G	O	■	F	R	E	E
P	E	E	P	■	P	E	N	■	Y	E	N	S

CROSSWORD 190

E	D	I	T		D	I	P		S	L	O	W
R	U	D	E		O	D	E		C	A	R	E
R	E	L	E	A	S	E	D		A	G	E	D
S	L	Y		L	E	A	D	E	R			
			A	D	S		L	A	Y	I	N	G
C	H	I	N	A		N	E	T		T	O	E
H	A	N	D		P	O	D		D	E	N	T
A	R	T		A	L	S		T	I	M	E	S
P	E	O	P	L	E		S	H	E			
			A	L	A	S	K	A		T	A	P
A	C	T	S		S	U	I	T	C	A	S	E
S	O	O	T		E	R	R		A	L	P	S
H	O	M	E		S	E	T		R	E	S	T

CROSSWORD 191

I	C	E		A	R	T		D	R	I	P	S
N	O	R		S	U	E		R	O	D	E	O
N	O	I	S	I	E	R		A	W	A	R	D
S	P	E	E	D		M	A	P				
			W	E	T		L	E	A	P	E	D
A	R	M			O	R	E		S	O	L	E
D	E	A	L		O	U	R		H	O	S	E
D	A	R	E		T	N	T			R	E	D
S	L	E	E	V	E		S	L	Y			
				O	D	D		Y	E	L	L	S
S	T	R	A	W		I	N	I	T	I	A	L
T	W	I	C	E		M	A	N		A	V	E
Y	O	D	E	L		E	G	G		M	A	D

CROSSWORD 192

C	A	S	H		D	E	W		S	T	O	P
R	I	L	E		A	S	H		T	A	X	I
E	D	E	N		S	K	I		A	M	E	N
W	E	E		S	H	I	N		G	E	N	T
		P	A	N		M	E	R	E			
A	S	I	D	E		O	D	E		F	I	B
C	A	N	O	E				C	A	R	R	Y
E	G	G		Z	I	P		A	L	I	K	E
			G	E	N	E		L	A	G		
W	I	S	E		H	E	A	L		H	A	S
H	O	P	E		A	L	P		I	T	C	H
O	W	E	S		L	E	E		N	E	R	O
M	A	D	E		E	D	S		K	N	E	E

CROSSWORD 193

S	E	A	L		B	A	T	H		B	R	O
I	D	L	E		O	H	I	O		R	I	D
R	I	T	A		Y	A	R	N		A	D	O
S	T	O	V	E	S		E	E	R	I	E	R
			E	A	C	H		Y	E	N		
B	A	R		R	O	A	D		D	I	A	L
A	L	E		L	U	R	E	S		E	V	E
G	A	P	E		T	E	N	T		R	A	T
		E	L	F		S	T	A	G			
S	N	A	K	E	S		I	R	I	S	E	S
H	U	T		A	L	P	S		L	O	R	E
O	D	E		S	O	R	T		L	A	I	N
W	E	D		T	W	O	S		S	P	E	D

CROSSWORD 194

R	I	P	S		B	L	O	W		B	I	T
O	R	A	L		R	U	D	E		A	D	O
W	A	D	E		U	S	E	D		T	E	A
			D	A	S	H				H	A	S
P	A	R		T	H	E	N		P	E	S	T
E	X	A	C	T		R	O	S	E			
R	E	P	A	I	R		W	E	T	T	E	R
			S	C	A	T		W	E	A	V	E
L	I	S	T		T	U	B	E		B	A	D
A	N	T				N	U	D	E			
I	D	O		T	H	I	S		A	L	S	O
R	I	O		A	U	N	T		R	E	A	L
S	A	D		P	E	G	S		L	E	N	D

CROSSWORD 195

I	C	E		E	C	H	O		S	C	A	T
D	A	Y		F	L	E	W		H	E	I	R
O	R	E		F	I	R	E		O	N	L	Y
L	E	S	S	O	N	S		C	O	T		
			A	R	T		B	A	K	E	R	Y
P	R	I	N	T		F	A	R		R	U	E
L	O	N	G		B	I	N		T	E	L	L
A	P	T		W	A	X		Y	O	D	E	L
N	E	E	D	E	D		D	E	W			
		R	I	B		G	R	A	N	D	M	A
A	D	E	S		L	I	A	R		R	U	G
D	U	S	K		E	V	I	L		A	L	E
D	O	T	S		D	E	N	Y		B	E	D

CROSSWORD 196

R	I	D		S	A	M	E		S	T	A	B
O	D	E		C	L	A	Y		T	O	L	L
L	O	S		R	A	T	E		A	U	T	O
E	L	I		A	N	T		A	R	R	O	W
		R	I	M		E	L	M				
S	P	I	N		E	R	I	E		C	A	B
O	I	N	K	E	D		E	N	T	I	R	E
B	E	G		V	I	E	S		O	N	C	E
				I	T	S		D	E	N		
S	M	A	L	L		C	U	E		A	I	L
L	E	N	A		C	A	S	E		M	O	O
A	R	T	S		A	P	E	D		O	W	N
T	E	E	S		T	E	D	S		N	A	G

CROSSWORD 197

T	A	G	S		S	P	A		S	W	A	N
O	X	E	N		A	L	L		T	R	U	E
P	E	T	E		L	O	T		R	E	N	T
			E	L	A	T	E		A	N	T	S
A	M	A	Z	E	D		R	O	W			
D	I	N	E	S		H	E	Y		F	A	D
O	L	D		S	L	E	D	S		A	N	Y
S	K	Y		E	A	R		T	W	I	N	E
			E	N	D		F	E	A	R	E	D
R	I	T	A		D	O	O	R	S			
O	D	E	S		E	R	R		H	A	T	E
S	O	R	E		R	A	T		E	V	I	L
E	L	M	S		S	L	Y		R	A	C	K

CROSSWORD 198

P	A	R	T	S		R	A	G		C	A	T
A	B	O	U	T		E	L	I		A	S	H
L	E	D	G	E		C	O	N		V	I	E
				M	O	O	N		S	E	A	M
E	L	F			D	R	E	A	M			
C	O	O		P	O	D		B	U	I	L	D
H	A	R	B	O	R		D	E	G	R	E	E
O	D	D	E	R		O	I	L		A	N	N
			S	T	A	I	R			N	A	T
T	I	N	T		A	N	T	S				
A	D	E		A	R	K		P	E	A	R	L
P	E	A		W	O	E		A	R	G	U	E
E	A	R		E	N	D		T	R	E	N	D

CROSSWORD 199

P	A	Y		F	L	A	T		S	T	A	B
A	L	E		R	I	P	E		M	A	M	A
P	A	N		A	N	T	E		O	X	E	N
A	S	S	U	M	E			A	G	I	N	G
			T	E	N	D	E	R				
E	D	I	T	S		W	A	T	C	H	E	D
L	U	R	E		B	E	T		H	A	V	E
F	E	A	R	F	U	L		W	O	M	E	N
				A	S	L	E	E	P			
S	P	O	O	N			L	A	S	S	I	E
L	A	W	N		C	H	A	P		T	O	Y
A	N	N	E		A	U	T	O		A	W	E
M	E	S	S		T	E	E	N		G	A	S

CROSSWORD 200

I	D	L	E		T	A	C		A	P	E	D
N	E	O	N		A	I	R		D	O	V	E
T	A	R	T		S	L	Y		D	R	E	W
O	L	D	E	S	T			A	S	P		
			R	H	Y	M	E	S		O	I	L
S	E	N	S	E		I	R	K		I	R	A
O	R	E			W	A	R			S	A	N
R	I	G		H	E	M		S	P	E	N	D
T	E	A		E	D	I	T	O	R			
		T	A	R			A	N	I	M	A	L
A	R	I	D		B	O	X		C	O	M	E
L	A	V	A		A	D	E		E	V	E	N
S	T	E	M		R	E	D		S	E	N	D

CROSSWORD 201

P	E	A		S	A	L	T		S	P	U	N
A	L	P		A	L	A	N		C	A	P	E
L	I	T	T	L	E	S	T		R	I	O	T
			E	A	R	S		F	E	R	N	S
R	O	B	E	R	T		S	E	E			
E	N	E	M	Y		O	P	E	N	I	N	G
A	C	T			I	D	A			T	O	E
R	E	S	P	O	N	D		C	H	E	S	T
			E	L	K		C	H	I	M	E	S
A	R	M	E	D		M	O	A	N			
N	A	I	L		J	A	N	I	T	O	R	S
N	I	N	E		A	M	E	N		D	U	O
S	L	E	D		B	A	S	S		E	N	D

CROSSWORD 202

H	E	Y		B	R	A	G		C	H	E	W
A	V	E		L	A	V	A		R	I	D	E
M	E	S	S	A	G	E	S		U	R	G	E
			A	M	E	N			S	E	E	P
A	L	O	N	E		U	N	I	T			
L	E	N	T		F	E	E	D		A	G	E
P	A	L	A	C	E		W	O	O	D	E	N
S	K	Y		O	A	T	S		W	A	N	D
			B	O	T	H		D	I	M	E	S
A	L	T	O			R	A	I	N			
S	O	A	R		Y	O	U	N	G	E	S	T
P	O	K	E		A	N	N	E		G	E	E
S	P	E	D		P	E	T	S		O	W	N

CROSSWORD 203

H	O	S	E		A	R	C	H		T	O	W
E	V	I	L		S	H	O	E		O	D	E
M	A	R	S		P	I	L	L		M	O	P
S	L	E	E	T		N	A	P		A	R	T
				E	G	O		S	A	T		
S	I	N		L	A	S	T		I	O	W	A
T	R	A	I	L	S		A	S	L	E	E	P
Y	A	R	D		P	E	C	K		S	E	T
		R	O	Y		S	K	I				
S	P	A		E	L	K		T	A	M	E	D
H	O	T		L	A	I	R		C	A	V	E
O	N	E		L	I	M	E		T	R	E	E
O	D	D		S	N	O	B		S	E	N	D

CROSSWORD 204

E	G	G	S		A	C	E		S	T	A	G
D	A	R	E		W	A	X		T	A	L	E
E	V	E	N		A	L	P		O	X	E	N
N	E	W	S		I	L	L		R	I	S	E
			E	A	T		A	S	K			
L	I	N	D	A		S	I	P		A	G	O
I	D	A		R	H	I	N	O		P	E	W
T	O	Y		O	U	R		K	N	E	E	L
			I	N	N		S	E	A			
L	I	P	S		T	W	O		P	R	O	D
A	D	E	S		E	R	A		P	A	P	A
M	E	N	U		R	A	P		E	V	E	R
B	A	S	E		S	P	Y		D	E	N	T

CROSSWORD 205

S	P	I	T		A	S	P		S	T	O	P
A	L	T	O		P	E	A		H	A	R	E
L	E	E	R		T	E	N	D	E	R	E	R
T	A	M	E	R		S	E	A				
				A	L	A		B	A	T	H	S
D	U	G		I	O	W	A		R	E	E	L
E	R	R	A	N	D		C	A	M	E	R	A
A	G	E	D		E	A	R	N		N	O	T
N	E	W	E	R		P	E	T				
				A	L	P		S	M	A	S	H
T	O	M	A	T	O	E	S		E	C	H	O
O	D	O	R		R	A	P		O	H	I	O
W	E	P	T		D	R	Y		W	E	N	T

CROSSWORD 206

R	O	S	E		H	E	M		S	P	I	T
I	D	E	A		A	V	A		T	O	R	E
T	E	E	T	E	R	E	D		A	L	A	N
A	S	K		Y	E	N		I	R	O	N	S
			T	E	S	T	E	D				
F	A	I	R				A	L	A	S	K	A
A	D	V	I	S	E		R	E	P	A	I	D
D	E	E	P	E	R				E	N	D	S
				T	A	S	T	E	S			
W	A	S	P	S		P	A	L		T	A	B
I	N	T	O		M	A	N	I	C	U	R	E
S	N	I	P		A	R	K		A	N	T	E
H	E	R	S		Y	E	S		R	E	S	T

CROSSWORD 207

E	N	D	S		O	P	E	N		T	I	N
R	I	O	T		F	I	V	E		O	R	E
A	C	N	E		F	R	E	E		M	O	O
S	E	E	P			A	N	D		A	N	N
			S	C	O	T		S	A	T		
L	O	T		A	B	E	L		L	O	G	S
E	U	R	O	P	E		A	S	L	E	E	P
D	R	A	W		Y	A	N	K		S	T	Y
		I	L	L		L	E	I	S			
P	A	N		A	H	A			N	A	P	S
A	L	E		M	A	S	H		A	C	R	E
U	S	E		B	I	K	E		C	H	E	W
L	O	S		S	L	A	M		K	E	Y	S

CROSSWORD 208

E	D	I	T		S	I	P	S		A	C	T
L	I	N	E		C	O	L	T		L	A	Y
M	A	T	S		A	W	A	Y		A	S	P
S	L	O	T		R	A	Y		A	N	T	E
			E	L	F		E	N	D			
T	R	A	D	E		P	R	I	E	S	T	S
O	U	R		A	R	O	S	E		P	I	E
E	N	T	E	R	E	D		C	R	A	N	E
			A	N	N		B	E	E			
S	P	A	R		E	V	A		A	N	T	S
C	A	R		I	W	I	N		P	A	R	E
A	I	M		W	E	E	D		E	V	E	N
T	R	Y		O	D	D	S		D	Y	E	D

CROSSWORD 209

C	A	R	T		C	O	B		A	L	S	O
O	D	O	R		O	W	E		R	O	A	D
T	A	L	E		A	N	D		M	O	L	D
S	M	E	A	R	S		R	H	Y	M	E	S
			T	A	T	T	O	O				
A	L	L	E	Y		W	O	W		Y	A	P
L	O	A	D		R	I	M		D	E	L	I
I	T	S		T	A	C		F	E	A	S	T
				N	I	E	C	E	S			
W	A	I	S	T	S		H	E	E	D	E	D
A	C	R	E		I	D	O		R	A	V	E
S	H	O	T		N	O	R		T	R	E	E
H	E	N	S		S	E	E		S	E	N	D

CROSSWORD 210

P	E	G	S		S	E	W		T	H	A	W
I	R	A	N		A	V	A		H	O	B	O
E	A	S	E		L	E	T		R	O	L	E
			E	R	A	S	E		O	D	E	S
A	M	A	Z	E	D		R	O	B			
R	E	N	E	W		H	E	R		I	V	E
T	N	T		A	S	I	D	E		R	A	G
S	U	E		R	O	D		G	O	I	N	G
			A	D	O		H	O	R	S	E	S
S	M	O	G		T	R	E	N	D			
T	A	X	I		H	E	N		E	D	E	N
A	M	E	N		E	A	R		R	U	L	E
G	A	N	G		D	R	Y		S	O	F	T

CROSSWORD 211

K	I	T	S		A	L	A	N		A	R	C
E	R	I	E		R	O	D	E		R	A	H
G	E	N	E		M	U	S	T		I	V	E
			M	O	O	D				S	E	A
B	A	T		C	R	E	W		G	E	N	T
A	D	O	R	E		R	A	K	E			
R	E	P	E	A	T		G	I	A	N	T	S
			S	N	A	P		C	R	O	O	K
S	W	A	T		R	A	N	K		R	O	Y
W	O	W				L	A	S	T			
E	R	A		S	L	A	M		A	L	D	A
A	R	K		P	A	C	E		N	E	A	R
R	Y	E		A	G	E	D		K	E	N	T

CROSSWORD 212

S	H	E		C	A	S	T		A	R	K	S
P	U	N		A	L	T	O		J	A	I	L
Y	E	T		B	A	R	N		A	N	T	E
		R	H	I	N	O		I	R	K	E	D
C	H	A	I	N		L	A	D				
R	I	N	G		G	L	U	E		M	O	W
A	R	C	H	E	R		N	A	T	I	V	E
B	E	E		R	I	O	T		O	N	E	S
				I	N	N		P	R	I	N	T
D	R	A	P	E		I	R	O	N	S		
I	O	W	A		B	O	I	L		T	A	B
S	P	A	T		A	N	N	E		E	Y	E
K	E	Y	S		A	S	K	S		R	E	D

CROSSWORD 213

C	A	M	P		F	A	C	T		B	E	G
O	D	O	R		I	D	L	E		A	X	E
W	A	V	E		B	E	A	M		S	A	N
S	M	E	A	R		S	U	P	R	E	M	E
			C	U	E		S	T	A	B		
N	I	G	H	T	L	Y		S	W	A	T	S
O	D	E				F	A	N		L	O	T
S	O	N	G	S		P	A	R	S	L	E	Y
		T	A	P	S		G	U	M			
W	A	L	L	E	T	S		N	I	C	K	S
H	U	E		N	E	A	R		L	A	N	E
I	T	S		D	E	L	I		E	V	E	N
P	O	T		S	L	E	D		D	E	E	D

CROSSWORD 214

L	I	M	E		C	A	S	H		S	L	Y
A	D	O	S		A	C	H	E		L	E	E
M	O	P	S		V	E	A	L		I	N	N
P	L	E	A	S	E		L	L	A	M	A	S
			Y	A	M		L	O	G			
W	H	I	S	P	E	R		S	O	A	P	S
H	E	R			N	A	G			L	I	P
O	M	E	N	S		P	A	R	S	L	E	Y
			A	P	T		R	U	T			
P	R	A	Y	E	R		M	E	A	D	O	W
L	I	D		N	O	T	E		L	O	D	E
A	P	E		D	O	W	N		E	V	E	S
Y	E	S		S	P	O	T		R	E	S	T

CROSSWORD 215

R	I	T	A		A	P	E		S	M	O	G
O	R	A	L		G	A	L		C	O	V	E
L	O	R	E		R	Y	E		A	L	A	N
E	N	T	R	E	E		C	A	N	D	L	E
			T	R	E	A	T	S				
R	A	R	E	R		P	E	P		H	I	S
O	W	E	D		S	A	D		A	U	T	O
W	E	D		F	A	R		P	R	E	S	S
				O	U	T	F	I	T			
B	R	I	N	G	S		R	E	I	G	N	S
A	I	D	E		A	T	E		S	L	I	P
B	L	O	W		G	E	E		T	U	N	A
E	E	L	S		E	N	D		S	E	E	N

CROSSWORD 216

J	A	D	E		S	P	A		P	R	A	Y
O	B	E	Y		N	O	S		H	O	L	E
G	E	N	E	R	O	U	S		O	W	L	S
S	L	Y		A	R	T	I	S	T			
			H	I	T		S	H	O	V	E	L
P	E	D	A	L		A	T	E		E	V	E
E	R	A	S		H	I	S		R	E	I	N
A	I	M		P	A	L		G	I	R	L	S
R	E	P	A	I	R		S	A	D			
			M	E	D	A	L	S		L	A	S
M	E	M	O		E	L	E	P	H	A	N	T
E	V	E	N		S	A	P		I	N	T	O
T	A	N	G		T	N	T		P	E	E	P

CROSSWORD 217

O	W	N	E	R		M	A	S		M	O	W
W	H	E	R	E		I	N	K		A	L	E
L	O	W	E	R		S	T	I	R	R	E	D
				U	N	T	I	D	Y			
	R	A	I	N	Y				E	A	S	T
S	I	G	N		L	I	T			T	W	O
O	V	E	N		O	D	E		S	T	E	M
F	A	N			N	A	P		H	I	P	S
A	L	T	O				E	L	E	C	T	
			I	S	R	A	E	L				
B	A	L	L	O	O	N		A	D	A	M	S
O	W	E		M	A	T		M	O	D	E	L
B	E	D		E	D	S		A	G	O	N	Y

CROSSWORD 218

R	A	F	T		A	L	P	S		A	R	K
A	B	L	E		H	O	O	K		D	U	E
T	E	E	M		E	A	S	Y		A	L	E
S	L	A	P		A	N	T		A	M	E	N
			L	I	D		M	I	X			
G	I	V	E	S		R	E	N	E	W	A	L
A	V	A		S	O	U	N	D		E	R	A
L	E	T	T	U	C	E		I	T	E	M	S
			N	E	T		C	A	R			
S	P	I	T		O	R	E		A	S	P	S
P	A	D		S	P	I	N		D	I	A	L
O	I	L		P	U	N	T		E	D	G	E
T	R	Y		A	S	K	S		D	E	E	D

CROSSWORD 219

N	A	P		L	A	S	H		O	D	E	S
E	G	O		I	N	T	O		S	I	L	O
I	R	K		S	N	U	G		C	A	I	N
G	E	E		T	E	N		S	A	M		
H	E	D	G	E				A	R	O	M	A
			U	N	T	I	D	Y		N	E	W
T	E	R	M		I	R	A		I	D	L	E
A	Y	E		O	P	E	N	E	D			
P	E	A	R	L				L	A	S	S	O
		P	O	D		P	R	O		C	U	T
O	H	I	O		F	L	I	P		A	R	T
A	U	N	T		E	A	S	E		L	E	E
K	E	G	S		D	Y	E	D		E	R	R

CROSSWORD 220

T	I	M		O	W	L	S		C	A	K	E
H	O	E		R	O	O	T		E	V	I	L
A	W	E		P	O	O	R		R	A	N	K
W	A	T	C	H		M	I	N	E			
			O	A	K		P	I	A	N	O	S
C	O	L	O	N	E	L		P	L	A	N	E
A	X	E			Y	E	N			I	C	E
B	E	N	C	H		T	A	T	T	L	E	D
S	N	A	R	E	D		B	O	O			
			E	Y	E	S		T	W	A	N	G
T	R	U	E		B	E	S	T		P	A	L
W	A	S	P		T	A	K	E		E	V	E
O	W	E	S		S	T	I	R		D	Y	E

CROSSWORD 221

H	I	M		A	S	I	A		A	C	T	S
E	R	A		W	A	R	N		I	O	W	A
N	O	T		A	P	E	D		S	M	O	G
S	N	E	A	K				A	L	P		
			N	E	O	N		D	E	A	L	T
S	P	A	N		H	I	P	S		R	A	H
W	A	D	E		I	C	E		M	E	N	U
A	I	D		P	O	E	T		O	D	E	S
P	R	I	C	E		R	E	S	T			
		T	A	G				T	H	U	M	B
S	W	I	M		L	A	D	Y		P	A	L
L	O	O	P		O	V	A	L		O	R	E
Y	E	N	S		G	A	M	E		N	E	W

CROSSWORD 222

E	D	G	E		E	G	G		T	H	A	T
C	E	L	L		M	O	O		E	A	C	H
H	E	A	D		P	O	T		L	I	M	E
O	D	D	E	S	T			A	L	L	E	Y
			R	H	Y	M	E	S				
G	O	L	L	Y		I	N	K		R	A	P
A	W	A	Y		F	A	D		F	A	C	E
Y	E	S		S	U	M		T	I	G	E	R
				U	N	I	T	E	D			
D	R	A	W	N			W	A	D	D	E	D
R	O	B	E		I	C	E		L	O	D	E
A	P	E	S		D	O	E		E	V	E	N
B	E	L	T		A	P	T		R	E	N	T

CROSSWORD 223

S	O	L	O	S		B	I	B		R	I	B
A	L	E	R	T		A	D	E		A	C	E
P	E	T	E	R		R	E	N	E	W	E	D
				I	S	R	A	E	L			
	H	I	P	P	I	E		A	M	E	N	
S	O	R	E		F	L	A	T		L	A	D
K	N	I	G	H	T		C	H	R	O	M	E
Y	E	S		O	S	L	O		O	P	E	N
	S	H	O	W		E	R	O	D	E	D	
			D	E	M	A	N	D				
T	H	I	E	V	E	S		O	M	I	T	S
E	A	R		E	R	E		R	A	D	I	O
A	S	K		R	E	D		S	P	A	N	S

CROSSWORD 224

H	A	T	S		R	I	P		A	R	C	S
U	N	I	T		I	D	A		D	E	L	I
T	Y	P	E		O	L	D		D	E	A	N
			V	O	T	E	D		E	L	M	S
W	A	T	E	R	S		L	E	D			
A	L	O	N	E		D	E	N		O	D	D
I	T	S		G	H	O	S	T		W	O	E
L	O	S		O	U	T		R	I	N	S	E
			I	N	N		S	E	N	S	E	D
L	I	P	S		D	O	M	E	S			
A	D	E	S		R	I	O		E	A	S	T
M	E	N	U		E	L	K		C	L	U	E
B	A	S	E		D	Y	E		T	I	E	D

CROSSWORD 225

R	O	B	E		A	C	T	S		S	E	E
O	V	E	R		S	H	I	P		W	A	X
D	E	E	R		P	A	R	E		E	R	A
E	N	T	E	R		P	E	A		E	L	M
			D	O	V	E		K	I	T		
A	L	P		A	I	L	S		R	E	A	D
P	A	R	A	D	E		O	R	A	N	G	E
T	W	I	G		D	I	M	E		S	O	W
		V	E	T		N	E	A	R			
A	H	A		A	S	H		L	O	W	E	R
S	E	T		R	O	A	R		W	A	D	E
I	R	E		T	A	L	E		E	V	E	S
A	D	S		S	P	E	D		D	E	N	T

CROSSWORD 226

H	I	D	E		R	I	G		S	H	O	P
I	R	A	N		E	V	A		L	O	N	E
T	E	N	D		V	E	T		A	L	E	S
			E	Y	E		E	R	N	E	S	T
S	P	I	D	E	R		S	A	T			
O	U	T		A	S	H		T	E	L	L	S
F	R	E	D		E	A	T		D	E	A	L
A	R	M	E	D		M	O	O		A	C	E
			S	O	S		N	I	P	P	E	D
S	A	F	E	T	Y		I	L	L			
O	V	E	R		R	A	G		U	T	A	H
D	I	E	T		U	G	H		M	E	N	U
A	D	D	S		P	E	T		P	E	T	E

CROSSWORD 227

A	C	M	E		U	S	E	S		S	P	A
S	L	A	M		G	O	A	L		T	A	G
P	U	M	P		H	O	S	E		A	C	E
S	E	A	T			T	E	E		R	E	D
			Y	E	A	H		P	E	T		
H	A	T		V	I	E	W		A	L	A	S
I	S	R	A	E	L		R	A	R	E	S	T
S	K	I	D		S	C	A	T		S	H	Y
		P	O	D		A	P	E	S			
P	A	L		I	N	N			O	W	E	D
I	C	E		S	O	A	P		R	A	V	E
T	N	T		C	O	D	E		E	D	E	N
Y	E	S		S	N	A	P		R	E	N	T

CROSSWORD 228

H	A	T		G	R	A	B		H	A	S	H
I	D	A		L	A	D	Y		A	C	H	E
T	O	R	T	O	I	S	E		N	E	O	N
			O	W	L			A	S	S	E	S
M	E	M	O		S	L	I	C	E			
E	X	I	T			A	N	T	L	E	R	S
R	A	N		T	A	N	K	S		V	I	E
E	M	E	R	A	L	D			K	E	N	T
			I	R	I	S	H		I	R	K	S
S	W	E	P	T			I	T	S			
H	I	D	E		A	R	R	E	S	T	E	D
O	N	E	S		L	I	E	S		E	R	A
T	E	N	T		P	O	D	S		D	R	Y

CROSSWORD 229

H	O	O	T		T	O	W		C	A	S	T
E	R	I	E		A	B	E		A	C	H	E
R	E	L	E	A	S	E	D		N	E	O	N
				S	K	Y		W	A	S	P	S
T	R	A	S	H		E	V	I	L			
R	I	L	E		E	D	E	N		J	A	B
A	P	P	E	A	R		S	E	C	U	R	E
Y	E	S		W	A	N	T		A	N	T	E
			E	A	S	E		D	R	E	S	S
A	N	G	R	Y		A	L	A				
S	O	A	R		P	R	O	M	I	S	E	S
P	E	T	E		O	L	D		R	A	G	E
S	L	E	D		D	Y	E		K	N	O	W

CROSSWORD 230

G	A	P	E		O	D	D		S	W	A	B
I	D	E	A		P	I	E		T	A	L	E
N	O	R	T	H	E	R	N		R	I	D	E
				O	N	E			A	L	A	N
A	L	L	O	W		C	L	A	Y			
S	A	I	D		S	T	A	R		S	H	E
I	N	V	E	N	T		S	K	A	T	E	R
A	D	E		O	A	K	S		P	U	R	R
			E	D	G	E		B	E	N	D	S
S	P	A	R			T	E	E				
M	A	M	A		S	T	A	N	D	A	R	D
O	R	E	S		A	L	S		O	H	I	O
G	E	N	E		G	E	T		T	A	M	E

CROSSWORD 231

H	O	T		P	L	A	Y		S	P	A	R
E	R	A		E	A	S	E		U	R	G	E
N	E	B	R	A	S	K	A		N	O	E	L
			A	S	H			B	U	D	D	Y
L	A	S	T				N	A	P			
A	C	H	E	D		D	O	T		T	W	O
P	R	O		I	R	I	S	H		R	I	D
S	E	E		V	I	E		E	R	A	S	E
			W	E	B				E	Y	E	S
S	T	O	O	D			B	A	A			
L	I	A	R		S	M	A	L	L	E	S	T
A	R	T	S		P	E	R	T		G	O	O
P	E	S	T		A	L	S	O		O	W	N

CROSSWORD 232

A	R	I	D		L	A	M	P		W	H	Y
D	O	N	E		A	B	E	L		H	O	E
D	O	T	S		G	E	N	E		A	L	A
S	M	O	K	Y				A	F	T	E	R
			S	O	S		I	D	A			
A	C	T		U	P	O	N		N	O	S	Y
D	O	E			A	N	D			W	E	E
S	O	D	A		R	E	I	N		L	E	T
			D	U	E		A	I	M			
O	F	T	E	N				P	E	C	K	S
R	I	O		C	A	P	E		L	A	N	E
A	V	A		L	I	E	D		O	V	E	N
L	E	D		E	R	R	S		N	E	E	D

CROSSWORD 233

T	W	I	N		T	E	E		S	T	E	M
N	O	N	E		H	A	Y		M	I	N	E
T	O	N	E		U	S	E		A	L	D	A
			D	O	M	E			R	E	S	T
S	U	P	E	R	B		N	A	T			
T	R	A	D	E		P	U	T		B	I	N
E	G	G		G	R	A	N	T		A	D	E
W	E	E		O	I	L		E	L	B	O	W
			A	N	D		K	N	E	E	L	S
A	L	A	S			K	I	D	S			
R	O	C	K		P	I	N		S	I	T	E
C	O	M	E		I	N	K		E	V	I	L
S	P	E	D		E	D	S		N	E	C	K

CROSSWORD 234

F	I	T		B	A	S	S		T	H	A	N
O	R	E		O	H	I	O		H	E	R	O
R	E	E	N	T	E	R	S		R	A	I	D
			A	H	A			M	O	L	D	S
D	E	L	I		D	R	A	I	N			
E	V	I	L			O	B	S	E	R	V	E
B	E	N		A	I	D	E	S		A	I	R
T	R	E	M	B	L	E			P	I	E	R
			A	L	L	O	W		E	N	D	S
S	T	A	G	E			I	R	A			
T	U	R	N		R	E	V	E	R	E	N	D
O	N	C	E		A	G	E	D		R	U	E
P	E	S	T		T	O	S	S		A	N	N

CROSSWORD 235

K	A	T	E		S	O	D		S	E	E	N
I	D	E	A		C	U	E		M	A	D	E
T	O	A	S	T	E	R	S		U	R	G	E
			T	I	N		S	I	G	N	E	D
A	C	T		P	E	T	E	R				
L	O	O	P			W	R	E	S	T	L	E
D	A	L	E		H	I	T		O	R	A	L
A	T	L	A	S	E	S			W	I	N	S
				P	A	T	C	H		O	D	E
T	O	M	C	A	T		H	E	Y			
O	V	A	L		E	M	E	R	A	L	D	S
L	E	N	A		R	O	W		R	E	A	L
D	R	E	W		S	O	S		D	E	N	Y

CROSSWORD 236

T	O	W		C	R	A	B		A	R	M	S
A	H	A		H	O	S	E		G	O	A	L
G	I	N		A	B	L	E		A	C	N	E
S	O	D		S	E	E		L	I	K	E	D
		E	Y	E		E	D	E	N			
T	I	R	E		U	P	O	N		B	I	N
A	R	E	N	A	S		C	A	S	I	N	O
C	A	R		D	E	C	K		A	R	K	S
			N	O	S	E		A	P	T		
A	C	M	E	S		R	A	N		H	I	S
C	L	A	W		P	E	C	K		D	O	E
T	I	M	E		E	A	R	L		A	W	E
S	P	A	R		G	L	E	E		Y	A	M

CROSSWORD 237

T	A	B		S	I	P	S		T	Y	P	E
U	S	E		A	D	A	M		H	E	E	D
B	I	G		N	O	S	E		R	A	T	S
E	A	S	E	D		T	A	L	E			
			G	A	L		R	O	A	S	T	S
J	U	G	G	L	E	R		S	T	O	R	E
O	N	E			D	I	G			R	U	E
G	I	A	N	T		D	O	N	A	T	E	D
S	T	R	E	A	M		T	O	W			
			A	G	E	S		D	E	A	L	T
S	P	A	R		O	W	E	D		B	E	E
P	A	I	L		W	A	V	E		E	N	D
A	N	D	Y		S	P	E	D		L	A	S

CROSSWORD 238

E	R	A	S	E	■	S	P	Y	■	I	D	A
D	A	V	I	D	■	E	R	A	■	D	O	C
S	H	A	P	E	■	C	U	P	■	E	L	M
■	■	■	■	N	O	O	N	■	S	A	L	E
A	L	L	■	■	K	N	E	L	T	■	■	■
D	O	E	■	D	A	D	■	E	A	R	T	H
D	O	N	K	E	Y	■	F	I	G	U	R	E
S	P	A	I	N	■	A	L	S	■	S	I	R
■	■	■	C	Y	C	L	E	■	■	H	O	E
B	A	R	K	■	H	A	W	K	■	■	■	■
U	S	E	■	S	O	S	■	E	R	R	O	R
D	I	N	■	A	R	K	■	P	I	A	N	O
S	A	T	■	P	E	A	■	T	O	T	E	D

CROSSWORD 239

P	O	P	■	D	R	A	W	■	S	T	E	P
A	W	E	■	R	U	L	E	■	T	I	R	E
T	E	R	R	I	B	L	E	■	I	D	L	E
■	■	■	A	L	S	O	■	G	R	E	E	K
U	N	T	I	L	■	W	A	R	■	■	■	■
S	E	E	D	■	A	S	I	A	■	V	I	A
E	R	A	S	E	R	■	D	Y	E	I	N	G
S	O	S	■	A	C	R	E	■	A	C	N	E
■	■	■	■	S	H	E	■	P	R	E	S	S
T	H	E	F	T	■	M	A	L	L	■	■	■
H	A	R	E	■	M	O	L	A	S	S	E	S
E	V	I	L	■	O	V	E	N	■	A	Y	E
M	E	E	T	■	M	E	S	S	■	P	E	T

CROSSWORD 240

G	E	T	■	A	L	P	S	■	A	N	N	S
A	L	I	■	P	O	L	O	■	P	A	U	L
S	I	M	M	E	R	E	D	■	R	I	D	E
■	■	■	U	S	E	D	■	A	I	L	E	D
D	I	A	L	■	■	G	I	L	L	■	■	■
I	D	L	E	■	S	E	T	S	■	S	K	I
S	E	E	S	A	W	■	C	O	P	T	E	R
H	A	S	■	L	A	S	H	■	L	I	N	K
■	■	■	F	A	M	E	■	■	A	R	T	S
S	H	O	E	S	■	V	E	S	T	■	■	■
L	E	N	A	■	R	E	D	H	E	A	D	S
A	R	C	S	■	U	R	G	E	■	R	I	O
M	E	E	T	■	N	E	E	D	■	M	E	N

CROSSWORD 241

F	O	G	■	■	W	A	R	■	■	H	A	S
A	B	E	■	T	A	P	E	■	R	A	I	L
C	O	N	■	U	S	E	D	■	E	M	M	Y
T	E	E	N	S	■	■	S	A	N	■	■	■
■	■	■	O	K	A	Y	■	C	O	A	T	S
■	B	U	S	■	N	I	C	E	■	J	O	E
Z	A	N	Y	■	T	E	A	■	M	A	R	T
A	L	I	■	E	E	L	S	■	U	R	N	■
P	E	T	A	L	■	D	E	N	T	■	■	■
■	■	■	U	M	P	■	■	U	T	T	E	R
T	H	A	N	■	A	R	I	D	■	I	V	E
R	U	N	T	■	D	A	R	E	■	L	E	S
Y	E	N	■	■	S	P	A	■	■	T	N	T

CROSSWORD 242

M	I	T	T	■	A	R	M	■	M	E	M	O
O	D	O	R	■	Y	E	A	■	O	V	A	L
B	O	N	E	■	E	A	S	T	W	A	R	D
S	L	E	E	P	■	S	K	I	■	■	■	■
■	■	■	■	I	D	O	■	P	U	T	T	S
O	F	F	■	T	A	N	K	■	G	O	A	T
A	L	L	E	Y	S	■	I	N	H	A	L	E
T	E	E	N	■	H	A	T	E	■	D	E	W
H	E	A	D	S	■	P	E	R	■	■	■	■
■	■	■	■	A	S	P	■	O	C	C	U	R
R	O	M	A	N	C	E	S	■	L	O	N	E
I	R	A	N	■	O	A	K	■	A	R	I	D
G	E	N	T	■	T	R	Y	■	P	E	T	S

CROSSWORD 243

A	N	N	E	■	S	H	Y	■	B	R	O	W
C	A	I	N	■	T	E	A	■	R	I	P	E
T	I	L	T	■	E	L	M	■	A	D	E	S
S	L	E	E	T	E	D	■	■	K	E	N	T
■	■	■	R	A	P	■	A	C	E	■	■	■
M	E	S	S	Y	■	O	I	L	■	P	A	T
A	L	E	■	L	A	D	L	E	■	A	D	O
P	I	T	■	O	N	E	■	V	E	R	S	E
■	■	■	D	R	Y	■	T	E	D	■	■	■
P	A	P	A	■	■	S	H	R	I	N	K	S
U	S	E	D	■	J	O	E	■	T	U	N	E
R	I	N	D	■	O	F	F	■	E	D	E	N
E	A	S	Y	■	B	A	T	■	D	E	E	D

CROSSWORD 244

C	H	A	T	■	E	C	H	O	■	H	A	T
L	E	N	A	■	D	R	O	P	■	E	G	O
A	R	T	S	■	S	A	L	E	S	M	E	N
P	O	E	T	S	■	T	E	N	T	■	■	■
■	■	■	E	A	S	E	■	S	O	D	A	S
O	F	F	■	F	I	S	H	■	R	U	L	E
W	E	A	S	E	L	■	A	L	M	O	S	T
E	A	C	H	■	L	A	V	A	■	S	O	S
D	R	E	A	M	■	S	E	W	S	■	■	■
■	■	■	L	A	S	H	■	N	I	C	K	S
L	O	L	L	I	P	O	P	■	G	O	A	L
E	R	A	■	L	O	R	E	■	N	O	T	E
D	E	W	■	S	T	E	W	■	S	P	E	D

CROSSWORD 245

L	A	V	A	■	S	P	A	T	■	H	E	M
O	W	E	D	■	P	A	T	H	■	E	V	A
R	A	T	E	■	O	V	E	R	■	A	I	R
D	Y	E	■	J	O	E	■	E	A	R	L	Y
■	■	R	E	A	L	■	P	A	R	■	■	■
A	L	A	R	M	■	H	A	T	C	H	E	T
L	E	N	A	■	O	I	L	■	H	A	L	O
L	E	S	S	O	N	S	■	D	E	N	I	M
■	■	■	E	Y	E	■	H	E	R	D	■	■
S	T	A	R	S	■	T	O	W	■	S	A	P
W	I	N	■	T	E	A	R	■	C	O	P	E
A	N	T	■	E	G	G	S	■	A	M	E	N
B	E	E	■	R	O	S	E	■	B	E	D	S

CROSSWORD 246

P	A	I	L	■	S	T	E	M	■	S	P	A
A	C	R	E	■	W	I	D	E	■	O	I	L
S	H	O	T	■	U	N	I	T	■	M	E	L
T	E	N	T	■	N	A	T	■	V	E	R	Y
■	■	■	E	G	G	■	O	D	E	■	■	■
A	D	O	R	E	■	W	R	I	T	T	E	N
V	O	W	■	E	R	A	S	E	■	A	Y	E
A	T	L	A	S	E	S	■	T	H	R	E	W
■	■	■	W	E	D	■	U	S	E	■	■	■
K	I	T	E	■	H	I	T	■	A	D	A	M
I	D	O	■	W	E	N	T	■	P	A	L	E
S	E	W	■	H	A	T	E	■	E	R	A	S
S	A	N	■	O	D	O	R	■	D	E	N	S

CROSSWORD 247

S	A	F	E	R	■	P	E	P	■	W	A	S
A	L	I	V	E	■	A	L	E	■	A	L	L
D	A	R	E	D	■	L	O	W	■	I	D	A
■	■	■	■	S	N	A	P	■	S	T	A	B
A	D	D	■	■	O	C	E	A	N	■	■	■
R	U	E	■	U	S	E	■	G	U	A	R	D
C	E	L	E	R	Y	■	D	E	G	R	E	E
S	T	I	N	G	■	S	O	D	■	M	E	N
■	■	■	V	E	S	T	S	■	■	S	L	Y
A	W	A	Y	■	N	O	E	L	■	■	■	■
D	A	N	■	N	O	W	■	A	M	A	Z	E
O	L	D	■	O	R	E	■	W	A	G	O	N
S	K	Y	■	T	E	D	■	S	T	O	O	D

CROSSWORD 248

P	A	N	D	A	■	R	O	B	■	S	A	G
A	V	O	I	D	■	O	W	E	■	I	D	A
D	A	T	E	D	■	A	N	N	■	L	O	P
■	■	■	■	S	A	M	E	■	D	O	S	E
E	D	S	■	■	M	E	R	C	Y	■	■	■
R	U	T	■	T	E	D	■	L	E	A	P	T
R	E	A	G	A	N	■	L	A	S	S	I	E
S	T	R	A	P	■	C	A	P	■	I	L	L
■	■	■	T	E	N	O	R	■	■	A	L	L
C	A	K	E	■	I	R	K	S	■	■	■	■
A	C	E	■	H	E	N	■	H	E	A	D	S
S	H	E	■	I	C	E	■	I	G	L	O	O
T	E	N	■	P	E	R	■	P	O	S	T	S

CROSSWORD 249

B	A	I	L	■	P	O	P	■	A	S	P	S
A	C	R	E	■	A	W	E	■	C	O	O	P
S	M	O	G	■	N	E	W	■	T	A	L	E
S	E	N	S	E	D	■	■	A	S	K	E	D
■	■	■	■	R	A	C	E	D	■	■	■	■
A	R	E	N	A	■	L	A	S	A	G	N	A
H	U	G	E	■	H	A	T	■	N	O	O	N
A	N	O	T	H	E	R	■	S	N	O	W	Y
■	■	■	■	A	N	K	L	E	■	■	■	■
D	E	L	A	Y	■	■	O	W	N	E	R	S
O	V	E	R	■	R	A	W	■	O	R	A	L
S	E	A	T	■	A	I	L	■	D	I	V	E
E	N	D	S	■	T	R	Y	■	S	E	E	D

CROSSWORD 250

ADO■STAB■ODDS
YOU■PURE■SOAP
ENTRANCE■COLE
■■■UTAH■PARED
GLAD■■EVER■■■
LANE■BRAT■NAP
UNTRUE■SEVERE
EDS■GENT■IRKS
■■■ALTO■■COST
ANGRY■TAPE■■■
SIRE■MINISTER
PLEA■ACNE■ERA
SEWS■DEER■DRY

CROSSWORD 251

MAIN■OATS■SHE
ACRE■DIAL■PAY
SHOE■ORGANIZE
TENDER■■NOTES
■■■INSISTS■■■
STAND■GAS■LAP
KING■ALP■FATE
ICY■EGO■GAYER
■■■TROOPER■■■
APRON■■READER
BRUNETTE■WOVE
LOG■SEAS■ASIA
EDS■TEDS■YELL

CROSSWORD 252

PIT■SWAM■STAR
IRE■TAPE■CURE
NOS■EVEN■ANTS
ENTREE■■BLAST
■■■ORDERED■■■
SHOWS■LUG■PEA
OUR■■TEE■■ILL
BEE■DOC■YANKS
■■■SOOTHED■■■
TASTE■■OLDEST
ALLY■PAUL■ATE
IDOL■ELSE■SUN
LATE■WEED■END

CROSSWORD 253

LID■CAT■RAKER
ODE■RIO■OLIVE
ALABAMA■DINED
NYLON■DIE■■■■
■■■BEE■ROAMED
APT■■ADO■CORE
READ■SUN■TWIN
MEMO■TOE■■SET
SLEEVE■DAN■■■
■■■■ERR■RAFTS
WASPS■INITIAL
AWAIT■LAS■VIA
RENTS■EYE■ELM

CROSSWORD 254

EDGE■LAMP■BED
LEER■IDEA■IRE
MEAN■NETS■KIN
SPREADS■SWEET
■■■SPA■PEA■■■
CRATE■PEDDLED
AIR■■TIP■■EVA
NOTHING■TOTEM
■■■ANT■DIP■■■
TROTS■VINEGAR
EAR■EDEN■NILE
ERA■CUTE■EVEN
MEL■TOSS■REST

CROSSWORD 255

HUM■SILL■SILO
ORE■TRIO■IRAN
ENTERING■LORE
■■■VAST■■ENDS
THREW■■HEN■■■
REIN■BREATHED
AIL■GAYER■IRE
PREPARED■SKIN
■■■ASK■■TWEET
STAR■■PLEA■■■
LACE■RAINBOWS
OPEN■ALAS■WOO
BEST■WERE■NEW

CROSSWORD 256

FAR■AWAY■PLEA
ELI■LODE■HELP
ASP■LOSS■RISE
TOSSED■■EASED
■■■OYSTERS■■■
RAINS■ALREADY
AID■■IRK■■BYE
PROTECT■SWEET
■■■WRESTLE■■■
INDIA■■WIDEST
NEAR■SKID■ALI
TOLL■PINE■RID
ONES■ADES■SPY

CROSSWORD 257

EDGE■ONCE■OFF
ROLL■DEAN■PAR
ALES■DIRT■PIE
SLEEP■GEE■OLD
■■■■UGH■RAN■■
SAP■CASH■LEAD
KNOCKS■ORANGE
INTO■POLO■TEN
■■ATE■BET■■■■
HIT■ACT■SCRAM
ADO■GOAL■LIME
SEE■ERIE■ACES
HAS■RENT■PENS

CROSSWORD 258

CANE■SOD■SHOE
UPON■ODE■MOVE
BEST■ADS■ABEL
■■■INK■ERRORS
THERE■TROT■■■
RUDER■EVA■SEW
AGE■VANES■ERA
YEN■OUT■TRAIN
■■■FUSS■EASED
INSIST■ADD■■■
DEAR■ROB■ITEM
LONE■ILL■SODA
ENDS■ADE■HOST

CROSSWORD 259

GLAD■AGES■APT
LACE■CART■NAY
OVEN■TRIO■NIP
WASTE■DEW■ODE
■■■SAFE■SAY■■
TAG■RIND■LIDS
APRONS■AVENUE
PEAR■HOLE■GOT
■■NEW■TEND■■■
OLD■HOT■TICKS
KIM■EVES■NOEL
AVA■RARE■GLEE
YES■ELSE■SEND

CROSSWORD 260

NEWS■ALS■CRAB
ADAM■CAP■OILY
GIVE■TRIANGLE
STEAK■INN■■■■
■■■RITA■NECKS
WAD■TOTS■ALAN
ISRAEL■POTATO
TIES■LOAD■WEB
HAWKS■BROW■■■
■■■■HAT■RACER
CABLECAR■SOLO
OHIO■RIO■TOMS
PANT■END■ELSE

CROSSWORD 261

■■YAP■■■TAB■■
■CORE■■TILES■
VODKA■SWEATER
ACES■AMID■TWO
SOL■SNUG■FEET
TASTING■PURRS
■■■ITS■LOS■■■
BOONE■HOLSTER
ACRE■TOOL■ALI
ICE■HUMP■SLOB
LUGGAGE■STEPS
■ROOTS■■PINE■
■■NOS■■■ART■■

CROSSWORD 262

S	C	O	T	■	D	A	B	■	A	L	T	O
I	O	W	A	■	E	Y	E	■	C	O	I	N
N	O	E	L	■	L	E	E	■	T	A	L	L
■	■	■	E	L	I	■	T	W	E	N	T	Y
A	R	E	N	A	S	■	L	A	D	■	■	■
C	E	N	T	S	■	P	E	T	■	T	E	D
M	A	D	■	T	E	A	S	E	■	R	A	Y
E	D	S	■	I	V	Y	■	R	O	U	S	E
■	■	■	O	N	E	■	T	E	P	E	E	S
D	E	S	I	G	N	■	A	D	E	■	■	■
O	V	A	L	■	I	T	S	■	R	A	I	N
T	I	L	E	■	N	E	T	■	A	L	D	A
S	L	E	D	■	G	A	Y	■	S	P	A	T

CROSSWORD 263

M	A	T	■	T	R	O	T	■	F	R	E	D
A	L	E	■	H	O	B	O	■	R	I	D	E
I	L	L	■	R	A	T	E	■	O	P	E	N
D	Y	E	■	E	R	A	■	■	W	E	N	T
■	■	V	O	W	■	I	R	O	N	■	■	■
R	A	I	N	■	S	N	O	W	■	C	A	T
I	N	S	E	C	T	■	B	E	F	O	R	E
B	Y	E	■	O	A	T	S	■	A	N	T	E
■	■	■	R	O	B	E	■	T	N	T	■	■
H	O	M	E	■	■	A	G	O	■	A	H	A
E	V	I	L	■	S	P	A	T	■	C	A	R
L	E	N	A	■	O	O	Z	E	■	T	I	M
P	R	E	Y	■	S	T	E	M	■	S	L	Y

CROSSWORD 264

B	O	O	M	■	H	A	T	■	D	E	E	P
A	I	D	E	■	E	V	A	■	I	D	L	E
A	L	D	A	■	L	A	G	■	R	I	S	E
■	■	■	N	A	P	■	■	O	T	T	E	R
W	I	L	T	S	■	C	O	W	■	■	■	■
I	D	O	■	K	N	O	W	N	■	L	A	D
S	E	T	■	■	O	R	E	■	■	A	C	E
H	A	S	■	P	O	N	D	S	■	S	H	E
■	■	■	■	A	N	Y	■	U	S	H	E	R
S	T	R	A	W	■	■	P	E	T	■	■	■
L	O	A	N	■	T	O	E	■	A	B	E	L
U	N	I	T	■	I	D	A	■	L	O	D	E
R	E	D	S	■	M	E	L	■	L	O	S	T

CROSSWORD 265

A	R	T	S	■	T	E	N	■	T	A	M	S
L	O	O	P	■	A	L	A	■	E	R	I	E
I	D	O	L	■	N	I	P	■	P	I	N	E
■	■	■	A	R	K	■	■	■	E	D	E	N
C	H	A	S	E	■	F	I	R	E	■	■	■
R	I	G	H	T	■	A	D	E	■	T	N	T
I	R	E	■	I	O	W	A	N	■	H	O	E
B	E	D	■	R	U	N	■	T	W	I	N	E
■	■	■	B	E	T	S	■	E	A	S	E	S
S	H	O	O	■	■	■	O	D	D	■	■	■
L	E	N	A	■	P	E	W	■	D	I	S	C
A	R	C	S	■	A	Y	E	■	E	C	H	O
P	O	E	T	■	W	E	D	■	D	E	E	D

CROSSWORD 266

R	I	T	A	■	F	I	B	■	A	H	A	B
I	R	I	S	■	O	R	E	■	R	I	C	E
D	O	E	S	■	G	A	G	■	E	T	N	A
E	N	D	I	N	G	■	■	E	A	S	E	D
■	■	■	S	A	Y	I	N	G	S	■	■	■
P	A	R	T	Y	■	R	U	G	■	B	I	D
A	L	A	S	■	P	A	N	■	T	U	N	A
W	E	T	■	F	I	T	■	S	O	N	N	Y
■	■	■	V	E	T	E	R	A	N	■	■	■
T	H	R	E	W	■	■	E	D	I	T	E	D
H	E	A	R	■	A	H	A	■	G	R	A	Y
A	R	C	S	■	S	O	D	■	H	I	R	E
W	O	K	E	■	H	E	Y	■	T	O	L	D

CROSSWORD 267

I	N	K	■	C	A	W	■	■	A	L	D	A
C	A	N	■	O	L	E	S	■	L	O	A	N
E	G	O	■	B	L	E	W	■	I	S	N	T
■	S	W	O	R	E	■	E	G	G	■	■	■
■	■	■	P	A	Y	■	D	O	N	O	R	■
S	P	A	T	S	■	L	E	T	■	M	A	P
I	L	L	■	■	B	A	N	■	■	I	V	E
R	U	E	■	C	A	D	■	C	A	T	E	R
■	S	C	O	U	R	■	D	O	G	■	■	■
■	■	■	V	E	T	■	I	R	O	N	S	■
A	C	R	E	■	E	D	E	N	■	E	L	F
V	A	I	N	■	R	A	G	E	■	W	A	R
E	B	B	S	■	■	D	O	T	■	S	P	Y

CROSSWORD 268

T	O	O	■	I	T	C	H	■	A	L	P	S
O	W	N	■	S	H	O	O	■	C	O	L	A
P	L	E	A	S	I	N	G	■	H	A	U	L
■	■	■	P	U	N	■	■	H	E	D	G	E
T	E	P	E	E	■	S	K	I	■	■	■	■
A	D	O	■	S	P	L	I	T	■	D	A	B
P	I	N	■	R	U	T	■	■	■	O	W	E
S	T	Y	■	S	O	R	E	R	■	M	A	D
■	■	■	■	A	D	S	■	O	B	E	Y	S
S	P	E	E	D	■	■	A	B	E	■	■	■
L	A	V	A	■	T	E	L	E	G	R	A	M
O	R	E	S	■	O	V	E	R	■	A	G	O
W	E	N	T	■	T	E	S	T	■	W	E	B

CROSSWORD 269

S	A	F	E	■	A	D	D	■	A	L	S	O
A	L	A	S	■	R	I	O	■	L	O	A	D
N	E	T	S	■	M	E	L	■	B	A	L	E
■	■	■	A	G	O	■	P	R	U	N	E	S
P	R	A	Y	E	R	■	H	E	M	■	■	■
L	A	S	S	O	■	T	I	C	■	P	O	P
A	R	K	■	R	H	I	N	O	■	I	D	A
Y	E	S	■	G	E	M	■	V	A	P	O	R
■	■	■	S	I	R	■	S	E	V	E	R	E
T	H	R	E	A	D	■	P	R	O	■	■	■
R	E	I	N	■	I	C	E	■	I	O	W	A
O	I	L	S	■	N	U	N	■	D	U	O	S
T	R	E	E	■	G	E	T	■	S	T	O	P

CROSSWORD 270

R	A	T	■	S	L	I	P	■	S	L	I	M
A	G	E	■	H	A	T	E	■	W	O	R	E
W	O	N	■	E	V	E	R	■	O	V	A	L
■	■	D	R	E	A	M	S	■	R	E	N	T
S	L	E	E	P	■	■	U	S	E	■	■	■
H	E	R	D	■	S	E	A	L	■	O	W	L
O	N	E	■	B	E	A	D	Y	■	P	I	E
E	A	R	■	A	N	T	E	■	F	O	R	E
■	■	■	A	R	T	■	■	W	I	S	E	R
B	E	L	L	■	E	R	R	O	R	S	■	■
R	A	I	L	■	N	E	A	R	■	U	G	H
A	C	M	E	■	C	A	N	S	■	M	O	O
T	H	E	Y	■	E	D	G	E	■	S	O	W

CROSSWORD 271

T	H	A	T	■	A	D	D	S	■	T	O	O
H	O	P	E	■	L	E	A	P	■	O	W	L
A	M	E	N	■	S	C	R	E	A	M	E	D
W	E	D	S	■	■	E	E	L	S	■	■	■
■	■	■	E	V	E	N	■	L	I	M	E	S
A	R	K	■	E	A	T	S	■	D	O	L	L
R	O	A	S	T	S	■	P	L	E	A	S	E
M	O	T	H	■	T	R	I	O	■	T	E	D
S	M	E	A	R	■	A	N	T	E	■	■	■
■	■	■	P	U	R	R	■	■	L	A	S	H
B	A	K	E	R	I	E	S	■	A	B	L	E
U	S	E	■	A	L	S	O	■	T	E	A	R
S	H	Y	■	L	E	T	S	■	E	L	M	S

CROSSWORD 272

H	A	R	E	■	S	O	B	■	S	A	F	E
A	L	A	S	■	T	W	O	■	T	R	A	Y
T	A	N	K	■	E	L	M	■	R	I	C	E
E	N	G	I	N	E	■	B	R	I	D	E	S
■	■	■	M	A	P	■	S	I	P	■	■	■
A	N	N	O	Y	E	D	■	B	E	A	N	S
H	U	E	■	■	R	A	G	■	■	W	O	E
A	N	T	E	S	■	D	E	S	S	E	R	T
■	■	■	L	I	T	■	R	U	T	■	■	■
T	H	R	O	N	E	■	M	E	A	D	O	W
H	E	A	P	■	E	R	A	■	M	I	N	E
U	R	G	E	■	M	A	N	■	P	A	C	E
S	E	E	D	■	S	T	Y	■	S	L	E	D

CROSSWORD 273

R	U	L	E	■	D	I	S	H	■	D	E	N
O	P	E	N	■	E	C	H	O	■	I	V	E
P	O	N	D	■	S	E	A	T	■	R	A	T
E	N	T	E	R	S	■	P	E	T	E	■	■
■	■	■	D	U	E	■	E	L	E	C	T	S
B	A	G	■	E	R	A	■	S	A	T	I	N
U	S	E	S	■	T	I	M	■	M	E	M	O
M	I	M	I	C	■	L	I	P	■	D	E	W
P	A	S	T	E	S	■	L	I	D	■	■	■
■	■	T	E	L	L	■	D	E	E	P	E	R
A	D	O	■	L	I	M	E	■	L	O	D	E
P	U	N	■	A	C	E	S	■	A	P	E	D
T	O	E	■	R	E	N	T	■	Y	E	N	S

CROSSWORD 274

L	A	V	A		P	R	A	Y		P	A	T
O	V	A	L		R	I	C	E		A	G	O
W	A	N	T		I	D	E	A		N	A	T
			O	O	Z	E				D	I	E
S	A	N		F	E	R	N		H	A	N	D
A	D	U	L	T		S	A	M	E			
P	O	N	I	E	S		B	E	A	M	E	D
			S	N	O	W		S	P	E	A	R
R	A	F	T		W	I	T	S		T	R	Y
E	R	R				D	A	Y	S			
G	E	E		A	D	E	S		L	I	P	S
A	N	T		L	O	S	T		E	V	I	L
L	A	S		P	E	T	E		D	E	N	Y

CROSSWORD 275

G	A	L		S	A	N	D		S	L	E	D
A	G	O		P	L	E	A		L	O	D	E
P	E	T	E	R	P	A	N		U	R	G	E
			V	A	S	T		O	R	D	E	R
A	L	L	E	Y		E	N	D				
L	O	A	N		T	R	I	O		I	W	O
D	O	C	T	O	R		C	R	O	W	E	D
A	P	E		W	E	R	E		V	I	E	D
				L	E	E		T	E	N	D	S
W	A	S	P	S		D	O	W	N			
E	C	H	O		P	U	N	I	S	H	E	S
T	R	O	T		A	C	E	S		I	R	A
S	E	W	S		R	E	S	T		D	R	Y

CROSSWORD 276

K	I	M		B	L	E	W		A	D	D	S
E	V	A		A	I	D	E		T	R	I	O
Y	E	T		S	K	I	T		L	I	A	R
		T	W	E	E	T		M	A	P	L	E
P	L	E	A			O	D	E	S			
E	A	R	L		G	R	I	M		T	W	O
T	W	E	L	V	E		S	O	R	R	O	W
E	N	D		I	N	C	H		E	A	R	N
			P	E	E	R			A	C	E	S
S	P	E	E	D		A	L	E	R	T		
A	L	A	S		I	D	O	L		O	D	D
F	A	S	T		C	L	A	M		R	O	Y
E	Y	E	S		Y	E	N	S		S	E	E

CROSSWORD 277

O	F	F		A	L	P	S		F	O	R	M
R	U	E		C	A	L	L		I	D	E	A
E	R	A		T	R	A	Y		L	O	A	N
		S	M	O	K	Y		M	E	R	R	Y
O	T	T	E	R		E	V	E	S			
R	U	I	N		A	D	A	M		S	P	A
A	N	N	U	A	L		S	O	F	T	E	R
L	A	G		R	A	F	T		L	E	A	K
			R	I	S	E		S	E	E	K	S
S	T	O	O	D		M	O	W	E	R		
P	A	P	A		T	A	X	I		I	D	O
A	P	E	S		A	L	E	S		N	O	W
T	E	N	T		P	E	N	S		G	E	E

CROSSWORD 278

E	D	I	T		S	T	Y		S	A	N	D
A	U	T	O		O	W	E		T	R	U	E
R	E	S	T		F	I	N		R	I	D	E
			I	R	A	N		F	A	D	E	D
C	R	A	N	E	S		L	I	P			
L	O	N	G	S		L	O	G		S	E	A
A	P	T		I	R	I	S	H		T	A	C
W	E	E		D	I	D		T	W	I	S	T
			P	E	P		H	E	A	R	T	S
A	W	A	R	D		G	I	R	L			
L	O	N	E		C	A	R		K	E	P	T
D	O	N	S		A	P	E		E	V	E	N
A	D	E	S		B	E	D		D	E	N	T

CROSSWORD 279

R	I	M	S		P	A	W		W	R	A	P
I	D	E	A		A	V	A		R	O	B	E
B	A	N	D	A	G	E	S		I	D	L	E
				Y	E	N			S	E	E	K
S	P	A	D	E		U	N	I	T			
L	A	V	A		P	E	A	R		S	H	E
A	N	I	M	A	L		Y	A	P	P	E	D
B	E	D		L	O	S	S		R	A	N	G
			M	I	T	T		W	O	R	S	E
A	L	T	O			R	I	O				
L	O	O	P		T	O	R	N	A	D	O	S
A	N	N	E		E	L	I		R	U	D	E
N	E	E	D		A	L	S		M	E	E	T

CROSSWORD 280

H	E	M		M	O	P	E		A	N	N	E
A	X	E		A	B	E	L		C	A	I	N
M	A	R		L	E	A	K		R	I	N	D
S	M	E	L	L	Y			S	O	L	E	S
			A	S	S	I	S	T	S			
L	I	M	B			R	O	A	S	T	E	D
E	V	A		T	W	A	N	G		W	A	Y
D	E	T	R	O	I	T			B	O	R	E
			H	O	N	E	S	T	Y			
A	P	R	I	L			P	R	E	T	T	Y
L	A	I	N		H	A	L	O		I	R	A
S	I	L	O		E	D	I	T		L	I	P
O	N	E	S		N	E	T	S		L	O	S

CROSSWORD 281

O	R	E		A	L	D	A		S	C	O	T
F	U	R		T	I	E	D		T	A	X	I
F	E	A	R	L	E	S	S		O	P	E	N
			E	A	S	E		A	R	E	N	A
G	A	I	N	S		R	A	C	K			
A	C	R	E		I	T	C	H		E	G	O
S	N	O	W	E	D		M	E	A	D	O	W
P	E	N		D	O	S	E		P	I	N	E
			B	E	L	T		H	A	T	E	D
S	P	O	O	N		E	V	E	R			
L	A	V	A		G	R	E	A	T	E	S	T
A	C	E	S		Y	E	A	R		Y	E	N
T	E	N	T		M	O	L	D		E	A	T

CROSSWORD 282

L	E	E		S	W	A	M		S	P	O	T
I	R	A		W	O	R	E		C	O	V	E
P	A	R		I	R	K	S		R	O	A	D
		L	O	R	D		S	P	E	L	L	S
C	H	I	L	L	S		I	R	E			
L	I	E	D			K	E	E	N	E	S	T
A	D	S		D	A	I	R	Y		L	A	W
W	E	T	T	E	S	T			D	E	L	I
			R	A	H		D	R	I	V	E	N
B	A	N	A	N	A		R	I	D	E		
A	R	I	D		M	E	A	N		N	A	T
A	C	N	E		E	G	G	S		T	W	O
S	H	E	D		D	O	S	E		H	E	M

CROSSWORD 283

B	O	S	S		T	O	L	D		S	A	M
U	P	O	N		E	R	I	E		O	W	E
M	A	L	E		L	E	A	N		M	E	L
P	L	E	A	S	E		R	I	P	E	S	T
			K	E	G	S		M	E	W		
W	E	D		E	R	I	C		T	H	A	N
I	R	E		K	A	Z	O	O		A	L	A
T	A	L	K		M	E	N	D		T	I	P
		A	I	D		S	T	O	P			
P	O	W	D	E	R		E	R	A	S	E	R
A	V	A		B	E	A	N		P	A	V	E
P	E	R		U	N	I	T		E	V	E	S
A	R	E		T	O	M	S		R	E	N	T

CROSSWORD 284

F	A	S	T		B	A	G	S		A	C	T
O	D	O	R		E	X	I	T		G	O	O
G	O	N	E		T	E	A	R		E	V	A
			N	E	W		N	E	E	D	E	D
C	R	A	D	L	E		T	A	X			
O	I	L		M	E	T		M	A	L	L	S
T	O	S	S		N	A	G		M	O	A	T
S	T	O	O	L		G	A	L		S	K	I
			L	A	S		M	A	S	T	E	R
M	A	K	E	U	P		B	Y	E			
O	R	E		G	O	A	L		W	E	D	S
P	I	G		H	O	P	E		E	V	I	L
E	D	S		S	L	E	D		D	E	N	Y

CROSSWORD 285

D	O	C		A	S	K		A	S	H	E	S
I	D	O		W	I	N		C	H	I	N	A
S	O	P	R	A	N	O		T	E	D	D	Y
C	R	E	E	K		W	H	O				
			D	E	W		O	R	E	G	O	N
R	I	B		N	E	R	O		L	A	N	E
I	D	O	L		T	A	R		M	I	C	E
G	E	N	E		T	H	A	N		N	E	D
S	A	D	D	L	E		Y	I	P			
				A	R	K		P	A	C	E	D
A	B	O	U	T		I	M	P	R	O	V	E
P	A	U	S	E		T	O	E		L	E	E
E	N	T	E	R		S	O	D		A	N	D

CROSSWORD 286

I	R	I	S	■	W	A	N	T	■	S	O	B
L	I	N	T	■	O	D	O	R	■	T	W	O
L	O	V	E	■	W	E	R	E	■	A	N	N
■	■	E	V	E	■	■	■	N	U	R	S	E
S	A	N	E	R	■	A	D	D	S	■	■	■
K	I	T	■	R	E	L	Y	■	E	A	S	T
I	D	O	■	S	A	L	E	S	■	T	O	Y
N	E	R	O	■	R	E	S	T	■	L	O	P
■	■	■	I	D	L	Y	■	I	R	A	T	E
A	N	G	L	E	■	■	■	R	U	N	■	■
L	A	Y	■	A	W	A	Y	■	S	T	A	G
D	I	M	■	L	O	N	E	■	T	I	L	E
A	L	S	■	T	O	T	S	■	S	C	A	T

CROSSWORD 287

A	L	T	O	■	C	O	B	■	A	L	S	O
L	O	A	N	■	A	V	A	■	G	O	L	D
D	A	L	E	■	B	E	L	I	E	V	E	D
A	D	E	■	H	I	R	E	D	■	E	D	S
■	■	N	O	O	N	■	S	E	T	■	■	■
B	E	T	W	E	E	N	■	A	R	M	O	R
O	V	E	N	■	T	A	G	■	A	I	D	E
W	A	D	E	D	■	P	R	A	I	S	E	D
■	■	■	R	U	N	■	A	N	N	S	■	■
A	S	H	■	M	E	A	N	T	■	O	U	T
C	H	E	A	P	E	S	T	■	D	U	N	E
T	O	R	N	■	D	I	E	■	I	R	I	S
S	P	E	D	■	S	A	D	■	M	I	T	T

CROSSWORD 288

S	A	L	T	■	A	L	A	■	W	H	A	T
A	L	A	N	■	N	O	D	■	E	A	C	H
D	I	S	T	A	N	C	E	■	L	I	M	E
■	■	■	■	S	E	A	■	A	L	L	E	Y
S	W	A	M	P	■	T	A	R	■	■	■	■
T	I	R	E	■	P	E	C	K	■	M	O	B
E	D	I	T	O	R	■	E	S	C	A	P	E
W	E	D	■	K	E	G	S	■	A	M	E	N
■	■	■	■	A	Y	E	■	G	R	A	N	D
S	P	R	A	Y	■	O	N	E	■	■	■	■
T	I	E	D	■	T	R	O	M	B	O	N	E
A	L	S	O	■	A	G	O	■	I	D	O	L
G	E	T	S	■	P	E	N	■	T	E	R	M

CROSSWORD 289

E	L	M	S	■	A	R	C	S	■	T	O	W
R	O	O	T	■	P	E	A	L	■	A	H	A
R	A	R	E	■	T	A	M	E	■	D	I	N
S	N	E	A	K	■	P	E	P	■	P	O	T
■	■	■	M	E	R	E	■	T	W	O	■	■
A	D	S	■	P	U	R	R	■	A	L	A	S
C	R	U	S	T	S	■	O	D	D	E	S	T
T	Y	P	E	■	T	R	A	Y	■	S	P	Y
■	■	P	A	L	■	E	D	E	N	■	■	■
W	H	O	■	I	T	S	■	D	I	T	C	H
H	I	S	■	G	R	I	M	■	C	A	R	E
A	D	E	■	H	U	G	E	■	E	X	A	M
T	E	D	■	T	E	N	T	■	R	I	B	S

CROSSWORD 290

N	E	W	■	P	R	A	Y	■	S	E	W	S
A	V	A	■	R	O	L	E	■	T	R	E	E
B	E	D	■	I	D	E	A	■	E	A	S	T
S	N	E	E	Z	E	■	■	T	E	S	T	S
■	■	■	L	E	O	P	A	R	D	■	■	■
T	A	S	K	■	■	E	X	I	S	T	E	D
A	I	L	■	S	L	E	E	P	■	A	G	O
C	R	Y	S	T	A	L	■	■	U	R	G	E
■	■	■	L	E	S	S	O	N	S	■	■	■
S	T	R	A	W	■	■	V	E	E	R	E	D
P	O	E	T	■	A	D	E	S	■	I	V	E
A	N	N	E	■	P	U	N	T	■	S	E	E
N	E	T	S	■	T	O	S	S	■	E	R	R

CROSSWORD 291

R	A	T	■	C	L	A	W	■	A	L	S	O
U	S	E	■	L	A	S	H	■	L	O	A	D
S	I	R	■	O	N	L	Y	■	T	A	M	E
T	A	R	■	S	E	E	■	Z	O	N	E	S
■	■	I	V	E	■	E	V	E	■	■	■	■
I	D	E	A	■	S	P	A	R	■	I	R	A
C	A	R	T	O	N	■	N	O	R	M	A	L
E	D	S	■	K	I	S	S	■	Y	I	P	S
■	■	■	■	A	P	T	■	B	E	T	■	■
S	T	R	A	Y	■	A	B	E	■	A	S	H
A	W	A	Y	■	W	R	E	N	■	T	O	Y
F	I	N	E	■	H	E	A	D	■	E	L	M
E	G	G	S	■	O	D	D	S	■	D	O	N

CROSSWORD 292

C	A	S	H						A	C	E	S
O	C	C	U	R				A	R	O	S	E
T	H	R	E	A	D		E	X	C	U	S	E
S	E	E	■	P	R	U	N	E	■	P	A	D
	D	A	M	■	A	N	D	■	C	O	Y	
		M	I	A	M	I	■	T	O	N		
			T	R	A	F	F	I	C			
		A	T	E	■	O	L	E	O	S		
	A	D	S	■	P	R	O	■	A	C	T	
H	I	M	■	R	U	M	O	R	■	R	I	O
E	D	I	S	O	N		D	O	N	A	L	D
R	E	R	U	N				T	A	P	E	D
E	D	E	N						B	E	D	S

CROSSWORD 293

I	R	A	■	S	L	O	T	■	I	D	E	A
R	O	B	■	M	E	N	U	■	G	O	A	L
A	L	L	■	E	V	E	R	■	L	E	T	S
N	E	E	D	L	E	■	T	W	O	■	■	■
■	■	■	I	L	L	■	L	O	O	K	E	D
H	O	N	E	Y	■	M	E	N	■	A	D	E
A	H	A	■	■	Y	E	S	■	■	T	E	E
N	I	P	■	P	A	L	■	S	P	E	N	D
G	O	S	S	I	P	■	S	H	E	■	■	■
■	■	■	P	E	P	■	T	I	T	L	E	S
R	I	T	A	■	I	R	O	N	■	O	R	E
O	V	E	N	■	N	I	N	E	■	F	I	N
W	E	A	K	■	G	O	E	S	■	T	E	D

CROSSWORD 294

B	A	N	■	A	B	E	L	■	S	P	A	T
U	S	E	■	R	O	D	E	■	H	A	L	O
M	I	X	■	E	A	S	T	■	I	D	L	Y
S	A	T	I	N	S	■	T	I	N	■	■	■
■	■	■	L	A	T	H	E	R	■	A	C	T
H	U	R	L	■	■	A	R	K	■	B	O	Y
E	G	O	■	S	W	I	S	S	■	L	I	P
A	L	P	■	A	I	R	■	■	G	E	N	E
D	Y	E	■	I	N	S	I	D	E	■	■	■
■	■	■	O	L	D	■	T	O	M	C	A	T
C	O	R	N	■	O	V	A	L	■	R	I	O
O	R	A	L	■	W	I	L	L	■	I	D	A
D	E	N	Y	■	S	A	Y	S	■	B	E	D

CROSSWORD 295

C	O	M	E	■	W	A	S	■	W	H	O	M
A	P	E	S	■	A	L	E	■	I	O	W	A
S	E	E	K	■	D	I	N	■	L	E	N	T
E	N	T	I	R	E	■	A	C	T	■	■	■
■	■	■	M	A	D	■	T	A	S	T	E	D
A	R	R	O	W	■	F	O	R	■	R	A	Y
B	A	A	S	■	S	I	R	■	S	U	R	E
E	G	G	■	M	I	X	■	S	P	E	N	D
L	E	S	S	E	N	■	R	U	E	■	■	■
■	■	■	A	L	A	■	H	E	L	M	E	T
L	O	A	F	■	T	W	O	■	L	O	D	E
E	D	G	E	■	R	E	D	■	E	V	E	N
D	E	E	R	■	A	B	E	■	R	E	N	T

CROSSWORD 296

R	I	M	S	■	W	I	G	■	T	A	C	K
I	R	A	N	■	E	V	A	■	O	V	E	N
P	A	P	A	■	P	E	P	■	T	I	L	E
■	■	■	R	U	T	■	■	L	A	D	L	E
A	C	H	E	S	■	B	A	I	L	■	■	■
J	O	E	■	E	L	E	C	T	■	A	N	N
A	L	A	■	■	A	I	M	■	■	R	I	O
R	E	D	■	F	I	N	E	R	■	I	C	E
■	■	■	S	I	N	G	■	Y	O	D	E	L
A	F	T	E	R	■	■	M	E	L	■	■	■
P	L	A	N	■	O	W	E	■	D	E	A	L
E	E	L	S	■	W	O	O	■	E	L	S	E
S	A	L	E	■	N	E	W	■	R	I	P	E

CROSSWORD 297

P	E	C	K	■	Y	A	M	■	S	W	A	Y
O	X	E	N	■	A	B	E	■	L	A	T	E
L	I	N	E	■	P	E	N	■	E	Y	E	S
O	T	T	E	R	■	L	U	M	P	■	■	■
■	■	■	L	E	D	■	■	A	T	T	I	C
S	O	N	■	D	I	A	R	Y	■	I	D	O
O	D	E	■	■	A	G	E	■	■	M	O	O
F	O	R	■	F	L	O	A	T	■	E	L	K
A	R	O	M	A	■	■	R	A	N	■	■	■
■	■	■	I	T	E	M	■	B	E	A	T	S
A	Y	E	S	■	A	I	D	■	E	C	H	O
L	E	N	T	■	S	L	Y	■	D	R	A	B
A	N	D	Y	■	T	E	E	■	S	E	T	S

CROSSWORD 298

W	E	T	■	A	T	O	P	■	S	A	G	A
A	G	O	■	N	E	A	R	■	W	R	E	N
G	O	O	■	I	N	T	O	■	A	G	E	D
E	S	K	I	M	O	■	P	E	R	U	■	■
■	■	■	C	A	R	■	H	A	M	M	E	R
A	N	G	E	L	■	P	E	R	■	E	V	A
L	O	I	S	■	M	A	T	■	K	N	I	T
P	E	G	■	A	I	D	■	T	I	T	L	E
S	L	A	N	T	S	■	O	W	L	■	■	■
■	■	N	O	E	S	■	W	I	N	N	E	R
P	E	T	S	■	I	R	I	S	■	A	V	E
E	R	I	E	■	L	I	N	T	■	P	E	N
A	R	C	S	■	E	G	G	S	■	E	R	E

CROSSWORD 299

J	A	M	■	O	R	A	L	■	P	L	E	A
A	G	O	■	B	O	N	E	■	E	A	R	N
N	E	W	■	E	A	T	S	■	D	I	R	T
E	S	S	A	Y	S	■	S	P	A	R	S	E
■	■	■	Y	E	T	■	O	I	L	■	■	■
O	W	N	E	D	■	O	N	E	■	A	P	T
W	O	O	■	■	W	A	S	■	■	D	I	E
L	E	D	■	I	R	K	■	B	L	O	N	D
■	■	■	A	D	E	■	M	O	O	■	■	■
A	R	O	M	A	S	■	I	N	S	E	C	T
P	O	P	E	■	T	H	A	N	■	D	O	E
E	D	E	N	■	L	I	M	E	■	G	I	N
D	E	N	S	■	E	D	I	T	■	E	N	D

CROSSWORD 300

H	A	M	■	S	P	A	R	■	C	A	W	S
A	L	E	■	T	A	X	I	■	A	L	O	E
W	A	R	■	U	S	E	D	■	I	S	N	T
K	N	E	A	D	■	■	E	A	R	■	■	■
■	■	■	G	Y	M	S	■	N	O	R	S	E
L	E	N	O	■	A	N	D	Y	■	I	L	L
A	D	O	■	■	P	I	E	■	■	L	O	S
V	I	E	■	A	S	P	S	■	P	E	T	E
A	T	L	A	S	■	S	I	T	E	■	■	■
■	■	■	S	H	Y	■	■	H	A	R	S	H
O	M	I	T	■	A	B	L	E	■	A	H	A
D	A	R	E	■	W	O	O	S	■	N	O	R
D	E	E	R	■	N	A	P	E	■	G	E	T

CROSSWORD 301

L	A	S	T	■	S	T	A	G	■	M	E	T
O	H	I	O	■	H	I	R	E	■	A	V	A
W	A	N	T	■	O	N	C	E	■	M	E	L
■	■	■	I	D	E	A	■	■	E	A	R	L
S	P	I	N	E	■	■	I	L	L	■	■	■
L	A	R	G	E	■	A	N	I	M	A	L	S
A	L	A	■	P	U	C	K	S	■	P	U	P
T	E	N	S	E	S	T	■	T	H	E	R	E
■	■	■	O	R	E	■	■	E	A	S	E	D
G	L	A	D	■	■	A	D	D	S	■	■	■
R	A	G	■	T	R	I	O	■	H	A	R	P
A	C	E	■	W	A	D	E	■	E	R	I	E
B	E	D	■	O	N	E	S	■	S	M	O	G

CROSSWORD 302

O	U	R	■	A	C	M	E	■	T	I	E	D
A	T	E	■	R	O	A	D	■	O	N	C	E
T	A	C	■	A	R	K	S	■	A	C	H	E
S	H	E	■	B	E	E	■	■	S	H	O	P
■	■	I	T	S	■	U	N	I	T	■	■	■
L	A	V	A	■	U	P	O	N	■	P	I	G
A	L	E	R	T	S	■	E	N	T	I	R	E
D	I	D	■	E	E	L	S	■	W	A	K	E
■	■	■	W	A	D	E	■	W	O	N	■	■
S	O	D	A	■	■	A	B	E	■	I	N	K
I	R	O	N	■	I	D	O	L	■	S	E	E
R	A	V	E	■	R	E	A	L	■	T	R	Y
S	L	E	D	■	E	R	R	S	■	S	O	S

CROSSWORD 303

P	L	O	T	■	A	S	P	S	■	B	A	R
L	O	V	E	■	R	A	R	E	■	R	I	O
O	R	A	L	■	T	H	A	W	■	A	D	D
W	E	L	L	S	■	A	Y	E	■	G	E	E
■	■	■	■	P	E	R	■	D	O	G	■	■
L	A	B	■	A	D	A	M	■	R	I	D	S
O	I	L	I	N	G	■	A	V	E	N	U	E
G	L	A	D	■	E	R	I	E	■	G	O	T
■	■	N	A	P	■	A	N	N	■	■	■	■
A	S	K	■	A	C	T	■	T	O	D	A	Y
C	U	E	■	T	O	T	S	■	W	I	S	E
M	E	T	■	H	A	L	O	■	E	V	I	L
E	D	S	■	S	T	E	W	■	D	E	A	L

CROSSWORD 304

B	R	A	T	■	B	A	L	L	■	R	O	W
E	A	S	E	■	A	S	I	A	■	E	V	A
A	R	K	S	■	A	L	E	S	■	M	E	L
N	E	S	T	S	■	E	D	S	■	I	N	K
■	■	■	■	W	E	E	■	O	W	N	■	■
T	I	P	■	A	L	P	S	■	A	D	A	M
A	L	L	E	Y	S	■	T	U	X	E	D	O
P	L	A	N	■	E	R	A	S	■	R	E	B
■	■	I	D	O	■	A	B	E	■	■	■	■
B	I	N	■	A	C	T	■	D	I	S	C	S
O	N	E	■	T	O	T	S	■	T	H	E	N
I	T	S	■	H	A	L	O	■	C	O	L	A
L	O	T	■	S	T	E	W	■	H	E	L	P

CROSSWORD 305

T	I	N	■	S	W	I	M	■	W	A	I	T
A	D	O	■	T	I	R	E	■	A	L	D	A
G	O	T	■	O	P	E	N	■	S	P	A	R
S	L	E	E	V	E	■	T	A	P	■	■	■
■	■	■	R	E	D	■	I	N	S	I	D	E
S	O	F	A	■	■	C	O	N	■	S	U	N
I	R	A	■	P	L	A	N	E	■	T	E	D
R	A	T	■	E	A	R	■	■	T	O	T	S
E	L	E	C	T	S	■	S	H	E	■	■	■
■	■	■	L	E	T	■	C	O	A	S	T	S
J	A	D	E	■	I	T	E	M	■	C	A	T
A	S	I	A	■	N	O	N	E	■	A	P	E
W	H	E	N	■	G	O	E	S	■	N	E	W

CROSSWORD 306

J	A	B	S	■	T	O	S	S	■	O	W	L
O	R	A	L	■	A	D	A	M	■	M	A	E
H	E	R	E	■	R	O	L	E	■	I	D	A
N	A	K	E	D	■	R	E	L	A	T	E	D
■	■	■	P	A	T	■	S	L	Y	■	■	■
P	R	E	S	S	E	D	■	■	E	R	A	S
O	A	R	■	H	A	R	S	H	■	A	L	A
D	Y	E	D	■	■	Y	E	A	R	N	E	D
■	■	■	O	D	D	■	E	L	I	■	■	■
V	I	R	T	U	E	S	■	O	P	A	L	S
A	D	E	■	N	A	I	L	■	P	L	E	A
S	E	A	■	E	L	L	A	■	E	D	E	N
T	A	P	■	S	T	O	P	■	D	A	R	E

CROSSWORD 307

F	A	D	S	■	F	A	D	E	■	T	W	O
E	D	I	T	■	A	C	I	D	■	R	A	W
E	D	G	E	■	T	E	N	D	■	U	R	N
■	■	■	A	G	E	■	■	I	T	E	M	S
A	R	O	M	A	■	■	K	E	Y	■	■	■
N	E	W	■	G	L	U	E	■	P	R	I	M
T	E	E	M	■	E	S	P	■	E	A	S	E
E	L	S	A	■	N	E	T	S	■	I	L	L
■	■	■	T	E	D	■	■	A	N	N	E	S
A	L	O	H	A	■	■	B	Y	E	■	■	■
R	O	B	■	R	O	P	E	■	E	R	A	S
T	O	E	■	T	R	E	E	■	D	I	S	H
S	P	Y	■	H	E	A	T	■	Y	O	K	E

CROSSWORD 308

O	N	C	E	■	C	O	P	■	S	C	O	T
W	E	L	L	■	A	X	E	■	L	O	R	E
E	X	A	M	I	N	E	D	■	E	D	E	N
S	T	Y	■	D	O	N	A	L	D	■	■	■
■	■	■	A	L	E	■	L	O	S	S	E	S
T	R	U	L	Y	■	F	E	W	■	E	V	E
H	A	R	P	■	P	A	D	■	W	A	I	T
E	G	G	■	P	A	N	■	S	I	L	L	S
M	E	E	K	E	R	■	D	O	G	■	■	■
■	■	■	E	R	A	S	E	D	■	A	S	P
A	C	N	E	■	D	I	S	A	G	R	E	E
S	O	A	P	■	E	L	K	■	A	M	E	N
H	O	P	S	■	S	O	S	■	G	Y	M	S

CROSSWORD 309

O	W	L	■	S	K	I	D	■	S	I	R	S
W	O	E	■	T	I	N	Y	■	T	R	U	E
E	N	T	R	A	N	C	E	■	E	A	S	E
■	■	■	H	I	G	H	■	R	E	N	T	S
A	C	T	O	R	■	E	V	I	L	■	■	■
W	O	O	D	■	U	S	E	D	■	S	A	T
A	P	P	E	A	R	■	R	E	S	C	U	E
Y	E	S	■	U	G	L	Y	■	H	A	T	E
■	■	■	K	N	E	E	■	B	A	T	O	N
G	R	A	N	T	■	A	J	A	R	■	■	■
R	O	L	E	■	S	N	A	C	K	I	N	G
A	B	E	L	■	P	E	C	K	■	R	O	Y
B	E	S	T	■	A	R	K	S	■	A	R	M

CROSSWORD 310

T	I	P	■	B	E	E	T	■	S	N	O	W
I	D	O	■	U	R	G	E	■	L	E	N	A
N	O	R	■	R	A	G	E	■	A	G	E	D
A	L	T	E	R	■	■	■	S	P	A	■	■
■	■	■	L	O	W	■	L	A	S	T	E	D
C	H	E	F	■	A	D	A	M	■	I	V	Y
O	I	L	■	G	L	O	B	E	■	V	I	E
O	R	E	■	A	L	T	O	■	H	E	L	D
P	E	C	A	N	S	■	R	U	E	■	■	■
■	■	T	U	G	■	■	■	N	Y	L	O	N
S	H	I	N	■	A	P	E	D	■	A	H	A
H	O	O	T	■	L	O	V	E	■	W	I	G
Y	E	N	S	■	S	T	A	R	■	S	O	S

CROSSWORD 311

B	U	D	■	R	O	B	E	■	A	D	A	M
A	P	E	■	O	W	E	D	■	S	O	D	A
B	O	B	■	A	N	N	S	■	L	O	O	K
E	N	T	E	R	E	D	■	V	E	R	S	E
■	■	■	R	E	D	■	P	I	E	■	■	■
A	W	A	R	D	■	S	E	E	P	I	N	G
C	A	T	■	■	S	O	N	■	■	V	I	A
E	Y	E	B	R	O	W	■	W	E	E	P	S
■	■	■	R	I	B	■	G	A	L	■	■	■
S	T	O	O	D	■	P	E	R	F	E	C	T
A	U	N	T	■	W	R	E	N	■	V	O	W
I	N	C	H	■	E	A	S	E	■	E	L	I
L	E	E	S	■	D	Y	E	D	■	R	A	N

CROSSWORD 312

F	O	G	■	A	J	A	R	■	W	I	C	K
A	W	E	■	D	O	S	E	■	R	O	L	E
D	E	N	■	M	I	L	D	■	A	W	A	Y
■	■	T	W	I	N	E	■	■	P	A	Y	S
S	P	L	I	T	■	E	R	A	S	■	■	■
T	O	E	S	■	U	P	O	N	■	A	V	A
U	P	S	E	T	S	■	O	Y	S	T	E	R
N	E	T	■	W	E	N	T	■	C	H	A	T
■	■	■	L	O	S	E	■	R	O	L	L	S
P	A	P	A	■	■	E	L	A	T	E	■	■
L	I	E	S	■	E	D	I	T	■	T	A	C
A	D	E	S	■	G	E	N	E	■	E	R	R
N	E	R	O	■	O	D	E	S	■	S	K	Y

CROSSWORD 313

J	E	F	F	■	T	O	M	■	A	S	K	S
E	V	I	L	■	A	P	E	■	C	H	I	P
T	E	L	E	G	R	A	M	■	T	O	T	E
S	N	E	E	R	■	L	O	G	■	W	E	D
■	■	■	T	A	B	■	S	A	F	E	■	■
P	E	A	■	B	A	G	■	L	U	R	E	D
A	L	D	A	■	T	A	C	■	N	E	R	O
D	I	D	N	T	■	S	U	N	■	D	A	N
■	■	I	T	E	M	■	B	A	R	■	■	■
S	E	T	■	A	I	D	■	M	O	T	H	S
A	R	I	A	■	L	I	F	E	B	O	A	T
L	I	O	N	■	E	E	L	■	E	L	L	A
T	E	N	D	■	S	T	Y	■	S	L	O	B

CROSSWORD 314

J	A	Y	■	A	C	R	E	■	O	D	D	S
A	G	E	■	F	L	A	G	■	N	E	R	O
B	O	A	S	T	I	N	G	■	C	L	A	W
■	■	■	K	E	P	T	■	R	E	I	G	N
O	S	C	A	R	■	E	L	I	■	■	■	■
R	O	O	T	■	A	D	O	S	■	D	R	Y
A	L	T	E	R	S	■	D	E	G	R	E	E
L	O	S	■	A	I	D	E	■	R	A	I	N
■	■	■	■	T	A	R	■	Y	A	W	N	S
A	W	O	K	E	■	A	C	E	S	■	■	■
C	O	I	N	■	S	P	L	A	S	H	E	S
H	O	L	E	■	P	E	A	R	■	A	R	K
E	L	S	E	■	A	S	P	S	■	T	R	Y

CROSSWORD 315

K	I	T	S	■	I	N	K	■	A	P	E	S
I	R	O	N	■	D	O	E	■	R	A	V	E
C	A	N	E	■	A	T	E	■	O	V	E	N
K	N	E	E	■	H	E	N	■	M	E	N	D
■	■	■	Z	O	O	■	E	R	A	■	■	■
C	O	M	E	T	■	A	S	H	■	T	A	P
O	W	E	■	T	A	S	T	Y	■	E	V	A
T	N	T	■	E	L	K	■	M	E	D	A	L
■	■	■	A	R	C	■	S	E	E	■	■	■
T	E	L	L	■	O	W	L	■	R	I	C	E
H	A	I	L	■	H	O	E	■	I	D	O	L
A	C	M	E	■	O	R	E	■	E	E	L	S
T	H	E	Y	■	L	E	T	■	R	A	T	E

CROSSWORD 316

A	C	T	■	S	L	A	M	■	S	W	A	M
S	U	E	■	H	A	V	E	■	P	A	C	E
P	E	N	■	O	V	E	N	■	R	I	M	S
■	■	C	L	E	A	N	■	S	A	L	E	S
G	L	E	E	■	■	U	G	L	Y	■	■	■
L	A	N	E	■	H	E	R	O	■	O	N	E
U	N	T	R	U	E	■	A	W	A	K	E	N
E	D	S	■	P	R	A	Y	■	G	L	A	D
■	■	■	D	O	E	S	■	■	E	A	R	S
B	R	A	I	N	■	H	A	R	S	H	■	■
L	I	V	E	■	R	O	L	E	■	O	L	D
E	D	I	T	■	I	R	A	N	■	M	O	O
W	E	D	S	■	G	E	N	T	■	A	P	T

CROSSWORD 317

C	O	P	E	■	S	H	E	■	S	T	A	G
O	V	E	R	■	C	A	N	■	P	O	L	E
L	A	W	N	■	R	U	G	■	E	A	S	T
E	L	S	E	■	A	L	I	■	A	D	O	S
■	■	■	S	A	M	■	N	O	R	■	■	■
W	I	L	T	S	■	B	E	T	■	A	D	D
E	V	E	■	I	R	I	S	H	■	C	U	E
B	Y	E	■	D	O	N	■	E	A	T	E	N
■	■	■	L	E	T	■	A	R	M	■	■	■
F	I	R	E	■	A	P	T	■	U	T	A	H
I	D	E	A	■	T	O	O	■	S	O	L	O
S	L	I	P	■	E	L	M	■	E	N	D	S
T	E	N	T	■	S	O	S	■	S	E	A	T

CROSSWORD 318

E	R	R	■	S	T	I	R	■	D	I	S	C
V	I	E	■	T	O	R	E	■	E	C	H	O
E	L	E	V	A	T	O	R	■	S	E	E	P
R	E	L	A	Y	■	N	U	N	S	■	■	■
■	■	■	T	E	E	■	N	I	E	C	E	S
A	C	E	■	D	A	B	■	P	R	O	V	E
R	O	D	S	■	T	U	B	■	T	R	E	E
C	L	E	A	R	■	N	A	P	■	E	N	D
S	A	N	D	A	L	■	N	O	D	■	■	■
■	■	■	D	Y	E	D	■	K	I	N	K	S
W	I	F	E	■	M	O	V	E	M	E	N	T
A	D	O	S	■	O	V	E	R	■	W	E	E
D	A	R	T	■	N	E	T	S	■	S	E	W

CROSSWORD 319

F	A	D	E	■	S	E	W	■	S	I	N	G
A	L	A	N	■	T	E	E	■	P	R	E	Y
C	A	R	D	■	O	L	D	■	R	O	O	M
E	S	K	I	M	O	S	■	■	A	N	N	S
■	■	■	N	A	P	■	F	L	Y	■	■	■
B	R	A	G	S	■	S	E	E	■	A	D	D
A	I	L	■	T	W	E	E	T	■	S	U	E
A	B	E	■	E	A	T	■	T	A	K	E	N
■	■	■	T	R	Y	■	T	E	N	■	■	■
L	O	V	E	■	■	S	H	R	I	N	K	S
O	V	E	N	■	G	O	O	■	M	E	N	U
R	A	T	S	■	E	D	S	■	A	R	I	D
E	L	S	E	■	M	A	E	■	L	O	T	S

CROSSWORD 320

E	V	E	S	■	N	I	P	■	F	A	R	E
R	I	N	K	■	O	R	E	■	O	R	A	L
R	A	D	I	A	T	O	R	■	L	E	N	S
■	■	■	E	V	E	N	■	S	L	A	T	E
S	T	A	R	E	■	■	O	H	O	■	■	■
P	I	T	S	■	S	I	D	E	W	A	L	K
A	D	O	■	B	A	K	E	D	■	B	E	N
R	E	P	T	I	L	E	S	■	G	E	N	E
■	■	■	A	B	E	■	■	A	L	L	O	W
B	O	M	B	S	■	P	O	L	O	■	■	■
I	D	O	L	■	L	U	K	E	W	A	R	M
T	O	N	E	■	I	R	A	■	E	R	I	E
E	R	A	S	■	D	R	Y	■	D	E	N	T

CROSSWORD 321

A	D	O	■	P	E	S	T	■	E	G	G	S
S	O	D	■	I	D	E	A	■	C	L	A	P
K	N	E	E	L	I	N	G	■	H	O	P	E
■	■	■	R	O	T	S	■	T	O	W	E	D
A	L	E	R	T	■	E	G	O	■	■	■	■
C	A	N	E	■	I	D	L	Y	■	Y	A	M
H	I	D	D	E	N	■	E	S	C	A	P	E
E	D	S	■	A	C	R	E	■	O	W	E	S
■	■	■	■	S	H	E	■	F	I	N	D	S
T	R	U	L	Y	■	D	A	R	N	■	■	■
R	I	S	E	■	P	U	N	I	S	H	E	S
O	P	E	N	■	A	C	N	E	■	A	L	A
T	E	D	S	■	N	E	E	D	■	T	I	N

CROSSWORD 322

P	R	I	M	■	M	U	G	■	E	L	M	S
R	A	V	E	■	I	R	A	■	R	A	I	L
O	P	E	N	I	N	G	S	■	R	I	L	E
■	■	■	■	T	E	E	■	B	O	R	E	D
G	R	A	S	S	■	N	E	A	R	■	■	■
R	O	C	K	■	S	T	A	B	■	H	O	E
A	D	M	I	R	E	■	C	E	R	E	A	L
B	E	E	■	U	T	A	H	■	A	R	K	S
■	■	■	D	I	S	C	■	T	H	O	S	E
R	E	R	U	N	■	T	W	O	■	■	■	■
O	D	E	S	■	S	U	I	T	C	A	S	E
S	E	A	T	■	E	A	T	■	A	B	E	L
E	N	D	S	■	A	L	S	■	B	E	E	F

CROSSWORD 323

B	A	N	■	S	H	O	W	■	A	D	D	S
A	L	I	■	H	O	P	E	■	N	E	R	O
A	L	P	H	A	B	E	T	■	N	E	A	R
■	■	■	■	U	P	O	N	■	L	E	D	G	E
S	T	A	G	E	■	E	G	O	■	■	■	■
P	I	L	E	■	A	D	E	S	■	W	H	O
A	N	D	R	E	W	■	N	E	P	H	E	W
T	E	A	■	V	A	S	T	■	R	E	A	L
■	■	■	■	E	Y	E	■	C	E	N	T	S
S	A	F	E	R	■	C	A	R	S	■	■	■
P	U	L	L	■	P	U	N	I	S	H	E	S
I	T	E	M	■	A	R	T	S	■	O	A	K
T	O	W	S	■	D	E	E	P	■	T	R	Y

CROSSWORD 324

K	I	N	■	T	E	E	N	■	L	A	S	H
I	R	A	■	U	G	L	Y	■	O	N	C	E
T	O	P	■	R	O	L	L	■	S	C	A	R
S	N	E	A	K	■	S	O	B	■	E	N	D
■	■	■	L	E	D	■	N	A	B	S	■	■
D	E	L	A	Y	E	D	■	R	I	T	A	S
I	R	I	S	■	W	I	N	■	C	O	L	T
M	A	S	K	S	■	E	A	G	E	R	L	Y
■	■	T	A	I	L	■	Y	E	P	■	■	■
H	O	E	■	S	O	S	■	O	S	C	A	R
O	W	N	S	■	W	H	I	R	■	A	L	I
S	E	E	P	■	L	O	N	G	■	S	O	N
E	D	D	Y	■	Y	O	K	E	■	T	E	D

CROSSWORD 325

G	I	F	T	■	N	O	S	■	C	R	I	B
O	D	O	R	■	A	C	E	■	A	I	D	E
L	E	N	A	■	T	E	A	S	P	O	O	N
D	A	D	S	■	■	A	L	I	■	■	■	■
■	■	■	H	O	R	N	■	P	A	P	A	S
A	S	K	■	W	I	S	E	■	R	I	L	E
R	O	N	A	L	D	■	L	A	T	E	S	T
C	L	I	P	■	E	A	S	T	■	S	O	S
H	O	T	E	L	■	V	E	E	R	■	■	■
■	■	■	■	I	C	E	■	■	I	T	C	H
B	A	R	I	T	O	N	E	■	P	A	L	E
E	X	I	T	■	M	U	G	■	E	X	A	M
T	E	D	S	■	B	E	G	■	R	I	M	S

CROSSWORD 326

G	A	S	P	S	■	G	U	Y	■	A	N	N
A	W	A	I	T	■	O	N	O	■	L	E	E
L	E	D	G	E	■	S	I	N	■	D	O	C
■	■	■	■	W	E	S	T	■	S	A	N	K
A	D	E	■	■	A	I	S	L	E	■	■	■
D	I	D	■	A	S	P	■	O	W	I	N	G
A	V	I	D	L	Y	■	P	O	S	T	E	R
M	E	T	A	L	■	S	I	P	■	E	R	A
■	■	■	S	Y	R	U	P	■	■	M	O	B
B	O	T	H	■	O	N	E	S	■	■	■	■
A	V	A	■	B	U	S	■	L	I	N	D	A
B	A	N	■	U	S	E	■	A	V	O	I	D
E	L	K	■	N	E	T	■	M	E	W	E	D

CROSSWORD 327

E	C	H	O	■	C	O	N	■	S	O	N	G
G	R	A	B	■	O	W	E	■	O	V	E	R
G	E	T	S	■	A	N	T	■	M	A	R	E
S	W	E	E	T	S	■	■	B	E	L	O	W
■	■	■	R	O	T	A	T	E	■	■	■	■
H	E	A	V	Y	■	R	A	G	■	R	A	H
E	R	I	E	■	Y	A	P	■	C	A	P	E
Y	A	M	■	W	E	B	■	P	O	W	E	R
■	■	■	■	E	A	S	T	E	R	■	■	■
A	S	K	E	D	■	■	R	A	N	G	E	R
L	E	N	A	■	A	B	E	■	C	O	V	E
D	E	E	R	■	D	A	N	■	O	N	E	S
A	D	E	S	■	D	A	D	■	B	E	S	T

CROSSWORD 328

G	R	E	W	■	W	A	R	■	H	E	L	D
L	I	V	E	■	O	D	E	■	E	R	I	E
A	P	E	S	■	O	D	D	■	R	A	K	E
D	E	N	T	E	D	■	■	P	O	S	E	D
■	■	■	■	A	S	I	D	E	■	■	■	■
S	T	A	I	R	■	T	Y	P	I	C	A	L
H	O	W	L	■	A	C	E	■	D	A	L	E
E	Y	E	L	A	S	H	■	C	A	B	L	E
■	■	■	■	S	H	Y	E	R	■	■	■	■
B	L	A	C	K	■	■	M	Y	S	E	L	F
E	A	C	H	■	A	S	P	■	I	D	E	A
N	I	N	E	■	N	E	T	■	R	E	A	D
D	R	E	W	■	D	A	Y	■	E	N	D	S

CROSSWORD 329

E	R	A	S	■	H	E	L	D	■	G	O	O
L	A	N	E	■	A	R	E	A	■	R	U	N
S	I	T	E	■	T	E	A	M	M	A	T	E
E	N	E	M	Y	■	■	D	E	E	D	■	■
■	■	■	E	A	R	■	■	S	O	U	P	S
W	A	R	D	R	O	B	E	■	W	A	L	L
I	R	A	■	D	O	O	R	S	■	T	E	E
R	I	D	E	■	F	O	R	E	H	E	A	D
E	D	I	T	S	■	■	S	T	Y	■	■	■
■	■	A	C	I	D	■	■	S	P	A	T	S
B	A	T	H	R	O	B	E	■	H	I	R	E
E	G	O	■	E	V	E	S	■	E	D	E	N
N	O	R	■	N	E	T	S	■	N	E	E	D

CROSSWORD 330

O	A	T	S	■	A	S	P	■	A	D	A	M
F	L	I	P	■	C	U	E	■	L	A	C	E
F	I	N	I	S	H	E	D	■	E	R	R	S
■	■	■	D	O	E	■	A	G	R	E	E	S
U	S	H	E	R	S	■	L	E	T	■	■	■
S	P	A	R	E	■	S	E	E	S	A	W	S
E	A	R	■	■	D	A	D	■	■	D	I	P
D	R	E	A	M	E	D	■	S	N	O	R	E
■	■	■	R	A	N	■	C	L	O	S	E	D
U	R	G	E	N	T	■	L	I	T	■	■	■
T	O	R	N	■	I	N	I	T	I	A	L	S
A	S	I	A	■	S	U	N	■	C	H	O	P
H	E	N	S	■	T	N	T	■	E	A	S	Y

CROSSWORD 331

O	V	A	L	■	S	A	I	L	■	S	H	E
D	E	L	I	■	N	I	L	E	■	P	E	A
E	A	T	S	■	I	D	L	E	■	A	L	S
S	L	O	T	■	F	E	E	■	A	N	D	Y
■	■	■	E	L	F	■	G	A	L	■	■	■
A	R	E	N	A	■	W	A	T	E	R	E	D
R	A	Y	■	S	M	A	L	L	■	I	R	E
C	H	E	E	S	E	S	■	A	C	O	R	N
■	■	■	L	O	S	■	A	S	H	■	■	■
W	I	C	K	■	S	O	W	■	E	C	H	O
I	R	A	■	T	I	N	A	■	S	H	O	W
F	O	R	■	N	E	C	K	■	T	A	M	E
E	N	D	■	T	R	E	E	■	S	P	E	D

CROSSWORD 332

B	R	A	T	■	T	W	O	S	■	S	P	A
E	A	S	E	■	O	H	I	O	■	T	A	P
A	R	K	S	■	W	E	L	L	■	A	G	E
N	E	S	T	S	■	E	Y	E	■	R	E	D
■	■	■	■	O	W	L	■	S	A	T	■	■
W	A	R	■	M	I	S	T	■	L	I	E	S
E	L	O	P	E	S	■	O	R	A	N	G	E
B	L	U	E	■	H	E	R	E	■	G	O	T
■	■	N	A	B	■	S	E	A	■	■	■	■
S	A	D	■	E	L	K	■	D	A	D	D	Y
H	U	E	■	G	A	I	T	■	L	O	R	E
I	T	S	■	A	C	M	E	■	E	V	E	N
N	O	T	■	N	E	O	N	■	S	E	W	S

CROSSWORD 333

A	H	A	■	A	R	E	A	■	F	I	T	S
D	A	B	■	D	A	R	T	■	E	D	I	T
A	L	E	■	O	H	I	O	■	N	O	S	Y
M	O	L	A	R	■	E	P	I	C	■	■	■
■	■	■	B	E	G	■	■	R	E	A	D	Y
D	E	A	L	■	O	N	C	E	■	S	E	A
E	D	G	E	■	N	O	R	■	L	I	A	R
L	E	E	■	P	E	T	E	■	E	A	R	N
I	N	D	I	A	■	■	W	O	N	■	■	■
■	■	■	S	N	A	G	■	V	O	I	C	E
A	P	E	S	■	U	R	G	E	■	D	O	N
P	E	R	U	■	T	E	E	N	■	O	L	D
T	R	E	E	■	O	W	E	S	■	L	A	S

CROSSWORD 334

C	O	B		G	L	O	W		W	I	T	H
A	B	E		I	O	W	A		I	D	E	A
L	E	D		R	A	N	G		R	O	L	L
M	Y	S	E	L	F			H	E	L	L	O
			A	S	S	U	M	E	S			
S	T	A	R			N	O	R		T	I	P
P	A	I	N		I	D	O		P	O	R	E
A	R	M		O	N	E			L	O	A	N
			S	U	N	R	I	S	E			
S	L	A	N	T			N	E	A	T	E	R
N	I	C	E		S	O	D	A		A	D	E
A	N	N	E		E	D	I	T		P	E	A
P	E	E	R		T	E	A	S		E	N	D

CROSSWORD 335

K	I	C	K		C	B	S		P	L	O	W
I	D	L	E		O	O	H		L	A	N	E
N	E	I	G	H	B	O	R		A	G	E	D
G	A	P		A	R	T	I	S	T			
			V	I	A		V	I	E	N	N	A
A	C	T	O	R		P	E	R		A	I	R
S	L	O	W		G	E	L		M	I	C	K
P	A	T		B	O	G		W	A	L	K	S
S	N	O	R	E	R		T	I	C			
			E	D	I	T	E	D		P	E	T
F	R	O	G		L	O	N	E	L	I	E	R
I	O	W	A		L	E	T		O	S	L	O
R	E	E	L		A	S	H		P	A	S	T

CROSSWORD 336

O	D	O	R		A	L	P		C	O	S	T
D	I	V	E		C	O	O		O	H	I	O
D	E	E	P		T	R	O	M	B	O	N	E
S	T	R	A	P		D	R	A	W			
			I	L	L			N	E	S	T	S
R	E	T	R	E	A	T	S		B	A	R	E
I	D	A		A	V	O	I	D		L	I	E
T	I	L	T		A	N	C	E	S	T	O	R
A	T	L	A	S			K	E	N			
			L	O	I	S		D	A	N	C	E
L	O	N	E	S	O	M	E		C	O	R	D
I	R	A	N		W	O	W		K	N	E	E
D	E	B	T		A	G	E		S	E	W	N

CROSSWORD 337

G	R	A	Y		A	S	P	S		I	L	L
R	A	T	E		N	O	E	L		R	I	O
A	R	T	S		T	R	A	I	N	I	N	G
B	E	E		B	E	T		V	E	S	T	S
		N	A	Y			P	E	W			
L	A	D	L	E		P	E	R		S	A	M
O	D	E	S		D	I	G		T	U	N	A
W	E	D		P	A	N		S	A	I	N	T
			R	E	D			A	C	T		
S	C	O	U	T		C	U	T		C	A	T
T	O	R	N	A	D	O	S		C	A	V	E
A	L	A		L	I	M	E		A	S	I	A
G	A	L		S	P	E	D		B	E	D	S

CROSSWORD 338

B	A	T		S	T	O	P		S	C	A	T
A	B	E		T	R	U	E		P	O	L	E
A	L	E		E	A	R	N		O	A	T	S
S	E	N	S	E	D			P	I	L	O	T
			P	R	E	T	Z	E	L			
M	E	N	U			Y	I	P		W	A	S
O	V	E	N		R	I	P		P	A	I	L
W	E	T		P	U	N			U	G	L	Y
			B	I	G	G	E	S	T			
I	S	S	U	E			L	I	T	T	L	E
T	O	L	L		A	B	E	L		R	O	D
C	R	A	B		D	O	C	K		I	V	E
H	E	M	S		D	O	T	S		M	E	N

CROSSWORD 339

B	E	A	T		P	L	U	G		S	I	P
A	C	M	E		R	I	T	A		N	O	R
T	H	E	N		O	A	T	S		O	W	E
S	O	N	S		O	R	E		A	W	A	Y
			E	L	F		R	I	B			
S	T	A	R	E		D	E	S	E	R	V	E
H	A	S		M	A	I	D	S		A	I	R
E	X	P	L	O	R	E		U	S	H	E	R
			A	N	T		P	E	P			
F	O	L	D		I	C	E		L	O	S	S
A	P	E		S	C	O	T		A	N	T	E
M	E	N		A	L	D	A		S	C	A	N
E	N	D		P	E	E	L		H	E	R	D

CROSSWORD 340

K	E	G	S		S	P	I	T		D	I	M
I	R	O	N		W	A	V	E		I	R	E
D	A	T	E		O	W	E	D		A	I	M
			E	R	R	S			A	L	S	O
F	R	O	Z	E	N		A	P	T			
L	I	V	E	S		S	L	E	E	T	E	D
I	C	E		C	H	O	S	E		H	A	Y
P	E	N	G	U	I	N		L	E	A	S	E
			Y	E	S		M	E	L	T	E	D
A	D	A	M			J	A	D	E			
N	E	W		S	P	A	R		C	R	O	W
T	E	A		P	A	I	R		T	U	N	A
S	P	Y		A	L	L	Y		S	E	E	D

CROSSWORD 341

S	A	G	S		H	A	S		S	I	D	E
E	V	E	N		E	R	A		O	R	A	L
T	A	M	E		A	C	T		F	I	R	S
			A	D	D			W	A	S	T	E
B	R	O	K	E		S	P	A				
L	A	W		N	E	W	E	R		A	N	T
O	R	E			Y	E	A			V	I	E
W	E	D		F	E	E	L	S		I	N	N
				A	S	P		A	I	D	E	D
C	H	E	E	R			O	D	D			
L	A	V	A		S	I	X		A	L	P	S
A	L	E	S		A	C	E		H	A	I	L
M	O	R	E		M	E	N		O	B	E	Y

CROSSWORD 342

D	A	M	S		B	O	Y	S		D	A	D
I	T	E	M		R	I	O	T		U	S	E
G	E	N	E		A	N	D	Y		S	I	N
			A	L	I	K	E		O	K	A	Y
S	N	O	R	E	D		L	E	D			
C	O	A	S	T		R	E	A	D	E	R	S
A	S	K		T	O	U	R	S		Y	A	P
R	E	S	P	E	C	T		T	H	E	R	E
			A	R	T		T	E	A	S	E	D
H	A	L	L		O	D	O	R	S			
I	V	E		A	B	E	L		H	A	T	E
D	I	E		D	E	A	L		E	V	I	L
E	D	S		E	R	R	S		S	A	N	K

CROSSWORD 343

A	U	N	T		A	R	T	S		S	O	B
S	T	I	R		D	E	A	N		A	W	E
P	A	L	E		S	A	L	E	S	M	E	N
S	H	E	E	T		D	E	E	P			
				A	P	E		R	I	L	E	D
A	R	C		N	E	R	O		C	O	D	E
G	A	R	A	G	E		V	O	Y	A	G	E
E	V	I	L		P	L	E	A		F	E	D
D	E	B	T	S		A	N	T				
			E	L	M	S		H	O	M	E	R
H	A	I	R	I	E	S	T		R	O	D	E
A	D	D		T	R	I	O		A	R	I	D
T	E	A		S	E	E	N		L	E	T	S

CROSSWORD 344

G	R	O	W		C	A	P		G	R	I	D
A	I	D	E		H	U	E		H	A	L	E
S	C	O	T	L	A	N	D		O	W	L	S
P	E	R		A	L	T	A	R	S			
			A	R	K		L	A	T	H	E	R
F	I	E	L	D		G	E	E		A	X	E
L	O	V	E		C	O	D		G	L	A	D
A	W	E		S	A	T		C	A	L	M	S
T	A	S	T	E	S		W	A	G			
			R	A	I	S	I	N		O	U	R
R	A	V	E		N	O	N	S	E	N	S	E
A	L	A	N		O	D	D		A	C	E	S
H	A	N	D		S	A	Y		T	E	S	T

CROSSWORD 345

L	O	V	E		S	I	N		S	L	O	T
O	V	E	N		A	D	E		T	A	P	E
T	A	R	T		N	O	W		E	V	E	N
S	L	Y	E	S	T			J	E	A	N	S
			R	O	A	S	T	E	D			
L	A	S	S	O		P	A	W		L	A	S
A	L	A		T	W	I	C	E		A	L	P
Y	E	T		H	A	T		L	O	W	L	Y
			M	E	S	S	I	E	R			
A	C	H	E	D			T	R	A	M	P	S
S	H	O	W		A	G	E		N	E	R	O
P	A	L	E		H	A	M		G	A	I	N
S	P	E	D		A	L	S		E	L	M	S

CROSSWORD 346

C	A	T		G	A	M	E		A	P	E	S
H	U	E		O	X	E	N		D	I	A	L
A	T	E		L	E	N	D		V	E	R	Y
P	O	S	E	D		D	E	L	I			
			L	E	D		D	O	C	T	O	R
C	H	I	M	N	E	Y		W	E	A	V	E
L	A	D			N	A	G			P	E	N
A	T	L	A	S		P	A	T	I	E	N	T
P	E	E	L	E	D		L	O	T			
			M	A	I	D		A	S	K	E	D
A	L	T	O		S	U	D	S		I	C	Y
L	I	E	S		K	N	I	T		S	H	E
S	P	A	T		S	E	E	S		S	O	S

CROSSWORD 347

S	A	G	S		A	S	K		T	R	O	T
A	D	A	M		I	C	E		R	I	P	E
N	O	S	E		M	A	T		U	S	E	D
			A	L	E	R	T		L	E	N	S
S	T	A	R	E	D		L	A	Y			
H	O	R	S	E		M	E	L		I	R	K
O	A	K		R	O	A	S	T		R	U	E
E	D	S		E	R	R		A	G	I	N	G
			O	D	D		C	R	U	S	T	S
S	P	A	T		E	R	A	S	E			
W	A	N	T		R	O	B		S	E	A	S
A	C	N	E		E	L	I		T	A	P	E
P	E	E	R		D	E	N		S	T	E	W

CROSSWORD 348

B	O	A	T		L	O	A	D		D	A	M
I	N	T	O		U	R	G	E		E	R	A
T	E	E	M		R	E	E	L		L	E	I
			A	Y	E	S		A	S	I	A	N
P	A	S	T	E	D		B	Y	E			
O	L	E	O	S		C	A	S	T	L	E	S
U	S	E			S	A	G			A	L	E
T	O	N	I	G	H	T		S	E	N	S	E
			C	U	E		G	U	I	D	E	D
S	H	E	E	T		A	U	N	T			
K	I	D		T	A	P	E		H	A	V	E
I	R	E		E	W	E	S		E	R	I	E
D	E	N		R	E	S	T		R	E	A	L

CROSSWORD 349

F	I	L	E		S	A	T		O	W	L	S
A	D	A	M		A	W	E		W	H	A	T
S	L	I	P		H	A	S		N	I	N	E
T	E	N	T		A	R	T	S		S	E	W
			Y	A	R	D		P	A	T		
L	A	S		G	A	S		R	I	L	E	S
O	S	C	A	R				A	L	E	R	T
S	P	A	D	E		A	L	I		D	R	Y
		T	O	E		V	A	N	E			
A	C	T		D	E	E	D		A	L	P	S
N	O	E	S		A	N	D		R	O	L	E
T	O	R	E		C	U	E		T	R	E	E
E	L	S	E		H	E	R		H	E	A	P

CROSSWORD 350

K	I	N		C	O	S	T		P	L	O	W
I	D	O		A	N	N	E		R	A	R	E
S	O	N		S	E	A	L		A	G	E	D
S	L	E	P	T		P	L	A	Y			
			E	L	I		S	C	E	N	T	S
R	E	S	P	E	C	T		T	R	O	O	P
O	A	K			Y	I	P			T	E	A
A	S	I	A	N		N	E	A	R	E	S	T
R	E	N	T	E	R		A	N	Y			
			T	W	I	G		G	E	R	M	S
H	A	T	E		P	I	L	E		E	A	T
U	P	O	N		E	V	I	L		A	D	E
M	E	N	D		R	E	D	S		D	E	W

CROSSWORD 351

A	N	T		T	W	O			F	A	L	L
W	E	E		R	O	L	E		I	D	E	A
E	X	A	M	I	N	E	D		R	E	D	S
	T	R	A	P		S	I	T	E			
			E	L	M		T	A	M	E	D	
P	E	R		E	A	R		P	A	R	E	D
E	R	A	S		D	E	W		N	I	N	E
A	R	M	O	R		F	O	R		E	Y	E
	S	P	R	A	T		W	E	B			
			C	H	U	M		G	Y	M	S	
S	O	M	E		R	E	T	R	E	A	T	S
P	I	E	R		F	L	E	E		S	A	P
A	L	L	Y			T	N	T		T	R	Y

CROSSWORD 352

N	A	G		E	L	M	S		B	A	S	S
O	W	E		L	E	A	P		E	R	I	E
D	E	N		V	E	R	Y		A	I	D	E
		T	W	I	S	T		A	D	D	E	D
B	A	L	E	S		I	D	L	Y			
U	S	E	S		K	N	I	T		P	R	O
L	I	S	T	E	N		S	O	A	R	E	D
B	A	T		D	E	C	K		L	E	N	D
			P	I	E	R		P	E	S	T	S
S	P	L	I	T		A	M	U	S	E		
W	A	I	L		A	D	A	M		R	A	P
A	C	N	E		C	L	I	P		V	I	A
N	E	E	D		T	E	D	S		E	R	R